The Idea of Greater ι

The Idea of
Greater Britain

Empire and the Future
of World Order, 1860–1900

Duncan Bell

PRINCETON UNIVERSITY PRESS

PRINCETON AND OXFORD

Library of Congress Cataloging-in-Publication Data

Bell, Duncan, 1976–
 The idea of greater Britain : empire and the future
of world order, 1860-1900 / Duncan Bell.
  p. cm.
 Includes bibliographical references and index.
 ISBN: 978-0-691-12865-8 (hardcover : acid-free paper)
 1. Great Britain—Colonies—History—19th century.
2. Imperialism—History—19th century. 3. National
characteristics, British. 4. Great Britain—Civilization—
19th century. I. Title.
DA16.B38 2007
909′.0971241081—dc22

                                          2007002911

British Library Cataloging-in-Publication Data is available

This book has been composed in Sabon

Printed on acid-free paper. ∞
press.princeton.edu
Printed in the United States of America

1 3 5 7 9 5 8 6 4 2

*This book is dedicated to the memory
of my father, Charles Julian Bell,
and my grandfather, Alexander Bruce.*

The old colonial system is gone. But in its place no clear
and reasoned system has been adopted. The wrong theory
is given up, but what is the right theory? There is only one
alternative. If the colonies are not, in the old phrase,
possessions of England, then they must be part of
England; and we must adopt this view in earnest.
—J. R. Seeley, *The Expansion of England:*
Two Courses of Lectures (1883)

Holding, as we must, that any reasonable security for
good order and civilisation in the world implies the
growing application of the federation principle in
international politics, it will appear only natural that the
earlier steps in such a process should take the form of
unions of States most closely related by ties of common
blood, language, and institutions, and that a phase of
federated Britain or Anglo-Saxondom, Pan-Teutonism,
Pan-Slavism, and Pan-Latinism might supervene upon the
phase already reached. There is perhaps a suspicion of
excessive logic in such an order of events, but a broad
general view of history renders it plausible and desirable
enough. Christendom thus laid out in a few great federal
empires, each with a retinue of uncivilised dependencies,
seems to me the most legitimate development of present
tendencies and one which would offer the best hope of
permanent peace on an assured basis of inter-Imperialism.
—J. A. Hobson, *Imperialism: A Study* (1902)

The essence of empire is control. To control, whether
of oneself or of others, everyone must bring a philosophy.
—A. P. Thornton, *Doctrines of Imperialism* (1965)

Contents

Acknowledgments

Writing this book would have been impossible without a great deal of support, and I would like to thank those who have facilitated and enriched the process. Firstly, a number of institutions have aided me financially. The Arts and Humanities Research Board funded the doctoral research on which this book is based, while the Fulbright Commission supported a year in the Department of Political Science at Columbia University. Colleagues in the Centre of International Studies, and in the Faculty of History, University of Cambridge, have helped to create intellectually vibrant environments in which to work, as well as offering excellent advice at key points. I would also like to thank the support staff (in particular Wendy Cooke) for all their help over the last five years. Jesus College provided a comfortable home for the early stages of the project. Finally, it is a great honor to have been elected to a Junior Research Fellowship at Christ's College. The college provides a beautiful environment in which to work, and I would like to thank the late Master (Malcolm Bowie), the current Master (Frank Kelly), the Fellows, and the staff, for their kind and generous welcome.

In my own experience academic research is a highly social activity, anchored in regular interaction with teachers and friends (often one and the same), and without them this project would probably never have started, let alone reached some sort of conclusion. I would especially like to thank Charles Jones, for his patient and erudite supervision of an ever mutating project, and Istvan Hont, for his brilliant scholarly guidance as well as for his steadfast support. My movement back and forth between international relations and the fresh pastures of intellectual history has been made much easier by both of them. Alan Bell, Peter Mandler, and Marc Stears have read all (or most) of the manuscript, and I am very grateful for their probing commentaries as well as their admirable endurance. Casper Sylvest has read it two or three times; his counsel has been consistently illuminating, and his own work on liberal internationalism has helped me to formulate and refine many of my own arguments. At the last minute Ged Martin provided pellucid comments on several chapters. Peter Cain has helped in navigating the choppy waters of Victorian imperialism. My doctoral thesis examiners, Richard Tuck and David Cannadine, offered some very useful suggestions for improving the text, and their kind assistance and subsequent encouragement is much appreciated. Michael Freeden, Quentin Skinner, and Gareth Stedman Jones, have all offered inspiration, as well as tremendously helpful advice, for my work on the history of political thought, and this project owes much to their own scholarly endeavours. I would also like to thank the following for their constructive comments on one (or more) chapters: David Armitage, Jens Bartelson, Michael Bentley, Antoinette Burton, Linda Colley, Stephen Constantine, Daniel Deudney, Heather Ellis, Zeev Emmerich, James Epstein, Sarah Fine, Matthew Grimley, Ian Hall, Joel Isaac, Stuart Jones, Duncan Kelly, Oswyn Murray, Karuna Mantena, Jeanne Morefield, Jeremy Morris, Maria Neophytou, Karen O'Brien, Jon Parry, Susan Pedersen, Jennifer Pitts, Simon Potter, David Reynolds, Julia Stapleton, John Thompson, David Worsley, and Brian Young. Finally, various friends and colleagues provided excellent advice, and I would like to thank them also: Tarak Barkawi, Mike Boyle, William Burke-White, John Burrow, Stefan Collini, Susanna di Feliciantonio, Inbali Iserles, Zaheer Kazmi, Martin O'Neill, Emma Rothschild, Andrea Sangiovanni, Mette Eilstrup-Sangiovanni, and Ricardo Soares de Oliveira. None of the above can be held responsible for any remaining scholarly infelicities. It has been a pleasure to work with Ian Malcolm, a brilliant editor.

I have benefited greatly from the comments and questions of audiences at seminars and conferences, including those at the British Academy; Institute for Historical Research; Cambridge; Oxford; Warwick; Pomona College; the University of California, Berkeley; Columbia, Sheffield Hallam; the International Studies Association annual conventions in Honolulu (2005) and San Diego (2006), as well as the American Political Science Association annual convention in Washington, D.C. (2005). Various portions of the book have appeared in print, sometimes in rather different forms. Elements of chapter 4 can be found in "The Victorian Idea of a Global State" in Duncan Bell (ed.), *Victorian Visions of Global Order: Empire and International Relations in Nineteenth-Century Political Thought* (Cambridge University Press, 2007). Some of the material from chapter 6 was published in "Unity and Difference: J. R. Seeley and the Political Theology of International Relations," *Review of International Studies*, 31/3 (2005). A version of chapter 3 appeared as, "Dissolving Distance: Empire, Space, and Technology in British Political Thought, 1860–1900," in *The Journal of Modern History*, 77/3 (2005), while a version of chapter 8, entitled, "From Ancient to Modern in Victorian Imperial Thought," appeared in *The Historical Journal*, 49/3 (2006). I would like to thank the editors and publishers (the University of Chicago Press and Cambridge University Press) for their kind permission to reprint this material.

Finally, for their exceptional support, I would like to extend my warmest thanks to my friends, especially Jude Browne; my partner, Sarah Fine; and my wonderful family, particularly Dorothy and Alex Bell, and Helen Bruce. This book is dedicated to the memory of my father and grandfather.

Abbreviations

Primary Sources

CR—*Contemporary Review*
ER—*Edinburgh Review*
FM—*Fraser's Magazine*
FR—*Fortnightly Review*
IF—*Imperial Federation*
LQM—*London Quarterly Magazine*
MM—*Macmillan's Magazine*
NC—*The Nineteenth Century*
NR—*National Review*
PRCI—*Proceedings of the Royal Colonial Institute*
QR—*Quarterly Review*
WR—*Westminster Review*

Secondary Sources

AHR —*American Historical Review*
EHR—*English Historical Review*
EJPT—*European Journal of Political Theory*
HJ—*Historical Journal*
HPT—*History of Political Thought*
JBS—*Journal of British Studies*
JCCH—*Journal of Colonialism and Colonial History*
JHI—*Journal of the History of Ideas*
JICH—*Journal of Imperial and Commonwealth History*
JMH—*Journal of Modern History*
MIH—*Modern Intellectual History*
OHBE—*The Oxford History of the British Empire (1998–1999)*
P&P—*Past and Present*
PT—*Political Theory*
TRHS—*Transactions of the Royal Historical Society*
VS—*Victorian Studies*

The Idea of Greater Britain

1

Introduction: Building Greater Britain

When we have accustomed ourselves to contemplate
the whole Empire together and call it England, we shall
see that here too is a United States. Here too is a
homogeneous people, one in blood, language, religion,
and laws, but dispersed over a boundless space.
—J. R. Seeley, *The Expansion of England* (1883)

A firm and well-compacted union
of all the British lands would form a state
that might control the whole world.
—Charles Oman, *England in the Nineteenth
Century* (1899)

THE HISTORY of modern political thought is partly the history of the attempt to confront increasing global interdependence and competition. *The Idea of Greater Britain* focuses on an important but neglected aspect of this chronicle: the debate over the potential union of the United Kingdom with its so-called settler colonies—the lands we know now as Australia, Canada, New Zealand, as well as parts of South Africa—during the late Victorian age. Straddling oceans and spanning continents, this polity was to act, so its advocates proclaimed, as a guarantor of British strength and of a just and stable world. I explore the languages employed in imagining the settler empire as a single transcontinental political community, even as a global federal state, with the intention of contributing to the history of imperial thought and Victorian intellectual life. I seek to shed light on the ways in which the future of world order—the configuration and dynamics of economic and geopolitical power, and the normative architecture justifying this patterning—was perceived in an age of vital importance for the development of politics in the twentieth century and beyond.

The quest for Greater Britain was both a reaction to and a product of the complex evolution of nineteenth-century international politics. The turbulent economic and political conditions of the era engendered profound anxiety, leading to the belief that a colossal polity was indispensable for preserving strength in a world in flux. In this sense it was reactive. But it was a product in the sense that the communications technologies facilitating increasing levels of economic interdependence also generated the cognitive shift that was necessary for people to conceive of the scattered elements of the colonial empire as a coherent and unified political unit, and even as a state.[1] In the last three decades of the century, a significant number of commentators responded to the widespread perception that the world was both shrinking and becoming increasingly competitive, and that this was a world in which Britain was losing (or had already lost) its midcentury preeminence.[2] A strong and vibrant Greater Britain was one of the most prominent solutions offered to the crisis of confidence in national supremacy. The debate signaled an important moment in the reconfiguration of national consciousness in a late Victorian world subject to the vicissitudes of international relations and a transfiguration of the prevailing norms of domestic political culture. It was driven in part by the perceived need to theorize and construct a bulwark against the encroachment of a powerful set of global challengers, most notably Germany, the United States, and Russia. As such it illustrates the disquieting effect that the impending loss of great power status had on a generation of thinkers. But the debate also constitutes a chapter in the intricate story charting the advent of democracy. Seen by many in Britain as a world-historical development, the emergence and spread of democracy (at least among the so-called civilized) was regarded as inevitable, as the culmination, whether intended or not, of many of the social, economic, and political trends of the previous two centuries, and it spawned a constantly mutating blend of optimism and anxiety. Imperial commentators reacted in divergent ways. For some, the spread of the Anglo-Saxon peoples across the face of the earth was the main engine of global progress; Greater Britain was, as such, a virtuous agent of democratic transformation. It foreshadowed the future. The majority, however, were more skeptical, and more nervous: the arrival of democracy prompted apprehension, and sometimes even fear. It was unclear what sort of path it would carve through the modern world, and in particular how both empire and state would be reconfigured. This group often saw Greater Britain as a counterrevolutionary response, capable of taming the transition to democracy. These concerns provided the fertile soil in which ideas about Greater Britain blossomed, flourished, and finally wilted.

---

[1] These lands were, of course, already occupied by various indigenous communities, nearly all of which suffered greatly at the hands of the settlers. On some of the methods of dispossession, see Julie Evans, Patricia Grimshaw, David Phillips, and Shurlee Swain, *Unequal Rights* (Manchester, 2003).

[2] "Britain" and "England" were often employed interchangeably during the eighteenth and nineteenth centuries, in large part due to the long-standing dominance of the English over the other realms. See here Paul Langford, *Englishness Identified* (Oxford, 2000), 11–15; and Krishan Kumar, *The Making of English National Identity* (Cambridge, 2003). Except where I deem it appropriate, I use "Britain."

The dates that I have chosen for the title of the book—namely c.1860–1900—act as a rough guide rather than a precise measure for the range of materials covered. In some chapters I reach further back in time, exploring dimensions of late eighteenth- and early nineteenth-century imperial thought, while in the conclusion I discuss some developments in the early twentieth century. The bulk of the text, however, focuses on the closing decades of Victoria's reign. Both the proximate cause of the explosion of interest in Greater Britain, and the shifts in the perception of the planet that helped underpin the idea of an integrated global polity, can be traced principally to the 1860s. The early 1870s saw a surge in proposals for an imperial federal system; during the 1880s this turned into a flood. From the mid-1890s confidence in the project of transforming the constitutional structures of the empire began to decline, as legislative success eluded the imperialists, as the leaders of the colonies displayed limited enthusiasm for such ideas, and as imperial priorities were increasingly focused on southern Africa. The war in South Africa (1899–1902) redirected imperial political thought in numerous ways, and it is for this reason that I stop at the turn of the century. Tracing the changes, as well as the various lines of continuity, would require another book.

The remainder of this introduction sets the scene for the following chapters. In the next section I explore some of the meanings of the term "Greater Britain." I then examine the role of the imperial federation movement within the wider discourse of Greater Britain and locate the book in relation to recent work in the history of political thought and imperial history. The final section provides an outline of the arguments presented, and a breakdown of the individual chapters.

THE BOUNDARIES OF IMPERIAL DISCOURSE: IMAGINING GREATER BRITAIN

During the 1830s and 1840s the relationship between the rapidly expanding settler colonies and London came under increasing scrutiny. The Canadian rebellions (1837–38) marked a watershed, catalyzing interest in conceding limited self-government to the settlers. The late 1840s and 1850s saw many of them granted "responsible government," which meant, in essence, the creation of limited representative institutions.[3] It

---

[3] By 1860 there were eleven self-governing colonies: Newfoundland, Nova Scotia, New Brunswick, Prince Edward Island, Canada (what is now Ontario and southern Quebec), New Zealand, New South Wales, Tasmania, South Australia, Victoria, and Queensland. The Cape of Good Hope turned down the offer of responsible government in 1854, but accepted it in 1872. The number of units was reduced by the creation of British North America (usually referred to simply as "Canada") in 1867 and the federation that produced Australia in

was generally assumed that such changes would eventually result in the independence of the colonies; the point of reform was to push such a moment far into the future and to make sure that when it came the terms of separation would be amicable. "Every colony," argued the radical politician J. A. Roebuck in 1849, "ought by us to be looked upon as a country destined, at some period of its existence, to govern itself," a point echoed in 1856 by Arthur Mills, an esteemed Tory colonial commentator, who stated that "to ripen those communities to the earliest possible maturity— social, political, and commercial—to qualify them, by all the appliances within the reach of a parent State, for present self-government, and eventual independence, is now the universally admitted object and aim of our Colonial policy."[4] During the 1860s, however, many watchful observers perceived an imminent threat to the empire. This trepidation resonated throughout sections of the British elite for the remainder of the century, shaping the debate over the aims and the structure of Greater Britain.

Two distinct but related fears helped to generate and sustain the debate. From the 1860s onward many imperial thinkers were concerned with the potential impact of a socially and morally corrosive "materialism" on the population as a whole, and on the Liberal party in particular. While this fear was sharpened by a growing awareness of the constraints on British global power, the chief source of alarm was domestic.[5] It was widely thought that under the pernicious influence of Cobdenite "Manchesterism" (as well as the rigor of Gladstonian fiscal prudence), the newly enfranchised middle and working classes would become increasingly selfish and introverted. Their sense of patriotism would evaporate. To such people, the empire would seem a burden rather than a source of greatness. Had not Adam Smith and many of his disciples derided the value of the colonies? Claiming to follow in his footsteps, the radical polemicist Goldwin Smith made a strident intervention in political debate with *The Empire* (1863), a collection of essays demanding the emancipation of the colonies. Gesturing in his direction, one exasperated imperialist complained that there "have been springing up of late years a number of half-politi-

---

1901. Most imperial unionists supported the federation of the individual colonies, as it reduced the problems of economic and political coordination. For a comprehensive overview, see John M. Ward, *Colonial Self-Government* (London, 1976). For general context, see Chris Bayly, *Imperial Meridian* (London, 1989); P. J. Cain and A. G. Hopkins, *British Imperialism, 1688–2000* (Harlow, 2001), ch. 8; and Susan Farnsworth, *The Evolution of British Imperial Policy During the Mid-Nineteenth Century* (New York, 1992).

[4] Roebuck, *The Colonies of England* (London, 1849), 170; and Mills, *Colonial Constitutions* (London, 1856), lxix. A prolific commentator on imperial issues, Mills served as a Conservative M.P. between 1857 and 1865 and 1873 and 1880.

[5] On the constraints on power, see Richard Millman, *British Foreign Policy and the Coming of the Franco-Prussian War* (Oxford, 1965), ch. 1. For the dynamics of domestic concerns, see J. P. Parry, *The Politics of the Constitution* (Cambridge, 2006).

cal charlatans, half ignoramuses, who are contending that the colonies are
of no use to the mother country."[6] It was feared that this attitude would
lead invariably to either benign neglect or explicitly "anti-imperial" legislation. In either case, the empire faced a dangerous challenge. Then, secondly, during the 1880s apprehension was heightened by further turmoil
over democracy, Irish Home Rule, and mounting economic and geopolitical competition. This was the decade in which "socialism" came to
be seen as an imminent threat to the body politic and in which the global
political horizon darkened perceptibly. The two fears inspired intense disquiet about the future stability and greatness of the polity.

A number of options were canvassed, and the period witnessed rivalry
between diverse conceptions of empire.[7] During the 1870s Benjamin Disraeli propounded a vision of a military empire focused on Asia, stressing
the value of India, the danger of Russia, and the imperative of bringing
"civilization" to "backward" peoples. It was this particular rendition of
a long-standing theme in British imperial thought and practice that served
as the target of Gladstone's successful Midlothian campaign (1879–80).[8]
Throughout the last three decades of the century, however, the focus increasingly shifted to the "Anglo-Saxon" empire. Grandiose visions of colonial unity found emotive and symbolic expression in poetry, prayer,
song, and major architectural projects, as well as through the more conventional media of political thought.[9] A small minority continued to
advocate independence for the settler colonies, most notably Cobden,
Bright, and Goldwin Smith;[10] others recommended limiting reform to

[6] Smith, *The Empire* (London, 1863); and M. H. Marsh, comments in the *PRCI*, I (1869–
70), 14–15.

[7] The vocabulary employed to talk about the empire lacked precision. The term "colony"
had a variable referent: for some it applied only to settler territories (the main focus of this
book), for others, any territory ruled by Britain. "Imperialism" was a term used for much
of the Victorian period to characterize the despotic municipal politics of France; it was only
in the late 1860s, and especially the 1870s, that it entered mainstream use to refer to policies of foreign conquest, and, even then, there was much confusion over its meaning as well
as its normative status. For further discussion, see Richard Koebner and Helmut Dan
Schmidt, *Imperialism* (Cambridge, 1964); Andrew Thompson, "The Language of Imperialism and the Meanings of Empire," *JBS*, 26 (1997), 147–77; and David Armitage, *The Ideological Origins of the British Empire* (Cambridge, 2000).

[8] C. C. Eldridge, *Disraeli and the Rise of a New Imperialism* (Cardiff, 1996); H.C.G.
Matthew, *Gladstone, 1809–1898* (Oxford, 1997), Part II, ch. 2; and Peter Cain, "Radical-
ism, Gladstone, and the Liberal Critique of Disraelian 'Imperialism'" in Duncan Bell (ed.),
Victorian Visions of Global Order (Cambridge, 2007).

[9] See, for examples, Alex G. Bremner, "'Some Imperial Institute,'" *Journal of the Society
of Architectural Historians*, 62 (2003), 50–73; John Clifford, *God's Greater Britain* (London, 1899); and Benjamin George Ambler, *Ballads of Greater Britain and Songs of an Anglo-
Saxon* (London, 1900).

[10] Peter Cain, "Capitalism, War, and Internationalism in the Thought of Richard Cobden," *British Journal of International Studies*, 5 (1979), 229–48.

minor tinkering, such as conferring more honors on colonial statesmen. Many still believed, even if they did not seek to support, an argument that since self-government had been awarded to the settler communities, it was inevitable that they would eventually become independent. Decreed by fate, this process should be left to follow its natural course.[11] The most persistent, ambitious, and from the perspective of political thought, the most interesting response, however, was the demand for a united Greater Britain.

During the late nineteenth century political theorizing was, as Jose Harris has observed, "virtually a national sport of British intellectuals of all ideological and professional complexions."[12] Debate over the empire was no exception and it drew in a wide range of participants. Who were the proponents of Greater Britain, and what was their intended audience? Most of the figures examined in this book can be classified, to employ Stefan Collini's felicitous phrase, as "public moralists."[13] They formed part of the elite class of academics, businessmen, lawyers, politicians, and journalists—often combining several of these roles simultaneously—who shaped public debate in London, the imperial metropolis. Some were prominent colonial politicians who entered the metropolitan intellectual fray only occasionally. A further category comprised the stalwarts of the organizations central to imperial debate—in particular the Colonial Society (founded in 1868)[14] and the Imperial Federation League (1884–1893)— who served as propagandists and prophets of a new world. Virtually all of the high-profile advocates were men; this was a heavily gendered discourse. The colonial unionists generated a vast amount of material, penning hundreds of books, pamphlets, speeches, and essays published in the leading periodicals of the day.[15] It is on these sources that I mainly focus.

[11] Herman Merivale, "The Colonial Question in 1870," *FR*, 7 (1870), 171; and Robert Lowe, "The Value to the United Kingdom of the Foreign Dominions of the Crown," *FR*, 22 (1877), 618–30.

[12] Harris, "Political Theory and the State" in S.J.D. Green and R. C. Whiting (eds.), *The Boundaries of the State in Modern Britain* (Cambridge, 1996), 16.

[13] Collini, *Public Moralists* (Oxford, 1991). The term "public intellectual" was not widely employed until the mid-twentieth century, although many of the people I explore fit this category. See here Stefan Collini, *Absent Minds* (Oxford, 2006), ch. 1. See also, for general context, Julia Stapleton, *Political Intellectuals and Public Identities in Britain since 1850* (Manchetser, 2001), Pt. I.

[14] This soon became the Royal Colonial Society (1869), but, following a complaint from the Royal College of Surgeons about possible confusion over initials, it quickly changed its name to the Royal Colonial Institute (RCI). See *PRCI*, 1 (1869), 9–10. On the foundation of the society, see Edward Beasley, *Empire as the Triumph of Theory* (London, 2005).

[15] I use the term "colonial unionist" throughout the book to denote individuals who advocated strengthening ties with the settler colonies in the late Victorian era. It does not imply adherence to any particular scheme or plan of action. Biographical details of most of the individuals covered can be found in the *Oxford Dictionary of National Biography*, or the relevant national biographies of Canada, Australia, South Africa, and New Zealand.

Although the movement itself stretched around the globe, with outposts located in the towns and cities of the empire, the debate centered on London, for it was considered vital to fight and win the ideological battle in the heart of the imperial system. The proponents of Greater Britain, and in particular the imperial federalists, represented one of a large number of competing and intersecting movements aiming to challenge and transform the way in which the British empire (and state) was understood. Expounding their views in the most high-profile outlets in British political culture, they succeeded in drawing the support, as well as the opprobrium, of some of the leading thinkers, public commentators, and politicians of the day.

Greater Britain meant different things to different people; therein resided both its wide appeal and ultimately one of its chief weakness. The term was employed in three main ways. Firstly, it could denote the totality of the British empire, the vast ensemble of disparate territories coloring the map of the world red.[16] Secondly, it could refer to the settlement colonies, which by the 1870s were growing very rapidly in population, economic power, and strategic importance. And thirdly, it could mean the "English-speaking," or Anglo-Saxon, countries of the world, encompassing not only the settlement empire but also the United States. This conceptual multivalency reflected conflicting views over the future direction of the empire, and it exposed some of the fault lines running through the political thought of the period. Although all three modulations circulated widely, the most frequent usage was in reference to the settler colonies. In his pioneering *Short History of British Colonial Policy* (1897), H. E. Egerton argued that "The Period of Greater Britain" commenced in 1886.[17] This was to place the starting point at least fifteen years too late, however, for intense argument over the future of the settler empire began in earnest in the early 1870s, drawing its terminological inspiration from Charles Dilke's best-selling travelogue *Greater Britain* (1868).[18] Some thinkers preferred other labels for the colonial empire. The celebrated historian J. A. Froude named this incipient polity "Oceana," in a deliberate republican echo of James Harrington's utopian vision. Another commentator

[16] This is the sense employed, for example, in Phiroze Vasunia, "Greater Britain and Greater Rome" in Barbara Goff (ed.), *Classics and Colonialism* (London, 2005), 34–68.
[17] Egerton, *A Short History of British Colonial Policy* (London, 1897), Book V. At the time, Egerton worked at the Emigrants' Information Office. In 1905 he became the first Beit professor of colonial history at Oxford. On his views, see J. G. Greenlee, "A 'Succession of Seeleys,'" *JICH*, 4 (1976), 266–83.
[18] Dilke, *Greater Britain*, 2 vols. (London, 1868). Other early texts include: [John Robinson], "The Future of the British Empire," *WR*, 38 (1870), 47–74; [John Edward Jenkins], "Imperial Federalism," *CR*, 16 (1871), 165–88; J. A. Froude, "England and Her Colonies," *FM*, 1 (1870), 1–16; and Andrew Robert Macfie, "On the Crisis of the Empire," *PRCI*, 3 (1871–72), 2–12. For some of the intellectual background to this shift, see Beasley, *Empire as the Triumph of Theory*.

suggested the creation of the "United States of England." Francis de La-
billlière, one of the most prolific advocates of colonial unity, referred to
a global "Federal Britain."[19] The most common appellation, however,
was "Greater Britain." The writings of Dilke, who soon rose to national
prominence as a radical politician and strategic thinker, exemplified both
the conflicting visions of political destiny common at the time and the in-
consistency of imperial vocabulary. In *Greater Britain* he initially employed the term as a synonym for the British empire as a whole, although
later in the book he declared that it should be confined to the "English-
speaking, white-inhabited, and self-governed lands." In his *Problems of
Greater Britain* (1890), he observed that the elements of the empire "vary
infinitely in their forms of government, between the absolutism which prevails in India and the democracy of South Australia and Ontario," but he
also lamented that "in popular usage" the term "Greater Britain" was "applied . . . chiefly to the English countries outside of the United Kingdom
remaining under British government."[20] This was problematic because he
thought that discussions of the past, present, and future of Greater Britain
ought to recognize the vital role of the United States.

The historian J. R. Seeley employed the term "Greater Britain" throughout *The Expansion of England* (1883), the most influential account of
colonial unity in the late Victorian age. Like Dilke, Seeley started by defining it very broadly, as encompassing four "great groups of territory" inhabited "either chiefly or to a large extent by Englishmen" and subject to
the sovereignty of the Crown—Australia, Canada, the West Indies, and
the Cape Territories—as well as India. Nevertheless, throughout his writings he was keen to stress the radical difference between the colonial empire and the empire in India, and to highlight the primary importance of
the former. And as with Dilke, his definition of Greater Britain underwent
a number of shifts. At one point in *The Expansion of England*, he claimed
that Greater Britain was (with a few minor exceptions) racially homogeneous, and as such it could not incorporate India. Later in the same book
he argued that there were actually two separate Greater Britains, one composed of the colonial empire, the other of India, and that they were antithetical in important respects:

> The colonies and India are in opposite extremes. Whatever political maxims
> are most applicable to one, are most inapplicable to the other. In the colonies

[19] Froude, *Oceana* (London, 1886); Harrington, *The Commonwealth of Oceana*, ed.
J.G.A. Pocock (Cambridge, 1992 [1656]); [Urquhart Forbes], "Imperial Federation," *LQR*,
4 (1885), 325–26; and De Labillière, *Federal Britain, or, Unity and Federation of the Empire* (London, 1894).
[20] Dilke, *Greater Britain*, II, 149; and Dilke, *Problems of Greater Britain* (London,
1890), I, 1 and 171; II, 157. See also Dilke, *The British Empire* (1899), 9–10. On Dilke's
tempestuous career, see David Nicholls, *The Lost Prime Minister* (London, 1995).

everything is brand-new. There you have the most progressive race put in the circumstances most favourable to progress. There you have no past and an unbounded future. Government and institutions are all ultra-English. All is liberty, industry, invention, innovation, and as yet tranquillity.

India, composing the other "Greater Britain," displayed the opposite characteristics; "it is everything which this is not." Indeed, "India is all past and, I may almost say, has no future." His priorities, as well as the main focus of his concern, were clear: "When we inquire then into the Greater Britain of the future we ought to think much more of our Colonial than our Indian Empire."[21] This theme was woven through the imperial discourse of the time; the colonial empire was seen anew as a space for transformative moral and political action, for the shaping of a patriotic imperial citizenry, and for the salvation of the endangered "mother country." To generalize about the role of "the empire" during the Victorian era is to miss the vital point that many contemporaries envisioned multiple empires, governed by different political systems, subject to assorted dreams and demands, and as a consequence holding diverse places in both their affections and schemes of political thought.

For Seeley, the material foundations of this global polity had already been laid in the previous decades, even centuries, of imperial expansion. But during the eighteenth century, the crucial period in the physical expansion of empire, "the idea that could shape the material mass was still wanting." All empires at the time, including the British, were "artificial fabrics, wanting organic unity and life." It was only in the late nineteenth century, and for reasons explored throughout this book, that Greater Britain came to be seen as an "organic unity." The first and most important step on the road to building Greater Britain was a cognitive one, involving a transformation in the way that people imagined the empire. "If Greater Britain in the full sense of the phrase really existed," insisted Seeley, "Canada and Australia would be to us as Kent and Cornwall."[22] Once this shift in political—as well as spatiotemporal—consciousness was achieved, the nature of imperial policy could be redirected. And all of humanity would benefit, for it was argued that a just and peaceful world order depended on the British to regulate and police its affairs.

Traditionally viewed as the keystone of empire, India played an ambiguous role in the debates over Greater Britain. While few colonial unionists demanded withdrawal from India, and though they often displayed the arrogant self-satisfaction about its possession so common

---

[21] Seeley, *The Expansion of England*, 10, 49, 176, and 11.

[22] Ibid., 61, 72, and 63. This was an example later repeated in Leo Amery, "Imperial Defence and National Policy" in C. S. Goldman (ed.), *The Empire and the Century* (London, 1905), 182.

among the Victorians, they tended to stress that in the long term it was of less importance for the greatness of Britain than the settlement empire. There were a handful of suggestions to incorporate India into an expansive federation, albeit on very different terms from the settler colonies, but they were peripheral, at least until the years following the First World War.[23] Greater Britain was to be an Anglo-Saxon political space, a racial polity. "It is hard to see," the historian Charles Oman proclaimed, how India "could be fitted into the scheme." Froude, meanwhile, argued that the "colonies are infinitely more important to us than even India—it is because the entire future of the English Empire depends on our availing ourselves of the opportunities which those dependencies offer to us."[24] Greater Britain was more important because it was seen as *British*; the settlement colonies were an extension of the British (or more commonly English) nation, constituting an "empire of liberty" that was to be transmuted into a single postimperial global formation. Important though it was to them, India was still an imperial possession, still alien. In a sense, though, the attention lavished on the Anglo-Saxon world represented a strange obfuscation of actually existing political conditions, for imperial activity in Asia and in particular in Africa was reaching new levels of intensity. This was, after all, the era of the rapacious "Scramble for Africa," the fateful period in which the European powers, Britain foremost among them, carved up the remaining territory of that vast continent. What is perhaps most surprising about the intellectual life of the closing decades of the nineteenth century is the relative lack of attention paid, at least in metropolitan political discourse, to theorizing what J. A. Hobson later termed the "[e]arth hunger" of the "new imperialism."[25]

Due to its unique combination of size and wealth, the difficulty of governing it internally and defending it externally, and the prestige attached to it, India remained an overriding concern for policy-makers.[26] The future of the settlement empire never fully supplanted the importance of India in the political calculations of Britain's ruling elite. I am not trying to replace one set of grand generalizations about Victorian political culture with yet another one—we have too many of those already. Instead,

[23] H. Mortimer Franklyn, *The Unit of Imperial Federation* (London, 1887); G. F. Bowen, "The Federation of the British Empire," *PRCI*, 17 (1886–86), 294; and C. L. Tupper, "India and Imperial Federation," *IF*, 7/7 (1892), 77–78. See also S. R. Mehrota, "Imperial Federation and India, 1868–1917," *Journal of Commonwealth Political Studies*, 1 (1961), 31.

[24] Oman, *England in the Nineteenth Century*, 259; and Froude, "England's War," *FM*, 3 (1871), 144.

[25] Hobson, *Imperialism* (London, 1902), 11.

[26] Sneh Mahajan, *British Foreign Policy, 1874–1914* (London, 2001). This was not universal, however, for as H.C.G. Matthew observed (*The Liberal Imperialists* [Oxford, 1973], 160), many liberal imperialist politicians at the turn of the century (including Rosebery), "showed remarkably little interest in India."

I want to complicate the picture, stressing that discussion of Greater Britain engaged and energized people across the political spectrum, including many of the leading public intellectuals of the day, and that in analyzing the contours of imperial discourse it is possible to illuminate some important and underappreciated aspects of Victorian political thought.

The creation of a global federal polity underpinned by a single nationality (or race) and governed by elective parliamentary institutions, represents one of the most audacious political projects of modern times. For much of the post-Renaissance period the legacy of Rome shaped conceptions of empire. Cicero, nearly two millennia before, had spoken in *De Republica* (51 ACE) of his compatriots as those "whose empire now holds the whole world."[27] In the sixteenth century the Spanish had briefly, in a similar vein, laid claim to dominion of the globe, *dominus totius orbis*. The drive for Universal Monarchy was motivated by the same impulse. In these bombastic claims, however, "universal" often meant little more than the lands of Europe, or perhaps the Mediterranean or Atlantic worlds.[28] (The only substantive tradition to claim true global dominion was that of the early modern canonists, determined to expand the temporal regulation of divine universality—and here the brute facts of geopolitics and the limitations of technology rendered their vision a fantasy.) In the nineteenth century the inheritance of Rome confronted that most potent of modern ideological developments, nationalism, and this was to have a profound influence on both the justification and practices of empire, as the increasingly self-conscious national states of Europe exported their regional ambitions throughout the world.[29] It is this genus of nationalistic imperialism that Michael Hardt and Antonio Negri argue has been dissolved by the corrosive forces of capital, migration, and technology, to be replaced by a formless, borderless postmodern global empire—an implausible argument that exaggerates the transformation of the state, but one symptomatic of the sense of radical novelty felt by many at the end of the twentieth century.[30] The tension between the demands of universality and the claims of the particular helped structure Victorian imperial

[27] See Anthony Pagden, *Lords of All the World* (New Haven, 1995), 23. See also Richard Tuck, "The Making and Unmaking of Boundaries from the Natural Law Perspective" in Allen Buchanan and Margaret Moore (eds.), *States, Nations, and Borders* (Cambridge, 2003), 143–71.

[28] On the boundaries of Roman political thought, see Tuck, "The Making and Unmaking of Boundaries," 144 and 149. For an illuminating comparison of the Spanish and British empires, see J. H. Elliott, *Empires of the Atlantic World* (London, 2006).

[29] Bayly, *Imperial Meridian*, esp. ch. 4. On how the rise of nationalism made "universal empire" within Europe unthinkable, see also Ernest Renan, "Qu'est-ce qu'une nation?" [1882], reprinted in Geoff Eley and Ronald Grigor Suny (eds.), *Becoming National* (Oxford, 1996), 43.

[30] Hardt and Negri, *Empire* (Cambridge, Mass., 2000).

discourse. On the one hand, the "civilizing mission" was anchored in an ancient notion of the prerogative, even obligation, of the most advanced societies to bring light to the dark corners of the earth. On the other, it was never seriously proposed that this meant, literally, global dominion, and the coexistence of various competing empires was taken for granted. The idea of a polity that would simultaneously dominate the earth and offer it stability and leadership, a beneficent Greater Britain, seemed to awkwardly straddle the two positions, expansive yet circumscribed, global and yet necessarily bounded.

GREATER BRITAIN AND IMPERIAL FEDERATION: VARIATIONS ON A THEME

The relationship between Greater Britain and imperial federation was complex and often confused. While virtually all federalists employed the language of Greater Britain, not all of the proponents of Greater Britain were federalists. Imperial federation attracted a number of renowned advocates including Seeley, Froude, James Bryce, Lord Rosebery, W. E. Forster, L. T. Hobhouse, J. A. Hobson, Alfred Tennyson, Joseph Chamberlain, W. T. Stead, and Cecil Rhodes. A galaxy of less prominent characters joined them. Opposition, meanwhile, emanated from many quarters, including such notables as A. V. Dicey, Dilke, E. A. Freeman, Goldwin Smith, Herbert Spencer, Robert Lowe, John Morley, John Bright, Gladstone, and Salisbury. The picture, though, was rarely as simple as this binary opposition might suggest, for many of the critics of federation (understood in a formal constitutional sense) were fervent advocates of a nonfederal Greater Britain. Dilke, for example, believed that federation was inappropriate as a mechanism for forging closer imperial bonds, as the colonists displayed little enthusiasm for it, and the moral and cultural foundations were already secure enough.[31] To tamper with the existing constitutional structure would undermine the project of global colonial unity. The demand for imperial federation was, then, a subset of the wider concern over the future of Greater Britain.

The quest for a global British polity was one of the most ambitious responses to the rupture in Victorian national self-confidence. It was seen as the answer to a plethora of problems. "Restless, disappointed, alarmed, a ray of light appeared," declared the Chichele Professor of Modern History at Oxford.[32] Not only was this "ray of light" born of anxiety, it grew dazzling under its veil, and finally dimmed as its utility and practicability

---

[31] Dilke, *The Problems of Greater Britain*, I, 458–59.
[32] Montagu Burrows, "Imperial Federation," *NR*, 4 (1884–85), 367.

appeared to recede. The proximate cause of the rise of the federalist movement was the largely unfounded suspicion that the Liberal government was intent on dismembering the empire in 1869–71. This triggered a strident campaign to "save" the empire, a drive that gathered steam during the 1870s and reached its peak in the late 1880s and early 1890s, by which time the status of the colonies was an issue firmly on the agenda of many politicians and political thinkers.[33] The IFL was created in 1884, during a "period of political unrest, agitation, and doubt."[34] Proponents of federation were the most vocal, innovative and ambitious, as well as the best-organized advocates of Greater Britain. This does not mean that they developed a coherent political vision on which all agreed—far from it—but rather that they offered some ambitious proposals for the future of world order, established organizations to agitate for federation (most notably the IFL), created a campaigning journal (*Imperial Federation*), and in general tried to present the semblance of unity and common purpose. It is for this reason that I will concentrate primarily on those who identified themselves as federalists.

The difference between antifederalists like Dilke and federalists such as Seeley was often one of temperament and tactics. The antifederalist proponents of Greater Britain were in general less concerned about the exigency and extent of the crises identified by the federalists, and more optimistic about the strength of the already existing ties binding the empire. They saw no need to overlay this flourishing entity with more formal political structures. At least some of them regarded the political independence of the settler colonies as unproblematic, even as potentially beneficial, arguing that racial and national commonalities were enough to keep Greater Britain united as a global force for the foreseeable future. Demanding independence for the colonies, J. A. Farrer, a leading expert on Adam Smith, argued that "the Separatist, too, may indulge in his dream of a greater Britain, of an English Empire coterminous with English speech, concentrated, not by unnatural and galling political bonds, but by the sympathies of free communities, and by the affections of equal al-

---

[33] For contemporary comments on the agitation, which was initiated mainly by the withdrawal of troops from New Zealand, see William Westgarth, "On the Colonial Question," *PRCI*, 2 (1870), 59–61; and Julius Vogel, "Greater or Lesser Britain," *NC*, 1 (1877), 809–10. As historians now argue, imperial policy was actually marked by continuity not rupture: C. C. Eldridge, *England's Mission* (London, 1973), chs. 3 and 4; Burgess, *The British Tradition of Federalism*, ch. 2; and Farnsworth, *The Evolution of British Imperial Policy*, ch. 6. While agreeing with this interpretation, in this book I am more concerned with the widespread shift in representations of the empire, of how it was conceived. This shift is portrayed convincingly in Beasley, *Empire as the Triumph of Theory*; and Beasley, *Mid-Victorian Imperialists* (London, 2005).

[34] William Greswell, "The Imperial Federation League," *NR*, 14 (1889–90), 186. See also E.H.H. Green, "The Political Economy of Empire," *OHBE*, IV, 358.

lies."[35] Goldwin Smith, as we shall see, outlined a similar argument. The federalists tended to view the world through a darker lens, and thought that the only way to secure and strengthen the empire lay in further formalizing the existing ties, locking the colonies into a permanent constitutional relationship with the United Kingdom.

The federalists themselves were divided over how much change was required. Ged Martin has sketched a useful tripartite distinction—one that will be employed throughout the book—between the different modes of federation that were proposed during the nineteenth century.[36] The most straightforward politically was "extra-parliamentary" federation, defined by the operation of an organized group of high-ranking individuals offering nonbinding advice on imperial affairs. This led to a proliferation of calls for the creation of imperial Advisory Councils in London.[37] An alternative, more complex and constitutionally demanding, was "parliamentary federalism," whereby the colonies were to send elected representatives to sit in London. This had been a common exhortation since the mid-eighteenth century. Finally, and generating the most ambitious proposals, "supraparliamentary federalism" demanded the creation of a sovereign federal chamber operating above and beyond the individual political assemblies of the empire, including that in Westminster. As such, so the argument went, the organization of the Anglo-Saxon colonies would resemble that of Switzerland, Germany (after 1871), and, in particular, the United States. In essence, it demanded the construction of a globe-spanning state.

The meaning of the concept of "empire" and the way in which the term "imperial federation" was employed fluctuated considerably. Such theoretical vagueness led to criticisms both at the time and in more recent analyses of imperial discourse.[38] Yet castigating the lack of conceptual precision displayed by the federalists—for example, emphasizing their

---

[35] Farrer, "The Problem of Empire", *FR*, 43 (1885), 344.

[36] Martin, "Empire Federalism and Imperial Parliamentary Union, 1820–1870," *HJ*, 15 (1973), 65–93. Various plans are outlined in Seymour Cheng, *Schemes for the Federation of the British Empire* (New York, 1931). For contemporary snapshots, see Frederick Young, "Schemes and Suggestions for Imperial Federation," *IF*, 1/3 (1886), 71–72; and F. P. de Labillière, "British Federalism," *PRCI*, 24 (1892–93), 95–120.

[37] See, for example, Earl Grey, "How Shall We Retain the Colonies?" *NC*, 5 (1879), 935–54; and John Douglas Sutherland, Marquis of Lorne, *Imperial Federation* (London, 1885). Lorne was the son-in-law of Queen Victoria, and served as governor-general of Canada (1878–83). He suggested that the agent-generals of the colonies be allowed the privileges of the House of Commons (such as making speeches) but without the power of the vote combined, in an unspecified manner, with a Privy Council–like board.

[38] Richard Jebb, "Imperial Organization" in Charles Sydney Goldman (ed.), *The Empire and the Century* (London, 1905), 333–36; J. E. Kendle, *Federal Britain* (London, 1997), ch. 3; and Burgess, *The British Tradition of Federalism*, 76.

failure to distinguish consistently between "federation" and "confederation"—obscures an adequate historical reconstruction of the intentions and languages employed in imagining the future of Greater Britain. It was the very elusiveness of the federalist agenda that allowed such a diverse group of thinkers to remain united by a common concern for so long, and the key point is not that the movement was too amorphous, or that it lacked intellectual coherence, or indeed that it collapsed when it did, but rather that the debate was maintained at a high level of intensity for over three decades and that its echoes resounded throughout the early years of the twentieth century. Visions of Greater Britain acted as a focal point and site of political contestation for a series of wide-ranging arguments over the nature of the British state and its claims to global leadership. This was not simply a chapter in the uneven history of British federalism, or even of the empire itself.

Most contemporaries viewed the movement for imperial federation as a failure. None of the main constitutional recommendations promulgated by its leading figures was realized at the time, and it collapsed in ignominy, divided among competing interest groups and visions of the future. Although it played a significant role in the establishment of a system of imperial conferences, the first of which convened in 1887, the movement was regarded as a disappointment by many of its supporters, whose ambitions had often been far greater. Despite the vocal backing of a large number of backbench MPs, and also the patronage of some senior parliamentary figures (including Rosebery, Forster, and Chamberlain), the issue was rarely taken seriously in the highest reaches of Westminster.[39] It was one thing for senior politicians to voice support, another for them to actually invest political capital in trying to revise imperial policy. Dilke commented once that it was "regarded as safe for Canadian politicians to talk enthusiastically about Imperial Federation in the abstract, provided it is understood no serious practical action is to be taken towards that end."[40] This point can be extended to include the British parliamentary elite. The federalists also suffered from their failure to attract the support of the two leading politicians of the late Victorian period. Salisbury characterized Chamberlain's enthusiasm for imperial federation as "so distasteful that all plans for it . . . would seem in detail impractical." This was a common rejoinder, and it highlighted the massive struggle that the federalists encountered in trying to convert skeptics to their cause.

[39] J. E. Kendle, *The Colonial and Imperial Conferences, 1887–1911* (London, 1967), 13–16; and Michael Burgess, "The Imperial Federation Movement in Great Britain, 1861–93," unpublished PhD, University of Leicester, 1976, ch. 3. Burgess notes the almost total absence of serious discussion in parliamentary debate between 1874–86 (81). Moreover, the movement also failed to find much favor in the Colonial Office.

[40] Dilke, *Problems of Greater Britain*, I, 100.

Neither was that other Victorian titan, Gladstone, impressed by formal federal schemes, going so far as to ridicule imperial federation as "chimerical if not a little short of nonsensical." He dismissed summarily the plan submitted for consideration by the IFL in April 1893.[41] The League broke up acrimoniously soon after, and by the outbreak of the South African War this phase of the debate was largely exhausted. Following the war, the emphasis shifted to designing proposals focusing on economic issues, or on minor political changes, rather than on significant constitutional engineering, although there were some notable exceptions to this rule.[42]

The bulk of federalist activity occurred outside Parliament. Arguments about Greater Britain were thus formulated, disseminated, and challenged mainly in the wider public sphere, composing an important dimension of what John Darwin labels the "information milieu" of Victorian imperial campaigning.[43] But here the limits of the federal endeavor, rooted in a problematic conception of the nature of political action, came to the forefront. While there were numerous federalist supporters among the colonial populations, the dominant attitude in the empire of settlement was one of indifference.[44] Dilke observed that while "many of the leading colonists and distinguished statesmen that Greater Britain has produced are in favour of Imperial Federation," it should also be understood that "some communities they represent on other questions seem on this one disinclined to follow their lead." Another critic of formal federation wrote that a "sentimental aspiration confined to what used to be called the governing class of this country cannot reverse the history of forty years."[45] Given the lack of parliamentary muscle that the federalists could command, this was a key failing. The more successful of Collini's "public

[41] Salisbury, letter to Henry Parkes, December 23, 1891, cited in David Steele, *Lord Salisbury* (London, 1999), 271; and Gladstone, as recorded by his private secretary Edward Hamilton in his diary, 19 November 1884; quoted in Michael Burgess, "The Federal Plan of the Imperial Federation League 1892?" in Andrea Bosco (ed.), *The Federal Idea* (London, 1990), 153. The text of the plan is reproduced in Arthur Loring and R. J. Beadon (eds.), *Papers and Addresses by Lord Brassey* (London, 1894), 289–301. Gladstone rejected it for a variety of reasons, including its lack of specificity and because it hinted at a challenge to free trade. See also Robert Beadon, "Why the Imperial Federation League Was Dissolved," *NR*, 22 (1893–94), 814–22.

[42] I return to this issue, and highlight some of the exceptions, in the concluding chapter.

[43] Darwin, "Imperialism and the Victorians," *EHR*, 112 (1997), 642.

[44] From an extensive literature, see Keith Sinclair, *Imperial Federation* (London, 1955); John Eddy and D. M. Schreuder (eds.), *The Rise of Colonial Nationalism* (London, 1988); Luke Trainor, *British Imperialism and Australian Nationalism* (Cambridge, 1994); and, for some cautionary words, Douglas Cole, "The Problem of 'Nationalism' and 'Imperialism' in British Settlement Colonies," *JBS*, 10 (1971), 160–82.

[45] Dilke, *Problems of Greater Britain*, II, 481; and Bernard Mallet, "The Whigs and Imperial Federation," *MM*, 61 (1890), 220.

moralists" were united in an intimate communion with their audience, and this gave their thought much of its influence and power. To a degree the same could be said of many of the federalists; they moved in the same circles, they published in the same periodicals, they were members of the same clubs. But there was a dissonance between their actual and their intended (indeed their necessary) audiences, for although they may have been at home in the comfortable rhythms of the London intellectual scene, they failed to grasp the altogether different dynamics, expectations, and ambitions of the multiple groups—comprising the politicians in Westminster, the British working classes, and the colonial settler populations—that they stressed the importance of converting to their creed. This triple failure proved fatal to most of their ambitions.

Colin Matthew has noted that by the late 1880s the IFL was dominated by Conservative parliamentary members.[46] But imperial federation was not solely, or even primarily, a conservative endeavor. As will be emphasized throughout the following chapters, advocates of Greater Britain spanned all the major political camps, making it one of the broadest and most diffuse of Victorian ideological projects. All of the leading promoters of Greater Britain argued that the future of the empire should be regarded as a nonpartisan issue, that it was simply too important to be left to the machinations of party politics. Nevertheless, the impetus and theoretical innovation in the quest for a global polity often came from liberals. This was a form of liberalism, however, that was frequently laced with traditional republican themes of virtue, patriotism, disdain for materialist luxury and excess wealth creation, agrarian nostalgia, and a striving for the common good above narrow self-interest. It combined anxiety about the future progress and moral character of the polity with a belief that the ultimate harmony of sectional interests could be secured through judicious constitutional engineering, promising the intellectual and political elite the institutional means to harness "improvement" while simultaneously taming radicalism and the damaging consequences of mass democracy. In drawing on such long-standing tropes in British political discourse, many of the colonial unionists sought to distinguish themselves sharply from what they saw as the corrosive liberalism of the "Manchester School" and the utilitarian political economists.

---

[46] Matthew, *The Liberal Imperialists*, 163, indicates that in 1888 of the 83 MPs on the IFL council, only 6 were liberals (this included James Bryce). It should be noted, though, that he does not indicate how many of the nonliberals were (ex-liberal) unionists. In the early days of both the League and of the Royal Colonial Institute, there was a very significant liberal presence. The list of the Council of the IFL in 1888 is reproduced in Loring and Beadon (eds.), *Papers and Addresses of Lord Brassey*, Appendix III, 283–89. On conservative ideology, see E.H.H. Green, *The Crisis of Conservatism* (London, 1995); and Michael Bentley, *Lord Salisbury's World* (Cambridge, 2001).

Traditionally, unions of states have been institutional responses to perceived military weakness. This strategic impulse continued to drive the
move to federate in the nineteenth century, especially after the American
experiment had demonstrated that it was possible to create a strong federal state (and not simply a loose confederal alliance). It was the leading
strand in imperial federalist thought. While economic considerations were
also important, and while some colonial unionists demanded the creation
of a commercial *Zollverein*, it was political and military concerns (infused
with claims about virtue, justice, and destiny) that predominated during
the period covered by this book.[47] And economic reasoning itself was
often inseparable from ethical prescription: specific policies—including,
in their conflicting ways, both laissez faire and protectionism—were often
justified at least partly on the grounds that they helped to shape the moral
character of individuals and communities.[48] During the late 1880s and
early 1890s the political and theoretical schisms that had always divided
the colonial unionists began to undermine the (at best limited) coherence
of the movement. Its diverse elements never attained sufficient ideological focus, force, or consensus, for the unionists differed over the goals of
federation, over the methods of persuasion to adopt, and, ultimately, over
how the empire should be constituted and governed.[49]

This book seeks to demonstrate that the debate over Greater Britain
was both more important and more interesting than has often been recognized—more important because during the last three decades of the
century the question of colonial unity was a pressing topic for many politicians and intellectuals; more interesting not because the arguments presented were highly sophisticated or original (although some were at least
the latter) but because they symbolized and helped to amplify many of the
tensions pervading Victorian political thought. The stakes seemed very

[47] For examples of a defense-oriented approach, see Lord Brassey, "Imperial Federation
as Recently Debated," *NC*, 30 (1891), reprinted in the *Papers and Addresses of Lord
Brassey*, 156–69; and J.C.R. Colomb, *Imperial Federation* (London, 1886). For imperial
preference, see Charles Tupper, "How to Federate the Empire," *NC*, 31 (1892), 525–37; S.
Bourne, "Imperial Federation in Its Commercial Aspect," *IF*, 1/1 (1886), 8–10; and, C. E.
Howard Vincent, "Inter-British Trade and Its Influence on the Unity of the Empire," *PRCI*,
22 (1891–92), 265–88. This was a minority position, however, at least in public. For a use-
ful account of the various types of economic reforms proposed, see Anthony Howe, *Free
Trade and Liberal England, 1846–1946* (Oxford, 1997), 213–22.

[48] Cain, "Character and Imperialism," *JICH*, 34 (2006), 177–200; and P. J. Cain, "Empire and the Languages of Character and Virtue in Later Victorian and Edwardian Britain,"
MIH, 4 (2007), 1–25.

[49] Following the dissolution of the IFL, competing organizations were established that
focused on either the military or economic aspects of a united empire. These included the
United Empire Trade League (1891), which pushed a preference agenda, the Imperial Federation (Defence) Committee (1894), which stressed military co-operation, and the British
Empire League (1896), composed of free traders.

high. For Seeley the future of Greater Britain was an issue of epochal significance: "what an enormous, intricate, and at the same time what a momentous problem is before us! . . . How much it surpasses in importance all those questions of home politics which absorb our attention so much!" Forster, Liberal statesman and first president of the IFL, proclaimed that failure to construct a federation would result in the "weakening of England, the increased probability of war among Christian nations, and—I do not think the words too strong—the throwing back of the progress of civilisation."[50]

Advocates of a global polity were often chastized for being utopian fantasists, their ideas detached from any secure anchorage in British political experience. The fact that they were generally unwilling to provide detailed plans for a federal Greater Britain, preferring instead to talk in elusive terms about reorienting public consciousness, was seen to confirm their crude idealism. This is not a portrait that they acknowledged. The federation of the English-speaking elements of the empire was not, argued one political radical, "of the character of a Utopian dream, but of the nature of an eminently practical and vital question."[51] For many, a federal Greater Britain served as a positive ideal, an inspirational model of the future necessary to crystallize transformative political action in the present. It functioned in a similar manner to Georges Sorel's "myth," as a powerful though largely indeterminate image that helped unify and motivate support.[52] They recognized the importance, indeed the necessity, of shaping public opinion and appealing to diverse audiences both at home and in the colonies, and their style of advocacy, as a consequence, emphasized the intuitive, emotional, and symbolic aspects of politics at the expense of the more laborious elaboration of detailed proposals. This notion of Greater Britain as motivational ideal triggered an avalanche of passionate but vague rhetoric about unity, glory, and destiny—the iconographic order of Greater Britain.[53] While this was a plausible strategy, and perhaps the only one with any chance of success, it led to significant problems. The chief impediment appeared in attempting to translate the nebulous idea of global unity, of a providentially ordained Greater Britain, into a widely acceptable practical scheme in an intellectual and political environment that was often skeptical of radical change (let alone the specific ambitions of the federalists) and unwilling to place the colonial em-

---

[50] Seeley, *The Expansion of England*, 165; and Forster, comments, *Imperial Federation* (London, 1884), 26.

[51] [Anon.], "The Federation of the British Empire," *WR*, 128 (1887), 485.

[52] Sorel, *Reflections on Violence*, ed. Jeremy Jennings (Cambridge, 1999 [1908]), 28–29 and 116–17. Cf. J.D.B. Miller, "The Utopia of Imperial Federation," *Political Studies*, 4 (1956), 195–97.

[53] Duncan Bell, "The Idea of a Patriot Queen?" *JICH*, 34 (2006), 1–19.

pire at the forefront of legislative priorities. Although the proponents of
a federal Greater Britain failed to achieve their proximate goals, they nevertheless succeeded in raising the colonial empire to a position in metropolitan political consciousness unmatched since the American secession.
The long-term repercussions of the debate were to have a pronounced (albeit indirect) effect on the shape of European and global politics in the
twentieth century.

EMPIRE AND IDEOLOGY

The most impressive studies of Victorian political thought have tended
to sideline issues of overseas dominion, focusing instead on the exploration of domestic intellectual movements.[54] Yet historically ideologies
of empire have not been sui generis, but rather important constituents of
broader constellations of political discourse; to examine them in isolation (or simply to disregard them altogether) is to lose much of the scope
and force not only of the ideas themselves but of political theory in general. It is therefore fortunate that the history of imperial political thought
has recently, albeit belatedly, attracted considerable attention; most of
this work, however, remains focused on the early modern period and the
eighteenth century. Although there are signs that this is beginning to
change, and the Victorians are being subjected to the same forensic scrutiny as that accorded thinkers of preceding centuries, work remains to be
done.[55]

Part of the problem is that imperial historians and historians of political thought rarely engage in sustained and constructive dialogue, with adverse consequences for both fields. The political theory of Greater Britain
has been unduly neglected. The imperial federation movement has generated a small but valuable scholarly literature. In particular, the work of
Ged Martin, Michael Burgess, and J. E. Kendle provides us with a comprehensive outline of the institutional dynamics of the movement, the
chronology of the agitation, and the wider political impact of the federalist movement—topics that I therefore do not engage systematically.[56]

[54] See, for example, John Burrow, *Whigs and Liberals* (Oxford, 1988); Burrow, Stefan
Collini and Donald Winch, *That Noble Science of Politics* (Cambridge, 1983); Collini, *Public Moralists;* Michael Freeden, *The New Liberalism* (Oxford, 1978); Peter Clarke, *Liberals
and Social Democrats* (Cambridge, 1978); and H. S. Jones, *Victorian Political Thought.*
[55] For recent contributions to the literature, see the essays in Duncan Bell (ed.), *Victorian
Visions of Global Order* (Cambridge, 2007); and also the work reviewed in Bell, "Empire
and International Relations in Victorian Political Thought," *HJ*, 49 (2006), 281–98. On
developments in India, see the special edition of *MIH* ("An Intellectual History for India"),
4/1 (2007).
[56] Martin, "Empire Federalism and Imperial Parliamentary Union, 1820–1870"; Bur-

Just as the understanding of the history of political thought is constrained by neglect of imperial and international affairs, so the understanding of imperial political theory is hindered by the lack of attention paid to the assorted contexts—political, social, cultural, theological and scientific—in which debates over the empire were situated. Only by interpreting the discourse of Greater Britain in relation to these fields of thought and practice is it possible to gain an adequate appreciation of the innovation and continuity, as well as the intentions and force, of the arguments. And because historians of political thought have largely ignored the idea of Greater Britain, there is a significant lacuna in our map of Victorian intellectual history. The questions raised by the notion of an intercontinental political community encompass several critical themes, including: theories of statehood, free trade, and competition; conceptions of race, culture, and nationality; attitudes to both territoriality and the sea; and relations with Ireland, continental Europe, and the United States. A study of such arguments offers important insights into the Victorian political imagination.

The Idea of Greater Britain is, in a sense, an examination of the complex and tension-ridden interface between political thought and public policy. Schemes for Greater Britain and imperial federation were not the product of political philosophers working away in secluded cloisters. They were political ideologies: "clusters of ideas, beliefs, opinions, values and attitudes usually held by identifiable groups, that provide directives, even plans, of action for public policy-making in an endeavour to uphold, justify, change or criticize the social and political arrangements of a state or other political community."[57] Ideologists are less concerned with logical coherence and rigor (much as this might also seem important to them) than with shifting the nature of practical politics by drawing on and manipulating existing discourses, by generating wide support among target groups, and by presenting their ideas as the only viable solution to a particular set of self-defined problems. While the advocates of Greater Britain usually did not display the philosophical skills required to stir the interest of most historians of political thought, they present a case study of an

---

gess, "The Imperial Federation Movement in Great Britain, 1861–93"; Burgess, *The British Tradition of Federalism;* Kendle, *The Colonial and Imperial Conferences,* ch. 1; and Kendle, *Federal Britain.* See also Andrew Thompson, *Imperial Britain* (London, 2000); A. L. Burt, *Imperial Architects* (Oxford, 1913), 64–103; Cheng, *Schemes for the Federation of the British Empire;* J. E. Tyler, *The Struggle for Imperial Unity, 1868–1895* (London, 1938); Sobei Mogi, *The Problem of Federalism* (London, 1931), I; and Murray Forsyth, *Unions of States* (Leicester, 1981).

[57] Michael Freeden, "Ideology, Political Theory and Political Philosophy" in Gerald Gaus and Chandran Kukathas (eds.), *Handbook of Political Theory* (London, 2004), 6. On politicians as political thinkers see Kari Palonen, "Political Theorizing as a Dimension of Political Life," *EJPT,* 4 (2005), 351–66.

equally significant mode of political thinking. Their efforts also illuminate the difficulties faced when attempting to translate ambitious political visions into practice. These are lessons from which many of the political theorists of our own time, enamored of an overly abstract fusion of moral philosophy and jurisprudence, could learn.

If we understand the history of political thought as an exercise in retrieval, as an archaeological reconstruction of the languages through which past generations conceived of the world and their relationship to it, a broad interpretative approach is required. The phrase "imperial political thought" is used throughout the book in a deliberately expansive sense, as encompassing the complex of arguments invoked to envisage, interrogate, and offer potential answers to the questions raised by the existence of empire. Imperial political thought was articulated via a number of different media: traditional forms of textual "political theory" (primarily books, pamphlets, and essays); work addressed to specific expert audiences (policy papers, reports); direct but usually transient interventions into political debate (speeches and forays into journalism); and literary and symbolic representations of the empire. I concentrate largely, but not exclusively, on the first three of these categories, partly to redress the imbalance in much recent imperial historiography, mainly because this is where most of the relevant material is found. An exclusive focus on the works of canonical figures—John Stuart Mill most obviously—obscures the wider patterns of Victorian political thought. The reason for this is simple: "great" figures are often unrepresentative (or are only partly so) of the intellectual currents of any given historical epoch. Anthony Howe has argued that the theoretical mutation of the ideology of free trade in the late Victorian period "has often bemused historians, for it took place not at the level of the towering waves of economic and social theory, but in the murky shallows of recondite policy debate." Likewise Boyd Hilton has demonstrated that focusing on the "towering waves" of economic and social theory led to a widespread misunderstanding of the ideological sources of nineteenth-century political economy, for lavishing attention on Adam Smith, Bentham, and Ricardo masked the fundamental role played by evangelical theology.[58] This is also the case with the political theory of Greater Britain. It is the "murky shallows," not only of policy debate but also of general political argument, that we must scour in order to enrich understanding of the way in which the empire was imagined, and the multiple and often contradictory roles that it played in Victorian

---

[58] Howe, *Free Trade and Liberal England, 1846–1946*, 195; and Hilton, *The Age of Atonement* (Oxford, 1988). See also Frank Trentmann and Martin Daunton, "Worlds of Political Economy" in Trentmann and Daunton (eds.), *Worlds of Political Economy* (London, 2004), 10.

intellectual life. Without comprehending the importance of ideas about Greater Britain, the picture of Victorian imperial discourse is radically incomplete.

A further gap in the intellectual history of empire relates to the evolution of languages of British national consciousness. There are two overlapping dimensions that here need to be separated. The first concerns Victorian perceptions of empire, the way in which it was conceived by the inhabitants of the metropole. The importance of the "empire of settlement" for the late Victorians has been underplayed in the imperial history boom of the last two decades.[59] Recent historiography, and in particular the "new imperial history," has been dominated by explorations of the ideologies, representations, and practices of British rule in Africa and India, as well as the considerable, even constitutive, impact that these had on Britain.[60] This scholarship has provided many valuable insights, confronting issues—race, class, gender, the everyday lives of imperial subjects, and the modes and mechanisms of domination and resistance—that were for too long sidelined by an often complacent Eurocentric field. But this laserlike focus has obscured even as it has revealed, opening up some topics while occluding others.[61] The second dimension overlaps with these developments, for interest in the cultural and subaltern aspects of the imperium has paralleled, and at times been intersected by, an intense debate over the various sources and permutations of British (and English) national identity during the eighteenth and nineteenth centuries. The empire unsurprisingly looms large in this literature. Linda Colley, for example, argues that a sense of Britishness was fashioned in opposition to Catholic France during the long eighteenth century, and increasingly during the nineteenth, through encounters with the "imperial other."[62] This

[59] Phillip Buckner, "Whatever Happened to the British Empire?" *Journal of the Canadian Historical Association*, 3 (1993), 3–32; and Carl Bridge and Kent Fedorowich (eds.), *The British World* (London, 2003). An important exception is Cain and Hopkins, *British Imperialism*. Although it is beset by other problems, this neglect was less true of the older imperial historiography: see, for example, the chapters by Ronald Robinson and W.C.B. Tunstall in *The Cambridge History of the British Empire*, ed. E. A. Benians, James Butler and C. E. Carrington (Cambridge, 1959), III, 127–79 and 230–53. Here, however, as with most work of the period, the empire is regarded in isolation from wider currents of thought, and their focus is therefore different from mine.

[60] For interesting examples, see Kathleen Wilson (ed.), *A New Imperial History* (Cambridge, 2004); and Antoinette Burton (ed.), *After the Imperial Turn* (Durham, N.C., 2003). Skeptical notes are sounded in Peter Marshall, "Imperial Britain," *JICH*, 23 (1995), 379–95; and Bernard Porter, *The Absent-Minded Imperialists* (Oxford, 2004).

[61] For an excellent discussion of these issues, pointing to both the strengths and weaknesses of postcolonial approaches, see Frederick Cooper, *Colonialism in Question* (Berkeley, 2005).

[62] Colley, "Britishness and Otherness," *JBS*, 31 (1992), 309–29; and, Colley, *Britons* (New Haven, 1992).

historiographical project goes some of the way to meeting J.G.A. Pocock's demand for a "new subject" of British history, encompassing the interactions of the various peoples and entities that have, over the centuries, expanded, contracted, and finally coalesced into what we know as the United Kingdom.[63]

The confluence of the new(ish) British history and the new(ish) imperial history has highlighted important dimensions of imperial experience and British social and political development. No longer can Britain be studied in isolation from the empire, or the empire separate from Britain. What is still missing, however, is an adequate account of the languages through which the empire—or, more precisely, the various sociopolitical formations that composed the imperial system—was imagined by its inhabitants and in particular by its ideological architects. While numerous scholars have argued that British identity was formed through a binary coding of difference in relation to an exotic "Other,"[64] many, perhaps even the majority, of late Victorian British theorists of empire were concerned as much (and sometimes more) with the projection and sustenance of a coherent sense of Britishness throughout the settler communities. While visions of Greater Britain were framed in relation to a putative global racial hierarchy, at the peak of which stood the Anglo-Saxons, they were also and equally focused on other factors, including fear of increasing competition from other "civilized" states, most notably France, Germany, and America, as well as anxiety about the dangers of socialism, the emergence of a degenerate "underclass," and the perceived growth of a self-interested utilitarian liberalism among the British middle classes and governing elite.

Eliga Gould claims that following the American revolution, the British would "[n]ever again . . . think of any part of their empire as an extension of their own nation."[65] Yet for many Victorian commentators the British national "self" was thought to extend across the planet. This diasporic imagined community was composed, contends Pocock, of "neo-Britains," of people defined by their "global Britishness." While this pic-

---

[63] Pocock, "British History," *JMH*, 47 (1975), 601–21; and Pocock, "The New British History in Antipodean Perspective," *AHR*, 104 (1999), 490–500. See also Armitage, *Greater Britain, 1516–1776*.

[64] Most influentially, Edward Said, *Orientalism* (London, 1978); and Said, *Culture and Imperialism* (London, 1993). For various criticisms, see John Mackenzie, *Orientalism* (Manchester, 1995); Peter Mandler, "The Problem with Cultural History," *Cultural and Social History*, 1 (2004), 94–118; Mandler, "What Is 'National Identity'?" *MIH*, 3 (2006), 271–97; and David Cannadine, *Ornamentalism* (London, 2001).

[65] Gould, *The Persistence of Empire* (Chapel Hill, 2000), 214. He adds the rather elusive qualifier, "at least not in the way they had before 1776." This may well be the case, strictly speaking, but I would argue that the sense in which the Victorians saw it was even stronger than before. See also Gould, "A Virtual Nation?" *AHR*, 104 (1999), 476–89.

ture distorts the "history of multi-ethnic and polyglot colonial societies far removed from the United Kingdom," it is nevertheless how such societies were painted by many late nineteenth-century colonial unionists.[66] Contemporaries viewed the idea of a seamless global nation—let alone a global state—as an innovative, indeed unprecedented, mode of political association. In a speech to the electors of Bristol (1780), Edmund Burke had preached the virtues of the great transatlantic "nation" comprising Britain and the American colonies, united as one body politic through the constitutional arterial system of virtual representation. But this was not a historical narrative (or a conception of the nation) affirmed by many late Victorians: as Seeley proclaimed, "[i]n the last century there could be no Greater Britain in the true sense of the word because of the distance between the mother-country and its colonies and between the colonies themselves."[67] Only with the advent of instantaneous communications, and through the re-imagining of the status and purpose of the colonies and their (Anglo-Saxon) occupants, was it possible to identify the intense sense of political and cultural consciousness necessary for a true global community. Although they differed over the conceptual relationship between state, nation, and empire, for many imperialists Greater Britain was bound intimately by commonality of race, institutions, sensibility, and citizenship. The demand for a global polity was one aspect of the belief in— or fantasy of—a global (national-racial) identity.

OUTLINE OF THE BOOK

The Idea of Greater Britain is not a chronological history of the movement pushing for colonial unity, but rather an analytical account of various aspects of late nineteenth-century political thought. It does not examine parliamentary debates over the empire or provide a detailed taxonomy of the many and varied plans for the future disseminated during the era. It makes no attempt to gauge the popularity of such plans in Britain or the colonies, or to trace the ways in which ideas circulated through the complex networks comprising the imperial system.[68] Instead it explores

[66] Pocock, *The Discovery of Islands* (Cambridge, 2005), 181–91 and 20; and for the criticism, Tony Ballantyne, *Orientalism and Race* (Basingstoke, 2002), 3.

[67] Burke, "Speech at Bristol Previous to Election" [1780] in *The Writings and Speeches of Edmund Burke*, ed. W. M. Elofson (Oxford, 1981), III, 464; and Seeley, *The Expansion of England*, 74.

[68] The study of the circulation of ideas and practices has generated some of the most innovative recent work on empire, including Ballantyne, *Orientalism and Race;* Richard Drayton, *Nature's Government* (London, 2000); and Alan Lester, *Imperial Networks* (London, 2001).

various facets of the theoretical discourse over Greater Britain as it
emerged and evolved at the political core of the empire, analyzing the motivations of its advocates, the assumptions that structured their ideas, the
conceptual and rhetorical moves that they made, and the cultural conventions that shaped their thought, and which they in turn sometimes attempted to challenge or remould.

There was no such thing as a "representative" proponent of Greater
Britain. Colonial unionists traversed, and as such collapsed, the pro-
crustean categories that have been employed traditionally to interpret the
Victorians: individualist versus collectivist; progressive or reactionary;
high, low, or broad church; Tory, Liberal, or Radical; free or fair trader;
and so forth. Consequently, analyzing in exhaustive detail the thought of
a small number of federalists would provide a misleading picture of the
project for a Greater British century. I employ what might be termed a
method of "hybrid contextualization," insofar as I present both detailed
portraits of individual thinkers and wide-ranging thematic studies of significant shifts in the theoretical perspectives shaping political consciousness. Without the former, an account of late Victorian imperial discourse
would lose sight of the nuance and complexity of individual intellectual
development, the specificities of sensibility, disposition, and temperament
so important in shaping political ideas, and the resulting depiction would
lack adequate depth and texture. But without the latter, detailed biography loses its anchorage in the intellectual fields that shape and constrain
the writing and dissemination of political thought, and especially in a debate as sweeping as that over Greater Britain the vital relationship to the
wider intellectual and political world would be lost.

Two general lines of argument frame the book, and set the context for
the various themes pursued in the individual chapters. The first of these
concerns the stimulus driving the advocates of Greater Britain. It has traditionally been argued that they were motivated overwhelmingly by apprehension about the rise of foreign competitors, both military and economic: the creation of an ambitious German state at the heart of Europe,
added to the post–Civil War vitality of America and alarm over Russia,
fueled anxiety about the destiny of Britain. This external pressure, so the
argument runs, when combined with fear that the empire was rapidly slipping off the political agenda, triggered the outburst of writing about
Greater Britain. While the rise of competitor states was certainly a key
motivational factor, it was not the only one. It is also essential to take account of the anxiety—and the exhilaration—spawned by the onset of
democracy, both in the United Kingdom and farther afield. Disquiet preceding the Reform Acts (of 1867 and 1884) was followed, in many quarters, by what Alan Ryan has termed "democratic disappointment," a
sense of disillusionment with the trajectory of political development. This

disenchantment should be read in light of the perceived intellectual tensions and transformations of the age. The shibboleths of Victorian self-confidence were under unremitting assault. The foundations of progress, the epistemic bases of religious and ethical belief, the sacred doctrines of political economy, even the unity and balance of the kingdom, all were challenged by advances in science, by social and political turbulence, by shifts in the philosophical current.[69] But others, usually political radicals, welcomed the coming of an age of democracy, and they looked to Greater Britain as both an exemplar and an agent of progressive change. For John Morley this was an age of "transition in the very foundations of belief and conduct," while A. V. Dicey, looking back over the century, wrote that during the closing decades of Queen Victoria's reign the country had witnessed that "singular phenomenon which is best described as the disintegration of beliefs, or, in other words, the breaking up of established creeds, whether religious, moral, political, or economical."[70] Visions of Greater Britain were partly a response to this ferment.

The second line of argument concerns the novelty of the federal discourse. Miles Taylor claims that neither the "supporters nor the opponents of the schemes for imperial federation differed very much from the ideas expressed by the colonial reformers of the 1830s."[71] Yet, while there was indeed a long tradition of demanding colonial unity, most commonly via parliamentary representation, and while there were various similarities between the two periods, the structure, intensity, and theoretical focus of the later debate was different. Seeley argued that "all the conditions of the world are altered now."[72] New ways of imagining and justifying the

[69] Ryan, "The Critique of Individualism" in Brian Barry, Archie Brown, and Jack Hayward (eds.), *The British Study of Politics in the Twentieth Century* (Oxford, 2003), 109; and, for general context, John Burrow, *The Crisis of Reason* (London, 2000). For shifts, during the 1870s, in moral philosophy, economics, epistemology, the philosophy of religion, and social theory, see the essays by James Allard, Ross Harrison, Geoffrey Hawthorn, Margaret Schabas, Peter Nicholson, and James Livingston, in Thomas Baldwin (ed.), *The Cambridge History of Philosophy, 1870–1945* (Cambridge, 2003).

[70] Morley, *On Compromise*, 2nd ed. (London, 1886 [1874]), 29; and Dicey, *Lectures on the Relation Between Law and Public Opinion in England During the Nineteenth Century*, 2nd ed. (London, 1914 [1905]), 444. Individuals on apparently opposing sides of the imperial debate concurred: Seeley, "Ethics and Religion," *FR*, 45 (1889), 501–14; and Goldwin Smith, "The Impending Revolution," *NC*, 35 (1894), 353–66.

[71] Taylor, "*Imperium et Libertas,*" *JICH*, 19 (1991), 13. Ged Martin makes the same argument: "Empire Federalism and Imperial Parliamentary Union, 1820–1870"; and Martin, "The Idea of "Imperial Federation" in Ronald Hyam and Ged Martin (eds.), *Reappraisals in British Imperial History* (London, 1975), 121–39.

[72] Seeley, *The Expansion of England*, 297. The colonial reformers concentrated more on propagating specific land reform proposals (following the writings of E. G. Wakefield) and on establishing functioning social hierarchies in the colonies in order to encourage emigration by members of all classes, than they did on general constitutional proposals for the colo-

empire followed from this belief. Although the plans for extraparliamen-
tary advisory councils predominated, supraparliamentary proposals took
center stage due to their ambition and ability to generate controversy. Parliamentary proposals, previously the most common form of argument, retreated into the wings. Furthermore, the growing awareness of the potential power of new communications technologies led to a shift in the
type of political community that could be envisaged as plausible. It had
by 1870 become possible to imagine a global nation-state, which would
before have been largely unintelligible. Graham Berry, a leading colonial
politician, proclaimed that science "has rendered that feasible which,
under conditions that prevailed half a century ago, would have been impossible."[73] The shifting perception of Britain's global role heightened the
urgency of the demands and also generated the audacious nature of many
of the solutions proffered. Combined, these shifts marked a significant
transition in imperial political thought.

Chapter 2 outlines the key political and intellectual contexts essential
for comprehending the anxiety over the future of the empire. It details the
insidious sense of apprehension, fueled by the fear of mass democratic
politics at home and increasing global competition, displayed by many
imperial thinkers during the closing decades of the century. It highlights
how ideas about emigration played a vital role in helping to transform the
perceived relationship between "home" and "abroad," "domestic and
"foreign," and it examines some radical ideas about colonial unity, demonstrating how the settler territories were seen by some people as spaces
for democratic experimentation and for spreading progressive politics.

Chapter 3 traces the impact that changing conceptions of time and
space had on imperial thought over the long nineteenth century. Scholars
have focused almost exclusively on geology and especially biology when
trying to unravel the manner in which science inflected political theorizing. This is certainly an important area of inquiry, for evolutionary ideas
influenced attitudes to competition, race, religion, time, and place, but
such a focus has neglected the role of more prosaic industrial technologies in shaping the contours of political theory. Yet these technologies have

---

nial empire, let alone on conceptions of a global nation or new understandings of the state.
See Wakefield, *Outline of a System of Colonization* [1829] and, *A View of the Art of Colonization* [1849], both in *The Collected Works of Edmond Gibbon Wakefield*, ed. M. F.
Lloyd-Prichard (Glasgow, 1968), 178–87 and 758–1040. See also Donald Winch, *Classical Political Economy and Colonies* (London, 1965), 90–155; Erik Olssen, "Mr Wakefield
and New Zealand as an Experiment in Post-Enlightenment Experimental Practice," *New
Zealand Journal of History*, 31 (1997), 197–218; and Michael J. Turner, "Radical Agitation and the Canada Question in British Politics, 1837–41," *Historical Research*, 79 (2006),
90–114.
  [73] Berry, "The Colonies in Relation to the Empire," *PRCI*, 18 (1886–87), 7.

been (and remain) a significant facet of political argument. While evolution fashioned ideas about the place of humanity in the cosmos, as well as insidious social Darwinist interpretations of human communal life, engineering (and particularly transport and communications) technologies engendered a profound transformation in the manner in which the world itself was perceived, shrinking it from a previously awesome scale to a manageable space in the minds of contemporary observers. The chapter explores the vital role played in the development of imperial discourse by what Walter Bagehot labeled the "new world of inventions"[74]—in particular the ocean-traversing steamship and the submarine telegraph. It also examines how the contrasting ideas about distance articulated by Edmund Burke and Adam Smith shaped debate for much of the ensuing century. This "new world" allowed what had seemed unbridgeable distances to be overcome; the very perception of the political limits prescribed by nature was transformed.

Chapter 4 charts how the question of federalism moved to the center of British political debate, and identifies a variety of ways of conceiving the empire as a state. In particular I outline Seeley's views on global statehood. The chapter also documents some of the conceptions of nation and race that helped structure late Victorian imperial discourse. Chapter 5 examines the way in which the perceived meaning and status of the constitution played an essential regulative function in imperial debate, and what this tells us about historical consciousness and political theory in the Victorian era. It also investigates what I term "civic imperialism," a distinctive republican vision of imperialism that permeated the debates over colonial unity, a vision exemplified by the work of historian J. A. Froude.

Chapters 6 and 7 examine in detail the thought of two of the most influential imperial commentators, namely Goldwin Smith and Seeley. These chapters have two primary aims: firstly, they seek to deepen our understanding of their political ideas; and secondly, they highlight the similarities in their ideological projects, the unity in difference. Smith and Seeley staked out positions that were seen as occupying distinct and opposed positions on the imperial spectrum. Seeley was the intellectual figurehead of Greater Britain, Smith of those resolutely skeptical of the value of the settler empire, let alone federation. As the liberal writer and politician John Morley argued, Smith's conclusions were "directly opposed" to those of Seeley.[75] This is how they continue to be interpreted in imperial historiography. However, although there were crucial differences between their projects, there were also many interesting parallels, and ultimately they should be understood as promoting similar ends, if by different

---

[74] Bagehot, *Physics and Politics* (London, 1896 [1872]), 1.
[75] Morley, "The Expansion of England," *MM*, 49 (1884), 242.

means. Both defended a global yet circumscribed Anglo-Saxon community; both, that is, sought to construct a barricade against the decline and potential fall of Britain as a global power. The gap between the proponents of a federal Greater Britain and many of their harshest critics was, as this juxtaposition suggests, not as wide as it might at first appear. The political thought of Seeley and Smith illustrates another point that emerges from the analysis of Greater Britain. The relationship between religion and visions of Greater Britain was a complex one: there was no single religious position on the empire, and people of all denominations (as well as those of none) were to be found supporting it. It should be remembered nevertheless that the core ambition of Greater Britain was the unity of the British Anglo-Saxon community, and that a key element of this identity was its Protestantism. In this sense at least, Greater Britain could be seen as the striving for a global church, with Seeley, as we shall see, the apostle of this vision. Ultimately, though, religion played an indeterminate role in the debates.

Chapters 8 and 9 return to thematic analysis, documenting a number of theoretical innovations that underpinned late Victorian imperial thought. In chapter 8 I examine how representations of antiquity helped determine the contours of debate. Rather than looking to the Romans and Greeks for intellectual authority and for models of political action, as was traditionally the case, many colonial unionists looked instead to the example set by the United States. In order to justify their proposals they constructed a confident and future-oriented narrative of modernity, one that escaped the vision of political self-dissolution that they associated with previous empires. Chapter 9 explores the diverse ideological functions played by ideas about America. It was utilized as an archetype for a federal empire, while also sending a warning shot from history about the dangers of mistreating colonists. And due to its increasing economic and geopolitical power, and the competitive challenge it represented, it also offered one of the key motivations for constructing a global polity. I explore the tensions between these views, and also look at plans to (re)unite the United States and Greater Britain. Finally, the Conclusion summarizes some of the key dimensions of the debate and traces some of its echoes in later British political discourse.

2

Global Competition and Democracy

> At the present time, almost everyone believes
> in the growth of democracy, almost everyone talks
> of it, almost everyone laments it; but the last
> thing people can be brought to do is to make
> timely preparation for it.
> —Matthew Arnold, "Democracy" (1861)

> Never, surely, was the English mind so confused,
> so wanting in fixed moral principles, as at present.
> —William Westgarth, "The Unity of the Empire" (1884)

THE VALUE placed on the colonial empire shifted considerably over the course of the nineteenth century. The distant lands frequently seemed an unnecessary drain on resources, offering little in return, and even among those who supported colonization, many doubted whether it would be possible to hold on to the colonies in the long term, even if this was desirable.[1] By the 1860s it was widely assumed that they were heading inexorably toward independence, for good or ill. Within a generation such views were seldom voiced, and both the necessity and the practicability of a strong, integrated, and durable imperial polity was proclaimed loudly across the political spectrum. Greater Britain, and in particular imperial federation, became a popular rallying cry.

Fear of apathy was a customary theme in imperial political thought. Imperialists argued that their compatriots often failed to grasp the precarious nature of British global power, or the roles and responsibilities associated with the possession of empire. Their writings and speeches were peppered with objections—usually exaggerated—about the failure of their interests and ambitions to register sufficiently with the government and the people. John Stuart Mill was expressing a common grievance when in 1859 he bemoaned the "indifference to foreign affairs" displayed by the public, and when a decade later he castigated the "indifference of

---

[1] Martin Lynn, "British Policy, Trade, and Informal Empire in the Mid-Nineteenth Century," *OHBE*, IV, 101–22; John M. Ward, *Colonial Self-Government* (London, 1976); A.G.L. Shaw, "British Attitudes to the Colonies, ca. 1820–1850," *JBS*, 9 (1969), 71–95; and W. P. Morrell, *British Colonial Policy in the Age of Peel and Russell* (Oxford, 1930).

official people in England about retaining the colonies."[2] In an early statement of supraparliamentary federalism, John Edward Jenkins, an Australian radical then living in London, warned of the dangers besetting British policy: "At this moment," he wrote, "we are drifting to the disintegration of our Empire."[3] In 1870 J. A. Froude claimed that the public was largely "alienated" from the colonies.[4] Indifference, so they thought, was leavened with ignorance, a lack of awareness about the nature and value of the empire. Speaking at the inaugural meeting of the Royal Colonial Society the Marquis of Normanby, an eminent colonial governor, argued that "[n]o person who takes an interest in colonial matters can help being struck with the extra-ordinary ignorance that exists in this country in regard to colonial matters," while at the same meeting Baillie Cochrane, a Tory MP and one of the original leaders of the "Young England" movement, criticized public and political "indifference."[5] Writing in the *Quarterly Review* in 1870 John Martineau crystallized the frustration of many imperialists when he lambasted the "carelessness and indifference with which the English Parliament, reflecting truly the apathy of the public, has treated the magnificent inheritance of our Colonial Empire."[6] The language of "crisis" was utilized to demonstrate the urgency of the prob-

---

[2] Mill, "A Few Words on Non-Intervention" [1859] in *The Collected Works of John Stuart Mill* (Toronto, 1963–91), XXI, 117; and Mill, letter to Henry Samuel Chapman, January 14, 1870, CW, XVIII, 1685. Hereafter I will refer to this edition as Mill, *CW*. See also Michael Bentley, *Politics Without Democracy*, 2nd ed. (Oxford, 1999), xviii and 182; Peter J. Durrans, "The House of Commons and the British Empire, 1868–1880," *Canadian Journal of History*, 9 (1974), 19–45; and Bernard Porter, *The Absent-Minded Imperialists* (Oxford, 2004).

[3] [Jenkins], "Imperial Federalism," *CR*, 16 (1871), 165 and 185. Jenkins, a barrister, was widely known to the public as the author of the social satire *Ginx's Baby* (London, 1871). He served as the first Agent-General for Canada in London (1874–1876), before being elected Liberal M.P. for Dundee (1874–80). Although he remained a liberal in most respects, he was so alarmed at what he saw as Gladstone's anti-imperialism, that he stood, albeit unsuccessfully, as a Tory parliamentary candidate in both 1885 and 1896.

[4] Froude, "England and Her Colonies," *FM*, 1 (1870), 4–5. For a similar complaint about India, see L. J. Trotter, "British India Under the Crown," *CR*, XV (1870), 113–32; and Frederick Young, "Emigration to the Colonies" *PRCI*, 17 (1885–86), 372. The evidence about indifference is mixed. See, for example, Jonathan Rose, *The Intellectual Life of the English Working Class* (London, 2001), ch. 6; Porter, *The Absent-Minded Imperialists*; and Catherine Hall, *Civilising Subjects* (Cambridge, 2002).

[5] Both men were commenting on Lord Bury's "Inaugural Speech" [March 15, 1869], reprinted in *PRCI*, I (1869–70), 51–62. George Phipps, Marquis of Normanby, had served as governor of Nova Scotia in the 1840s; during the 1870s and 1880s he was governor of Queensland, New Zealand, and Victoria. For similar sentiments, see Robert Andrew Macfie, "On the Crisis of the Empire," *PRCI*, 3 (1871–72), 3; and, a decade later, Granville Cunningham, *A Scheme for Imperial Federation* (London, 1895), 1–2.

[6] [John Martineau], "New Zealand and Our Colonial Empire," *QR*, 128 (1870), 135. See also, [Urquhart Forbes], "Britannic Confederation and Colonisation," *LQR*, 19 (1893), 245.

lem, to insist on its immediacy and magnitude. This emotive idiom made possible the claim that sweeping change was imperative, that without it the empire, and British power itself, would dissolve.

The question of colonial unity had assumed a significant place in political debate by the mid-1870s; and there it remained until the end of the century and beyond. In 1878 the Earl of Carnarvon, the Tory colonial secretary, argued that the colonies "are growing up—those great countries—and the main question which men now debate, is how this vast empire is to be held together, and how we are to prevent those particles from flying, as it were, into political space."[7] J. A. Farrer grumbled that the "movement for Imperial Federation has grown apace. Within a very brief period it has taken such possession of the press that it is now a household word in politics." Indeed by the mid-1880s Robert Stout, intermittent premier of New Zealand and harsh critic of federal plans, could complain that it "may truly be said that Imperial Federation is in the air"—a phrase repeated a decade later, this time enthusiastically, by Joseph Chamberlain,[8] then serving as secretary of state for the colonies. H. E. Egerton suggested that "a new spirit has appeared upon the scene." This spirit, he argued, "shows itself, in the case of the self-governing colonies, on the side of the Mother Country in a deepened sense of their value and of their claims; on the side of the Colonies in a wider Imperial Patriotism, and in a more serious recognition of the difficulties entailed upon the Mother Country by her European and Imperial responsibilities." Apathy appeared to be on the retreat. In the opening year of the new century the idealist philosopher J. H. Muirhead wrote that the previous two decades had witnessed a "great awakening" and the development of a "new form of national consciousness," a realization of the true importance of the organic unity of empire, a vision that, he maintained, was symbolized by the publication of Seeley's *The Expansion of England* and Froude's *Oceana*.[9] He warmly embraced this development. Whatever the ultimate impact of the movement, both critics and supporters regarded it as an important dimension of political debate.

What had generated this "new form of national consciousness"? The prominence of arguments over Greater Britain can be understood ade-

---

[7] Carnarvon, "Imperial Administration," *FR*, 24 (1878), 753. See also the recollections of the period in Lord Brassey, "Introduction" to William Parr Greswell, *Outlines of British Colonisation* (London, 1893), x.

[8] Farrer, "The Problem of Empire," *FR*, 37 (1885), 338; Stout, "A Colonial View of Imperial Federation," *NC*, 21 (1887), 351; and Chamberlain, *Proceedings of a Conference Between the Secretary of State for the Colonies and the Premiers of the Self-Governing Colonies, at the Colonial Office, London, June and July 1897*, (1897), LIX, 631.

[9] Egerton, *A Short History of British Colonial Policy* (London, 1897), 451; and Muirhead, "What Imperialism Means" [1900], reprinted in David Boucher (ed.), *The British Idealists* (Cambridge, 1997), 240 and 242.

quately only in the context of apprehension over the shifting bases of
British national identity in an age of disquiet over both mounting international competition and the possibly deleterious consequences of mass
democracy. As a correspondent wrote in *Imperial Federation* in 1886,
"[t]he United Kingdom is vexed and harassed to-day by a grim catalogue
of disorders. A commercial depression singularly prolonged, a consequent
widespread industrial distress, a land question, and sundry minatory
eruptive tremors of Socialism, are evils sufficient to engage the mind of
every English thinker."[10] Greater Britain was to act as a bulwark against
the cacophony of threats. Such an enormous concentration of wealth and
geopolitical power would allow the British to face the industrial and military challenge of competitor states. Moreover, through a policy of systematic emigration and the generation of an ethos of imperial patriotism,
the threat of socialism (and class struggle more generally) could be diffused. Democracy could be tamed and directed along imperial lines.

Scholars of colonial unity have paid insufficient attention to the importance of the symbiotic relationship between the "domestic" and the
"international" during this period, preferring instead to focus on the
threat from shifts in the balance of global power politics.[11] But this is to
miss half the story. "Home" and "abroad" were so closely linked in the
imagination of the colonial unionists that the categories lose much of their
analytical value when trying to determine the conceptual structure of imperial discourse. Greater Britain was, after all, viewed as a single political
unit, spanning the planet. It was for this reason that Julius Vogel, a former premier of New Zealand, objected to the argument that the colonies
were "foreign" territories; they were instead "part of a mighty nation."[12]
The advocates of Greater Britain sought to collapse the neat distinctions
between domestic and colonial, home and abroad, while simultaneously
emphasizing the important differences between the settler colonies and
the rest of the empire. In so doing they both reflected and helped to reinforce this divide. This chapter analyzes some of the contexts shaping these
arguments. The next section charts the widespread sense of anxiety over
the rise of military and economic threats to British preeminence. Follow-

[10] R. Bryce Bruce, "English Evils and Imperial Remedies," *IF*, 1/9 (1886), 248.
[11] See, for example, William Roy Smith, "British Imperial Federation," *Political Science Quarterly*, 36 (1921), 274–97; J. E. Tyler, *The Struggle for Imperial Unity, 1868–1895* (London, 1938); Hedley Bull, "What Is the Commonwealth," *World Politics*, 11 (1959), 583–84; Trevor Reese, *The History of the Royal Commonwealth Society, 1868–1968* (Oxford, 1968); J. E. Kendle, *The Colonial and Imperial Conferences, 1887–1911* (London, 1967), 1–2; Kendle, *Federal Britain* (London, 1997), xi–xii and ch. 3; and Michael Burgess, *The British Tradition of Federalism* (London, 1995), 28 and 35–37.
[12] Vogel, "Greater or Lesser Britain," *NC*, 1 (1877), 813; and also Vogel, "The British Empire," *NC*, 3 (1878), 617.

ing this, I investigate the domestic challenges perceived in an age of reform. The final two sections explore the stabilizing function that emigration played in proposals for bolstering Greater Britain, and outline a number of visions articulated by political radicals, most notably Joseph Chamberlain and J. A. Hobson.

Balances of Power: Global Threats and Imperial Responses

Defined by "stability, optimism, social solidarity, relative affluence, and liberality," the 1850s and 1860s, it is often argued, saw national self-confidence reach its peak.[13] Yet even though the domestic scene was relatively calm, especially when compared to the turbulence of the 1820s and 1830s, there was growing concern about the country's status as a great power. When delivering his lectures on international law in Cambridge in 1887, Henry Maine argued that the mid-Victorian generation, the "generation of William Whewell," "may be said to have had a dream of peace" to which the atmosphere in the years surrounding the Great Exhibition (1851) contributed. But the "buildings of this Temple of Peace had hardly been removed when war broke out again, more terrible than ever," and Maine pointed to the Crimean War (1853–56) as inaugurating a new period of conflict, which to believers in peace was "a bitter deception."[14] British failure to help the Danish (as had been promised) over Schleswig-Holstein in 1864–65; the devastating Prussian victory over Austria at Königgrätz in 1866; and increasing unease at the potential bellicosity of Napoleon III all fueled fears that British power was eroding dangerously. This trend was exacerbated during the closing three decades of the century.

To pessimistic observers, Britain appeared to enter a spiral of decline. In his *De l'Esprit des Lois* (1748), Montesquieu had declared that a sense of disquiet—"a certain difficulty in existence"—was an animating component of the English character.[15] Despite its anchorage in a dubious claim about the conditioning power of the natural environment, this was a prescient comment, for anxiety concerning impending national decline has shadowed British political discourse for much of the modern era.[16] Speaking in New York in 1890 the liberal scholar and politician James

---

[13] Lawrence Goldman, *Science, Reform, and Politics in Victorian Britain* (Cambridge, 2002), 59. See also Philip Harling, "Equipoise Regained?" *JMH*, 75 (2003), 890–918.

[14] Maine, *International Law* (London, 1888), 3–5.

[15] Charles de Secondat, Baron de Montesquieu, *The Spirit of the Laws*, ed. Anne M. Cohler, Basia Carolyn Miller, and Harold Samuel Stone (Cambridge, 1989), 241.

[16] David Cannadine, *In Churchill's Shadow* (London, 2002), 26–45; and John Darwin, "The Fear of Falling," *TRHS*, 5th series, 36 (1986), 27–45.

Bryce described the rise of a "spirit of discontent" throughout Europe, a spirit radically different from the more optimistic views that had predominated "twenty or thirty years" before.[17] Britain was faltering in its self-appointed task as leader of the "civilized" world; the march of progress was becoming sluggish. New and fearsome competitors were starting to draw near. Conservatives saw their fears about political life, both local and global, materializing before them, and many liberals lost the air of easy confidence that had so often marked their thought. The shift in mood was later recounted by the leading "new liberal" thinker L. T. Hobhouse: "Whether at home or abroad those who represented Liberal ideas had suffered crushing defeats. . . . Its faith in itself was waxing cold."[18] More a loss of nerve than a transformation of belief, this melancholy stance reinforced the drive to secure the future of Greater Britain. There were two major sources of uncertainty: global competition, both economic and geopolitical; and the onset of democracy. They reinforced each other, and the quest for Greater Britain cannot be understood adequately without comprehending this intricate dialectic.

Europe was in flux. Economically, British dominance was thought to be under sustained assault from across the Atlantic and, closer to home, from the recently established and rapidly industrializing Germany. Bismarck's newly forged state was, moreover, apparently enthusiastic to flex its muscles on the world stage, while Russia was regarded as an imminent threat to British primacy in Asia. Italy, the subject of obsessive speculation and the target of many liberal political fantasies, had finally unified. France was regarded warily. The Christian socialist leader J. M. Ludlow warned in 1870 that his compatriots had not yet perceived the full importance of these developments, "the vastness of the spectacle which vitally affects every State." This alleged incomprehension was not to last. "The pulse of Europe is unquestionably beating rather quick," a correspondent noted in the *Contemporary Review* in 1876.[19] With it beat the pulse of many British commentators. Three countries in particular generated concern: Germany, Russia, and the United States.[20] Although the perceived threat differed in each case, the collective power—military and industrial—of this triad led to a reappraisal of Britain's global role, and spurred the de-

[17] Bryce, "An Age of Discontent," CR, 49 (1891), 14–30.

[18] Hobhouse, *Liberalism*, in Hobhouse, *Liberalism and Other Writings*, ed. James Meadowcroft (Cambridge, 1994 [1911]), 103.

[19] Ludlow, "Europe and the War," CR, 15 (1870), 648; and M. E. Grant Duff, "The Pulse of Europe," CR, 28 (1876), 338. See also Emile de Laveleye, "The European Situation," FR, 18 (1875), 1–21; and C. C. Chesney, "Our Panics and their Remedy," MM, 23 (1871), 448–57.

[20] For examples, see [Jenkins], "An Imperial Confederation," CR, 17 (1871), 66; John Douglas, "Imperial Federation from an Australian Point of View," NC, 16 (1884), 854; and also [John Robinson], "The Future of the British Empire," WR, 38 (1870), 66. In most cases the danger was seen to emanate from one country in particular; all also had active admirers.

velopment of a mosaic of schemes for colonial unity. I will return to the more ambivalent and complicated response to America in chapter 9, focusing here on the other two. Germany was now ascendant on the continent: a country admired previously for its cultural dynamism, its biblical and historical scholarship, its sublime music, romantic poetry, and arcane philosophy, was transfigured into a menacing competitor. Commenting on the Europe-wide concern engendered by the unification of his homeland, Friedrich Nietzsche proclaimed in 1887 that "we see again even today" the "deep and icy mistrust which the German arouses as soon as he comes to power." While few concurred with Nietzsche's explanation for this mistrust—it represented, he declared, the "aftermath of that inextinguishable horror with which Europe viewed the raging of the blond Germanic beast for centuries"[21]—many in Britain were perturbed. Frederic Harrison, acolyte of positivism and ardent critic of empire, warned in 1880 that, "Europe is still in arms: each nation matching every other with suspicion, jealousy, or menace," and like many of his contemporaries he regarded Germany as an "empire of the sword," a country that "worst of all . . . fills the air with its spirit, and the sense of foreboding."[22] For Dilke, writing in the early 1890s, "European militarism," and in particular Germany, presented an imminent threat, while Bryce talked of Europe as a "vast camp," poised to explode.[23] The Honorary Secretary of the IFL, Francis de Labillière, warned that "[w]e cannot turn to the newspapers of the day without reflecting and feeling that it is quite possible that within a short period we may find ourselves at war with one, if not two, of the great powers of Europe."[24] But Britain, so many feared, was unprepared. Even the Royal Navy, that previously indomitable guarantor of British independence, was subjected to a relentless campaign to expose its deficiencies from the late 1880s onward. It is no coincidence that this agitation was partly the work of an outspoken imperial federalist, the notorious journalist W. T. Stead.[25]

---

[21] Nietzsche, *The Genealogy of Morality* [1887] ed. Keith Ansell-Pearson (Cambridge, 1994), 25.

[22] Harrison, "Empire and Humanity," *FR*, 27 (1880), 288; as well as Ludlow, "Europe and the War," 650 and 661; and Ludlow, "Principles and Issues of the War," *CR*, 15 (1870), 348–63. The general context is sketched in Paul Kennedy, *The Rise of Anglo-German Antagonism, 1860–1914* (London, 1982), Parts I–III. Admiration for Germany had reached its peak between 1851–70, a period characterized by Matthew Arnold as one of "Teutomania": Peter Mandler, *The English National Character* (London, 2006), ch. 3.

[23] Dilke, *Problems of Greater Britain*, I, 6; and Bryce, "An Age of Discontent," 22.

[24] Labillière, commenting on Graham Berry, "The Colonies in Relation to the Empire," 33; and W. E. Forster, "A Few More Words on Imperial Federation," *NC*, 17 (1885), 552.

[25] Frederick Whyte, *The Life of W. T. Stead* (London, 1925), I, 99–100, 106–107, 112–13, 145–59. Even John Stuart Mill worried about British military weakness: letter to J. E. Cairnes, August 22, 1871, *CW*, XVII, 1828–29. See, in general, Andrew Thompson, *Imperial Britain* (London, 2000), ch. 5; and Bernard Semmel, *Liberalism and Naval Strategy*

Russia acted as a further source of anxiety. Already demonized in the public imagination due to the disastrous war in the Crimea, it was viewed, especially during the 1880s, as dangerously expansionist and intent on challenging Britain over the vast spoils of India. "We should be prepared at all points against an aggressive power like Russia," one imperial federalist warned.[26] The "Eastern Question" convulsed British policy-makers and political commentators: "Afghanistan and Central Europe," the *Fortnightly Review* told its readers in 1880, "still keep English observers in the state of tension which is becoming normal with us, and which is inseparable from the fact of our living in an armed period." But fear of Russian intentions was not confined to the possible invasion of India. "With the colossus of the North striding South," Australia was also facing danger, de Labillière counseled.[27] The perception of a military threat emanating from Europe—whether in the guise of the German regime or on the distant eastern reaches of the continent—was a constant motif in imperial discourse. Greater Britain was regarded as essential for strategic purposes: the resources and sheer size of an intercontinental polity would act as a deterrent to the ambitions of potential rivals. "Both Russia and Germany are the European argument for Imperial Federation. The United States provides the Transatlantic argument."[28]

Such fears found powerful expression in a new and very popular genre of fictional writing: elaborate narratives predicting the outbreak and course of future wars. Seeking to entertain, to frighten, and to highlight the weaknesses of existing policy-making and strategic thought, literary, journalistic, and military expertise combined to construct evocative stories of conflicts yet to come. These stories proved an instant success with the public; the most popular sold tens of thousands of copies, raced through multiple editions, and were translated into numerous foreign languages. As was intended, they acted as a powerful form of political advocacy. Starting with Lt.-Colonel George Chesney's short story "The Battle of Dorking" (1871), which foresaw a weak and complacent Britain defeated by an aggressive German state, and which prompted Gladstone to publicly denounce the alarmism that it catalyzed, the genre reached its most sophisticated form in a collaborative narrative detailing the

---

(London, 1986), ch. 6. Cf. T. H. Farrer, "The Strength of England," *FR*, 23 (1878), 383–403.

[26] William Greswell, "Imperial Federation" in *England and Her Colonies* (London, 1887), 22; see also W. J. Courthope, "Problems of Greater Britain," *NR*, 15 (1890), 444.

[27] Anon., "Home and Foreign Affairs," *FR*, 27 (1880), 309; and de Labillière, *Federal Britain* (London, 1894), 241. See also Graham Berry, "The Colonies in Relation to the Empire," *PRCI*, 18 (1886–87), 6–7. On the "Eastern Question" in British politics, see J. P. Parry, *The Politics of Patriotism* (Cambridge, 2006), ch. 7.

[28] William Greswell, "The Imperial Federation League," *NR*, 14 (1889–90), 196.

"The War of 189-" (1892), where Britain ended up fighting Russia and France.[29] The editor of the illustrated weekly *Black and White* introduced the latter story as an important political intervention at a time of heightened alert. "The air is full of rumours of war. The European nations stand fully armed and prepared for instant mobilization. Authorities are agreed that a GREAT WAR must break out in the immediate future, and that this War will be fought under novel and surprising conditions."[30] The story explored those very conditions and, in so doing, made a case for stronger national and imperial defense. Among the leading contributors to this proliferating literature were a number of prominent advocates of Greater Britain, including the imperial federalist Admiral P. H. Colomb, who coordinated the team writing "The War of 189-," a team that also included Dilke. Another imperial federalist, Hugh Arnold-Forster, launched a political career on the back of his literary success, with one of his stories in particular—"In a Conning Tower" (1888)—introducing him to a large and appreciative audience.[31] Such narratives simultaneously articulated and helped to intensify the political fears of the age.

Anxiety about geopolitical weakness was linked closely to concern about the state of the economy. The rise of strong competitor states coincided with a severe depression in British trade and agriculture.[32] The promise of expansive and inevitable growth, predicted by the Panglossian political economists of preceding generations, was apparently unfulfilled.[33] The supremacy of free trade in Britain was not challenged seri-

---

[29] "The Battle of Dorking," published originally in *Blackwood's* in April 1871, is reprinted in I. F. Clarke (ed.), *The Tale of the Next Great War, 1871–1914* (Liverpool, 1995), 27–74. The controversy it generated is examined in I. F. Clarke, *Voices Prophesying War*, 2nd ed. (Oxford, 1992), ch. 2. "The Battle of 189-," published originally in *Black and White* in 1891–92, is reprinted in I. F. Clarke (ed.), *The Great War with Germany, 1890–1914* (Liverpool, 1997), 30–72. The genre is also analyzed in Charles Gannon, *Rumors of War and Infernal Machines* (Liverpool, 2005), chs. 1–2.

[30] "Editorial Introduction," cited in Clarke (ed.), *The Great War with Germany*, 30.

[31] Arnold-Forster, "In a Conning Tower; How I Took *HMS Majestic* to Victory," published originally in *Murray's Magazine* (1888), is reprinted in Clarke (ed.), *The Tale of the Next Great War*, 139–62. Arnold-Forster was the nephew of Matthew Arnold; this story was much admired by Kipling. Arnold-Forster served as a Liberal Unionist MP and eventually secretary of state for war under Balfour. Admiral Colomb's views on imperial federation were heavily influenced by the writings of his brother, the leading imperial federalist J.C.R. Colomb. Both men were also important figures in the agitation over the state of the navy.

[32] Cormac O'Gráda, "British Agriculture, 1860–1914" in Roderick Floud and Donald McCloskey (eds.), *The Economic History of Britain Since 1700*, 2nd ed. (Cambridge, 1994), II, 145–72.

[33] For complaints along this line, see Daniel Grant, *Home Politics* (London, 1870); and Jehu Mathews, *A Colonist on the Colonial Question* (London, 1872). Unsurprisingly, Mathews ended up as a supporter of imperial federation: "Nature and Need of Imperial Federation," *IF*, 1/4 (1886), 94–96.

ously until the Edwardian Tariff Reform movement launched its divisive campaign. Yet, the general rise of neomercantilist economic policies throughout the world, combined with an increase in the intensity of imperial expansion, meant that this was, as Anthony Howe argues, a period of "deglobalization."[34] Although the majority of the advocates of Greater Britain (and of imperial federation) remained supporters of free trade, a significant minority argued that this position was unsuited to the new political and economic environment. They demanded "fair trade," the introduction of preferences, tariffs, or some combination of the two, in order to shield the British and colonial economies from growing foreign competition.[35] The balance between free traders and their opponents switched after the turn of the century, with supporters of tariff reform gaining the upper hand in the wake of the South African war. The divisions over the theoretical foundations of political economy were a symptom of the fear of economic failure—and of the geopolitical consequences that followed from this. The doubts of the time now appear exaggerated; the British economy remained dynamic and powerful.[36] But it was no longer unreservedly preeminent, and the loss of relative power, and the apparent fear of falling behind, bred apprehension. Perceptions were vital. Compared with the extraordinary growth and dynamism of the American economy, the pivotal strategic position and industrial might of Germany, and the ostensibly aggressive intent of the Russians, it became imperative to many in Britain to seek solace in the verities of scale—to try and maintain Britain's position by welding the United Kingdom and its outlying colonial possessions into a formidable unit.

DEMOCRACY AND THE MORAL ECONOMY OF EMPIRE

The dynamics of domestic, international, and imperial politics were mutually reinforcing, generating a feedback loop of anxiety that served only to amplify the fear of precipitous decline. Democracy, as both incipient

[34] Howe, "Free Trade and Global Order" in Duncan Bell (ed.), *Victorian Visions of Global Order* (Cambridge, 2007). Howe also labels it a period of "imperial globalisation." See also Frank Trentman, "The Strange Death of Free Trade" in Eugenio Biagini (ed.), *Citizenship and Community* (Cambridge, 1996), 219–51.

[35] For a defense of free trade from a convinced critic of imperial federation, see T. H. Farrer, *Free Trade versus Fair Trade* (London, 1882). The I.F.L. established a committee to examine proposals by fair-traders (for example, a uniform customs code), which concluded that they were impracticable due to considerable local variation within the empire. The data was collected in Sir Rawson W. Rawson, *Sequel to Synopsis of the Tariffs and Trade of the British Empire* (London, 1889).

[36] The British economy in 1914 was still the most powerful the world had ever seen: Floud, "Britain, 1860–1914" in Floud and McCloskey (eds.), *The Economic History of Britain Since 1700*, II, 1.

practice and evocative vision, shaped political consciousness, spawning wild fantasies of a world on the verge of transformation, for better or worse, as well as more sober assessments of the reverberations affecting most spheres of social and political life. Excitement was often superseded by anxiety: disillusionment with democracy was one of the defining features of intellectual life in the closing decades of the century.[37] This was compounded by a general, albeit ill-defined, sense of the inevitability of change; as Tocqueville had argued, once the process of democratic reform had gained momentum it was impossible to halt.[38] This seemed to be the destiny of the "civilized" world. Liberals and conservatives often joined, although for different reasons, to voice their concerns about this future.[39] The powerful residue of whiggish prudence, exemplified by Walter Bagehot, was discernable in the venerable argument that it was better to represent interests than individuals.[40] For many "advanced liberals" it was not so much democracy per se that was the problem—and indeed they were prominent in encouraging the metastasis of democracy throughout the body politic—but rather the uncertainty that made judging its consequences on the British polity exceptionally difficult. As Seeley wrote in 1870, "something has happened, we do not yet know what; we have seen the flash, but the report has not yet reached us."[41] It was as much an epistemological problem as a purely political one. The specter of revolution stalked the British political imagination, the continental tumult of 1848 still a vivid memory. Perhaps all would be well; but at worst, it was feared, the very institutions and beliefs that had made Britain great would be dissolved. It was often claimed that the finely tuned and delicate engine of the British constitution had prevented a descent into chaos. Were the moral and cultural foundations of the country now under threat from the "leveling" and materialistic ethos of democracy? The Third Reform Act (1884) crowned this foreboding. Despite the fact that women (as well as up to 40 percent of adult men) were still denied the vote by the outbreak of the First World War, it was commonly perceived that the country had finally entered the democratic age.[42]

The qualms about the potentially damaging, even catastrophic, impact

---

[37] Christopher Harvie, *The Lights of Liberalism* (London, 1976), ch. 8; Christopher Kent, *Brains and Numbers* (Toronto, 1978), 142–51; Mandler, *The English National Character*, ch. 4.

[38] Tocqueville, *Democracy in America*, trans. Henry Reeve (London, 1862), I, 50.

[39] There were, of course, many who welcomed the developments. See, for example, Richard Ashcraft, "Liberal Political Theory and Working-Class Radicalism in Nineteenth-Century England," *PT*, 21 (1993), 249–72.

[40] Bagehot, *The English Constitution*, ed. Paul Smith (Cambridge, 2001 [1867]).

[41] Seeley, "The English Revolution of the Nineteenth Century," *MM*, 22 (1870), Part I, 241.

[42] The figures are from Jose Harris, *Private Lives, Public Spirit* (Harmondsworth, 1994), 13–17.

that the expansion of democracy might have on political stability were indivisibly linked to concern over the deteriorating international environment, for an internally weak state would find it difficult to face the challenge of foreign competitors. Visions of Greater Britain were, at least in part, a response articulated in order to ameliorate this complex of fears. The intellectual pessimism of the liberals when combined with the more traditional pessimism of the conservatives provided a strong platform from which to launch a campaign for colonial unity. In particular, the political mainstream, liberal and conservative alike, lived in fear of "socialism," the purported nemesis of liberty, stability, and progress.[43] It was against this backdrop that Herbert Spencer warned in 1891 that the country was being propelled from "freedom to bondage." Two years later the jurist A. V. Dicey complained that "socialistic sentiment, if not doctrine, has passed from the workshops into the drawing-rooms, and from the mouths of men on the pavement to the speeches of Members of Parliament."[44] It was percolating rapidly throughout society. Socialism threatened to corrode the patriotism, and in particular the fidelity to the constitution, that bound many of the members of the Victorian political and intellectual elite.

A conservative imperial federalist, the acclaimed poet and literary scholar W. J. Courthope, warned that "political supremacy has now passed to the working classes."[45] As a result of this shift in the political landscape, he argued, their views and voice must be accounted for in discussing the future of the empire. Labeling imperial federation a "noble and lofty dream," a writer in the Tory *Quarterly Review* argued in 1884 that the extension of the franchise was a danger to the empire because the vote was being handed to "many men who care extremely little for it [the empire], and are certainly from their position and knowledge, unable to express a valuable opinion upon [issues] of imperial interest." A federal empire would, he argued, "protect us from the danger of the one-man tyranny to which open democracies and veiled democracies alike are liable."[46] Charles Gavan Duffy, once a radical in Ireland and subsequently

---

[43] Socialism in the late nineteenth century was, however, a vague term. See, for example, the usage in J. E. Thorold Rogers, "Contemporary Socialism," *CR*, 47 (1884), 52. A slightly more balanced account of the nature of late Victorian socialism can be found in Emile de Laveleye, "The Progress of Socialism," *CR*, 43 (1883), 561–82. See also the essays by Gregory Claeys and Gareth Stedman Jones in Claeys and Stedman Jones (eds.), *The Cambridge History of Nineteenth-Century Political Thought* (Cambridge, 2007).

[44] Spencer, "From Freedom to Bondage" [1891] in Spencer, *The Man Versus the State*, ed. Albert Jay Nock (Indianapolis, 1982), 487–518; and Dicey, "Alexis de Tocqueville," *NR*, 21 (1893), 776. See also Goldwin Smith, "The Organization of Democracy," *CR*, 47 (1885), 319.

[45] Courthope, "Problems of Greater Britain," *NR*, 15 (1890), 434.

[46] [William Greswell], "England and Her Second Colonial Empire," *QR*, 158 (1884), 159 and 152; and Greswell, "Imperial Federation," 38.

a colonial politician in Victoria, argued in 1890 that the political machinery of an imperial federation might prove a useful instrument for dampening the worst excesses of populist democracy in Britain and throughout the colonial empire. A federal political system would require the operation of two chambers, the imperial one dealing with the great issues of war and peace, commercial relations, and diplomacy, the other with more mundane local concerns. He continued by comparing such a system to that operating already in France and the United States. "Is it too heavy a strain on public faith to assume that double election, which the two great republics find sufficient to exclude crude theories and angry prejudices from the Senate in countries where crude theories grow in extraordinary abundance, would be as effectual in Westminster as it is in Washington or Paris?"[47] Carefully calibrated institutional design, he suggested, could dissipate the powers and prejudices of the newly enfranchised people, their "crude theories" rendered harmless through the mechanisms of an efficient political federation.

It is no coincidence that the IFL was established in 1884. It had become increasingly obvious that the advocates of Greater Britain had to appeal to the widest possible constituency, or at the very least that they had to speak in the name of society as a whole. The people—the global British people—had to be persuaded. This required an organizational locus, and a platform for agitation. Michael Burgess has argued that the IFL never made an explicit effort to reach out to the working classes.[48] While true in institutional terms, at least insofar as the organization never systematically campaigned on the issue, it is notable that many individual imperialists (including the most prominent) argued that it was essential to persuade the working classes that Greater Britain benefited everybody. Seeley, Froude, and Rosebery, among others, stressed the importance of mobilizing the support of the workers.[49] Nor does it detract from the powerful role played by fear about the unintended consequences of democracy in generating, shaping, and sustaining the wider debate. Such concerns can be seen also in the persistent demands for both a national program of education focusing on the advantages of colonial unity, and for a policy of systematic emigration throughout the settler territories. Echoing the common complaint about apathy, one unionist wrote that the "working men are indifferent to the present and future of our colonies, but they need to

[47] Duffy, "Some Fruits of Federation," *IF*, 5/3 (1890), 68.
[48] Burgess, "The Imperial Federation Movement in Great Britain," 143–44.
[49] See "Sir John Seeley and National Unity," letter quoted by H. F. Wilson, *Cambridge Review*, 16 (1895), 197; Seeley, "Political Education of the Working Classes," *MM*, 36 (1877), 143–45; and Froude, "England and Her Colonies," 16. See also the three brief essays by an anonymous writer on "What We Offer to the Working Classes," in *IF*, 1/2 (1886), 50–51; *IF*, 1/3 (1886), 77–78; and *IF*, 1/4 (1886), 105–106; as well as William Macnaught, *Federation of the Empire . . . Especially Written for the Working Classes* (Liverpool, 1887).

be instructed as to the true value of their inheritance."[50] This was a necessity because of their newfound political role. Many of the promoters
of Greater Britain endeavoured to convince the working classes of the various benefits of a united empire (or at least to persuade themselves that
the workers would benefit). Proselytizing imperial federation in a speech
to the Trades Union Congress in 1884, Rosebery declared that the question of working-class emigration was "more important than the franchise
question which is now agitating the country," and that colonial unity was,
in general, the most pressing issue facing Britain.[51] Often, though, the failure to engage can be seen as a matter of complacency flavored with ignorance or wishful thinking. Vogel proclaimed that a "very large proportion
of the adult working classes hold the colonies in high, though mystical,
veneration." And Lorne, again without citing any evidence, stated that
the "hand-workers of the industrial classes" displayed great enthusiasm
for imperial federation.[52] Aware that working-class support was essential, they simply assumed that it was already secured. Such complacency
helps explain both the lack of active campaigning engaged in by the IFL
and the eventual failure of the movement.

For democracy to be made safe, it was argued that it had to be conditioned by the wisdom of British political virtue, and embedded within the
constellation of institutions that had both saved the country from revolution and propelled it to a dominant position in world politics. Victorian
political thinkers disagreed over whether society was held together by self-
interest or more expansive forms of social solidarity.[53] Although their
views were rarely as narrow as their opponents alleged, many political
economists thought that the answer lay primarily in the unintended effects of (self) interest.[54] This position was savaged by those who thought
that it inculcated a spirit of hedonism and augured the destruction of communal values and individual virtue. And the spread of democracy, so it
was often claimed, only encouraged such views. Imperial discourse reflected and deepened this division. Virtually all arguments advocating Greater
Britain stressed the importance of both interests—economic and political—and the more intangible links of race nationality and sentiment. Although the balance between them varied considerably among individuals,
it was the latter that dominated debate. Imperial discourse was permeated
with maudlin claims about the bonds—of blood and heart, culture, and

---

[50] [L. J. Jennings], "Travels in the British Empire," *QR*, 162 (1886), 466.

[51] Rosebery, speech to the Seventeenth Trades Union Congress, 11 September 1884,
reprinted in George Bennett (ed.), *The Concept of Empire* (London, 1953), 289–90.

[52] Vogel, "Greater or Lesser Britain," 816; and Lorne, *Imperial Federation*, 11.

[53] H. S. Jones, *Victorian Political Thought* (Basingstoke, 2000), 43–44.

[54] Emma Rothschild, "Political Economy" in Claeys and Stedman Jones (eds.), *The Cambridge History of Nineteenth Century Political Thought*.

history—uniting the Anglo-Saxons, but also, and perhaps more intriguingly, it was structured by arguments about the political efficacy of such sentimentality. The cold logic of economic and political "rationality" was bypassed by, or at least subsumed under, unadorned appeals to emotion. "The motive power which governs the world, whatever cynics may say, is, after all, the *heart*, not the head," wrote a radical unionist. Forster concurred: "sentiment has ruled the world since time began; and moreover, history informs us of this noteworthy fact: that wherever there is a deep and prevailing and powerful national sentiment, there are almost sure to be found strong economical and material grounds in its favour."[55] In particular, it was frequently suggested that sentiment provided the catalyst for patriotism, and in light of the weak constitutional bonds connecting Britain to its colonial empire, it was the power of this patriotism (premised as it was on the notion of a global people) that was the key to future consolidation. "Patriotism," proclaimed Froude, "may be sentimentalism, but it is a sentimentalism nevertheless which lies at the root of every powerful nationality, and has been the principle of its coherence and growth."[56] What the critics of Greater Britain saw as one of the key weaknesses of their opponents, many advocates of the idea regarded as a strength; to ignore, or to deprecate appeals to the heart was to miss the very foundation stone of the global polity, indeed of politics itself.

E.H.H. Green suggests that it was economic factors that shaped the debate over imperial federation, just as they did the latter disputes over tariff reform.[57] This exaggerates the continuities, important though they were, as well as underplaying the role played by noneconomic factors. Some Victorian colonial unionists did follow a primarily economic line of reasoning, focusing on the material benefits of closer cooperation. This sometimes led to calls for the tenets of economic policy and, in particular, free trade, to be rethought, although such demands usually fell on deaf ears. There was little support for a *Zollverein*, only slightly more for preferential treatment, and most advocates of Greater Britain (and indeed of

[55] Anon., "The Federation of the British Empire," WR, 128 (1887), 492 (italics in original); and Forster, "Imperial Federation," NC, 17 (1885), 205. See also Dilke, *Problems of Greater Britain* (London, 1890), I, 458–59; and A. V. Dicey, *Lectures on the Relation Between Law and Public Opinion in England During the Nineteenth Century* (London, 1905), 459. For an alternative view, stressing the priority of interests and downplaying colonial sentiment, see John Morley, "The Expansion of England," MM, 49 (1884), 254–57.

[56] Froude, "England and Her Colonies," FM, 1 (1870), 6. See also, Forster, "Imperial Federation," 216; and Seeley, "Our Insular Ignorance," NC, 18 (1885), 868–70.

[57] Green, "The Political Economy of Empire, 1880–1914," OHBE, III, 346–71; and Green, *The Crisis of Conservatism* (London, 1995), 35–41. On the economic arguments for and against empire, see John Cunningham Wood, *British Economists and the Empire* (London, 1983); Donald Winch, *Classical Political Economy and Colonies* (London, 1965); and Bernard Semmel, *The Rise of Free Trade Imperialism* (Cambridge, 1970).

imperial federation) remained free traders, at least until the turn of the
century. The most novel economic justifications for colonial unity were
advanced by an emerging school of "historical economists," a group that
included W. J. Ashley, William Cunningham, W.A.S. Hewins, and L. L.
Price. Critical of the abstract deductive methods of neoclassical economics, and motivated by a concern with social reform, a number of the leading historical economists supported imperial federation. They viewed the
empire as the most appropriate unit for enacting economic and social policies, as well as for maintaining British power and prestige. But the divisions within their ranks highlighted the wider splits over the economic rationale of empire. Cunningham, for example, remained an advocate of a
"cosmopolitan" free-trading empire until 1903, when he joined the others in backing Chamberlain's campaign for tariff reform. The key turning
point for him, as with many of his compatriots, was the war in South
Africa.[58] When combined with the notable lack of enthusiasm for ambitious political plans displayed by the leaders of the colonies, this generated a shift to nonconstitutional visions of unity; the emphasis moved increasingly to issues of economic efficiency and coordination, and to
strengthening informal connections.[59] But even here, economic arguments were interwoven with ethical considerations, permeated as they
were with concerns over character, glory, and virtue.[60] The majority of
Victorian colonial unionists, however, thought that focusing primarily on
"materialistic" questions was antithetical to a true imperial sentiment.
The advocacy of Greater Britain needs, then, to be understood as an element of the wider debate over the future of the British state in an age of
transition.

EMIGRATION AND THE SOCIAL QUESTION

Two primary fears about British political order were woven through the
debates over colonial unity. The first, a late flowering of Malthusian paranoia, focused on overpopulation and pauperism as a combined weight

[58] Gerard M. Koot, *English Historical Economics, 1870–1926* (Cambridge, 1987), 99,
118–19, and 151. See also Green, *The Crisis of Conservatism*, 162–63 and 176–83; and
Bernard Semmel, *The Liberal Ideal and the Demons of Empire* (Baltimore, 1993), ch. 4.

[59] Dilke notes the beginnings of this shift in 1899: *The British Empire* (London, 1899), 11.

[60] Peter Cain, "Empire and the Languages of Character and Virtue in Later Victorian and
Edwardian Britain," *MIH*, 4 (2007). For Chamberlain, this had always been the case; see,
for example, his speech on "Relations with the United States and the Colonies," Devonshire
Club, April 9, 1888, in Charles W. Boyd (ed.), *Mr Chamberlain's Speeches* (London, 1914),
I, 322. I return to this issue in the concluding chapter.

dragging Britain downward; the second concerned the dangers of social-ism. The latter was often seen as a political response to the socioeconomic conditions engendered by the former. According to this picture, Britain was plagued by an ever expanding mass of wretched humanity from within the ranks of which severe disquiet (and, in the very worst case, rev-olution) might grow. The "terrible" population pressures at home, Seeley argued in *The Expansion of England*, were "giving rise to most anxious politics."[61] Lord Brabazon, president of the National Association for Pro-moting State-Directed Colonization, warned that the "malady has reached a crisis, and some change will have to occur, either for the better or for the worse; and if for the worse, woe to society! If a Social Revolution is to be avoided some measures of relief to suffering humanity will have to be devised." The United Kingdom, the imperial federalist William Gres-well argued in 1883, needed to "utilise to the utmost the circumscribed area we possess, and, in the face of pauperism, competition, and the evils of a rapidly growing population, hold our position among the nations of the world."[62] The impact of these multiple challenges was powerful. The period marked a shift from an age of equipoise to an age of anxiety, para-doxically at the moment of Britain's greatest global reach.

Seeley insisted that the "whole question of emigration is wrapped up in the closest imaginable manner with Imperial Federation," arguing that alongside trade it was one of the "vast uniting forces" of Greater Brit-ain.[63] Two immediate benefits, it was claimed, would follow from an in-crease in the levels of emigration. First, it would swell the populations of the individual colonies, adding both to their own dynamism and to the military strength and economic productivity of Greater Britain as a whole. And secondly, it would help to relieve pressure on the overstretched labor market in the United Kingdom, thus helping to neutralize possible sources of unrest among the recently (or soon to be) enfranchised working classes. In an impassioned essay published in 1870 Froude focused on the neces-sity for emigration throughout the colonial empire, insisting that "Most of all it is the concern of the working men." One of the most important

[61] Seeley, *The Expansion of England*, 297. See also, Patrick H. W. Ross, *Federation and the British Colonies* (London, 1887), 29.

[62] Brabazon, "State-Directed Colonization," *NR*, 9 (1887), 525; and Greswell, "Imper-ial Federation," 6. Brabazon, 12th Earl of Meath, was a well-known philanthropist. On the return of the "social question" in the 1880s, see Jose Harris, *Unemployment and Politics* (Oxford, 1972).

[63] Seeley, "The Journal of the League," 4. See also Seeley, "The Object to be Gained by Imperial Federation," *IF*, 1/6 (1886), 206; Seeley, "Introduction" to *Her Majesty's Colonies*, (London, 1886), x and xxii–iii; Seeley, "The Eighty-Eights," *Good Words* (1888), 380; [Robinson], "The Future of the British Empire"; Froude, "England and Her Colonies"; Forster, "Imperial Federation," *NC*, 17 (1885), 201–18; de Labillière, *Federal Britain*; Cun-ningham, *A Scheme for Imperial Federation*, 64; and Parkin, *Imperial Federation*.

reasons for this was that in "relieving the pressure at home [it] may end the war between masters and men, and solve the problems of labour which trade unions can never solve."[64] In another early essay, Jenkins complained that neither the Liberals nor the Tories were grappling successfully with the "drift" that had characterized recent British policy, whether foreign or domestic. Both parties, he mocked, were "eddying round and round here in a Reform whirlwind, tossed out of the way there by an Irish gust, spun around by a German-French tempest, inanely watching the play of a Russian nor'-easter." Britain was already "overstocked," and if the importance of imperial federation was not recognized, and if as a consequence the empire fragmented, "[w]e should have thrown back upon us at home those serious problems to which the increasing exodus of our people has seemed to afford the healthiest solution." In response he proposed a supraparliamentary federation, granting equal citizenship to all its members, and governed by an imperial senate. Therein, "the ideal distinctions between 'home' and 'the colonies' would vanish away."[65] At the inaugural meeting of the Royal Colonial Society Lord Alfred Spencer Churchill observed that "[w]e are weighted down here by paupers, which cramps our energies in every direction," while the vice president of the RCS also pointed to the dangers of overpopulation. For both, the issue served as one of the central concerns of the new organization, a problem that was as pressing (if not more so) than at any time in the past.[66] Anxiety over democracy haunted these debates, for not only was the population too large, and hence discontented, but more and more people were going to be eligible to vote. This might spell disaster. Vogel identified where the real danger lay, warning the "propertied" classes that the "maintenance of those institutions they most prize, the safety of their order, of their lands and their family possessions depend upon the colonies remaining as outlets for surplus home population."[67] These fears were often stoked by exaggerated demographic projections. Forster, for example, suggested that the population of the United Kingdom would rise from 31.5 million to 63 million between 1871 and 1950, exerting great pressure on the limited space available. During the same period the colonies would grow much faster, climbing from 6.8 million to 82 million, but due to their enormous scale this would, he argued, "still leave room for indefinite increase."[68] In order to relieve growing pressure at home, as well

[64] Froude, "England and Her Colonies," 16.

[65] [Jenkins], "Imperial Federalism," CR, 16 (1871), 165; [Jenkins], "An Imperial Confederation," 69 and 70; and [Jenkins], "Imperial Federalism," 178.

[66] Comments, PRCI, I (1869–70), 47; and Alexander Galt, "The Relations of the Colonies to the Empire," 393.

[67] Vogel, "Greater or Lesser Britain," 820.

[68] Forster, Our Colonial Empire (Edinburgh, 1875), 13 and 16.

as to utilize the potential of the expanding colonies, systematic emigration and colonial unity were vital.

The "dangers" of socialism lurked, above all, in the vast industrial cities—those ultramodern spaces, simultaneously sources of peril, excitement, and energy, so central to the Victorian imagination. Noting with alarm the weak physical state of city dwellers, and arguing that the colonies (united in an imperial federation) could act as a suitable outlet, the Liberal MP Robert Macfie warned in 1870 that increasing foreign competition was only exacerbating the problem.[69] He thus managed to blend fear of foreign progress with that of British decline, neatly encapsulating the dynamics of the culture of imperial anxiety. Writing a decade later William Torrens, another Liberal MP, asserted that "it is wholly impossible that the population of even one portion or segment of the realm can be in a state of perennial discontent, destitution, and despair, without thereby becoming a well-head of danger, of distress and of deterioration to other more fortunate parts of the kingdom." The cities, argued Stephen Bourne, were nurturing an "enfeebled and debased" underclass, while Greswell insisted that the "overcrowded" country was "faced by endless social difficulties" and that this pointed to "extreme national peril."[70] In 1886 one Colonel Sir Francis W. de Winton cautioned that the steady "trickle" of emigrants leaving the country was not enough to quell the troubles that lay ahead. "Its movement," he continued,

> . . . is powerless to arrest the decaying germs which have already manifested themselves in our national life; or to destroy the growth of socialism fed by starvation, want of work, or the abandonment of hope. Add to discontent that decay which in its withering influences leads to despair, and then, can we wonder at starving men and women turning, in their revenge, on the system under which they live, and strong in their hate and passion, to rend and destroy it.

Subjected to a range of pressures, the working classes would "at no distant date" be driven "into the hands of socialism." The problem seemed acute. Writing in the Tory *National Review* the leading trade-union activist George Potter warned that the condition of the labor market was a "danger to the State." The reason for this was straightforward: "a feeling of deepest indignation is beginning to stir in the breasts of those who have

[69] Macfie, "On the Crisis of the Colonies," *PRCI*, 3 (1871–72), 5.
[70] Torrens, "Imperial and Colonial Partnership in Emigration," *PRCI*, 12 (1880–81), 180; Bourne, "Extended Colonisation a Necessity to the Mother Country," *PRCI*, 11 (1879–80), 23; Greswell, "Colonization and the Friendly Societies," 689. See also, Torrens, "Transplanting to the Colonies," *NC*, 9 (1881), 536–56.

hitherto been quiescent in their misery."[71] Simultaneously a warning and
plea, this image resonated with (and chilled) many of the promoters of
Greater Britain. A deteriorating international environment, economic depression, the extension of the franchise, urbanization: all combined to
form a potent brew.

The majority of colonial unionists seem to have been in favor of granting fairly high levels of state aid to assist emigration, covering both the
transportation costs and some of the financial burdens of settlement.[72] The
advocates of emigration could draw on a considerable body of theoretical
support for their arguments, for throughout the nineteenth century, political economists had emphasized the economic value of colonization. While
James Mill and Malthus had been skeptical about the benefits of colonial
emigration, from the 1830s onward opinion began to shift, and Wakefield,
Nassau Senior, Robert Torrens, and Herman Merivale, among others, defended the aquisition and maintenance of colonies.[73] In his *Principles of
Political Economy* (1848), John Stuart Mill argued for state intervention,
under the wise guidance of "philosophical legislators," to support colonization. He thought that this was so important that it should proceed independently of any material benefits that it might produce, but he nevertheless insisted that there existed a sound socioeconomic rationale.

> The question of government intervention in the work of Colonization in-
> volves the future and permanent interests of civilization itself, and far out-
> stretches the comparatively narrow limits of purely economic considerations.
> But even with a view to those considerations alone, the removal of popula-
> tion from the overcrowded to the unoccupied parts of the earth's surface is
> one of those works of eminent social usefulness, which most require, and
> which at the same time best repay, the intervention of government.[74]

[71] Winton, "Practical Colonisation," *PRCI*, 18 (1886–87), 309; and Potter, "Imperial
Emigration," *NR*, 1 (1883), 204. Potter was no Tory, but the editors of the journal invited
him to contribute, as they thought their readership should be exposed to such views. He was
the leader of the pro-emigration London Working Men's Association. The *National Review*
supported imperial federation: *NR*, 4 (1884–85), 365. For a Tory slant on the problem, see
William Fielding, "Imperial Migration and Settlement," *NR*, 8 (1886–87), 777–95.

[72] For a sample of views, see Burrows, "Imperial Federation," 379; comments, *PRCI*, II
(1870–71), 117–53; Frederick Young, "Emigration to the Colonies," *PRCI*, 17 (1885–86),
369; Walter Hazell, "Practical Means of Extending Emigration," *PRCI*, 19 (1887–8), 48–
64; William Gisbourne, "Colonisation," *PRCI*, 20 (1889–90), 53–69; and Fielding, "Imperial Migration and Settlement." There were dissenters from this position—see, for example, Winton, "Practical Colonisation."

[73] Senior, *Remarks on Emigration* (London, 1831); Senior, *An Outline of a Science of
Political Economy* (London, 1836); Torrens, *Colonisation of South Australia* (London,
1835); Torrens, *Self-Supporting Colonization* (London, 1847); and Merivale, *Lectures on
Colonisation and Colonies*, 2 vols. (London, 1841).

[74] Mill, *Principles Political Economy*, CW, III, 963.

Theoretical arguments were bolstered by practical developments; the imperialists were not shouting vainly into the wind. It was, after all, an age of massive emigration: from the 1840s until the 1930s the United Kingdom lost more people per year to emigration than it gained through immigration. The peak periods of emigration were during the 1870s and the 1890s, straddling the debate over the destiny of Greater Britain.[75] Emigration was, moreover, an issue that organized labor took seriously, and until very late in the century there was considerable trade-union support for state-aided emigration, which was seen as one way of ameliorating the plight of the working classes.[76] Realizing the possibilities that this heralded, one correspondent in *Imperial Federation* argued that the Friendly Societies and the Trade Unions might provide a great boost to the federation movement. Not only did they already support the idea of emigration, they had access to a transcontinental network of institutions and personal connections with which to facilitate it.[77] This was an attitude (as well as an organizational foundation) upon which many imperialists hoped to build, although ultimately they were unsuccessful in mobilizing the necessary support for their project(s). It was, after all, one thing to reiterate endlessly the necessity of class harmony and colonial unity, another actually to do the work essential to secure it, even if it were possible.

As with so much else in Victorian political thought, the issue of character, both individual and collective, was central to virtually all of the diverse visions of Greater Britain.[78] It was a commonplace of colonial unionist argument that British patriotic virtue was under threat from a combination of vulgar commercial self-interest and a debased and amoral

[75] For the dating of these peaks, see Harris, *Private Lives, Public Spirit*, 44. In general, see Marjory Harper, "British Migration and the Peopling of the Empire," *OHBE*, III, 75–88; and Colin G. Pooley and Jean Turnbull, *Migration and Mobility in Britain since the Eighteenth Century* (London, 1998), 276.

[76] Charlotte Erickson, "The Encouragement of Emigration by British Trade Unions, 1850–1900," *Population Studies*, 3 (1949), 248–73; Pamela Horn, "Agricultural Trade Unionism and Emigration, 1872–1881," *HJ*, 15 (1972), 87–102; and Howard L. Malchow, "Trade Unions and Emigration in Late Victorian England," *JBS*, 15 (1976), 92–116. The National Emigration League was created in 1870, following the union of the National Emigration Aid Society and the Working Men's Emigration Society. There was an initial but brief agitation in 1869–70, and a more powerful and sustained one in the 1880s under the auspices of the National Association for Promoting State-Directed Colonisation (formed in 1884). See here Malchow, *Population Pressures* (Palo Alto, 1979). Cf. Porter, *The Absent-Minded Imperialists*, 27–30.

[77] Anon., "Working Men Federationists," [sic] *IF*, 2/9 (1887), 205–26. See also the discussion in William Greswell, "Colonization and the Friendly Societies," *NR*, 11 (1888), 685–700.

[78] On the role of character, see especially Stefan Collini, *Public Moralists* (Oxford, 1991), ch. 3; H. S. Jones, *Victorian Political Thought* (London, 2000), ch. 2; and Mandler, *The English National Character*.

ethic—a combination that, as I will argue in chapter 5, led to the reiteration of long-standing civic humanist themes. In broad terms, this was related to the transformational quality of industrial capitalism, and the changing way in which the working and middle classes were imagined by the political and intellectual elites. In the eighteenth century it had been common to argue that as a consequence of living a hardy and rugged agrarian life the lower "ranks" were healthy and strong. The broad-shouldered agricultural worker was pictured as a backbone of the country. As urbanization intensified, however, and as the manufacturing sector created increasing numbers of jobs, leading to mass migration into the towns and cities and often unregulated work in factories, the image of the working classes was transformed.[79] The bodies of workers became objects of fear as much as sites for the projection of paternalistic ideals. Skilfully anatomized by Charles Dickens and passionately investigated by Charles Booth, the harsh realities of life in the city saw the representation of the "masses" assume a more variegated hue. Images of a prosperous and respectable artisan class—the main target of the state-aided colonization movement—coexisted alongside images of a more dangerous (under) class often conceived in sanitary terms as festering, disease ridden, and thus as a challenge to the "hygiene" of the body politic.[80] No longer hardy and content, they were instead decaying and degraded. In *National Life and Character* (1893), Charles Pearson went so far as to claim that the stagnation increasingly common in towns was partly the result of the lack of will (and space) to further colonize the planet.[81] Nostalgic as ever, Froude regarded urbanization as an imminent danger to the country. London, like all cities, was permeated by "mendacity and misery," while the agricultural strength of the country was declining catastrophically. Not only were sections of the working class being driven to drink and to corruption more generally, but the very physical robustness of the population was subjected to unrelenting assault.[82] The agrarian ideal had transmuted into its antithesis—a grim blend of urban squalor and a depressed and pauper-strewn countryside.

[79] On domestic population movements, see David Feldman, "Migration" in Martin Daunton (ed.), *The Cambridge Urban History of Britain* (Cambridge, 2000), III, 185–207; and R. J. Morris, "Urbanization" in Morris and Richard Rodger (eds.), *The Victorian City* (London, 1993), 43–73.

[80] Gareth Stedman Jones, *Outcast London* (Oxford, 1971); Daniel Pick, *Faces of Degeneration* (Cambridge, 1992), Part III; and Mandler, *The English National Character*, ch. 4. This grim imagery was employed in the promotion of emigration from the 1830s onward: Robert Grant, *Representations of British Emigration, Colonisation, and Settlement* (London, 2005), ch. 6. Visions of the urban poor were also shaped by racial tropes derived from the imperial encounter, especially with India: John Marriott, *The Other Empire* (Manchester, 2003).

[81] Pearson, *National Life and Character* (London, 1893).

[82] Froude, "England and her Colonies," 9–14.

Emigration throughout a united empire would solve a vital practical problem and in doing so call upon and reinforce the virtues necessary for national greatness. Colonization was intended "materially to conduce to mental elevation and moral advancement"; after all, "from time immemorial it has always required a certain self-sacrifice and hardihood for men and women to root up old ideas and associations and face the unknown conditions of a new world."[83] A strong and "healthy" character, defined by self-reliance and self-control, would be forged through a shift in environment—from industrial slum to frontier territory—for character and context were intertwined in an intricate dialectic in Victorian political thought; character was shaped by circumstance, but a good character was one that could cope with demanding circumstances. "It is quite consonant with the Anglo-Saxon character to evolve prosperity from adverse conditions, to thrive best when combating trials and overcoming difficulties."[84] The colonies offered just such an opportunity for challenge and reform. Alexander Galt, high commissioner of Canada, exhorted potential emigrants with an encomium: "Free farms await you in the extending prairies of the West—leave behind you the cares and troubles of the past, and accept the reward of honest labour, contented home, free from anxiety for the children growing up around you."[85] The wretched urban poor were subject to the temptations of socialism; life in the colonies, on the other hand, was held to offer the chance for transfiguration into ruggedly independent settlers, imbued with the spirit of imperial patriotism.

Brabazon observed that the poor were being taught to read and write, and, moreover, "to think," and if "those of them who are in actual want of the necessities of life are once impressed with the notion that their condition is not inevitable, but is the result of bad social and political arrangements, it will not be long before they will arise in wrath, and make their influence felt." The influx of workers from the depressed countryside into the already overflowing cities had to be diverted: ideally the "flow of this stream of strong healthy life could be directed to the Colonies before it had become polluted by contact and mixture with the foul cesspools of the city."[86] He concluded by drawing attention to the large number of eminent individuals who had expressed support for the project, including Rosebery, Seeley, and Froude. Elsewhere he warned of the "grave social

---

[83] John Robinson, "The Social Aspect of Colonisation," *PRCI*, 1 (1869), 152; and [Greswell], "England and Her Second Colonial Empire," 138.

[84] Bourne, "Extended Colonisation a Necessity to the Mother Country," 25.

[85] Galt, "The Future Destiny of the Dominion of Canada," *PRCI*, 12 (1880–81), 107. For similar views about Australia, see Lord Brassey, "On Work and Wages in Australia" in Arthur Loring and R. J. Beadon (eds.), *Papers and Addresses by Lord Brassey* (London, 1894), 235–37.

[86] Brabazon, "State-Directed Colonization," 525, 531, and 537.

and political dangers" facing the country, arguing that without planned colonization, Britain would fall prey to "some fatal national catastrophe." His proposals were backed by Lord Monkswell, who in an article published in the *Fortnightly Review* in 1888, proceeded to make explicit the link to imperial federation. "In the colonies," he argued, "energy and abilities must come to the forefront": "Faculties that are stunted and underdeveloped here from want of exercise, flourish and expand in the Virgin soil of our Colonies." State-funded colonization, he continued, "would do perhaps more than anything else to consolidate the Empire. Colonisation is as it were the pulse of the nation. It provides a perpetual circulation throughout the body politic," and, he argued, it is "bringing the question of federation more and more within the range of practical politics."[87]

One of the main problems facing the proponents of Greater Britain was that the majority of emigrants traveled to the United States rather than the outposts of empire.[88] Froude argued that Britain's lifeblood was draining away and that America was the main beneficiary. "They constitute the one great Power whose interests and whose pretensions compete with our own, and in so far as the strength of nations depends on the number of thriving men and women composing them, the United States have been made stronger, the English empire weaker, to the extent of those millions [of emigrants] and the children growing of them." The "extirpated swarms" were forever lost to England.[89] There could only be one victor in this race: if the Americans won, the British lost. Desperate to evade this problem, the colonial unionists sought to harness and redirect emigration, simultaneously depriving the United States of potential citizens while accelerating the population growth of the outlying provinces of Greater Britain.

There was a problem with plans for state-aided emigration, however, for many in the colonies were worried about unchecked emigration. It

[87] Brabazon, "State-Directed Emigration," *NC*, 16 (1884), 766 and 787; and Monkswell, "State Colonization," *FR*, 43 (1888), 397. Brabazon's opening paragraph paraphrased and then endorsed Seeley's main arguments about Greater Britain in *The Expansion of England* (764). Support also came from a Westminster Reviewer: Anon., "State-Directed Colonization," *WR*, 128 (1887), 71–82. For further discussion of the idea of "practical politics," see chapter 5.

[88] Due to the massive distances involved, most of the people who emigrated to Australia and New Zealand employed companies specially formed to aid migrants; those heading across the Atlantic only needed to purchase a ticket. Eric Richards, "How Did Poor People Emigrate from the British Isles to Australia in the Nineteenth Century?" *JBS*, 32 (1993), 250–79. See also Stephen Constantine, "Empire Migration and Social Reform 1880–1950" in Colin Pooley and Ian Whyte (eds.), *Migrants, Emigrants and Immigrants* (London, 1991), 62–86.

[89] Froude, "England and Her Colonies," 1.

seemed to them that the "best" of the working classes (let alone the other classes) remained in Britain, and that the colonies were simply being used as a dumping ground for British social problems—as indeed they often were. In his *Problems of Greater Britain*, Dilke presented this as a serious impediment to plans for the free flow of people throughout the colonies, and he also argued that it was an unpopular idea among many of the British working class, as they saw emigration as a cheap substitute for concerted social reform at home—as indeed it often was. "It is difficult to combine the two objects of promoting emigration from Great Britain for the sake of England, and of using it for the purpose of strengthening the tie between the United Kingdom and her colonies."[90] Some federalists responded by stressing the need to select particular types of individuals for emigration, and others, like Wakefield before them, made the distinction between emigration (unplanned and poorly regulated) and colonization (specifically targeted at the interests of the empire).[91] Whatever form it took, though, emigration was a central component of the idea of Greater Britain.

RADICAL VISIONS OF GREATER BRITAIN

Despite the complex of fears that animated the project for colonial unity, Greater Britain also offered radicals of various stripes a global stage on which to act out their visions of alternative political futures. Imperial federation could be viewed as a model for new and progressive types of political association, the colonies acting as laboratories for ideas and practices that, if judged successful, could be imported back into Britain.[92] For Dilke, these new economic and political practices "may one day be imitated by ourselves." The democratic nature of the colonial empire, according to such a view, might help to catalyze change at home. Democracy would finally be released from the shackles imposed on it by an

---

[90] Dilke, *Problems of Greater Britain*, I, 28–9 and II, 317–18. C. P. Lucas also notes that many colonists were wary of emigration for similar reasons: Lucas, "Introduction" to George Cornewall Lewis, *An Essay on the Government of Dependencies* (Oxford, 1891 [1841]), lli.

[91] Malchow, "Trade Unions and Emigration in Late Victorian England," 102; and, for earlier discussions, Grant, *Representations of British Emigration, Colonisation, and Settlement*, ch. 7.

[92] Dilke, *Problems of Greater Britain*, II, 576–77. On the way in which the colonies could be seen as test-beds for various political models, see Carl Bridge and Kent Fedorwich, "Mapping the British World," *JICH*, 31 (2003), 5; and Daniel Rodgers, *Atlantic Crossings* (Cambridge, Mass., 1998), ch. 2. According to Forster, for example, the settlers were conducting "democratic experiments which help us to solve the problems with which we know we must deal." Forster, *Our Colonial Empire*, 23.

aristocratic political system and the residues of feudalism. Furthermore, a globe-spanning democratic federal polity might help to transform the nature of international politics, channeling it in a more stable and pacific direction. But most radicals were not converted to the colonial unionist cause, remaining hostile to what they saw as a dangerous set of arguments about global domination.

An Australian colonist claimed that imperial federation, "appeals more strongly to the democratic imagination than any other movement of the day," because it focused on maintaining unity while simultaneously defending local self-government.[93] An anonymous contributor to the *Westminster Review*—a radical journal whose editorial line was strongly pro-imperial federalist[94]—demanded full manhood suffrage throughout an "imperial federated democracy," noting that the "questions of empire and citizenship are one and indissoluble." This would require a new directly elected legislative chamber.

> Such, we believe, will be the completed genesis of the British Constitution, and to this end we are not a day too soon in bringing up the mighty conservative and revolutionary energies of the masses. In this sense it may even be said that the British Constitution is in its infancy, for it has to solve larger and even larger problems of government, so as to become adjusted to the mental, moral, and material developments of its people.

"It is," the writer warned for good measure, "a race against time."[95] After noting that many radicals were skeptical about the value of the empire, another contributor to the *Westminster* argued that the democratic orientation of colonial constitutions, and the ideal of federation itself, boded well for the future of British liberalism and radicalism: "the constitutions of all our self-governing colonies are decidedly democratic in principle to a degree by no means reached in this country, even after all recent measures of reform. It may, therefore, naturally be expected that a more intimate union with such communities could tend to accelerate the course of progress on Liberal and Radical lines."[96]

An eminent radical and an arch-imperialist, Joseph Chamberlain was a vociferous proponent of imperial federation during the last two decades of the century—support that later translated into his famous campaign

[93] Henry D'Esterre Taylor, "The Advantages of Imperial Federation," *IF*, 3/6 (1888), 130.

[94] This position can be discerned from the editorial comments preceding the printing of an article critical of federation: William Lobban, "Is Imperial Federation a Chimera?" *WR*, 136 (1891), 54.

[95] Anon., "*Imperium et Libertas*," *WR*, 57 (1880), 98 and 94–95. Italics in original.

[96] Anon., "Home Rule and Imperial Federation," *WR*, 132 (1889), 229. Prominent radical federalists included Jenkins and Cunningham.

for tariff reform. He was also one of the most elusive federalists, offering strong support at times, remaining silent at others. His arguments oscillated between economic and politico-military justifications, but they were always flavored by concerns over social reform, as well as fantasies of racial superiority and national glory.[97] Chamberlain entered politics, in the 1870s, with his eyes trained firmly on domestic affairs but during the 1880s, worried by the direction of British policy and fearful about the future, he turned increasingly to international and especially imperial issues, a movement directed in part by his great admiration for Seeley's writings.[98] He never fell into the troughs of pessimistic despondency about domestic politics that seemed to afflict many of the advocates of Greater Britain; his account of British politics flatly contradicted Froude's dark utterances. "Let us, then, have confidence in the future," he declared to the assembled dignitaries at the Royal Colonial Institute in 1897: "I do not ask you to anticipate with Lord Macaulay the time when the New Zealander will come here to gaze upon the ruins of a great dead city. There are in our present condition no visible signs of decrepitude and decay."[99] He tended to focus on converting people to the idea of imperial federation— the "great dream" as he called it—rather than on elaborating detailed proposals. As he argued in Toronto in 1887, "[i]f imperial federation is a dream . . . it is a grand idea. It is one to stimulate the patriotism and statesmanship of every man who loves his country; and whether it be destined or not to perfect realisation, at least let us . . . do all in our power to promote it." It was, he reiterated in an important speech in 1896, the "most inspiring idea that has ever entered the head of British statesmen."[100] Nothing could be allowed to stand in its way. Decrying proposals for Irish Home Rule, he suggested that one of the main problems with Gladstone's plan was that it helped derail the federation of the empire.

> I hope we may be able sooner or later to federate, to bring together, all these great independencies of the British Empire into one supreme and Imperial

[97] On Chamberlain's conjoining of economic themes with more traditional ideas about character and virtue, see Peter Cain, "Empire and the Languages of Character and Virtue."

[98] For an early indication of Chamberlain's support for imperial federation, see "Relations with the United States and the Colonies," 322–23. For the impact of *The Expansion of England* on his thinking, as well as Dilke's writings, see J. L. Garvin, *The Life of Joseph Chamberlain* (London, 1929–68), I, 494 and 434.

[99] Chamberlain, "The True Conception of Empire," Annual Royal Colonial Institute Dinner, Hotel Metropole, March 31, 1897, in Boyd (ed.), *Mr Chamberlain's Speeches*, II, 5.

[100] Speech, December 30, 1887, cited in Peter Marsh, *Joseph Chamberlain* (London, 1994), 295; and his speech on "Commercial Union of the Empire," Congress of the Chambers of Commerce of the Empire, June 9, 1896, in Boyd (ed.), *Mr Chamberlain's Speeches*, I, 368. On his repeated use of the language of the "great dream" see Garvin, *The Life of Joseph Chamberlain*, III, 177–83. Further discussion of this understanding of the role of the federation movement can be found in chapter 5.

Parliament, so that they should all be units of one body, that one should feel what the others feel, that all should be equally responsible, that all should have a share in the welfare, and sympathise with the welfare of every part. That is what I hope, but there is very little hope for it if you weaken the ties which now bind the central portion of the Empire together.[101]

Chamberlain never retreated from advocacy of imperialism, or indeed of colonial unity, although his ideas about the most effective form of rule mutated over the years. He remained, for example, a committed free trader well into the 1890s. Following the dissolution of the IFL in 1893, though, he "suspended the quest for a constitutional answer, leaving that to 'gradual development.'"[102] Political unification was shunted aside, left to the progressive movement of history to bring about at some future date. He proposed instead an imperial *Zollverein*, a free trade area protected by a wall of tariffs, thinking that this might help to generate support for the creation of an imperial council, and eventually, he added, a full federation. In a speech to the Canada Club in 1896 he argued that such commercial links were the only way to properly secure colonial unity: "That is the principle of the German *Zollverein*, that is the principle which underlies the Federation of the United States of America; and I do not doubt for a moment that if it were adopted it would be the strongest bond of union between the British race throughout the world." But this idea was quashed at the Colonial conference of 1897, as was the immediate ambition to aim for a reform of the representative institutions of the empire, for the gathered colonial premiers were hostile to such plans.[103] And so, in the context of war in South Africa, he changed tack again, in 1900 proposing the establishment of an Imperial Council in London, with the emphasis this time on imperial defense.[104] Once again, this failed to attract sufficient political support; his next major move took him down the route of wholesale tariff reform.[105]

Two of the leading "new liberal" thinkers argued that imperial federation offered the institutional architecture to deepen democracy at home

[101] Chamberlain, speech at Rawtenstall, July 8, 1886, in Boyd (ed.), *Mr Chamberlain's Speeches*, I, 279.
[102] Marsh, *Joseph Chamberlain*, 421. The IFL was dissolved on the 24th November 1893.
[103] Garvin, *The Life of Joseph Chamberlain*, III, 182 and 191; Kendle, *The Colonial and Imperial Conferences*, 26–27. See also, Chamberlain, "Commercial Union of the Empire," 367–68 and 371–72.
[104] Garvin, *The Life of Joseph Chamberlain*, III, 629–31. The members of the Council would be granted the rank of either privy councillors or life peers.
[105] See here the speeches collected in Boyd (ed.), *Mr Chamberlain's Speeches*, II, Pt. VI; and the analysis in Marsh, *Joseph Chamberlain*, chs. 18–19; and Green, "The Political Economy of Empire," 346–71.

and help secure peace in the international system.[106] "It is quite evident," J. A. Hobson wrote in his classic study *Imperialism* (1902), that during the preceding decades "a strong and increasing desire for imperial federation has been growing among a large number of British politicians."[107] Although he was wary of Chamberlain and critical of his vision of imperial reform, believing that it would simply enrich rapacious capitalists, Hobson contended that a properly constituted imperial federation would benefit Britain, the colonies, and the wider world.[108] Britain and the colonies would remain tied together, evolving in parallel, while the unity of the empire could act as a spur to the evolution of a stable world divided between "great federal empires." Bound by free trade and interlocking political institutions this alternative vision of union was the best hope for creating a more tranquil world. "[We] may easily agree that a voluntary federation of free British States, working peacefully for the common safety and prosperity, is itself eminently desirable, and might indeed form a step towards a wider federation of civilised states in the future."[109] It would provide both an institutional template and encourage further striving. For Hobson, one of the main drawbacks of the "new imperialism," exemplified by the pernicious "Scramble for Africa" and the South African War, was that it helped block the creation of a viable imperial federation—it performed, in other words, the same destructive role that Chamberlain had attributed to Home Rule. If a federation had already been in place it would have acted as a brake on jingoistic imperialism because, he argued, the newly empowered colonies would have vetoed costly militaristic adventures.[110] This was yet another reason to act. The main problem standing in the way of federation concerned incentives. It was necessary to persuade the colonists that it was in their best interest to join a federation, yet the "democratic spirit" prevailing in the colonies was pushing in the direction of independence. The power of sentiment, and "the moral bonds of community of language, history, and institutions" linking Britain and

---

[106] On the "new liberalism," see Michael Freeden, *The New Liberalism* (Oxford, 1978); Stefan Collini, *Liberalism and Sociology* (Cambridge, 1979); and Avital Simhony and David Weinstein (eds.), *The New Liberalism* (Cambridge, 2001).

[107] Hobson, *Imperialism* (London, 1902), 350.

[108] His criticisms of tariff reform are clearest in Hobson, "The Inner Meaning of Protectionism," *CR*, 84 (1903), 365–74. In the 1890s he had been an admirer of Chamberlain and his views: Peter Cain, *Hobson and Imperialism* (Oxford, 2002), 61–62.

[109] Hobson, *Imperialism*, 351. See also the discussion in David Weinstein, "Consequentialist Cosmopolitanism" in Bell (ed.), *Victorian Visions of Global Order*.

[110] Hobson, *Imperialism*, 351 and 356–57. Some liberal colonial unionists feared that, whatever its value as an ideal, imperial federation had been hijacked by the Tories, and should therefore be opposed. For a discussion, and a rebuttal, of this view, see J. A. Murray Macdonald, "The Imperial Problem," *CR*, 80 (1901), 489–90.

the colonists, were insufficient to generate the necessary level of support, not because they were unimportant or weakening, but rather because they would remain strong whatever political direction the empire took, including dissolution. Yet the two main "inducements" that the British could offer to the colonists—preferential economic treatment or involvement in the imperial government of the "lower races"—would, if they were pursued, be counterproductive and even dangerous. According to Hobson they would throw progress into reverse, either alienating Britain's existing trading partners, thus stoking mistrust and threatening conflict, or empowering local oligarchic elites, thus stunting the spread of democracy in the colonies. Imperial federalists, then, had to hope that colonial leaders would grasp the "net utility" of federation, especially in light of the threatening rise of other great "empires," especially France, Germany, and the United States. If they failed in this task, Canada and the United States would probably federate, and Australia and South Africa would seek independence. But even if this happened, all would not be lost, for there would then exist the foundation for a "possible future re-establishment of loose political relations in an Anglo-Saxon federation."[111] It would still be in the interests of all to enter a federal alliance. However, the Edwardian years saw Hobson turn increasingly pessimistic about the wisdom of this grand vision, and he repudiated his earlier support for imperial federation, writing that "Those British Imperialists who, with the events of the last few years before their eyes, still imagine a closer Imperial federation in any shape or form practicable, are merely the dupes of Kiplingesque sentimentalism." The dream had died.[112]

L. T. Hobhouse offered a rather more ambivalent account of imperial federation. In *Democracy and Reaction*, a book published in 1904 but largely based on journal articles written in 1901–92, he launched a vitriolic assault on the combined forces of domestic and international "reaction," a process that had reached its apogee during the war in South Africa. This was partly a tale of democratic disillusionment, charting the way in which the reforming ambitions of the 1860s generation had been shattered as the working classes threw their support behind imperial expansion. But it contained within it a defense of the idea of a properly democratic imperial form. This started with a rejoinder to those who claimed (in a modern echo of an old republican argument) that democracy was not compatible with great geographic extent. The invention of federalism, he argued, had succeeded in neutralizing this problem. There were different types of federalism, however, ranging from the "strict" kind exempli-

---

[111] Hobson, *Imperialism*, 370, 359, 354, and 371–72.
[112] Hobson, *The Crisis of Liberalism* (London, 1909), p. 238.

fied by the United States to the "loose form" binding the British colonies. Following the war in South Africa, and as a result also of the "nationalist aspirations of the component parts," he was uncertain about the future of the colonial empire, but he continued to believe that federalism was "the natural means whereby over large areas unity can be reconciled with the conditions of popular government." Summarizing a fairly common radical line, while also signaling the important disciplining function played by race in such arguments, Hobhouse concluded that, "[d]emocracy may be reconcilable with Empire in the sense of a great aggregation of territories enjoying internal independence while united by some common bond, but it is necessarily hostile to Empire in the sense of a system wherein one community imposes its will on others no less entitled by race, education, and capacity to govern themselves."[113] For Hobhouse imperial federation was in principle defensible while traditional forms of imperialism were unjust, gross anachronisms more suited to an earlier and less enlightened age.

Other radicals offered powerful criticisms of the calls for imperial federation. In an essay published in 1885, William Clarke, a prominent socialist journalist, attacked the imperial federalists for their "vague talk" and their failure to recognize the "legitimate" interests of the colonists, despite any protestations to the contrary. "It is such an honour, they think, to be connected with England, that they assume that the interest of the Colonies must lie in such a union." This was an accurate description of widely held imperial attitudes. He also suggested that the idea of federating the far-flung colonies was itself a chimera, as none of the conditions identified in *The Federalist* existed in the British empire. But most importantly, for Clarke federation was just another element of the general spread of "Jingo" sentiment, the arrogant desire, fed by the upper classes and the rapacious capitalists, to dominate and exploit.

> It is, stripped of all the pretentious verbiage and vague rhetoric with which it has been adorned, an attempt on the part of certain interests to maintain their hold over mankind. The military and aristocratic class has joined hands in this matter with a large section of the capitalist class in order to secure the promotion of English financial interests, and to strengthen, if possible, English Imperialism.

Although he recognized that at least some of the federalists were "well meaning," he concluded that the demand for colonial unity nevertheless offered a potent boost to the fortunes of capitalist reaction, and that as

---

[113] Hobhouse, *Democracy and Reaction*, ed. Peter Clarke (Brighton, 1972 [1904]), 153–54, 155, and 156–57. On Hobhouse's "anti-imperialism," see Stefan Collini, *Liberalism and Sociology*, 81–90.

such it was a threat to the spread of democratic ideals and practices. Despite the good intentions of many of its members, the "real character" of the movement needed unmasking, for it represented, he argued, the "greatest, because most insidious, danger that the cause of democracy in England has to face."[114]

[114] Clarke, "An English Imperialist Bubble" in *William Clarke*, ed. H. Burrows and J. A. Hobson (London, 1908), 76, 81, and 88–89. The article was published originally in the *North American Review* in July 1885. It would be interesting to know what Hobson (an editor of Clarke's writings) made of his views of the federalists. For other critical comments from liberal-radicals and socialists, see the debates in the sixth session of the Rainbow Circle Meetings (1899–1900), in Michael Freeden (ed.), *Minutes of the Rainbow Circle, 1894–1924* (London, 1989), 69–79.

3

Time, Space, Empire

> The inventions of science have overcome the great
> difficulties of time and space which were thought to
> make separation almost a necessity, and we now feel
> that we can look forward, not to the isolated
> independence of England's children, but to their
> being united to one another with the mother-
> country, in a permanent family union.
> —W. E. Forster, *Imperial Federation* (1884)

THIS CHAPTER engages one of the most persistent yet overlooked themes in the history of political thought: the problem of constructing and governing an integrated political system over large distances. The obstacles presented by physical space—and in particular by the relative difficulty in traversing or communicating across it—have presented a set of recurring problems for political thinkers. Some revolve around administrative (and coercive) reach. In the days before efficient state agencies existed, for example, it was often extremely difficult for a central government authority to maintain control over the outlying districts of its territory, and the conditions for effective sovereignty identified by Max Weber were, as such, unattainable, for it was impossible to secure a monopoly on legitimate violence within a given space.[1] A different set of issues helped shape the debates over Greater Britain. Both the colonial unionists and their critics assumed that a durable polity required a high degree of social, cultural, and political homogeneity.[2] The critics claimed that the fragmented form and vast extent of the colonial empire rendered such homogeneity an impossible dream. Distance prohibited the development of the sense of communal identity necessary for effective citizenship. However, the advocates of a global polity argued that the problem of distance had been transcended by the power of innovative communications technologies, that conventional understandings of the relationship between geography and

---

[1] Weber, "Politics as a Vocation" [1918/19], in Weber, *Political Writings*, ed. Peter Lassman, trans. Ronald Speirs (Cambridge, 1994), 309–10. This had been a central theme in defining the state since the high Renaissance: Quentin Skinner, *Visions of Politics* (Cambridge, 2002), II, 376–77.

[2] I explore this argument in more detail in the next chapter.

political temporality were obsolete. This revolution transformed the manner in which political possibilities were (and could be) envisioned. Technology shaped not only on the material structures of social and political life, but also the cognitive apprehension of the world, the modes of interpreting and reacting to the natural environment and the political potential contained therein.

The eighteenth century witnessed the birth pangs of globalization: it was increasingly recognized that many of the communities of the world were becoming increasingly interdependent, that events in one place had far-reaching and often unanticipated effects in another. The planet was being transformed into a single space for economic exchange and political action. This shift in perception was to have a monumental impact on the conception of the empire. In the wake of the Seven Years War (1756–63), viewed by many observers as the first truly global conflict, the British empire was increasingly regarded as a semi-integrated political-economic system. The existence of a pan-Atlantic British community bound by the political technology of "virtual representation" was frequently asserted.[3] Arthur Young contended in 1772 that the American colonists and those residing in the home islands constituted "one nation, united under one sovereign," while Edmund Burke suggested that the Thirteen Colonies and Britain comprised one great nation, with America branded "that most growing branch."[4] Proposals for parliamentary representation of the colonists abounded. The period witnessed the articulation of a powerful, albeit minority, discourse of transatlantic British identity, emphasizing the commonality of legal and political traditions, and in particular the centrality of constitutional liberty.[5] However, advocates of economic integration and the diffusion of political rights continually ran into the difficulties presented by the vast distances separating the component communities of the (settler) empire. Indeed it was Burke, as we shall see, who was the most eloquent theorist of the spatial limitations imprinted by nature.

Before the 1870s a highly integrated *global* polity (let alone one ruling over a single self-conscious nation) was rarely, if ever, considered a feasible political option; afterward, it became a frequent demand. In sketching his plans for a supraparliamentary federation in 1871, John Ed-

---

[3] On the competing visions of empire during this period, see H. V. Bowen, "British Conceptions of Global Empire, 1756–83," *JICH*, 26 (1998), 1–27; and P. J. Marshall, "Britain and the World in the Eighteenth Century, IV," *TRHS*, series 6, 11 (2001), 1–15.

[4] Young, *Political Essays Concerning the Present State of the British Empire* (London, 1772), 1; and Burke, "Speech at Bristol Previous to Election" [1780] in *The Writings and Speeches of Edmund Burke*, ed. W. M. Elofson (Oxford, 1981), III, 464.

[5] Jack P. Greene, *Peripheries and Center* (Athens, Ga., 1986); and Eliga Gould, *The Persistence of Empire* (Chapel Hill, N.C., 2000).

ward Jenkins wrote that it "is likely that I shall be met with the familiar sneer that I have dreamed a magnificent dream."[6] And yet, he continued, the dream could finally be translated into reality with the necessary political will, for the world had changed irrevocably. This sense of novelty pervaded the debates over Greater Britain, triggering an outburst of extravagant theorizing about vast political agglomerations and hybrid colonial-state structures. Views on the nature of distance transcended the numerous political, cultural, and theological divisions between individuals. What mattered most was their relative optimism concerning the present and future opportunities engendered by new technological developments. This was as much a matter of sensibility, and of imagination, as of partisan political conviction. But the reaction to technological change was not unequivocal: at every stage there were dissenters, skeptics, critics. Technology may influence the broad outlines of political-economic development, it may even occasionally shape it by establishing the boundaries within which certain political forms are considered plausible and desirable, but it does not fully determine it. Nor does it propel it in a unilinear direction. The technological shift was a necessary but not sufficient condition for the imagining of a global polity.

When examining the complex relationship between technology and empire, historians have focused traditionally on the economic, administrative, or military aspects of imperial expansion and rule. In this vein Lewis Pyenson, for example, suggests that it is essential to concentrate on "how science has been used to further the overseas political goals of imperial nations in their colonies and spheres of influence."[7] What this mode of analysis neglects is the fundamental prior effect that the shifting perception of nature, and of the spatiotemporal dimensions of the world itself, had on the political imagination; shifts in the cognitive apprehension of political possibilities are elided by concentrating on efficiency, conquest, and administration. Technological change was important not only because it helped to meet imperial "goals," but because it reshaped the very identity of the goals themselves. Political theorists, meanwhile, have tended to generalize about the indispensable function of technology in the constitution and legitimation of modernity, of the ways in which technical rationality and the immanent drive to master nature have stripped hu-

---

[6] [John Edward Jenkins], "Imperial Federalism," *CR*, 16 (1871), 185.

[7] Pyenson, "Science and Imperialism" in R. C. Olby et al. (eds.), *Companion to the History of Modern Science* (London, 1996), 928. See also Daniel Headrick, *The Tools of Empire* (New York, 1981); Headrick, *The Tentacles of Progress* (Oxford, 1988); and Headrick, *The Invisible Weapon* (Oxford, 1991). For a wider perspective, see Richard Drayton, *Nature's Government* (London, 2000).

mans of their individuality and freedom of action.[8] While this argument
may be plausible at a rarefied level of abstraction, it does not help to dis-
entangle and situate the often contradictory conceptions of the limits
placed by nature—and challenged by technology—on the boundaries of
political association during the modern era. This problem is brought into
sharp relief by studying the transformation of nineteenth-century imperial discourse.

In the following section I chart the way in which questions of scale
helped to shape the nature of the fraught arguments over the American
colonies following the Seven Years War. This debate foreshadowed the
concerns of the later advocates of Greater Britain, and some of the leading thinkers involved in the dispute, notably Adam Smith and Edmund
Burke, were called upon routinely as authoritative voices throughout the
subsequent decades; they set the tone as well as the terms for much nineteenth-century theorizing. I then chart developments in the early and mid-
nineteenth century, arguing that a series of material and theoretical shifts
acted as a generative backdrop for the late Victorian debates over Greater
Britain. Justifications of empire, as well as the general drift of policy itself, were often related directly to differing views about the present and
future impact of technology. In the final section I explore the role of technological projections in the imperial discourse of the last thirty years of
the century, illustrating how the panegyrists of Greater Britain deployed
novel vocabularies to envisage the globe. This discursive shift followed
from a wildly optimistic interpretation of science and technology as agents
capable of ameliorating the problems that distance posed to community.

"THE ETERNAL LAW": EMPIRE AND THE VICISSITUDES OF DISTANCE

Following the Treaty of Paris (1763), which attempted to draw a veil over
the Seven Years War, there was a heated debate over the manner in which
the empire was to be governed. The war had seen the size and nature
of the empire transformed dramatically, challenging the previously dominant mercantile vision of a maritime, commercial colonial system, which
stressed the importance of the colonies for wealth generation, and which
understood wealth generation itself as the key to security in a viciously
competitive world. The inherent tension between the traditional metro-
politan-centered understanding of community and national interest, on the

---

[8] From a vast literature see, for example, Langdon Winner, *Autonomous Technology*
(Cambridge, Mass., 1977); Andrew Feenberg, *Critical Theory of Technology* (Oxford,
1986); and, perhaps most influentially, Theodor Adorno and Max Horkheimer, *Dialectic of
Enlightenment* (London, 1997 [1944]).

one hand, and the devolved and increasingly individualistic conception of liberty and rights propounded by the disaffected colonists, on the other, led ultimately to the fracture of the bond between Britain and its American territories.[9] It was a debate whose contours, dynamics, and outcome were to resonate powerfully over the coming century. In order to grasp the full complexity of the debate it needs to be understood in the context of a series of arguments revolving around the scope of individual reason and common interest, the limits of religious toleration, the meaning and practice of political representation, and so forth. For our present purposes, however, it is useful to isolate one of the key elements, namely the role that distance played in theorizing the most suitable form of connection.

Adam Smith, described by his friend David Hume as being "very zealous in American affairs," considered the colonial system both economically and morally unjustifiable.[10] He argued that the colonies had thrived despite themselves; that their wealth developed in spite of their being colonies, not because of it. One of the crucial reasons for this success was distance, which allowed them to escape the chains of domination to a degree unimaginable in past empires.

> In the plenty of good land, the European colonies established in America and the West Indies resemble, and even greatly surpass, those of antient Greece. In their dependency upon the mother state, they resemble those of antient Rome; but their great distance from Europe has in all of them alleviated more or less the effects of this dependency. Their situation has placed them less in the power of their mother country.[11]

The problems of communication and political administration between Europe and the "immensely remote" American and West Indian colonies allowed the colonists greater independence than had traditionally been the case, and this spawned healthier conditions for generating wealth.[12]

[9] For an analysis of arguements over the political economy of eighteenth-century empire, see Istvan Hont, *Jealousy of Trade* (Cambridge, Mass., 2005); Anthony Pagden, *Lords of All the World* (London, 1995), ch. 7; and for debates about American independence, Peter Miller, *Defining the Common Good* (Cambridge, 1994).

[10] Hume to Adam Smith, February 8, 1776 (Letter 149), in *The Correspondence of Adam Smith*, ed. E. Mossner and I. Ross (Oxford, 1977), 186. Hume was a critic of the war, and of the empire in general: Hume, "Of the Balance of Power" in Hume, *Essays, Moral, Political, and Literary*, ed. Eugene F. Miller (Indianapolis, 1987), 339 and 340. He comments on the problems of governance in "enormous monarchies" in his "Balance of Power," *Essays*, 341ff.

[11] Adam Smith, *An Inquiry into the Nature and Causes of the Wealth of Nations*, ed. W. B. Todd (Oxford, 1976), Book IV, Ch. VII, 567 (and, 568–71ff). On distance, see also Emma Rothschild, "Global Commerce and the Question of Sovereignty in the Eighteenth-Century Provinces," *MIH*, 1 (2004), 6, 13, and 15–16.

[12] Smith, *Wealth of Nations*, 559. See also his letter to Sir John Sinclair of Ulbster (October 14, 1782), *The Correspondence of Adam Smith*, 262.

Smith nevertheless remained skeptical of the economic and (interwoven with this) moral utility of the colonial system, arguing that although the British colonies enjoyed greater civil and commercial liberties than those of the other European powers and the "Antients," they still embodied "a manifest violation of the most sacred rights of mankind." The mercantile trading system distorted the British economy dangerously, exposing it to potential destruction. Overall, "folly and injustice" marked European colonial policy, he concluded, and ideally the whole system should be abolished. Such a radical break would not trigger economic adversity, as the colonial advocates frequently claimed, for the "natural affection" between the ex-colony and the "mother country" would "quickly revive" and the two independent countries could develop an extensive and prosperous relationship, based on free trade and friendly sentiment.[13] He thought that national "pride" would block such a policy, and as a consequence he recommended modifying the existing administrative structures of the empire, arguing in particular that the colonists should help pay for their own defense. But in a discussion over how best to set the levels of taxation and collect the revenue, he noted the impossibility of coordinating such a complex process across a geographically extensive and fragmented political system: "the distance of the colony assemblies from the eye of the sovereign, their number, their dispersed situations and their various constitutions would render it very difficult to manage them in the same manner, even though the sovereign had the same means of doing it."[14]

The sheer size of the empire precluded it from functioning as a unified polity. The fact, moreover, that there was no sentimental bond between the occupants of the different colonies (itself primarily a function of distance), indeed that they were "strangers" to one another, made it highly unlikely that such a dispersed form of governance could ever work. Smith argued that London should remain the locus of decision-making, and it was thus necessary to have the colonies represented in Parliament. Drawing on the example of the Dutch confederation, he proposed the "union of Great Britain with her colonies."[15] He believed, in other words, that a

[13] Smith, *Wealth of Nations*, 582, 606–17. In an unpublished document, Smith suggested, in a bold stroke of realpolitik, that following the dissolution of the colonial bond, and in the event that natural affections did not revive quickly enough, it might be beneficial to hand Canada over to the French and Florida to the Spanish, so as to surround the Americans with potential enemies and thus force them into alliance with their old rulers. See "Smith's Thoughts on the State of the Contest with America, February 1778," ed. David Stevens, in *The Correspondence of Adam Smith*, 377–85. This plan had also occurred to Samuel Johnson: *Taxation no Tyranny*, in, *Works*, ed. D. Greene (New Haven, 1977), 10 and 451.

[14] Smith, *Wealth of Nations*, 616–17 (cf. 946–47); 619.

[15] Ibid., 622 and 624. This is the kind of "Dutch model" discussed in David Hume, *An Enquiry into the Principles of Morals*, in Hume, *Enquiries*, ed. P. H. Nidditch (Oxford,

form of constitutional "federal union" (more precisely a confederation) cemented with American political representation would be the most suitable compromise solution to the crisis.[16] While he was aware that the Americans would still regard distance from the heart of government as a problem, he did not think that this predicament would endure, for as the population of the United States grew, so too would the size of its representation. Eventually, the body responsible for coordinating the "united states," the "assembly which inspects and superintends the affairs of the whole empire," would migrate across the Atlantic.[17] Writing over a century later, J. Shield Nicholson, professor of political economy at the University of Edinburgh, claimed that Smith had formulated the "most definite and most practicable scheme ever yet published of Imperial Federation."[18] At the time, however, it seemed far from practicable and Smith remained understandably pessimistic about the general acceptance of such a solution.

> Unfortunately . . . the plan of constitutional union with our colonies and of American representations seems not to be agreeable to any considerable party of men in Great Britain. The plan, which, if it could be executed, would certainly tend most to the prosperity, to the splendour, and to the duration of the empire, if you except here and there a solitary philosopher like myself, seems scarce to have a single advocate.[19]

Smith's ideas for a "constitutional union" cannot be seen as promoting the idea of an intercontinental British state predicated on strong and resilient communal bonds, let alone a homogeneous national community. Indeed the logic of his argument points to the impossibility of such an entity, owing to the fact that the fragmented nature of the empire rendered its members "strangers" to one another. Smith sought colonial representation in order to generate taxation, and he had no desire to forge an ocean-straddling Greater Britain.

Smith was not, however, a lone voice in the wilderness; there were other "solitary philosophers" arguing for radical solutions. Thomas Pownall, for example, proposed a scheme of American parliamentary representation, at least in the early editions of *The Administration of the Colonies* (1764–77), claiming that the colonies and Britain were bound by a common commercial "interest," and that together they formed a "grand ma-

---

1975), 206. This is a reprint of the 1777 edition. I would like to thank Istvan Hont for discussion on this point.

[16] Smith, "Thoughts on the State of the Contest with America," 383; he comments on the problems of distance, 382.

[17] Ibid., *Wealth of Nations*, 625–26, 620.

[18] Nicholson, "Tariffs and International Commerce" in A. S. White (ed.), *Britannic Confederation* (London, 1892), 122.

[19] Smith, "Thoughts on the State of the Contest with America," 382.

rine dominion."[20] The colonies were to be self-governing entities within the British imperium. Richard Price, dissenting minister and the bane of Edmund Burke, also advocated an innovative confederal solution to the crisis, one that foreshadowed, albeit in an anemic form, the later idea of a federal Greater Britain. However, his visionary scheme was not (and could not have been) considered plausible given the prevailing conception of "nature" and the tyranny of distance, and it sank without trace. In his "Observations on the Nature of Civil Liberty" (1776) he defined impediments to civil liberty as "any will distinct from that of the majority of a community which claims a power in making laws for it and disposing of its property." He continued, "it is an immediate and necessary influence that no one community can have any power over the property or legislation of another community which is not incorporated with it by a just and fair representation." If the community was not governed by its own popular will, through the practice of direct political representation, it languished in "a state of slavery." As a potential solution to this dilemma, Price recommended establishing a "general confederacy" that would have at its heart a "senate" composed of delegates appointed by the individual states. This was a plan that he had earlier described as appropriate for the peaceful governance of Europe.[21] He thus shifted the locus of power away from a reconfigured parliament in Westminster, as the proponents of colonial representation were demanding, and to a superordinate body. In his discussion of European politics, he had suggested that rather than letting one country dominate all the others and in the process destroy civil liberty, it was advisable to "let every state, with respect to all its internal concerns, be continued independent of all the rest, and let a general confederacy be formed by the appointment of a senate consisting of repre-

[20] Pownall, *The Administration of the Colonies* (London, 1864), 6. Pownall supported American representation in the six editions of his *Administration* published between 1764 and 1777, but in a speech in the House of Commons on December 1778 he changed his position, proposing instead American independence. For details of this switch, see David Stevens, "Introduction" to Appendix B, *The Correspondence of Adam Smith*, 379–80. See also, G. H. Guttridge, "Thomas Pownall's *The Administration of the Colonies*," *The William and Mary Quarterly*, 26 (1969), 31–46; and Miller, *Defining the Common Good*, 211–13 and 235–38. Later, in *A Memorial Most Humbly Addressed to the Sovereigns of Europe* (London, 1780), Pownall advocated a loose confederation—a "League"—consisting of Britain, the United States, and the (potentially) independent states of Latin America. For some other plans, see Neil York, "Federalism and the Failure of Imperial Reform, 1774–1775," *History*, 86 (2001), 155–79.

[21] Richard Price, "Observations on the Nature of Civil Liberty" [1776] in ibid., *Political Writings*, ed. D. O. Thomas (Cambridge, 1991), 23, 25, 30. For Price, "perfect" civil liberty was only possible in small communities, and larger ones had to rely for their protection on representation, and this led to great problems in America and Britain. See also Price, "Additional Observations," in *Political Writings*, 78, 93.

sentatives from all the different states." In both Europe and, he added in a novel twist, the wide reaches of the British empire, such a senate would ideally "possess the power of managing all the common concerns of the united states" acting as a "common arbiter or umpire" in disputes between clashing interests. In order to carry out such a monumental task, it would have "under its direction the common force of the states to support its decision." The result would be "an empire of freemen" not "an empire of slaves."[22]

These were all very ambitious schemes, sketching the outlines of an incipient transoceanic polity, but they were also marginal—as much signs of desperation at the loss of British prestige as of plausible ideas for government policy. Although he exaggerated his isolation, Smith was correct to claim that those in favor of American representation, let alone anything more radical, occupied a sparsely populated and deeply unpopular flank on the spectrum of opinion.[23] The period in which the globe haltingly came to be seen as a single space for political action witnessed the adumbration of a number of schemes for polities stretching across great distances; but space itself was still seen by most, if not all, as a serious and perhaps permanent impediment to such grand ambitions.

Edmund Burke railed eloquently against the doctrine of colonial representation. He wished to retain the empire, but he was skeptical of the practicability or desirability of closer political union with the colonists. His writings on the American crisis are pervaded by a powerful sense of the immoveable role that "nature" played in determining the contours of political action. In an essay written in response to a pamphlet on the "Present State of the Nation" (1769), he wrote of his interlocutor, William Knox, that it "costs him nothing to fight with nature, and to conquer the order of Providence, which manifestly opposes itself to the possibility of . . . Parliamentary Union." And because Knox was so imprudent as to challenge nature, his plans could be dismissed with contempt: "Enough of this visionary union; in which much extravagance appears without any fancy, and the judgement is shocked without anything to refresh the imagination. It looks like the author has dropped from the moon, without any knowledge of the general nature of this globe, of the general nature of its inhabitants, without the least acquaintance with the affairs of this country." He leveled the same criticisms at Pownall's ideas.[24] Burke's clearest

---

[22] Ibid., "Observations on the Nature of Civil Liberty," 25 and 34–35.

[23] See H. T. Dickinson, "Britain's Imperial Sovereignty" in Dickinson (ed.), *Britain and the American Revolution* (London, 1998), 64–97; and Paul Langford, "Property and 'Virtual Representation' in Eighteenth-Century England," *HJ*, 31 (1988), 83–115.

[24] Burke, "Observations on a Late Publication Intituled 'The Present State of the Nation'" [1769] in *The Writings and Speeches of Edmund Burke*, ed. Paul Langford (Oxford, 1981), II, 180–81.

articulation of the recurrent problem of governance over distance can be found in his great speech to the House of Commons on March 22, 1775. "*Opposuit natura*—I cannot remove the barriers of the creation."[25] The art of statesmanship, however skillfully performed, offered no possibility of overcoming barriers embedded so deeply "in the natural constitution of things."

> Three thousand miles of ocean lie between us and them. No contrivance can prevent the effect of this distance, in weakening Government. Seas roll, and months pass, between the order and the execution, and the want of a speedy explanation of a single point is enough to defeat a whole system. . . . Who are you, that should fret and rage, and bite the chains of Nature?—Nothing worse happens to you, than does to all Nations, who have extensive Empire; and it happens in all the forms into which Empire can be thrown. In large bodies, the circulation of power must be less vigorous at the extremities. Nature has said it. . . . This is the immutable condition; the eternal law, of extensive and detached Empire.[20]

The distance separating the colonies and Great Britain was, argued Burke, simultaneously one of the main reasons why the Americans were threatening rebellion and the chief impediment standing in the way of many of the ingenious plans for union that were offered as a response. This speech, and in particular this passage, was regarded as the most authoritative statement of the power of nature in nineteenth-century debates over the empire.

Other thinkers saw the Atlantic as a bar to any form of connection. Thomas Paine commented plaintively that the "distance at which the Almighty hath placed England and America is a strong and natural proof that the authority of one over the other, was never the design of Heaven."[27] Jeremy Bentham was likewise deeply skeptical about the possibility of governing colonies over great distances.[28] In writings produced between the 1790s and the 1830s, he highlighted the absurdity of attempting to

---

[25] Burke, "Speech on Conciliation with America" (March 22, 1775), *The Writings and Speeches of Edmund Burke*, ed. W. M. Elofson with John A. Woods (Oxford, 1996), III, 152. The phrase is taken from Juvenal, *Satires*, x: "Nature is opposed." Burke later argued that distance "has caused much misrepresentation of mutual sentiments" between the colonists and the British: "Address to the Colonists" (January 1777), in *Writings and Speeches*, III, 285. This once again points to the lack of communal unity identified by Smith.

[26] Burke, "Speech on Conciliation with America," 124–25. See also Paine, *Common Sense*, 67

[27] Paine, *Common Sense* [1776], ed. Isaac Kramnick (Harmondsworth, 1986), 87.

[28] Note that Bentham tended not to distinguish between the different types of colony that the British administered. For an insightful overview of his arguements, see Jennifer Pitts, *A Turn to Empire* (Princeton, 2005), ch. 3.

control a global empire, going so far as to compare the difficulties that Spain faced ruling over its colonial possessions with those of ruling the moon: "It has its Peninsular part and its Ultramarian part! It has its *earthly* part: it has its *lunar* part."[29] Bentham opposed colonies for a battery of reasons. In regard to distance, he sketched three main lines of argument. First, he emphasized that a large and dispersed empire, the product of "unnatural domination," was extremely hard to defend. Empires generated weakness not strength. *"Oh but they are a great part of our power*—Say rather, *the whole part of your weakness.* In your own natural body you are impregnable: in those unnatural excrescences you are vulnerable: Are you attacked at home? Not a man can you ever get from them: not a sixpence." He also presented a political-economic case, arguing that distance increased the cost of war, especially through the need to maintain and provision an expensive navy. "Are they attacked? They draw upon you for fleets and armies."[30] The burden on the state was not, in a final utilitarian calculus, worth this amount of expenditure and danger. And finally, he reiterated the familiar argument that distance rendered political leaders insensitive to the wants and needs of colonial populations: like Smith, he stressed that it was impossible to properly understand the life of those "strangers" living in remote lands. As such, colonial rule was both unjust and politically imprudent.

> Is it then for their advantage to be governed by a people who never know, nor ever can know, either their inclinations or their wants? What is it you can ever know about them? The wishes they entertain? The wants they labour under? No such thing: but the wishes they entertained, the wants they laboured under two months ago, wishes that may have changed, and for the best reasons: wants that may have been relieved, or become unrelievable.[31]

At the end of his life Bentham observed that the best argument for the independence of America was not one couched in the language of natural rights, the language that he had fought so hard against, but rather "the impossibility of good government at such a distance, and the advantage of separation to the interest and happiness of both parties."[32] Indeed he hoped that by the end of the century Australia would be transformed from

[29] Bentham, "Rid Yourselves of Ultramaria!" (1820–12) in ibid., *Colonies, Commerce, and Constitutional Law*, ed. Philip Schofield (Oxford, 1995), 52. Italics in original.

[30] Bentham, "Emancipate Your Colonies!" (1793) in ibid., *Rights, Representation, and Reform*, ed. Philip Schofield, Catherine Pease-Watkin, and Cyprian Blamires (Oxford, 2002), 296 and 305. Italics in original. Initially circulated privately, this pamphlet was finally published by Bentham in 1830, with the argument unchanged.

[31] Ibid., 292 and 293.

[32] Ibid., "Memoirs of Jeremy Bentham" in *The Works of Jeremy Bentham*, ed. John Bowring (Edinburgh, 1843), 10, 63.

a "dependency on the English Monarchy, into a Representative Democracy."[33]

These critical arguments were all recycled throughout the following decades, helping to structure debates over the nature and meaning of the empire. But over the course of the nineteenth century things were to change drastically, as the problem of distance was confronted in novel ways. The notion of an extensive political union populated by "strangers" was supplanted by visions of a tightly integrated global Anglo-Saxon community.

NATURE IN FLUX, C. 1830–1870

> We can remove mountains, and make seas our
> smooth highway; nothing can resist us.
> —Thomas Carlyle, "Signs of the Times" (1829)

The early and middle decades of the nineteenth century witnessed a comprehensive technological revolution, encompassing communications, materials, armaments, and medicine. The results were monumental and multifaceted. At the end of the century Nietzsche argued that the modern world was characterized by hubris, and he despaired of "our rape of nature with the help of machines and the completely unscrupulous inventiveness of technicians and engineers." Earlier Thomas Carlyle, in a more ambiguous vein, had intoned that "[w]e war with rude Nature and, by our restless engines, come off always victorious, and loaded with spoils."[34] Carlyle's threnody to a pre-industrial, Arcadian past was issued originally as a challenge to the obsession with trying to wrest the control of nature from the hands of God.[35] This epic undertaking was both an intellectual and a practical exercise, combining a scientific assault focused on deci-

---

[33] Bentham, "Postscript" (1829) included with "Emancipate your Colonies," 314. Bentham was not entirely consistent here, though, as he also produced at this time (following an invitation from E. G. Wakefield) an unpublished plan for the creation of a new colony in Australia, modeled partly on America: Philip Schofield, *Utility and Democracy* (Oxford, 2006), ch. 8.

[34] Nietzsche, *On the Genealogy of Morality* [1887], ed. Keith Ansell-Pearson (Cambridge, 1994), 86; and Carlyle, *Critical and Miscellaneous Essays* (New York, 1896), II, 60, quoted in Michael Adas, *Machines as the Measure of Men* (Ithaca, 1989), 213.

[35] While recognizing the heroic grandeur of the task, Carlyle was one of the many Victorians who remained deeply skeptical about the benefits of this struggle. See John Burrow, "Images of Time" in Stefan Collini, Richard Whatmore, and Brian Young (eds.), *History, Religion, and Culture* (Cambridge, 2000), 219.

phering the tangled and elusive codes of the physical world with the subsequent exploitation of such discoveries through the development of novel engineering practices—the remaking of Nature in the image (and at the service) of "Man." The political imagination was likewise being reshaped.

The era of the French revolution and of Napoleon was one of conservative reaction in Britain.[36] Fighting the French, repressing internal dissent, and keeping the remaining elements of its empire from rebelling, as both Ireland and a number of Caribbean Islands did, albeit unsuccessfully, in the 1790s, became priorities of the ruling elite. The empire was seen increasingly in terms of hierarchy and subordination, rather than, as the American colonists had often viewed it, an "empire of liberty." An aristocratic and martial ethos prevailed, and the idea of incorporating elements of the empire into the sacred realm of Britain was anathema to the temper of the times.[37]

Throughout the first half of the century the combination of geographical dispersion and poor communications shaped attitudes to an empire that, even by 1848, largely "remained out of sight and out of mind."[38] But during the late 1830s and 1840s long-standing assumptions about the restraints placed on the effective functioning of political communities by physical space came under increasing scrutiny. For some commentators, particularly those with an eye fixed on the future, the nascent steamship technology led to a reevaluation of Burke's purportedly unassailable "eternal law." For the majority of imperial theorists, however, distance remained a salient obstacle to constitutional and communal integration, and other forms of government had to be developed. It was partly as a result of the then dominant belief in the impossibility of effective rule over great distances that the doctrine of colonial "responsible government" appealed so strongly to those intent on retaining the empire.[39] The "colonial reform" movement was animated by similar concerns. Explicitly drawing on Bentham, the political economist and prophet of "systematic

[36] For general context, both in Britian and the empire, see C. A. Bayly, *Imperial Meridian* (London, 1989); Mark Francis, *Governors and Settlers* (London, 1992); Eliga H. Gould, "The American Revolution in Britain's Imperial Identity" in Fred M. Leventhal and Roland Quinault (eds.), *Anglo-American Attitudes* (Aldershot, 2000), 23–38; and Boyd Hilton, *A Mad, Bad, and Dangerous People?* (Oxford, 2006), esp. chs. 1–5.

[37] Michael Duffy, "War, Revolution and the British Empire" in Mark Philp (ed.), *The French Revolution and British Popular Politics* (Cambridge, 1991), 118–45; and C. A. Bayly, "The First Age of Global Imperialism, c.1760–1830," *JICH*, 26 (1998), 28–42.

[38] Miles Taylor, "The 1848 Revolutions and the British Empire," *P&P*, 166 (2000), 151.

[39] The role of distance in shaping midcentury policy was clear to later Victorian observers: John Colomb, "A Survey of Existing Conditions" in White (ed.), *Britannic Confederation*, 6.

colonization," E. G. Wakefield was adamant that rule at a distance was detrimental to colonial development, because it took months to communicate with the "mother country," and the officials in London barely knew or cared about what was transpiring thousands of miles away. This worry was one of the main sources for his argument in favor of "local self-government." As he wrote in *England and America* (1833), "[l]et colonies be societies in new places, and they will have the power to choose between self-government and government from a distance. That they would choose to govern themselves cannot be doubted by any one who is at all acquainted with the evils of being governed from a distance."[40]

The imaginative revolution wrought by new technologies, and in particular by transoceanic steamships and the electric telegraph, changed the direction of debate. The first steamship crossing of the Atlantic, made by the *Royal William* in 1833, heralded the inauguration of a new era in global communications, although the widespread practical impact of the technology was not felt until later in the century, as there was a considerable lag between showcasing a prototype and producing a commercially viable product and all the necessary supporting infrastructure. The early decades of the century may well have been, in Carlyle's suggestive phrase, the "Age of Machinery," of the brutal arrival of industrialization and (for him) all its accompanying sins, but the new machinery was only put to use extensively, and momentously, in reconfiguring global communications in the mid- and late-Victorian era.[41] Patented only four years after the *Royal William* sailed, the telegraph also came as a revelation—its impact, unlike that of steam, more revolutionary than evolutionary—allowing near instantaneous communication across vast distances. And yet, like steam, the telegraph took years of further development before it could make a significant contribution, first to domestic society and then to global politics. The English Channel was first traversed with a functioning cable in 1851, and the Atlantic only properly in 1866.[42] The key to the shifts in political thinking lay not so much in the practical details or timing of the new technological developments, but in the new imaginative possibilities they engendered. Rudyard Kipling, the court poet of imperialism, later proclaimed that, "Here in the womb of the world—here

[40] Wakefield, *England and America* [1833], in *The Collected Works of Edward Gibbon Wakefield*, ed. M. F. Lloyd Prichard (Glasgow, 1968), 580.

[41] Carlyle, "Signs of the Times," 100–101.

[42] Contemporary newspaper responses can be found in Kenneth Chew and Anthony Wilson, *Victorian Science and Engineering Portrayed in the Illustrated London News* (Stroud, 1993), 35 and 38–40. There had been a short-lived Atlantic cable in 1858. Cables reached Australia in 1872, New Zealand in 1876, and South Africa in 1879. See here the comments in C. P. Lucas, "Introduction" to George Cornewall Lewis, *An Essay on the Government of Dependencies* (Oxford, 1891 [1841]), xli.

on the tie-ribs of the earth / Words, and the words of men, flutter and flutter and beat." "They have," he boasted of the telegraph cables, "killed their father Time."[43]

Lord Durham, the great hope of the colonial reformers, stressed the increasing role of technology in his famous 1839 report on the Canadian rebellions.[44] The report contained two main recommendations: firstly, that Upper and Lower Canada be reunited, and secondly, that this new entity be granted "responsible government." Durham was alive to the importance of distance in his plans, and he was critical of the lack of an internal communications infrastructure in the vast Canadian territories, insisting that new technological discoveries could play a vital role in his scheme for uniting the British and French colonists. He was likewise aware of the future possibilities engendered by the recent "success of the great experiment" in which the *Royal William* had negotiated the Atlantic, although he did not develop these at any great length.[45] The report appeared at a time when the perception of distance and its relationship to the world was in flux: conflicting ideas about the potential for "conquering" nature led to radically different conceptions of the future of the empire. The imaginative impact of new technologies was more pronounced in George Cornewall Lewis's influential *Essay on the Government of Dependencies* (1841). He argued that distance explained why Britain needed to form a system of dependencies, as opposed to imposing direct rule, for if the lands were within easy reach, they could be incorporated fully into the dominion of the superior parliament.[46] "[N]otwithstanding the facilities for communication afforded by the art of modern civilisation, the point is soon reached, even in the present time, at which it becomes im-

[43] Kipling, "Deep-Sea Cables" [1896] in *Rudyard Kipling's Verse, 1885–1932* (London, 1934), 173.

[44] The report was regarded during the nineteenth century, however inaccurately, as a defining moment in imperial policy: see, for example, Charles Oman, *England in the Nineteenth Century*, 248; and Lucas, "Introduction," xxvii. For a revisionist debunking of this claim, see Ged Martin, *The Durham Report and British Policy* (Cambridge, 1972). Wakefield was a key influence on the drafting of the report.

[45] See, for example, *Lord Durham's Report on the Affairs of the British North American Colonies*, ed. C. P. Lucas (Oxford, 1912 [1839]), II, 204, 213, and 316–19. He wrote that "the great discoveries of modern art, which have, throughout the world, and nowhere more than in America, entirely altered the character and channels of communication between distant countries, will bring all the North American colonies into constant intercourse with each other" (*Report*, II, 316). See also Appendix C, 327, in volume 3.

[46] Cornewall Lewis, *An Essay on the Government of Dependencies* (London, 1841), 183. He here also relies on, and quotes widely from, Burke's speech on "Conciliation with the Colonies" (379–400). A prolific political writer, Lewis was later to serve as Chancellor of the Exchequer. For an insightful assessment of him as a "shrewd and solid thinker," see Walter Bagehot, "George Cornewall Lewis" (1863) in Bagehot, *Biographical Studies*, ed. R. H. Hutton (London, 1889), 206–47.

possible for the most powerful community to govern a territory without interposing a subordinate government between it and a supreme government." Distance was, then, "the cause which renders it necessary for the supreme government to govern it in that form." He drew explicitly on Burke to demolish the veracity of Adam Smith's plan for colonial representation: "The main objection to the plan (an objection which its author has not noticed) lies in the distance of the colonies from England. Where a supreme government is prevented by distance . . . from communicating rapidly with any of its territories, it is necessary that the distant territory should be governed as a dependency."[47] Arthur Mills, another leading colonial commentator, likewise drew on Burke's arguments about distance in formulating his criticisms of plans for colonial representation. But he also recognized that new technologies were going to have a transformative impact on the empire. "It is not by dreaming of systems [parliamentary representation] which would be valueless even if they were within our reach," he argued, "but by the gradual expansion of those powers of self-government already conceded to our Colonial Legislatures, and in bringing those Colonies which are geographically remote, closer to us by the appliance of all the arts of modern navigation, that our real bond of union is to be found."[48]

Opinion was divided between those who took account of the latest technological developments and then extrapolated their potential into a plan for the future, and the more cautious majority, who preferred to focus instead on the uncertain present. The specter of Burke still haunted, even shaped, the understanding of the political possibilities engendered by nature. But for those prepared to scan the horizon of the future, there were signs of radical change to be divined. In arguing for Canadian representatives to sit in London, G. A. Young wrote in 1839 that as a result of the steamship, the "objection urged by Mr. Burke to a similar scheme cannot now be maintained."[49] Herman Merivale, Drummond Professor of Political Economy at Oxford, was similarly optimistic. Indeed he provides an illuminating bridge between the disintegration of the British American empire and the later expansionary period. His *Lectures on Colonization and Colonies* (1841) embodied both the pessimism of the present and the

[47] Cornewall Lewis, *An Essay on the Government of Dependencies*, 187 and 301. His claim about Smith not noticing the dangers of distance in his plan for representation is technically inaccurate (see Smith, "Thoughts on the State of the Contest with America," 382) although he would not have had access to Smith's then unpublished manuscript.

[48] Mills, *Colonial Constitutions* (London, 1856), lxviii. The book was reprinted posthumously in 1891. Mills also served as a Tory MP (1857–65 and again in 1873–80). On the evolution of his ideas about empire, see Edward Beasley, *Mid-Victorian Imperialists* (London, 2005), ch. 2.

[49] Young, "The Canadas," *The British and Foreign Review*, 8 (1839), 328.

utopianism of the future that defined much nineteenth-century imperial theorizing. In an introductory discussion of the settler colonies, published in 1839, he focused on their potential for growth, observing that the only regions that combined the three "chief conditions of prosperity," "are those removed from us by half the circumference of the globe. And, with our present means of transport, all our improved skill and increased enterprise has not been, nor can be, successful in overcoming this great obstacle of distance." The costs were simply too high, and the "tediousness of communication with the mother-country causes much embarrassment to commerce, produces much disinclination on the part of the better class of colonists to remove there, and impedes the moral and intellectual advance of the community."[50] But Merivale was far from glum, for he noted abruptly and with evident excitement that "we are just on the eve of a revolution." Steam and telegraph were forging a brave new world, a world in which the colonial system would finally be placed on secure foundations: "The next fifty years, therefore, will, in all probability, see a change analogous in character, and more equal in extent, to that which effected in the first half century after the landings of the Spanish in America."[51]

Writing less than a decade later, two young revolutionaries were also marveling at the political impact of technological developments: "The bourgeoisie, by the rapid improvement of all instruments of production, by the immensely facilitated means of communication, draws all, even the most barbarian nations, into civilisation." For Marx and Engels, the world-breaking and world-making power of capitalism was propelled by innovative technologies, which simultaneously enhanced global communications and precipitated "social revolution" in the most backward societies. This violent yet necessary rupture helped pave the way for a bright post-capitalist future.[52] For most imperial advocates it was still courting ideo-

---

[50] Merivale, *Introduction to a Course of Lectures on Colonization and Colonies* (London, 1839), 12. The rather ambiguous chief conditions of prosperity were: "room and soil for a rapid increase of population," "natural advantages for the production of wealth," and "a secure dependence on the mother country, at least in the first stage of their existence" (12). A staunch liberal, Merivale later served as permanent undersecretary at both the Colonial Office (1848–60) and then the India Office (1860–74). On his ideas and career, see Beasley, *Mid-Victorian Imperialists*, ch. 3.

[51] Merivale, *Introduction to a Course of Lectures*, 16.

[52] Karl Marx and Friedrich Engels, *The Communist Manifesto* [1848], ed. Gareth Stedman Jones (Harmondsworth, 2002), 224. Marx's views on the need for a "social revolution" in India, and the way in which the British were inadvertently bringing one about, were sketched in articles he wrote for an American newspaper during the 1850s. See, for example, "The British Rule in India" (June 25, 1853) and "The Future Results of the British Rule in India" (August 8, 1853), both in the *New York Daily Tribune*, and reprinted in *Karl Marx and Friedrich Engels on Colonialism* (Moscow, 1960), 31–36 and 76–82. Marx, however, shifted his position during the 1870s, becoming more critical of the impact of the empire. For the shift, see Gareth Stedman Jones, "Radicalism and the Extra-European World: The

logical unintelligibility to argue for the construction of a homogenous, centrally administered, global federal polity. In his *Considerations on Representative Government* (1861), John Stuart Mill employed the Burkean refrain in an unqualified manner. He criticized plans for colonial representation in Parliament, and for creating a full colonial federation, arguing that,

> The feelings of equity, and conceptions of public morality, from which these suggestions emanate, are worthy of all praise; but the suggestions themselves are so inconsistent with rational principles of government that it is doubtful if they have been seriously accepted by any reasonable thinker. Countries separated by half the globe do not present the natural conditions for being under one government, or even members of one federation.

This was a view he reiterated just before his death.[53] Two years after Mill published the *Considerations*, Goldwin Smith, a self-professed disciple of Adam Smith, made the great distances separating the British colonial possessions one of the central themes in his controversial call for "colonial emancipation" and in so doing he ended up falling in line with Burke, in so many other respects his political nemesis. Adopting a distinctly Burkean tone, he argued that, "we need scarcely discuss in detail the possibility or expediency of summoning from the ends of the earth people who could not be involved in less than six months, to decide whether England should go to war upon some question affecting herself, and not admitting perhaps an hour's delay."[54] As a consequence, Smith was scathing about schemes for parliamentary federation, singling out for criticism the great Scotsman's plan.

A generation later such arguments had lost much of their force. A Promethean confidence in the power of technology catalyzed and structured the debates over Greater Britain, leading to a fundamental recasting of imperial possibilities. Nature was no longer seen as the immutable, inscrutable foe that had confronted Burke so forcefully; it had been overcome, defeated, tamed.

Case of Karl Marx" in Duncan Bell (ed.), *Victorian Visions of Global Order* (Cambridge, 2007).

[53] Mill, *Considerations on Representative Government*, CW, XIX, 564. Mill, letters to Arthur Patchett Martin, October 10, 1871, and Henry Kilgour, August 15, 1870, CW, XXII, 1758–59 and 233. In 1865 Viscount Bury also drew on Burke's arguments about distance in his *Exodus of the Western Nations* (London, 1865), II, 424–25, concluding that the "laws of nature are against permanent union" (426).

[54] Smith, *The Empire* (Oxford, 1863), 85.

IMPERIAL POLITICAL THOUGHT IN THE AGE
OF SCIENTIFIC UTOPIANISM, C. 1870–1900

[I]n these days we can break with Burke's objection,
NATURA OPPOSUIT, by merely pointing to what
science has done, and relying on what we
know that it yet will do.
—H. R. Nicholls, "The Prophetic
Objections to Federation" (1886)

The second half of the nineteenth century was infused by a commanding belief in the power of science and technology to solve the manifold problems of society. This was a time in which the search for a "science of society" (or polity) to match the unprecedented advances of the natural sciences was at its peak, and the scientific method, broadly understood, offered a powerful and culturally authoritative way of thinking about how to both understand and govern the country.[55] The sweeping political claims made on behalf of new technologies found a receptive audience.

In 1870 John Edward Jenkins warned that the empire was facing "dissolution," and that an imperial federation was the only adequate response. He realized that such a proposal had to overcome the argument from nature. "A solitary difficulty, like the pillar of salt, stands up—a sign of retrospective despair, of dead, inane deficiency of hope. Distance, enchantress of the far-off view is looked upon as the intractable witch of confederation."[56] But, he insisted, nature's "eternal law" was no longer an immutable obstacle. Action was needed to save the empire, and circumstances had changed: the advent of steam and the telegraph had "destroyed the obstacles of distance." The witch had been banished, and Jenkins looked optimistically to the future:

> It may be said that every year we advance nearer to our dependencies both in time and facility of intercourse. At no very distant date steam communication with Australia will be so frequent, regular, and rapid, and the telegraph system so enlarged and cheap, that no practical difficulty would impede the working of a representative federal government.[57]

---

[55] The 1860s also witnessed a transformation in the way in which speculative literature represented the world, highlighting the role of speed and new communications technologies in the acceleration of everyday experience. Nicholas Daly, *Literature, Technology, and Modernity, 1860–2000* (Cambridge, 2004).

[56] Jenkins, "An Imperial Confederation," *CR*, 17 (1871), 78.

[57] Ibid., "Imperial Federalism," *CR*, 16 (1871), 179; and Ibid., "An Imperial Confederation," 78.

This argument was repeated by W. E. Forster in "Our Colonial Empire," an address on the future of the empire delivered in Edinburgh in 1875. Forster discussed a number of themes pervading imperial political thought during the decade. First, in his opening remarks he was quick to point out that he was only going to talk about the settlement colonies. Second, he noted with obvious satisfaction the shift in the terms of imperial discourse: "Who talks now of casting off the Colonies? What more popular cry at present than the preservation of our Empire?" And most tellingly, he waxed lyrical on the surmounting of temporal and spatial obstacles in the face of global union: whereas in the past, "the difficulties of time and space would . . . drive them [the colonies] to independence," this was no longer the case, for contrary to Burke's proclamation, "science has brought together the ends of the earth, and made it possible for a nation to have oceans roll between its provinces."[58] He concluded by arguing for an imperial advisory council. In a later essay, in which he heralded the establishment of the IFL, Forster answered a rhetorical question about the plausibility of establishing a viable political community divided by huge expanses of water. "Yes," he argued, "it may be a novelty; but there is another novelty, and that is the political effect of steam and electricity." This point was echoed by the barrister Francis de Labillière, a former New Zealand colonist and prominent advocate of supraparliamentry federation, who suggested that new technologies rendered the "*oceanus dissociabilis*" objection to federation redundant, and it was repeated at the Westminster Palace Hotel Conference (1884), out of which the IFL grew, when the Conservative MP W. H. Smith remarked that, for "all practical purposes the electric telegraph and steam have brought the most distant and the most remote colony into nearer relations, and certainly into greater sympathy, with the interests of Government in the capital of London than the distant and remote portions of Great Britain were some 100 or 200 years ago." In his introduction to the 1891 edition of Cornewall Lewis's *Essay on the Government of Dependencies*, the historian C. P. Lucas argued that many of the points made by Lewis in the 1840s had been superseded by new technologies, and he explicitly challenged Burke's argument, which had been central to Lewis's position, stating that "[m]odern science is a fact which vitiates all comparisons between past and present times, and makes all calculations as to the future uncertain."[59]

[58] Forster, "Our Colonial Empire," as reported in the *Times*, Monday, November 6, 1875, 9. See here Burke, "On Conciliation with the Colonies," 9. For similar sentiments, see also the *Times*, 25 October 1872. On the importance of Forster's speech, see F. P. de Lablillière, "British Federalism," *PRCI*, 24 (1893), 110.

[59] Forster, "Imperial Federation," *NC*, 17 (1885), 206; Labillière, "The Contraction of England and Its Advocates," *NR* [June 1884], reprinted in Labillière, *Federal Britain* (Lon-

The most authoritative expression of this shift in imagination flowed from Seeley's pen. In *The Expansion of England* he argued that the construction of a true Greater Britain was something that could have been contemplated only in the second half of the nineteenth century, as previously distance acted as an unbridgeable "impediment" to political unity. Spread so widely, the empire had been "practically dissolved by distance." The impediment had been transcended, however, for "[s]cience has given the political organism a new circulation, which is steam, and a new nervous system, which is electricity." Seeley might have gone further and noted that following the logic of this argument a fully fledged Greater Britain would have been impossible even thirty years before. He observed that in the "eighteenth century Burke thought a federation quite impossible across the Atlantic Ocean," but that this was no longer a feasible position to hold for "since Burke's time the Atlantic Ocean has shrunk till it seems scarcely broader than the sea between Greece and Sicily." Labillière, writing in 1894 proclaimed that the "question of distance is almost superseded" by steam and the telegraph, "so that the prospect of a Federal Empire, which five-and-twenty years ago appeared very remote, and which fifty years since seemed almost a chimera, now assumes a pressing and tangible shape."[60]

One of the most useful ways to chart the changing nature of political argument is to highlight the shift in the languages used to imagine the world. The fundamental transformation in the ontological precepts shaping conceptions of the planet was matched by the proliferation of novel methods and vocabularies drawn on to portray it. Imperial political thought after 1870 was injected with fresh metaphors and evocative phrases that served partly to remap a new understanding of the relationship between the size of the planet and the political destiny of the empire, and served also to add a touch of urgency, romance, or inevitability to the future. Adulatory odes to the near miraculous power of technology abounded. Two forms of linguistic innovation are of particular interest: the widespread employment of organic (and particularly bodily) metaphors to describe the empire; and the common reference to "space and time" (or vice versa) being annihilated, destroyed, rendered obsolete. The

---

don, 1894), 160 (italics in original); Smith, in *Imperial Federation; Report*, 33; and Lucas, "Introduction," xli and xlii. Although critical of radical plans for federation, Lucas suggested allowing the Colonial agents to sit in a reconfigured second chamber. Also referring to the shifting status of the oceans, Joseph Chamberlain argued that the colonies were "joined to us by the seas that formerly seemed to divide us." Chamberlain, "The True Conception of the Empire," speech at the Annual Royal Colonial Institute Dinner, Hotel Metropole, March 31, 1897, in Charles W. Boyd (ed.), *Mr Chamberlain's Speeches* (London, 1914), II, 2.

[60] Seeley, *The Expansion of England*, 74–75; and Labillière, *Federal Britain*, 12.

former of these signified the final emergence of a truly unified colonial empire, the latter the defeat of nature by the power of human reason and ingenuity. Neither of these modes of expression was truly original, for they were both parasitic upon traditional state-centered discourses; the imperial theorists borrowed, elaborated, and extended to the whole world modes of expression previously utilized only in relation to contiguous political communities. Today's language of globalization, replete with claims of radical novelty and the "annihilation of space and time," often simply replicates the ways in which the late Victorians interpreted the dynamics of global politics.

The increasingly widespread employment of the conjoined pair "time and space" in imperial political thought was borrowed from a language that first emerged as a way of registering the profound impact of the railways. As the railway boom served as an early indicator of the power of technology in re-shaping the imagination, so it had also brought about a revolution in the languages used to capture this shift. The phrase "the annihilation of space through time," so resonant with the sheen of modernity and encoded in a vocabulary of scientific authenticity, became widespread in the 1840s, although it had a long and distinguished provenance.[61] The railways "shrank" the size of the advanced industrial states of western Europe and the United States, shattering previous conceptions of distance, speed, and national geography. Commenting on the opening of a rail link between Paris and Rouen in 1843, the poet Heinrich Heine proclaimed that the "elementary concepts of time and space have begun to vacillate. Space is killed by the railways, and we are left with time alone." He had witnessed, he thought, a "providential event."[62] The horizons of political possibility were transformed in the wake of these developments.

This scientistic language was adopted and adapted by imperial political theorists. "The inventions of science," Forster declared at the Westminster Conference, "have overcome the difficulties of time and space which were thought to make separation almost a necessity." Following the initial success of the Pacific cable in 1872 the *Times* declared that the "At-

---

[61] Quoting Alexander Pope, Edmund Burke once wrote: "The Ocean remains. You cannot pump this dry; and as long as it continues in its present bed, so long will the causes which weaken authority by distance will continue. 'Ye gods, annihilate but space and time, and make two lovers happy'—was a pious and passionate prayer;—but just as reasonable, as many of the serious wishes of very grave and solemn politicians." Burke, "Speech on Conciliation with America," 131. The (unidentified) passage is attributed to Pope in a footnote by Burke's editors.

[62] Quoted in Wolfgang Schivelbusch, *The Railway Journey* (Oxford, 1986), 37. On the dating of "time and space," see Michael Freeman, *Railways and the Victorian Imagination* (London, 1999), 21 and 150–71.

lantic Cable annihilates about two thousand miles of space; the Australian telegraph annihilates no less than twelve thousand." The Honorary Secretary of the RCI, Frederick Young, claimed that the "marvellous and mysterious help of telegraphy" had "worked a veritable revolution in the affairs of the world."[63] As a consequence of the world-historical transformation engendered by new technologies, Lucas argued that "generalisations on political questions will have to be perpetually recast with the ever-changing meaning of space and time."[64] No longer an eternally imprinted set of fetters, nature was now the subject of "annihilation," of forceful overcoming by the mind and practical works of humanity. Lord Norton, a sympathetic Tory critic of the federalists, employed the same terminology in defending the existing constitutional relations between the colonies and London; the "moral union" of the empire was already strong, he contended, and the "more time and space are annihilated, the closer does this sort of union become."[65] The historian E. A. Freeman was adamant that the federal project was bound to fail, based as it was on implausible claims about the ability to forge a common political identity between such disparate groups. But he was clear about the impact of steam and telegraph: "modern science has annihilated time and space . . . [so] that it takes no longer to get to Westminster from the most distant British colonies, than at the time of the Union of England and Scotland, it took to get from Shetland to London."[66] The political indeterminacy of the language of time and space resulted from uncertainty over the consequences of the perceived "shrinkage" of the planet. For some this was a jejune point, heralding little significant change in the possibilities of political organization; for others it was an unprecedented invitation to novelty.

   David Harvey, in *The Condition of Postmodernity* (1989), conflates the two distinct periods in which the language of "time and space" began to

---

[63] Forster, comments reported in *Imperial Federation: Report*, 27; the *Times*, November 16, 1772, reprinted in *PRCI*, 3 (1872), 36; and Young, comments printed in the *PRCI*, 8 (1876–77), 118–19. See also Lord Rosebury, *Imperial Federation: Report*, 36. Young was an indefatigable campaigner for colonial unity. See the brief biographical comments in Young, *A Pioneer of Imperial Federation in Canada* (London, 1902), 215, and, for the extent of his advocacy, see his prolific correspondence with newspapers on imperial topics in the Young Papers, University of Cambridge Library, RCMS, 54/III/21.

[64] Lucas, "Introduction," xlii.

[65] Lord Norton, "Imperial Federation—Its Impossibility," *NC*, 34 (1884), 514. In a former incarnation, Norton was Charles Adderley, a leading colonial reformer, as well as a founder of the Colonial Society. For his views on empire, which encompassed a nonfederal moral union of the Anglo-Saxons, see Edward Beasley, *Empire as the Triumph of Theory* (London, 2005), ch. 7. See also Norton, *Imperial Fellowship of Self-Governing British Colonies* (London, 1903).

[66] Freeman, "The Physical and Political Bases of National Unity" in White (ed.), *Britannic Confederation*, 52. For more on Freeman's views, see chapter 4.

signify a shift in the perception of the world. He argues that 1848 should
be regarded as the key marker, and that the midcentury years witnessed a
rapid acceleration in the spatial expansion of capitalism: "capitalism became embroiled in an incredible phase of massive long-term investment
in the conquest of space."[67] Harvey is correct to stress the critical role
played by the transformation in the representation of the planet, but in
claiming that the 1840s witnessed a re-imagining of "space and time" he
misses the vital point that during the nineteenth century the perception of
space underwent two distinct transformations. In the 1830s and 1840s, it
was "wounded" fatally when discrete national spaces appeared to "shrink"
in the wake of the railway revolution. But it was only during the closing
decades of the century that it was to be "annihilated" on a global scale.
The world as a whole appeared to contract.[68] When Victoria ascended
to the throne in 1837, Labillière wrote, "[n]o visionary had then even
dreamed of the opening of telegraphic communication with Australia, or
that men would be able to travel, in a fortnight, from London to the Pacific shores of Canada."[69] The lag in the changing terminology of imperial discourse reflects the fact that the two shifts in imagination were separated by a generation.

The second shift in the semantics of empire saw the extensive employment of organic metaphors to describe the totality of the colonial empire.
Organic ideas were of course far from novel, comprising one of the sta-
ple languages of late Victorian political thought, and imperial discourse
was once again drawing from a more widely employed lexicon. However,
the idea of the "biological" growth of the empire was previously uncommon, as the idea of an organic entity presupposes the interdependency of
the parts constituting the "life-form." As a result it was generally understood that there would be contiguity between the elements, thus allowing,
for example, territorially bounded states to be conceived as organisms. It
was steam (through the medium of transoceanic shipping) and electricity
(through the medium of the telegraph) that was now perceived to have
provided the means to envision the empire as one, as linked together and
capable of functioning as a highly integrated body politic. In particular,
this form of expression specified an intimate connection between the empire and the mammalian (presumably human) body: hence Seeley's "new
circulation" for the "political organism," the Marquis of Lorne's discussion of political shocks spreading instantaneously through the imperial

---

[67] Harvey, *The Condition of Postmodernity* (Oxford, 1989), 241, 252, 261, and 264.

[68] See, for an early example, J. Stephen, "The Atlantic Telegraph and its Lessons," *FR*, 5
(1866), 442; and [Anon.], "Atlantic Telegraph," *CM*, 12 (1865), 364–73. For some comments on the relationship between communications technologies and organic languages, see
also Laura Otis, "The Metaphoric Circuit," *JHI*, 63 (2002), 105–29.

[69] Labillière, *Federal Britain*, 251.

"limbs," and the Tory MP John Henniker-Heaton's claim that "the tele-graph and the post are the nerves and arteries of the whole." Seeley thought that the colonies were "not self-contained, they are limbs, the life of which depends on a heart and brain outside themselves."[70] For Jen-kins, the endangered empire represented a "hazardous organism," while for Egerton it was simply a "single organism."[71] Outlining a case for strengthening the ties between London and the South Pacific, the Aus-tralian politician Henry Parkes argued that it was essential "to bind the body and limbs" of the empire "in one great self-sustaining, consan-guineous political organism," while the idealist philosopher J. H. Muir-head, drawing on the organic idiom popularized by his philosophical al-lies, declared that "[n]ew arteries and nerve systems were beginning to be formed" between the various sections of the English race.[72] Forging an even more direct analogy, another observer claimed that, "[n]owadays, the whole earth resembles, in a measure, one of our own bodies. The elec-tric wires represent the nerves, and messages are conveyed from the most distant regions to the central plane of government, just as in our bodies, where sensations are conveyed to the sensorium."[73]

Burke's imposing presence still made itself felt. Labillière claimed that had he lived a century later, Burke would undoubtedly have been an im-perial federalist.[74] Surveying two decades of intense debate over federa-tion, and what he saw as the rising tide of support for the idea, Labillière asserted that technology had "marvellously removed the impossibilities of the past."[75] Burke had been premature to characterize the laws of na-ture as "immutable," as indelible barriers to union. Since the problem of distance had been removed, a closer and more productive association be-

[70] Lorne, *Imperial Federation* (London, 1885), 113; Henniker-Heaton, "The Postal and Telegraphic Communication of the Empire," *PRCI*, 19 (1888), 172; and Seeley, "Introduc-tion" to *Her Majesty's Colonies* (London, 1886), xxiii. Henniker-Heaton had spent a con-siderable amount of time working as a journalist and then public official in Australia; he served as a Tory MP (for Canterbury) from 1885 until 1910.

[71] [Jenkins], "An Imperial Confederation," 77; and Egerton, *A Short History of British Colonial Policy* (London, 1897), 451.

[72] Parkes, "Australia and the Imperial Connection," *NC*, 15 (1884), 869; and Muirhead, "What Imperialism Means" [1900] reprinted in *The British Idealists*, ed. David Boucher (Cambridge, 1997), 243.

[73] Gabriel Stokes, reply to a speech by Lord Salisbury, reprinted in *The Electrician*, No-vember 8, 1889, 13.

[74] Labillière, "British Federalism," 96. For other examples of the Smith-Burke debate being employed to structure arguments, see: George Ferguson Bowen, "The Federation of the British Empire," *PRCI*, 17 (1885–86), 290; Frederick Young, *On the Political Relations of Mother Countries and Colonies* (London, 1885), 16–17; W. M. Greswell, "Prize Essay" in *England and Her Colonies* (London, 1887); and the comments in John Morley, "The Ex-pansion of England," *MM*, 49 (1884), 252.

[75] Labillière, "British Federalism," 97.

tween the various elements of the colonial empire was not simply possible or desirable, it was necessary to secure British greatness. And Burke, he suggested, would have recognized this.

Skepticism about the ameliorative powers of technology coexisted alongside the panegyrics. The telegraph was often slow, had limited coverage, and was very expensive. It was a common complaint that monopolies dominating the telegraph system rendered it inaccessible to the vast majority of the population, and the most forceful opponent of such monopolies, John Henniker-Heaton, protested that as a result imperial communications were "denied to all but a wealthy few." The potential for technology to help strengthen the ties of empire was being squandered. He was nevertheless a firm believer in the power of communications, and of the increasing interdependence that the telegraph in particular could engender, for it provided "the means of intensifying and perpetuating the sympathy that is the basis of union." Ascribing near magical powers to the new technologies, he tendered an ode to the new age: "stronger than death-dealing war-ships, stronger than the might of legions, stronger than wealth and genius of administration, stronger than the unswerving justice of Queen Victoria's rule, are the scraps of paper that are borne in myriads over the seas, and the two or three slender wires that connect the scattered parts of her realm." As a result of this fragile copper girdle enveloping the empire, "[n]ot a misfortune, or a cause of rejoicing, of hope, astonishment or apprehension," could occur anywhere in the world without a "thrill of sympathy" cresting like a wave over the earth's surface.[76] The role of the new communications technologies in not only dissolving distance but also (as a consequence) forging a sense of community through bringing people into more frequent and intimate contact with one another was considered essential by many of the proponents of Greater Britain, for it was believed to foster a sense of unity between the colonists and the people of the United Kingdom, as well as between the different colonies. Referring to the new technologies, James Bryce stated that "[n]o such means of gathering, diffusing, and concentrating public opinion, of quickening its formation and strengthening its action, had ever been dreamt of before our own time." The result was, wrote another federalist, "an extraordinary condition of contactiveness."[77] An action in one part of the globe resonated powerfully and almost concurrently in another. The generation and maintenance of a communal identity stretching over the planet was (or so it seemed) finally possible.

[76] Henniker-Heaton, "An Imperial Telegraph System," 907–10; and Henniker Heaton, "The Postal and Telegraphic Communication of the Empire," 172. On the realities of imperial communication, see Simon Potter, *News and the British World* (Oxford, 2003).

[77] Bryce, "An Age of Discontent," *CR*, 59 (1891), 19; and Francis de Winton, "Address," *Proceedings of the Royal Geographical Society*, 11 (1889), 621. Winton was speaking in his capacity as president of the Geographical Section of the British Association.

The power of the revolution in political discourse is illustrated in the arguments adduced by those critical of a federal Greater Britain. Whereas distance had for centuries been a central plank in the case of the opponents of closer constitutional ties, it was after c.1870 employed far less frequently, and always in a heavily qualified manner. The silences, as ever, speak loudly. There were certainly those who drew on such arguments, notably Freeman, but they tended to insist that although the world had indeed shrunk in important respects, it did not follow that it was feasible to build an intercontinental political community. For Freeman, the problem was not simply distance, but the fact that the "ideal nation" required a "continuous territory . . . inhabited by a people under one government." Instantaneous communication, important as it was in other respects, did not transform the nature of the state. Morley took a similar view, and following Mill's discussion of the "rational principles of government" in the *Considerations on Representative Government* he argued that despite the development of new communications technologies, the "vast geographical distances" involved still presented an insurmountable problem for the unification of the colonial empire. Pointing to America as a precedent for such a union was deeply misleading, he contended, as it was a "geographically solid" state, its component parts not scattered across the world.[78] Responding to Forster's impassioned plea for federation, meanwhile, Lorne thought that it was imperative to ask what the colonists themselves actually thought of the future direction of government policy, and he suggested that rash suprafederal proposals were perhaps unrealistic in meeting their desires. But he also emphasized that it was now easy to direct such questions to them, as "telegraphic communication makes Australia as near to the Colonial Office as Victoria Street."[79] Both the opponents and proponents of federation tended to be united in their assumptions about what was necessary for a healthy political community; they differed in their interpretation of the impact that technology had in challenging the political limits imposed by nature.

REMAKING THE GLOBAL POLITICAL IMAGINATION

Whether or not people were opposed to the new technologies or the new ideals of imperial order, the success of the Victorian engineers catalyzed a fundamental shift in the manner in which people viewed the world and their relationship to it. No longer, it was argued, should the traditional in-

[78] Freeman, "The Physical and Political Bases of National Unity," 35 and 52; and Morley, "The Expansion of England," 256–57.

[79] Lorne, "Unity of Empire," *NC*, 17 (1885), 403. This essay was written as a skeptical riposte to Forster's federalist agenda; in the same vein, and in the same edition, see also Viscount Bury, "The Unity of the Empire," 381–96.

junction about the vast and insurmountable size of the empire determine policy toward other parts of the globe. In retrospect the critics were correct about the impractical, hubristic view of technology entertained by many of the promoters of Greater Britain, for the fact that it is possible to communicate with somebody on the other side of the planet does not necessarily engender a sense of community or common feeling, let alone common interests. The relentless rise of colonial nationalism, as well as the widespread colonial distrust of the federal idea, serves as a reminder of this. But these were not issues that appeared to disturb the glibly optimistic advocates of technology. The more breathless advocates of contemporary globalization would do well to learn from this episode.

Lord Salisbury, prime minister and foreign secretary, gave the inaugural speech at the founding dinner of the Institute of Electrical Engineers in 1889. His comments no doubt pleased those who had invited him, for they comprise one of the most striking statements of the intimate links between science and global politics in the Victorian era. It was a paean to an age of unrestrained confidence in the ability of human ingenuity to defeat the ancient problems of political governance. He started by hymning the "enormous benefits which electrical science confers upon mankind," claiming that at the Foreign Office, "we positively exist by virtue of the telegraph," and boasting that the telegraph had, "as it were, assembled all mankind upon one great plane, where they can see everything that is done, and hear everything that is said, and judge of every policy that is pursued at the very moment these events take place." Electrical engineers had thus, "combined together almost at one moment, and acting at one moment upon the agencies which govern mankind, the opinions of the whole of the intelligent world with respect to everything that is passing at that time upon the face of the earth." In conclusion, he proclaimed that this was the "most conspicuous feature in the politics of our time."[80]

The "long" nineteenth century witnessed a transformation of the ways in which the world was imagined. Although this transformation was always contested, always questioned, and although it generated varying interpretations of its possible consequences, during Victoria's protracted reign the planet appeared to shrink before the eyes of many observers. It was finally made small and manageable. This change in the structure of consciousness catalyzed a shift in the nature of political thought, revolutionizing the manner in which political communities in general and the settler empire in particular were, and indeed could be, conceived. In the period between the end of the Seven Years War and the dawn of the nineteenth century, the debate over distance and political community had, despite a brief flowing of ambitious visions of transatlantic "unions," been

---

[80] Marquis of Salisbury, Speech, printed in *The Electrician*, November 8, 1889, 13.

fairly one-sided, dominated by the view expressed most powerfully by Edmund Burke: nature was an immutable antagonist, circumscribing political projects. But as the century unfolded, this picture began to blur and as new communications technologies were invented and then became the driving engines and symbolic markers of the Victorian imperial state, so political thinkers recast their views on the spatial limits of viable communities. For the first time, the idea of a global polity, even a state, became a seemingly reasonable proposition. But the transition was slow and uneven: the middle decades of the century were pervaded by confusion and theoretical conflict over the coming of the age of steam and electricity. The signs of the times were hard to decipher, the future unclear. For some, this was a period of uncomfortable adjustment; the developments seemed either too fantastic or too limited to make much of a difference. They were the heirs of Burke. For others, however, the new technologies presented great opportunities, and they grasped them with relish. It was only in the second half of the century, and mainly from the 1870s onward, that the "annihilation" of "time and space" became a commonplace idea. The imperial federation movement, and the wider ideal of Greater Britain, was the most prominent articulation of this shift in political imagination.

4

Empire, Nation, State

A firm and well-compacted union of all the
British lands would form a state that might
control the whole world.
—Charles Oman, *England in the
Nineteenth Century* (1899)

THE DEBATE over Greater Britain encompassed questions about nationality, statehood, federalism, and race, as well as forms of imperial rule. Seeking to consolidate what they saw as the existing strengths of the colonial
bond, the unionists simultaneously prosletyzed a vision of moral order in
which a superior Anglo-Saxon race offered stability and leadership,
benevolently but firmly, to a chaotic world. Proposals ranged from the
moderate to the extremely ambitious, from reinforcing the existing ties
linking the colonies and the "mother country" to the construction of an
integrated global state, a giant polity to dwarf those of the history books.
A number of leading figures, including J. R. Seeley and W. E. Forster, argued explicitly for such a state, although the majority deliberately eschewed this provocative claim. The more sweeping proposals generated
considerable hostility, even incredulity, but a barrage of criticism failed to
dampen the enthusiasm for grandiose visions of the future among imperialists, and fantasies of a global polity were to permeate British political
thought almost until the era of decolonization. J.G.A. Pocock wrote once
that the "Atlantic Ocean is a great channel across which continents confront one another, but the Pacific is the true surface of the planet Aqua."[1]
In confidently bestriding "planet Aqua" many of the proponents of Greater
Britain envisaged a novel form of political association.

Visions of a global polity were not simply projections of the future,
dreams of a time yet to come. It was argued frequently that the contours
of this entity could be discerned in the existing configuration of the empire, but only in a ghostly form, and that in order to secure the greatness
of Britain this immanent structure needed to be put on a different constitutional footing. The argument assumed two basic forms. One deemed the
settler colonies important external appendages of the British state, and
sought to strengthen the intricate web of connections between them. The

---

[1] Pocock, "Between Gog and Magog," *JHI*, 48 (1987), 334.

other viewed them as integral elements of the British state itself, and as such it entailed an ambitious reordering of the potentiality of statehood. Both were premised on the dissolution of distance explored in the previous chapter. Nationality was also a fundamental concern, although again it could point in different directions: some unionists regarded the colonies as independent or embryonic nations, others saw Greater Britain as constituting a single indissoluble nationality. The latter view embodied a radical claim about the globalization of the nation, insisting that a tightly integrated and self-consciously cohesive political community could now spread across the face of the earth, escaping the spatial restrictions that had traditionally delimited such visions. Greater Britain could be characterized, then, as either a sophisticated political structure composed of semi-autonomous (and sometimes even independent) states underpinned by a common nationality, or alternatively as a multinational polity. Both positions were anchored in claims about the racial unity of the British people. The permutations were complex and sometimes conflicting, the variation reflecting both the multiplicity of conceptions of Greater Britain in circulation and the wider lack of consensus over the meaning and scope of nationality, statehood, federalism, and race.

This chapter explores some of this political and theoretical variety. In the following section I stress how the idea of federation moved from the margins to the center of British political discourse. Subsequently I highlight how the empire could, according to the conventions of Victorian political thought, be considered a state, and I examine in detail Seeley's conception of the "world-state." The final section investigates some of the different views of nationality and race that framed imperial debate.

The Turn to Federalism

> The aspect of the whole world suggests that we are
> passing from a nation epoch into a federation epoch.
> —George Parkin, *Imperial Federation* (1812)

The use of the term "federation" in late nineteenth-century imperial discourse was often, although certainly not always, inaccurate, the plans traveling under its name not federal in any strict sense.[2] Even when erro-

---

[2] A criticism made in Henry Thring, "The Fallacy of Imperial Federation," *NC*, 19 (1886), 22; and Richard Jebb, "Imperial Organization" in Charles Sydney Goldman (ed.), *The Empire and the Century* (London, 1905), 333–6. In the *Oxford English Dictionary* (www.oed.com), the second definition of the term "federation" is a reference to none other than: "b. Federation of the (British) Empire, Imperial Federation: a proposed readjustment of the relations between the various parts of the empire, by which the colonies would have shared with the mother country the control and the cost of all measures taken for the safety and well-being of the empire as a whole." Michael Burgess argues that ideally federalism

neous it was nevertheless a significant act of labeling, marking as it did a
shift in the conventions of British political thought. What had once been
considered alien had become a legitimate element of the vocabulary of
politics. Confederal arrangements had long been regarded with skepticism, and for much of the nineteenth century there was also considerable
doubt about the pioneering American national-federal variant. Tocqueville, for one, suggested that federation was not a suitable form of government for European states to adopt, and that it worked in America only
as a result of unusually propitious circumstances, and in particular the relative isolation of the country.[3] Modern Britain was a composite state, and
a federal structure seemed to offer little advantage over the post-1688
constitutional fudge, appearing fragile in the face of internal and external
threats. The "discourse of federalism," argues Pocock, "lies outside—if
only just outside—the history of political discourse which is British; it was
precluded, if at the same time mysteriously invented, by everything which
had shaped English history and the Anglo-British mind."[4] This argument
was employed by many of those opposed to a federal Greater Britain. According to George Baden-Powell, the "[f]ederal principle does not take
root in British soil. The tendency has always been towards national
unity."[5] This was true until the middle decades of the nineteenth century,
during which federalism became a topic of mounting interest among
British political thinkers. It was seen as an answer to many of the problems confronting a new and dangerous period in world history. Pocock
suggests that the period 1780–1830 should be seen as a "sattelzeit," an
era of flux and upheaval in patterns of discourse and conceptions of the
sociopolitical universe. It signaled the end of "early modernity" and the
birth of the modern, generating along the way a novel political terminology.[6] Federalism entered British political discourse, albeit at an oblique

and federation need to be distinguished, the former denoting a positive valuation of diversity, the latter a specific form of government. Burgess, "Federalism and Federation" in
Burgess and Alain-G. Gagnon (eds.), *Comparative Federalism and Federation* (London,
1993), 3–14; and also Preston King, *Federalism and Federation* (London, 1982), ch. 1. In
this chapter, however, I am using the terms interchangeably, as they were at the time.

[3] Tocqueville, *Democracy in America*, trans. Henry Reeve (London, 1862), I, ch. 8, esp.
192.

[4] Pocock, "Political Theory in the English-Speaking Atlantic, 1760–1790: (2)," in Gordon J. Schochet and Lois G. Schwoerer (eds.), *The Varieties of British Political Thought,
1500–1800* (Cambridge, 1993), 296. Historians of imperial federation argue likewise: J. E.
Kendle, *Federal Britain* (London, 1997), 41; and Michael Burgess, *The British Tradition of
Federalism* (Leicester, 1995), 17.

[5] Baden-Powell, "National Unity," *PRCI*, 16 (1884–85), 53.

[6] Pocock, "Political Theory in the English-Speaking Atlantic, 1760–1790: (2)," 311. The
term "sattelzeit" is taken from Reinhart Koselleck, *Futures Past*, trans. Keith Tribe (Cambridge, Mass., 1988).

angle, following the end of this period of "early modernity," as ideas about federation were first revitalized and then put into experimental practice in the former British colonies in North America. By the end of the century arguments about the virtues, and even the necessity, of federalism were a commonplace of political debate.

The growing importance of federalism seems to have been driven by two interwoven considerations: the spectacular trajectory of the United States and concerns over the future of the empire. For admirers of federalism it was primarily the model of the America state that appealed, not that of the (pre-*Bund*) loose agglomeration of German kingdoms. The Civil War (1860–65) provided the key test case. For some, the calamity seemed to prove once and for all that the American model was bankrupt, that it was simply too weak to restrain the social forces that a highly centralized sovereign authority could manage.[7] This position was adopted by, among others, the writers in the Tory *Quarterly Review*. As the young Robert Cecil (later Lord Salisbury) proclaimed in its pages, the war was "the most ignominious failure that the world has ever seen."[8] This was, however, a minority position. The success of the North, and the postwar economic dynamism of the country, suggested to many observers that federalism was a robust form of government. Edward Freeman, widely regarded as the leading expert on federal unions, refused to blame the pathologies of federalism for the outbreak of war, focusing instead on a historically contingent set of factors, notably the social divisions catalyzed by the moral and political economy of slavery. "All that these facts [about the war] prove is the indisputable truth that a Federal constitution is not necessarily a perfect constitution, that the Federal form of government enjoys no immunity from the various weaknesses and dangers which beset all forms of government."[9] The conflict did not challenge federal principles per se, and the fact that the United States survived the disaster, and even appeared to emerge stronger from it, demonstrated that federations could be extremely resilient. Federalism was vindicated as America flourished.[10]

From the 1830s onward debate over the future of the colonial empire also helped propel ideas about federation into mainstream politics. The

---

[7] See, for example, J. M. Farrar, "The Rise and Decline of the Confederate Government," *CR*, 40 (1881), 229–45.

[8] [Robert Cecil], "The Confederate Struggle and Recognition," *QR*, 112 (1862), 545.

[9] Freeman, *History of Federal Government* (London, 1863), 91 and 110–14. See also Freeman, "Federation and Home Rule," *FR*, 16 (1874), 173; and Freeman, "Some Impressions of the United States," II, *FR*, 32 (1882), 325; as well as J. N. Dalton, "The Federal States of the World," *NC*, 16 (1884), 115–17.

[10] John Burrow, "Some British Views of the United States Constitution" in R. C. Simmons (ed.), *The United States Constitution* (Manchester, 1989), 124; and Paolo Pombeni, "Starting in Reason, Ending in Passion," *HJ*, 37 (1994), 319–41. See also chapter 7.

granting of "responsible government" to the colonies triggered debate over how best to organize the internal structures of the colonies as well as the imperial system itself, a process that culminated in the perceived success of Canadian union in 1867–68. From then on federation was an established marker in imperial theory and practice. This development formed part of the intellectual backdrop to the debates over a federal Greater Britain and also for the contestation over Irish Home Rule.[11] An air of preordination surrounded these debates: the world seemed destined to be federal. Both the proliferation of actually existing federations and a widespread belief in the general tendency toward large omni-competent political units—a theme explored further in chapter 9—bolstered this conviction. "When we turn our gaze from the past to the future," Henry Sidgwick wrote in the mid-1890s, "an extension of federalism seems to me the most probable of the political prophecies relative to the form of government." Dilke concurred: "Our own age," he wrote in 1890, "has been a federal age." J. A. Hobson, meanwhile, explicitly linked democracy with the evolution of federal state forms, contending that the "democratic movement, both now and in the future, seems closely linked with the formation of federal States."[12] Federation had become a new dimension, even the endpoint, of progress. Many liberal internationalists, including Sidgwick, Herbert Spencer, Hobson, and L. T. Hobhouse, argued that a federation of "civilized" states was the most effective institutional arrangement for securing global peace and democracy.[13] For some of them, Greater Britain could serve as a means on the way to this end.

The main sources drawn upon in analyzing federalism were *The Federalist*, Tocqueville, John Stuart Mill, and, above all, Freeman, author of the leading Victorian text on the subject, the *History of Federal Government* (1863). The most enthusiastic support tended to emanate from liberals and radicals, although from the 1880s onward the American constitution appealed increasingly to Conservatives as it was seen to offer (through its system of checks and balances) a means of placing a break on ambitious plans pursued by the executive.[14] This is not to suggest that such admiration was universal, for there remained many ardent defend-

[11] J. E. Kendle, *Ireland and the Federal Solution* (Kingston, 1989).

[12] Sidgwick, *The Development of European Polity*, ed. Eleanor Sidgwick (London, 1903), 439; Dilke, *Problems of Greater Britain* (London, 1890), I, 97; and Hobson, *Imperialism* (London, 1902), 350. Sidgwick's book is based on lectures delivered in the mid-1890s.

[13] Duncan Bell and Casper Sylvest, "International Society in Victorian Political Thought," *MIH*, 3 (2006), 1–32; see also, Bart Schultz, *Henry Sidgwick* (Cambridge, 2004), 619.

[14] Murray Gerlach, *British Liberalism and the United States* (London, 2001); and John Pinder, "The Federal Idea and the British Liberal Tradition" in Andrea Bosco (ed.), *The Federal Idea* (London, 1991), I, 99–118. On conservative support, see Burrow, "Some British Views of the United States Constitution."

ers of the unitary state. John Austin, whose Bentham-inspired jurisprudence came to prominence only posthumously, and A. V. Dicey, whose arguments against federalism were colored by his staunch views on Irish Home Rule, offered two of the strongest defenses in their influential writings.[15] Confederation never gained extensive support, as it was regarded as a weak form of government, and it was singled out for criticism by most of those who went on to offer positive accounts of federal government. It did nevertheless gain occasional backing in imperial debate. Writing in 1901, Bernard Holland claimed that his ideal "is not a Federal State, and it is not a mere alliance, but it is a thing between the two, viz., a Confederation of States held together by the union of each to the Crown."[16]

Freeman distinguished the "system of confederated states," where the federal authority acted only on the constituent governments, from the *"composite state"* that had a "supreme federal government" exercising authority over individual citizens.[17] Only the latter of these could be classified as a federation proper. Although most authors recognized the difference between confederations and federations (even if their use of the terms was often cavalier), there remained considerable ambiguity over their respective attributes and over the way in which to characterize various intermediate structures. Indeed Sidgwick, like Seeley, thought that the distinction between confederation and federation had been given "perhaps undue importance," for it was hard to specify with any precision. Instead he saw them as broadly sequential, confederations tending to lead to federations.[18] In recognition of the ambiguity, Sidgwick coined the term "federality," "*i.e.* of the plan of uniting communities for certain important purposes of government, while they are separate and independent for certain other important purposes." Such a condition applied across a range of cases where power was devolved significantly, but the "decisive model of federality" was to be found in the United States.[19] This is a term that would have been very useful for the imperial federalists.

The debate over Greater Britain encompassed a variety of different un-

---

[15] John Austin, *The Province of Jurisprudence Determined* (London, 1832); Dicey, "Home Rule from an English Point of View," *CR*, 42 (1882), 66–86; and Dicey, *Lectures Introductory to the Study of the Law of the Constitution* (London, 1885). See also, Christopher Harvie, "Ideology and Home Rule," *EHR*, 91 (1976), 298–314.

[16] Holland, *Imperium et Libertas* (London, 1901), 301. See also, John Colomb, "A Survey of Existing Conditions" in Arthur White (ed.), *Britannic Confederation* (London, 1892), 3.

[17] Freeman, *History of Federal Government*, 10–13. Italics in original.

[18] Sidgwick, *The Development of European Polity*, 433. See also his discussion in *The Elements of Politics*, 4th ed. (London, 1919), 530–39. This edition is virtually unchanged from the 2nd edition of 1896.

[19] Ibid., *The Development of European Polity*, 428, 430, and 435. Italics in original; and Sidgwick, *The Elements of Politics*, 532–33.

derstandings of federalism, but in general the term signified the ambition to simultaneously defend unity and diversity, to protect and often reinforce the position of the colonists in relation to the "mother-country" while securing the means, whether political or economic, to coordinate the units within an overarching and durable structure.

STATEHOOD AND EMPIRE

If the emergent language of federalism offers one context in which to locate the theorists of empire, so too does that of the state. I am less concerned with what Herbert Spencer described as the "proper sphere of government," with the degree to which state institutions should intervene in society and economy, than with the widely held (and usually undertheorized) assumptions about the necessary and sufficient conditions of statehood.[20] As a descriptive category, the state referred to a particular genus of political unit—a unit distinguishable (ideally) from empires, regions, colonies, cities, counties, provinces, and simple political societies. But beyond this, Victorian accounts of the state, including and perhaps especially those of the global state, usually embodied pronounced moral or metaphysical dimensions. It was far more than an instrumental-functional set of institutions. Greater Britain was not conceived of as simply a mode of political organization, a marker in an Aristotelian classificatory matrix, but as one that articulated a moral purpose in the eyes of its proponents.

It used to be thought that the Victorians lacked a vocabulary of the state. As James Meadowcroft has demonstrated, however, the period stretching roughly from 1880 to 1914 witnessed a "theoretical turn towards the state."[21] While the word "state" was employed sporadically during the eighteenth and early nineteenth centuries, it was simply one among a collection of often interchangeable terms: "commonwealth," "nation," "government," "body politic," "political union," "sovereign," and so forth. Although these terms, and especially "government" and "nation," continued to feature throughout the nineteenth century, during the closing decades of Victoria's reign, discussion about the nature of political organization orbited around the concept of the state. As Henry Sidgwick lamented in a review of the translation of the Swiss jurist Johann Casper Bluntschli's influential *Theory of the State*, this newfound interest

---

[20] Spencer, "The Proper Sphere of Government" [1843] in *The Man Versus the State* (Indianapolis, 1982), 181–265.

[21] Meadowcroft, *Conceptualizing the State* (Oxford 1995), 3. See also, Cécile Laborde, "The Concept of the State in British and French Political Thought," *Political Studies*, 48 (2000), 540–57.

rarely led to great sophistication or conceptual novelty.[22] It established, nevertheless, the linguistic context for imagining aspects of the empire as a state, and it is one of the arguments of this chapter that much of the debate over Greater Britain should be seen as a manifestation of this efflorescence of interest in statehood.

The "state" was a multivalent concept, and to some it still seemed an unnecessary or exotic term.[23] (This partly explains why, when describing Greater Britain, some thinkers openly employed the word "state," while others who described it in otherwise identical terms, refrained from doing so.) Despite the proliferation of meanings attached to it, the most common understanding was fairly straightforward: it identified a delimited sovereign space, an independent political community that had reached a certain level of "civilization."[24] A number of basic assumptions underpinned this understanding, and although not all thinkers subscribed to all of the assumptions, it is possible to trace a family resemblance in the preconditions considered necessary for successful statehood. Four in particular are important: the state was defined by its sovereignty, understood broadly as its autonomy in decision-making over key aspects of domestic and international affairs, and the recognition of this autonomy by other states; it was in some sense regarded as natural (and often either as an outgrowth of or analogous to the family); it covered an easily identifiable and contiguous territorial space; and it was thought to require a high degree of social and cultural homogeneity, often phrased in the language of nationality and/or race.[25]

According to the understandings of statehood common at the time all supraparliamentary imperial federalist schemes—and indeed most parliamentary ones—could be viewed as demanding the creation of a state, a political-economic entity composed of people belonging to the same nation and/or "race," governed by a single, albeit devolved, system of representative institutions subordinate to a supreme federal legislative chamber. It would be federal in the sense that, due to the division of powers, the local legislatures would have a high degree of autonomy over specified and territorially delimited domains of policy. It would be centralized

---

[22] Sidgwick, *EHR*, 1 (1886), 378–82. See here Bluntschli, *The Theory of the State*, trans. D. G. Ritchie, P. E. Matheson, and R. Lodge (Oxford, 1885). This was a translation of the sixth German-language edition. On Bluntschli, see Martti Koskenniemi, *The Gentle Civiliser of Nations* (Cambridge, 2001), ch. 1.

[23] On some of the different meanings of "the state," see the comments in Sheldon Amos, *The Science of Politics* (London, 1883), 63–67.

[24] For a clear statement, see Sidgwick, *The Development of European Polity*, 1 and 25–28.

[25] For further elaboration of these categories, see Duncan Bell, "The Victorian Idea of a Global State" in Bell (ed.), *Victorian Visions of Global Order* (Cambridge, 2007).

in the sense that supreme authority would reside in either a newly created "senate" or a reconfigured parliament in Westminster. This body would determine questions of war and peace, trade, and any other general issues that concerned the whole polity. It would lack power over many local issues. The constituent units would meet Sidgwick's conditions of "federality." All of this was underpinned by the "annihilation" of distance. Both the colonies and the British state itself were reimagined, as the imperial federalists stipulated the transition from an unequal to an equal league, avoiding the incorporating state in favor of a federal alternative. This was a situation recognized by Dicey, one of the most implacable critics of imperial federation, who complained that such proposals implied the creation of a "new federated state."[26] The politician John Bright, also noting the consequences of such arguments, scoffed that the "idea . . . in my opinion is ludicrous that the British Empire—that is, the United Kingdom with all its colonies—should form one country, one interest, one undivided interest for the purposes of defence."[27] The case of the extra-parliamentary advocates is less straightforward, for they were trying to re-animate the existing structure, and were far less willing to promote transformative constitutional engineering, let alone the creation of new assemblies—even though it is also the case that although they tended to be cautious about the present, many of them also imagined radical developments in the future. Nevertheless, as we shall see, some of these individuals also insisted on labeling Greater Britain a state.

While a number of the federalists directly confronted the idea of transfiguring the empire into a state, many vacillated, remaining wary about how they characterized their plans. They made frequent admiring references to the United States, the archetypal federal state, employing it as a template for their ideas, and they often described their proposals in terms that fell squarely within the language of state theory. Offering a limited extra-parliamentary proposal, for example, the Australian historian and politician William Westgarth argued for "one great, complete, indivisible power" under "one . . . government."[28] But many unionists remained wedded, either through custom or through caution, to the language of em-

---

[26] Dicey, *Introduction to the Study of the Law of the Constitution*, 8th ed. (London, 1915), lxxxiv. This criticism falls in a discussion of the constitutional innovations proposed during the preceding thirty years. Dicey labeled the ideal of imperial federation a "delusion," offering a battery of reasons for its implausibility, including the differentials in wealth, power, and interests between the units, the lack of defensive necessity and of territorial contiguity, and, finally, the fact that federalism was intrinsically a weak form of government.

[27] John Bright, speech on January 29th, 1885, Birmingham, cited in W. E. Forster "A Few More Words on Imperial Federation," *NC*, 17 (1885), 552–53.

[28] Westgarth, "The Unity of the Empire," *NR*, 4 (1884), 507. A liberal free-trader, Westgarth was a prolific historian and political writer who moved to England in the late 1850s. He was one of the founders of both the Colonial Society and the IFL.

pire, a language forged and reproduced in relation to very different types of political organization. This presented a recurring set of challenges, most notably in reconciling political subordination and equality. The core of the problem was identified, in classical republican style, by J. A. Froude: "One free people cannot govern another free people." Wary of the constitutional plans of the most ambitious federalists, Froude (whose ideas will be examined in greater detail in the next chapter) preferred to draw on an older language; his ideal future lay in a "commonwealth" of "Oceana," a polity "held together by common blood, common interest, and a common pride in the great position which unity can secure."[29] Oceana would not be an empire, based (by definition) on subordination, but a single structure offering political equality to its constituent parts. From a critical standpoint Freeman argued that imperial federation was a "contradiction in terms": "What is imperial cannot be federal, and what is federal cannot be imperial."[30] A polity defined by domination could not be governed simultaneously by a system of devolved legislative powers and equal representation. This was a theoretical and practical problem neatly sidestepped by those who openly branded Greater Britain a state.

By the late nineteenth-century the settler colonies were often viewed as the product of the natural, even inevitable, diffusion of the English people across the unpopulated or under-utilised spaces of the planet. This view helped spawn the idea that the constituent units of the settlement empire could be seen as forming an organic unity. "If there is nothing highly glorious in such an expansion," argued Seeley, "there is at the same time nothing forced or unnatural about it."[31] This understanding of colonialism as an almost cosmically ordained process united figures as diverse as Seeley, Hobson, and Goldwin Smith. As colonialism was the spread of the English people, and not the imposition of a set of institutions and values on alien cultures, it could be conceived of as both natural and potentially more robust than other aspects of empire building. Indeed, it could be seen as an element of state building. It is no coincidence that the closing decades of the century witnessed an outburst of historical writing on the colonial empire, generated, as one commentator noted, largely by *The Expansion of England.*[32] In order to provide an adequate account of the present, and a foundation on which to build the future, it was essential to

---

[29] Froude, *Oceana* (London, 1886), 2 and 12. See also, George Parkin, *Imperial Federation* (London, 1892), 15–19.

[30] Freeman, "The Physical and Political Bases of National Unity," 45. For a similar argument, see William Lobban, "Is Imperial Federation a Chimera?" *WR*, 136 (1891), 55–56.

[31] Seeley, *The Expansion of England*, 296. There were critics of this view, though. John Morley, for example, argued that the colonial system was a weak "artificial empire." Morley, "The Expansion of England," *MM*, 49 (1884), 252.

[32] H. Morse Stephens, book review, *AHR*, 4 (1899), 712.

illuminate the teleological trajectory of imperial growth, to both naturalize it and locate it in time.

Greater Britain, moreover, would be a sovereign power. Those in favor of Advisory Councils left the constitutional structure of Britain largely intact. The parliamentary federalists called for the recasting of the franchise and a transformation of the constitutional status of the colonies, but not for the creation of any new legislative chambers. Such a vision could still be seen as pointing to a global state. A colonial supporter of federation, demanding a "really Imperial Parliament" in place of the "English, Scotch, and Irish one that wrongly goes by that name," suggested that if given representation, the colonists would "feel themselves part of one great state."[33] The real novelty, however, lay in the proposals of the supraparliamentary federalists, whose vision—when they bothered to sketch it in any detail—often included the creation of a new chamber (sometimes labeled a "senate") and the simultaneous downgrading of the power and scope of Westminster, which would be re-organized as a local legislature overseeing domestic British issues. Drawing on John Stuart Mill's discussion of federalism in chapter 17 of the *Considerations on Representative Government*, George Ferguson-Bowen, a former governor of Victoria, demanded a fully fledged federal polity, with an imperial council "analogous to the Congress of the United States, and to the Reichstag of United Germany." Francis de Labillière was fully cognizant of the constitutional implications of his own plans: "a second parliament and executive would therefore have to be formed."[34] An Australian federalist, meanwhile, stated that it "seems perfectly plain, and certainly only reasonable, that if we are to have Imperial Federation, we must of necessity create some imperial chamber to carry it on." Frederick Young advocated "a complete and equitable representative system in an imperial Parliament." This required the creation of a new senate. Such a federation—which he compared to America and labeled a "state"—would "mean an equal participation in the government of the empire, as a whole, and a full share in the exercise of its power." Greater Britain should be, he wrote elsewhere, "one, equal, indivisible." His ambitions for this polity

[33] [A Colonist], "A Proposed Reform of the English Constitution," FM, 8 (1873), 602.
[34] See Ferguson-Bowen, "The Federation of the British Empire," PRCI, 17 (1885–86), 287; and De Labillière, "Present Aspects of Imperial Federation," IF, 1/1 (1886), 5. For a sample of supraparliamentary proposals, see: Jenkins, "Imperial Federalism," CR, 16 (1871); and, Jenkins, "An Imperial Confederation," CR, 17 (1871), where he demands a "Federal Legislative Union under a Supreme Federal Government (78); [Urquhart Forbes], "Imperial Federation," LQR, 4 (1885), 334; Dalton, "The Federal States of the World"; Daniel Cooper, *A Federation of the British Empire* (London, 1880); Samuel Wilson, "A Scheme for Imperial Federation," NC, 17 (1885), 590–98; and Edward Salmon, "Imperial Federation," FR, 68 (1900), 1009–19.

were not modest: "It seems the mission of Greater Britain to be, by the Providence of God, the principal colonising country of the world."[35]

Plans for Greater Britain often drew on ambiguity over the existing quasi-federal structure of the British empire, and indeed over the nature of federalism itself. The exact constitutional status of the colonial empire was a source of widespread ignorance and confusion, as was noted by Alpheus Todd in his respected *On Parliamentary Government in England* (1867), and it was not until Todd wrote his sequel, *Parliamentary Government in the British Colonies* (1884), that a comprehensive text on the subject existed.[36] This lack of clarity was perhaps unsurprising given that the empire comprised a complex jigsaw of economic, judicial, and political institutions and practices—an ensemble once described as a "political museum comprehending specimens of almost all races and languages, and fragments of almost every extinct and existing nation of the habitable world."[37] Many commentators regarded the colonial empire as a federal (or quasi-federal) structure, albeit a weak and partial one. Hobhouse, for example, referred to the "loose, informal, quasi-Federalism of the British Colonial Empire," comparing it with the "strict" American variant, and emphasizing how in "true British fashion" the "lines of demarcation are not clearly marked, and much is left to tacit understanding."[38] Sidgwick argued that in principle federation proper was *prima facie* applicable" to such a political system, although he considered the differentials in size and power between the constituent units probably made it unwise. "If, for this or other reasons," he continued, "a Federal union is out of the question, the best temporary substitute seems to be to constitute the colony self-government within a sphere somewhat similar to that of a part-state in a Federation, but without any formal control over the operations of the central government of the state of which it is a part."[39] The ambiguities had been crystallized, as was so often the case, in the writings of John Stuart Mill, who had argued nearly forty years before that the colonial empire comprised "an unequal federation."

[35] W. J. Bradshaw, "Imperial Federation" in, *England and Her Colonies*, 79–80; Young, *On the Political Relations of Mother Countries and Colonies* (London, 1883), 14 and 15; and Young, *Imperial Federation of Great Britain and Her Colonies* (London, 1876), 43 and ix. See also Granville Cunningham, *A Scheme for Imperial Federation* (London, 1895), 11.

[36] Todd, *On Parliamentary Government in England* (London, 1887 [1867]), x–xii; and Todd, *Parliamentary Government in the British Colonies* (Boston, 1880).

[37] Arthur Mills, *Colonial Constitutions* (London, 1856), xxxix.

[38] Hobhouse, *Democracy and Reaction*, ed. Peter Clarke (Brighton, 1972 [1904]), 154. See also J. R. Seeley, "Georgian and Victorian Expansion," *FR*, 48 (1887), 136. The leading Australian journalist and civil servant Robert Garran, in *The Coming Commonwealth* (London, 1897), 110–11, argued that the British empire was "semi-federal" in form.

[39] Sidgwick, *Elements of Politics*, 548. On the need for rough parity in the size of the units, see also Sidgwick, *The Development of European Polity*, Lecture XXIX.

Every colony has . . . as full power over its own affairs, as it could have if it were a member of even the loosest federation; and much fuller than would belong to it under the Constitution of the United States, being free even to tax at its pleasure the commodities imported from the mother country. Their union with Great Britain is the slightest kind of federal union; but not a strictly equal federation, the mother country retaining to itself the powers of a Federal Government, though reduced in practice to their very narrowest limits.

It was this retention of powers that would disappear under (most) parliamentary and (all) supraparliamentary schemes. Mill realized the consequences of introducing colonial representation: "On this system there would be perfectly equal federation between the mother country and her Colonies, then no longer dependencies." Such a move would transform the nature of the constitutional relationship to such a degree that the old vocabulary would be inappropriate, and a new one required. No longer dependent, the colonies could be considered an integral and equal part of the polity, and this opened the door for characterizing the colonial empire as a state. Mill, however, was not prepared to argue in favor of this shift: noting proposals for an "equal federation" between the colonies and the "mother country," he dismissed them as laudable but ultimately inconsistent with the "rational principles of government." In particular, he argued, they failed to take account of the lack of common interests between such far-flung lands, and the impossibility of adequate deliberation between their elected representatives. "Even for strictly federative purposes," he wrote, "the conditions do not exist, which we have seen to be essential to federation."[40] He reiterated this point in a letter written in 1871: "I do not think that the federal principle can be worked successfully when the different members of the confederacy are scattered all over the world; & I think the English people would prefer separation to an *equal* federation."[41] The advocates of a federal Greater Britain sought to refute such arguments, and they did so, as we saw in the previous chapter, by arguing that conditions had changed sufficiently for such charges to be rendered obsolete.[42] They challenged the sociopolitical analysis underpinning Mill's normative arguments.

[40] Mill, *Considerations on Representative Government*, CW, XIX, 565. He elsewhere referred to the colonial empire as a "modified federation": letter to John Plummer, January 24, 1864, CW, XXXII, 146. Sidgwick also raised similar concerns about the lack of coordinate interests in fragmented empires, in *The Elements of Politics*, 547–48. Note that Mill talked about federation as the ideal solution to the problems of the Greek empire: "Grote's *History of Greece* [IV]," *The Spectator*, March 10, 1859, CW, XXV, 1128–34.

[41] Mill, letter to Arthur Patchett Martin, October 10, 1871, CW, XXII, 233. Italics in original.

[42] Mill's discussion in the *Considerations* was criticized by empire federalists; see for example, William Greswell, "Imperial Federation" in London Chamber of Commerce, *En-*

This ambiguity was further reinforced in Freeman's *History of Federal Government*, a book that drew from and in large part synthesized the theoretical points elucidated in *The Federalist*, and by Tocqueville and Mill.[43] It was utilized by both critics and supporters of Greater Britain. For a government to be classified as federal, Freeman argued, it had to meet two conditions: "On the one hand, each of the members of the Union must be wholly independent in those matters that concern each member only. On the other hand, all must be subject to a common power in those matters which concern the whole body of members collectively." This led to his widely employed definition of an ideal-type federation: "A federal Commonwealth, in its perfect form, is one which forms a single state in its relations to other nations, but which consists of many states with regard to its internal government."[44] As such, a federation could be seen simultaneously as a state and a collection of states, as singular and plural. It all seemed to depend on the angle of vision. Given the prominence of Freeman's writings, this ambiguity over the status of federalism helped open up the space that allowed Greater Britain to be conceived of as a state. Unlike Sidgwick and Mill, however, Freeman was clear that the colonies were not part of a federation, for despite their high degree of internal independence their "relations towards other nations are determined for [them] by a power over which neither the Colony nor its citizens have any sort of control."[45] The Crown in Parliament retained ultimate authority. It was this asymmetry that was challenged by the most ambitious federalists.

Forster, whose moderate vision encompassed the creation of an advisory council, drew directly on Freeman's definition—while ignoring his claims about the nature of the existing empire. His ambition was to see "a federation of peaceful, industrious, law-abiding commonwealths."[46] Yet he also insisted that the British colonial empire could already be seen,

---

gland and Her Colonies* (London, 1887), 2. Critics of federation also drew on it for support: John Morley, "The Expansion of England," 255–57.

[43] In particular, Freeman was an admirer of *The Federalist;* as he wrote to Bryce, "Tis one of the wisest books ever written. I used to call Polybius and it the Old and New Testament on the subject." Letter, July 10, 1884, in *The Life and Letters of Edward A. Freeman*, ed. W.R.W. Stephens (London, 1895), II, 324. He was, however, pessimistic about how well the complexities of federalism were understood by his compatriots—as he wrote to Bryce, "so few know." Letter, May 22, 1887, in *Life and Letters*, II, 367.

[44] Freeman, *History of Federal Government*, 3 and 9. "It is enough," he wrote, "for a commonwealth to rank . . . as a true Federation, that the Union is one which preserves to the several members their full internal independence, while it denies to them all separate action in relation to foreign powers" (15). Criticizing Freeman's definition, Murray Forsyth argues that once a polity is federal it takes on its own statelike properties and cannot be seen in this bifocal manner: Forsyth, *Unions of States* (Leicester, 1981), 7.

[45] Freeman, *History of Federal Government*, 3, 9, 26.

[46] Forster, *Our Colonial Empire* (Edinburgh, 1875), 31; and Forster, "A Few More Words on Imperial Federation," 555.

in some sense, as a single polity, for it comprised "the realm of one state in relation to other states." "I do not say that we are trying by federation to make the empire one commonwealth in relation to foreign Powers, because at present time it is one commonwealth." It formed, though, an "imperfect, incomplete, one-sided federation," and it was essential to complete and perfect it.[47] Freeman directly repudiated Forster's use of his definition. And he argued, moreover, that Forster was calling not for the "perfect" type of federation, the *Bundesstaat*, but the weaker "imperfect" form, the *Staatenbund*, a mode of political organization that was bound to fail due to its inherent weakness.[48] As was common among the extra-parliamentary federalists, however, Forster appeared ambivalent about whether to discount the future creation of an imperial senate, and he once stated that he foresaw a time when a council would be superseded by a full parliament.[49] But among such moderates, it was rare to explicitly label Greater Britain a state. This was largely for tactical reasons: they were determined to stay within the realm of what was archly termed "practical politics" (a trope analyzed in the next chapter), and the idea of a globe-spanning state, and especially one endowed with fully representative institutions and a new governing senate, seemed to many to fall into the realm of fantasy.

Charles Dilke's views on the desirability of federal unions underwent significant changes, partly illustrative of the wider shift in attitudes. In *Greater Britain* he advocated the "confederation" of the Australian colonies, although he thought this would probably lead to their independence.[50] "The bearing of confederation upon imperial interest is a simple matter. Although union will tend to the earlier independence of the colonies, yet, if federated, they are more likely to be a valuable ally than they could be if remaining so many separate countries." Like Goldwin Smith, he claimed that the "strongest argument in favour of separation is the somewhat paradoxical one that it could bring us a step nearer to the virtual confederation of the English race." He also expounded the standard criticisms of federation, however, arguing that "[l]ike all other federal constitutions, that of New Zealand fails to provide a sufficiently strong, central power to meet a divergence of interests between several

[47] Ibid., "Imperial Federation," *NC*, 17 (1885), 201 and 202. See also ibid., comments, in *Imperial Federation League, Report on the Adjourned Conference and of the First Meeting of the League* (London, 1884), 12. Freeman's definition was also employed in Jenkins, "An Imperial Confederation," 72–73; and De Labillière, *Federal Britain*, 64 and 94–95.

[48] Freeman, "Imperial Federation," *MM*, 51 (1885), 433–44 and 441.

[49] Forster, comments, Executive Committee meeting of the IFL, January 27, 1885, in the IFL Minute Book, British Library, Add Ms., 62778, 43.

[50] Dilke, *Greater Britain* (London, 1868), II, 108–109 and 156. Note that here, as was quite common, the terms "confederation" and "federation" are used interchangeably.

states." The system had also failed in Greece, Germany, and America, and "it may be said that, in these days of improved communications, wherever federation is possible, a still closer union is at least as likely to prove lasting."[51] By the time he wrote *Problems of Greater Britain*, nearly twenty-five years later, his position had altered. Firstly, he discerned a general shift toward federalism, pointing to the 1865 "victory of the principle in the United States"; the Canadian experiment; the creation of the German federal state in 1870; the adoption, in 1874, of a new Swiss constitution; and, finally, the laying of the foundations of an Australian federation in 1885. Looking to what he saw as the success of Canadian federation, he now wrote that "no difficulties are too great to be conquered in this fashion."[52] It was in this context that he spoke of living in a federal age. Once again he advocated the federation of Australia (including New Zealand), although he remained skeptical about the more ambitious plans for an overarching imperial federation.

Dilke's main hope seemed to lie in the continuance of the existing imperial relations until the conditions for closer union somehow fell into place. His ideal solution was a (nonparliamentary) "union upon equal terms between self-governing states," although he was vague about the details of this structure. This union would require an increase in the power of the Crown, however, and as such was unlikely to be popular with the British electorate, and he therefore put his hope in the nonpolitical ties linking the colonies. Even if the "young nation" of Australia became independent, he suggested, the connection between it and Britain "rests mainly on sentiment" and "it may still last indefinitely."[53] Dilke's writings were pervaded by a theme common to imperial discourse: the idea of the empire as an engine of education. One again, ideas associated with the family infused discussions of political association. There were two modulations of this educative vision. When referring to the empire in India and Africa it was routine to talk of the infancy of the people under British control.[54] The point of the civilizing mission was, so it was argued, to foster, encourage, and cajole the populations of "backward" places until they reached a level of "civilization" suitable to govern themselves. Mill wrote that the imperial power should act in a "parental" manner, guiding its "pupils" on the road to self-government in order to help propel them to a "higher stage of improvement."[55] The primary target of this tutelary system, and the locus of the problem it sought to rectify, was the mind of

---

[51] Ibid., II, 108–109 and 157; I, 344. On Smith, see chapter 7.
[52] Ibid., *Problems of Greater Britain*, I, 60.
[53] Ibid., I, 458–59.
[54] Uday Singh Mehta, *Liberalism and Empire* (Chicago, 1999), 28–36.
[55] Mill, *Considerations on Representative Government*, CW, XIX, 394–95, 567.

the "barbarian." Discussion of Greater Britain was permeated with the imagery of childhood, except here the referent was different. The target was not the people, who were after all descendants or relations of the inhabitants of Britain, but rather the polities in which they lived. It was the collective not the individual, the whole not the part, which was in need of supervision. It was Australia, Canada, and New Zealand that were "young" and "immature." The analogy could be pressed in different directions. For some, even when maturity had been attained, formal unity was a prerequisite of strength and glory. For others, including Dilke and Smith, it presupposed the eventual independence of the colonies, because the idea of childhood implied that the children would grow into self-determining adults. The aim of prudent policy was to ensure that the various family members remained close, and the main difficulty lay in continually recalibrating relations between the parents and the increasingly autonomous offspring. It was here that sentiment played such an important role. If this parenting task was performed badly, if too much was demanded—and Dilke included here the enforcement of an unwanted "imperial federation"[56]—then the colonies would become estranged from Britain.

J. R. SEELEY AND THE "WORLD-STATE"

In his writings of the 1880s and 1890s Seeley repeatedly insisted that the nature of the British state and the empire had been misunderstood. Considered "as a state," argued Seeley, "England has left Europe altogether behind it and become a world-state."[57] Although such a structure could already be traced in outline, it comprised only the foundations of his ambitious vision, for he sought the creation of a "great and solid World-State," an enduring polity that was yet to be brought into being.[58] Seeley nowhere discussed the specific constitutional structure that he had in mind, but his views on empire, his discussion of federalism in his posthumously published lectures, the *Introduction to Political Science* (1896), and especially his great admiration for the United States, point toward a vision of a supraparliamentary global polity, a United States of Great Britain.

[56] Dilke, *Problems of Greater Britain*, 458: "The best friends of the mother-country in the colonies hold that the attempt to create a common imperial Parliament would of itself destroy the empire; and I agree with them that if we are ever to have a council of the empire it will have to be very unlike a Parliament."
[57] Seeley, *The Expansion of England*, 293. See also Seeley, "Georgian and Victorian Expansion," 133.
[58] Ibid., *The Expansion of England*, 169 and 75.

Meadowcroft has observed that Seeley initially sketched a remarkably broad definition of the state in the *Introduction to Political Science*, so that it encompassed just about all forms of human community.[59] As such, it might be argued that there was nothing unusual in Seeley claiming that Greater Britain was a state, at least in a minimal sense. This would be a mistake, however, for in assessing the status of Greater Britain he was drawing on a much narrower understanding of the "nation-state." In *The Life and Times of Stein* (1878), his three-volume history of one of the key figures in modern German history, he wrote that the state "is merely a machinery by which a number of men protect their common interests." Following Fichte, he argued that the bonds of the nation "are more instinctive, and as it were, more animal" than those of the state, and consequently that the "state which is also a nation is an organism far surpassing in vigour and vitality the state which is only a state." This fusion of two distinct but complementary ideas—state and nation—was a recent development in the evolution of human societies, and it was, he argued, a rare phenomenon.[60] Greater Britain was a state in this specific sense.

Such states, wrote Seeley, "are composed of men who are in some sense homogeneous, and not only homogeneous in blood and descent, but also in ideas or views of the universe."[61] He maintained that there were three essential preconditions for (nation) state unity: the existence of a "community of race," a "community of religion," and a "community of interest."[62] The first two conditions, he claimed, obviously existed in the colonies: "If England and her colonies taken together make, properly speaking, not an Empire but only a very large state, this is because the population is English throughout and the institutions are of the same kind."[63] But there existed also a unity of interests, economic, political, and moral, in a way that previously had been impossible. This argument was a response to one of the main criticisms leveled at the idea of a federal Greater Britain, namely that even if the widely scattered communities exhibited cultural commonalties, there were few, if any, substantive

---

[59] Meadowcroft, *Conceptualizing the State*, 45–47; and Jens Bartelson, *The Critique of the State* (Cambridge, 2001), 52. See also, Seeley, *Introduction to Political Science*, 17; and Seeley, *Natural Religion* (London, 1882), 185.

[60] Seeley, *The Life and Times of Stein, or Germany and Prussia in the Napoleonic Age* (Cambridge, 1878), II, 17 and 35. See also Seeley, "History and Politics, II," *MM*, 40 (1879), 297; and "Georgian and Victorian Expansion," 126. On the importance of the state in Seeley's thought, see H.A.L. Fisher, "Sir John Seeley," *FR*, 60 (1896), 193.

[61] Seeley, *Introduction to Political Science*, 137.

[62] Ibid., *The Expansion of England*, 11, 50, and 220; and also ibid., *Introduction to Political Science*, 68–70, although see below for his vacillation on this issue.

[63] Ibid., *The Expansion of England*, 301. To confuse matters, he also once labeled Canada and Australia "great English continental states": ibid., "Introduction" to *Her Majesty's Colonies* (London, 1886), xxii.

interests that joined them.[64] This had been one of the main points of Mill's argument about the conditions of "rational government," and Seeley sought to confront it by suggesting that the existence of religious and racial unity generated a unity of interests. Without such unity, Seeley recognized, a successful federation was impossible—and federation was, after all, "an arrangement so extremely difficult" to construct.[65] In the "United States of Europe" (1871), a speculative quasi-Kantian essay about the potential for peace in Europe, Seeley had argued that a full continental federation was the only solution to the problem of incessant warfare between states. But he was deeply skeptical about the chances of success.[66] European federation would fail as the interests of the individual states diverged too much and, more fundamentally, because there was no common identity, based on language, religion, or race, that could serve as a foundation for unity. Such problems did not afflict Greater Britain, which was, "on the whole free from that weakness which brought down most empires, the weakness of being a mere mechanical forced union of alien nationalities."[67] According to such a view, the interests of the individual colonies and Britain were aligned, because they were rooted in the shared culture of the English "race."

Greater Britain was, then, a global political space occupied by millions of people united by a common history and common institutions. Colonists were not simply migrants to distant, alien lands, but citizens of a "world-Venice, with the sea for the streets."[68] While in the past there had been a Greater France, a Greater Spain, and a Greater Holland, the experience of the late Victorian British was unique, and the expansion of England, he maintained, "can be paralleled by nothing in the history of any other state."[69] Previous empires had neither the geographical extension nor the degree of cultural and political unity exhibited by Greater Britain. Nor

[64] See, for example, Robert Lowe, "The Value to the United Kingdom of the Foreign Dominions of the Crown," *FR*, 22 (1877), 618–30; and Morley, "The Expansion of England." Commonality of interests was a theme emphasized in, for example, De Labillière, *Federal Britain*, 198; George Parkin, *Imperial Federation*, 37–43; and Jenkins, "An Imperial Confederation," 69.

[65] Seeley, *Life and Times of Stein*, III, 238.

[66] Ibid., "The United States of Europe," *MM*, 23 (1871), 436–48. For his views on war, see Duncan Bell, "Unity and Difference," *Review of International Studies*, 31 (2005), 559–79.

[67] Seeley, *The Expansion of England*, 46.

[68] The evocative phrase can be found in ibid., 288. In "A Toccata of Galuppi's" [1855] Robert Browning wrote of Venice: "Ay, because the sea's the street there; and 't'is arched by ... what you call / ... Shylock's bridge with houses on it, where they kept the carnival: / I was never out of England ... it's as if I saw it all." Browning, *Poetical Works*, ed. Ian Jack (Oxford, 1970), 579.

[69] Seeley, "Introduction," xv.

did they exist in a world where space had been "annihilated." The fragments of the first British empire, separated by vast distances, and working under a warped mercantile economic system, did not and could not share the same vital interests.

> These were circumstances in which, though there might be colonies, there could be no Greater Britain. The material basis of a Greater Britain might indeed be laid, that is, vast territories might be occupied, and rival nations might be expelled from them. In this material sense Greater Britain was created in the seventeenth and eighteenth centuries. But the idea that could shape the material mass was still wanting.[70]

The advent of free trade and the development of new technologies had transformed material and cognitive conditions, and the time was now ripe for an idea to animate the mass. In an age that had finally realized the power of the "nationality doctrine" a new form of global British political consciousness was beginning to emerge, fusing the scattered components of a global state. Greater Britain, wrote Seeley,

> . . . is a vast English nation, only a nation so widely dispersed that before the age of steam and electricity its strong natural bonds of race and religion seemed practically dissolved by distance. As soon as it is proved by the example of the United States and Russia that political union over vast areas has begun to be possible, so soon Greater Britain starts up, not only a reality, but a robust reality.[71]

The people of Greater Britain faced a choice, and Seeley phrased it, in terms typical of the time, as a stark binary: separation or federal unification. "Such a separation would leave England on the same level as the states nearest to us on the continent, populous, but less so than Germany and scarcely equal to France."[72] Shorn of its dominions, England would be dwarfed. "The other alternative," he suggested, was that "England may prove able to do what the United States has done so easily, that is, hold together in a federal union countries very remote from each other." If it achieved this goal, Greater Britain would become, "in time far greater than any political union the world has known."[73] As if to prove his disinterested "scientific" curiosity about the subject, he proclaimed that, "[w]e ought by no means to take for granted that this is desirable."[74] His lectures sought, he stated, to explore the two options in order to divine

[70] Ibid., *The Expansion of England*, 72.
[71] Ibid., 75. Seeley referred to America as a "world state" (293). See also Seeley, "Georgian and Victorian Expansion," 138–39.
[72] Ibid., *The Expansion of England*, 15–16.
[73] Ibid., "Introduction," xi and xii.
[74] Ibid., *The Expansion of England*, 16.

which was best for the country. The answer, though, was predetermined by the very language, structure, and tone of his analysis. And it was underpinned by his suggestion that the aim of British policy should be to secure "the foundation of a solid and permanent union."[75]

Although he did not relate it directly to the British empire, Seeley's most thorough examination of federalism is found in the *Introduction to Political Science*, edited by his friend and colleague Henry Sidgwick. He discussed the different forms that federation could assume, drawing principally on *The Federalist*, Tocqueville, and Freeman.[76] He argued that the strict distinction drawn between "federal" and "unitary" states was misleading, as it was "too purely formal and verbal." Since all large countries were ultimately composite states, in the sense that they were composed of a number of semi-autonomous administrative units, it did not make sense to sharply distinguish them from federations.[77] "I deny, then, that between the unitary state and the federation or federal state there is any fundamental difference in kind; I deny that the one is composite in any sense in which the other is simple." The key to judging the state under examination was simply to assess the degree of authority vested in local government. "Where locality prevails, we can call this federal, where centralization prevails, we can call this unitary."[78] Indeed, he proclaimed that every "political union which has not sufficient central power to deserve the name of a unitary state must in our system be called federal," and he therefore surmised that "almost all very large empires" are federations, "because in them the central power cannot act vigorously at such a great distance." This echoes Sidgwick's conception of "federality." The ambition of the imperial federalists was to capitalize on, and to make tangible and strengthen, these bonds. But he had something more concrete, and more powerful, in mind for Greater Britain. It was essential, he argued, to distinguish between two different types of federal entity: the "federal state" and the "system of confederate states." Seeley was very critical of confederations, arguing that they were intrinsically weak. Most empires

---

[75] Ibid., "Georgian and Victorian Expansion," 139. This claim to disinterest certainly fooled some people: Walter Frewen Lord, *Lost Empires of the Modern World* (London, 1897), 355, praises Seeley's "language of frozen impartiality."

[76] Note that, like many other federalists, Seeley used the terms "federation" and "confederation" interchangeably (see for example, *Introduction to Political Science*, 63, 85, 205). However, as his later discussions made clear, he was well aware of the differences between them.

[77] Ibid., 94–95. Given that all major modern states were composite states, he argued that there was "no fundamental difference in the kind of union" between French departments, American states, and British counties.

[78] Ibid., 95. Rather confusingly, Seeley then proceeds to identify two kinds of unitary state, the centralized and decentralized, before moving on to discuss different types of federation (97).

fitted this category. Federal states, on the other hand, could prosper, but they required "a complete apparatus of powers, legislative, executive and judicial . . . raised above all dependence on the State governments."[79] He pointed to the United States as a "vigorous, strongly and sufficiently organised" example.[80] Greater Britain was to be a federal state in this grand sense.

RACE AND NATION

Greater Britain was conceived of not merely as a set of globe-spanning political institutions—whether a quasi-state, or one yet to come. It was viewed also as a community bound by shared norms, values, and purpose, and it is here that ideas about race and nation entered the picture. Then as now, the use of these terms was frequently muddled and lacked precision. Nation and state were also often employed interchangeably.[81] Despite this semantic confusion, however, a number of distinct patterns can be discerned. It was almost universally asserted that Greater Britain was populated largely by people of the same race, that it formed what Seeley labeled an "ethnological unity."[82] It was, as such, a racial polity. But there were two different interpretations of the same broad conception of nationality at work. For some Greater Britain consisted of multiple independent nations; for others, it comprised one nation. The division was not based on countervailing definitions of the content of nationality, but rather on the potential elasticity of the nation itself. This aspect of the debate focused, that is, on the question of whether or not it was possible to translate a sense of national self-consciousness across global distances.

Ideas about race and nationality intersected in complex and often confusing ways. It is a common argument that during the closing decades of the century, a new biologically informed mode of theorizing race superseded a more benign universalistic and monogenetic vision, associated in particular with the eighteenth century, in which all races were in principle created equal, but had over time progressed at significantly different rates due to the contrivance of extrinsic factors. The more virulent "sci-

[79] Ibid., "The United States of Europe," 440.

[80] Ibid., *Introduction to Political Science*, 97–99. Perhaps rather unsurprisingly given his Prussophilia, Seeley preferred the German terms for the different types of federation, *Bundesstaat* and *Staatenbund* (97). See also the discussion in Seeley, "The United States of Europe," 440–43.

[81] Ironically, this mirrored the intellectual genealogy of nationalism, for the nation of Sieyès was indistinguishable conceptually from Hobbes's idea of the state, as Istvan Hont argues in his, *Jealousy of Trade* (Cambridge, Mass., 2005), 447–529.

[82] Seeley, *The Expansion of England*, 50.

entific racist" ideology is held to have acted as a precondition for the rise in imperial aggression during the middle of Queen Victoria's reign. The difference between the two conceptions is marked: the former precluded the possibility of equality or progress, while the latter allowed it, at least in principle. This picture is, however, problematic—it both exaggerates the degree of uniformity and sympathy among "enlightenment" thinkers and overstates the theoretical rupture in the mid-nineteenth century.[83] Biological forms of racism certainly played a role in some imperial arguments, and no doubt in much imperial practice, being employed to justify the natural superiority of white Europeans over their colonial subjects. Racism and ignorance pervaded Victorian representations of the world. And influenced in particular by the Sepoy Rebellion (1857) and the Governor Eyre controversy (1865), the tone of racial discourse shifted, becoming (even) more aggressive, resulting in an increasingly toxic combination of hostility and defensiveness. But it is less clear that the underlying theoretical assumptions about civilization, progress, race, and society, underwent a fundamental transformation, at least until the very end of the century.

The racial conception of Greater Britain fitted into these wider debates. Greater Britain was underpinned, so it was thought, by a common race, where race was defined primarily by the beliefs, traditions, institutions, and behavioral characteristics associated with being "English" (or British or "Anglo-Saxon"). These were, in general, mutable and shaped by history rather than nature—although the space opened up by this mutability was (usually) implicitly delimited by the boundaries of "whiteness."[84] Nor was this language stable, as we can witness in Seeley's account of the preconditions necessary for a strong state. In *The Expansion of England* he presented three distinct claims. He started by arguing that, alongside a community of religion and a community of interest, it was essential that there exist a "community of race"; then he substituted the latter for a "community of nationality"; and finally, he talked of a "community of race, or rather the belief in a community of race," which, "when it ap-

[83] See also Peter Mandler, "'Race' and 'Nation' in Mid-Victorian Thought"; Mandler, *The English National Character* (London, 2006); and Stuart Jones, "The Idea of the Nation in Victorian Political Thought," *EJPT*, 5 (2006), 12–21.

[84] On various modulations of the elusive content of "Anglo-Saxonism," see Krishan Kumar, *The Making of English National Identity* (Cambridge, 2003), 206–207; Julia Stapleton, "Citizenship Versus Patriotism in Twentieth Century England," *HJ*, 48 (2005), 155–56; Mandler, *The English National Character*, ch. 3; and Paul Rich, *Race and the British Empire* (Cambridge, 1986), ch. 1. Mandler argues that the "Anglo-Saxonism" that dominated the imperial federation debate was less "Teutonized" than that of many mid-Victorians (*The English National Character*, ch. 4), although among advocates of Greater Britain there were exceptions, including Dilke and Goldwin Smith.

pears on a large scale, is identical with community of language." His examples of such linguistic "races" are the "English" and "French." Once again conflating ethnic and national classifications, he argued that the "nationality" of Greater Britain was strong enough to accept the presence of "a good many French and Dutch and a good many Caffres and Maories" without "marring the ethnological unity of the whole."[85] Dilke's writings, meanwhile, slipped repeatedly between biological and constructionist conceptions of race.[86] Such slippage was a common feature of much Victorian political writing.

The presence of xenophobia, and the role of racism, was also indicated by an act of silencing. The debate over Greater Britain was conspicuous for the relative lack of attention paid to the position of indigenous populations within the proposed polity—populations that often suffered enormously under colonial rule, arguably to the point of genocide in parts of Australia.[87] While other aspects of the empire, and especially India, could simply be bypassed in discussing Greater Britain, occupying as they did an obviously different category of rule, the same strategy could not be employed in relation to the populations that the colonists had driven violently from their lands. Most had little or nothing to say on this topic, or on the related one of the position of French settlers in Canada or the Boers in South Africa, and when discussion did arise it was frequently perfunctory and evasive.[88] Imperialists sometimes expressed brutally violent contempt. Froude once advocated (in a private conversation) the "extermination" of "Zulus and Kaffirs" who threatened to kill the "white men" who ruled them.[89] In a move common at the time, Dilke placed the "races" he met on his travels on a scale of civilization. While he was almost entirely negative about the Australian aborigines and the "debased" "Red Indians," he was at his most positive when waxing orientalist about the Maoris. *Greater Britain* was notable for its cruel condescension, and at one point he observed that the "gradual extinction of the inferior races is not only a law of nature, but a blessing to mankind."[90] This was an example of an argument, fairly common during the century, and found also in Froude, which claimed that many of the "weaker" peoples of the world

---

[85] Seeley, *The Expansion of England*, 11, 50, and 220.

[86] Compare, for example, Dilke, *Greater Britain*, I, 24–29 and, I, 123, 268, and 298.

[87] A. Dirk Moses (ed.), *Genocide and Settler Society* (Oxford, 2004).

[88] It was a topic raised occasionally by critics: Morley, "The Expansion of England," 255–56.

[89] This statement, made during a dinner conversation with Lord George Hamilton in 1879, is quoted in full in Michael Bentley, *Lord Salisbury's World* (Cambridge, 2001), 225.

[90] Dilke, *Greater Britain*, I, 130. See also Dilke, *Greater Britain*, I, 123, and ch. 5; II, 96–97. On the putative scale, see M. Hickford, "'Decidedly the Most Interesting Savages on the Globe,'" *HPT*, 46 (2006), 122–67.

would inevitably die out as a result of contact with the forces of "civilization," and that this was ultimately of benefit to humanity.[91] Despite his (limited) admiration for the Maoris, this was a fate he thought would invariably befall them.[92] This trope effaced both responsibility and choice, supplanting effective agency with the inevitability of iron laws of history. Liberals who drew on this line of argument, including Dilke, emphasized that the destiny of the doomed peoples should not be artificially accelerated, and indeed they were often critical of settler violence, but they nevertheless thought that it was pointless to offer serious resistance: fate could not be defeated.

The idea of nationality, and of national character more generally, played a central though often ambiguous role in Victorian political thought. It was generally assumed that a properly functioning state required a strong sense of national identification. But what did this mean? Mill's definition of nationality would have been uncontroversial:

> A portion of mankind may be said to constitute a Nationality if they are united among themselves by common sympathies which do not exist between them and any others. . . . This feeling of nationality may have been generated by various causes. Sometimes it is the effect of identity of race and descent. Community of language, and community of religion, greatly contribute to it. Geographical limits are one of its causes. But the strongest of all is identity of political antecedents; the possession of a national history, and consequent community of recollections; collective pride and humiliation, pleasure and regret, connected with the same incidents in the past. None of these circumstances, however, are either indispensable, or necessarily sufficient by themselves.[93]

This depiction is notable both for the range of specified characteristics associated with nationality and for its failure to rank them in importance or to stress how particular combinations cohere or might come into conflict. This reflected the common practice of using nationality to cover a wide range of phenomena. What unites many of the features, though, is the view of nationality as an artifact of consciousness, and as the most important form of social solidarity for securing political stability. During the middle and late nineteenth century liberals in particular were drawn to the nation, often stressing its democratic credentials, its emancipatory potential, and its compatibility with the "love of humanity." The antonym of national, in the dominant strands of Victorian political thought, was

---

[91] Patrick Brantlinger, *Dark Vanishings* (Ithaca, 2003).

[92] Dilke, *Greater Britain*, I, 392.

[93] Mill, *Considerations on Representative Government*, CW, XIX, 546. See, in general, Georgios Varouxakis, *Mill on Nationality* (London, 2002).

not the foreign or the cosmopolitan, but instead the provincial, the parochial, the narrow. It was a step on the road to the universal, not a retreat from it, and nationalism of this sort, which is to say support for the self-governing autonomy of groups identified as nations, was frequently understood as constitutive of a broadly internationalist vision.[94]

For some imperial thinkers, the colonies were in the process of forming new nations, or had even done so already. This process of differentiation from the originary British nation was regarded as a consequence of the radically different physical environments, social structures, economic systems, and nascent cultural traditions in which the colonists were enmeshed. Recognition of the increasing power of colonial nationality could lead in several directions. It could give strength to the view that the colonies should be allowed to separate, even that this was now inevitable, and that the future of Greater Britain lay in a moral community of the Anglo-Saxon race. This was, as we shall see in chapter 7, the view of Goldwin Smith. Dilke emphasized the national variability that overlay the commonalities of race. He held an environmental conception of national character, where physical and social conditions, in dynamic combination, shaped the personality of individuals and collectives alike: Canadians and Americans were very different in "type." But this "type" was anchored in the same foundations, in a "Saxondom" that incorporated both the United States and Greater Britain: "That which raises us above the provincialism of citizenship of little England is our citizenship of the greater 'Saxondom' which includes all that is best and wisest in the world."[95] Race and nation were often hard to separate in his thought; Greater Britain was united, he argued in 1899, by a "sentiment of common nationality and of racial patriotism."[96] But the belief in the growing strength of colonial "nationalism" also motivated urgent calls to halt, slow down, or at least redirect, this dangerous process. This was perhaps the main response among imperialists who recognized the power of colonial claims to national self-determination. Once again, however, this could lead to different visions of the future. It could either arrest the budding diversification, seeking to lock the colonists back into the primal nationality from which they had sprung, or it could underpin a vision of Greater Britain as a multinational polity held together by some form of federal constitutional structure. Stressing the urgency of unity, Seeley held fast to the former po-

---

[94] See here Jones, "The Idea of the National in Victorian Political Theory"; Jones, *Victorian Political Thought*, 49; Bell and Sylvest, "International Society in Victorian Political Thought"; and Georgios Varouxakis, "'Patriotism,' 'Cosmopolitanism,' and 'Humanity' in Victorian Political Thought," *EJPT*, 5 (2006), 100–18. As Varouxakis notes, there was no clear distinction made between nationalism and patriotism at the time.

[95] Dilke, *Greater Britain*, II, 150 and 156.

[96] Ibid., *The British Empire* (London, 1899), 139.

sition. The latter one was sketched by, among others, Rosebery, who in a
speech delivered in Adelaide in January 1884 argued that Australia could
no longer be seen as a colony, but was instead "a nation not in aspiration
or in the future, but in performance and fact." The empire, he maintained,
should be regarded as "a commonwealth of nations."[97]

In the Edwardian era, visions of a multinational commonwealth began
to eclipse the Seeleyan idea of a global nation-state, in recognition of the
burgeoning colonial demands for national autonomy. In other words,
while the dream of a global state never disappeared, it was increasingly
decoupled from the idea of a singular global nation. In 1905 W. F.
Monypenny, a leading journalist with *The Times*, conceived of the empire
as a "world state," a polity defined by cultural homogeneity and unity of
interests. This was, he claimed, the embodiment of a "new political conception" that "transcends nationality" while simultaneously allowing the
flourishing of separate nationalities within it. By escaping the clutches of
both a petty-minded "national exclusiveness" and a grim centralized
"Caesarian despotism" it pointed the way to a new form of political order,
a truly "cosmopolitan ideal."[98] Leo Amery wrote of the colonial empire
as a "single united whole, a great world-State, composed of equal and independent yet indissolubly united States." This was, he proclaimed, a
"new ideal," a "great federation" that corresponded to the "wider out-
look and broader humanity of advancing civilization."[99] Richard Jebb argued for a loose confederation of equal national parliaments under the
uniting force of the crown, which would act as a figurehead and symbol
of intimate connection.[100] The idea of an Anglo-Saxon commonwealth
was, meanwhile, central to the Round Table movement, because, as Lionel Curtis wrote in 1916, "Canadians, Australians, and South Africans
each think of themselves as nations distinct from the people of the British
Isles, just as the British think of themselves as a nation distinct from the
citizens of the United States." They had acquired, that is, a "national consciousness of their own."[101]

[97] Speech in Adelaide, January 18, 1884, reprinted in George Bennett, *The Concept of Empire*, 2nd ed. (London, 1962), 283. For similar phrasing, see also, Forster, "Imperial Federation," NC, 17 (1885), 201. On the problem of characterizing a growing sense of na-
tionality as antithetical to imperial loyalty, see Douglas Cole, "The Problem of 'Nationalism' and 'Imperialism' in British Settlement Colonies," JBS, 10 (1971), 160–82.

[98] Monypenny, "The Imperial Ideal" in C. S. Goldman (ed.), *The Empire and the Century* (London, 1905), 23 and 27.

[99] Amery, "Imperial Defence and National Policy" in Goldman (ed.), *The Empire and
the Century*, 181–82. See also Leo Amery, "Imperial Unity," speech, July 15, 1910, in
Amery, *Union and Strength* (London, 1912), 2.

[100] Richard Jebb, *Studies in Colonial Nationalism* (London, 1905), 300. See also Jebb,
The Britannic Question (London, 1913). For earlier aspects of the role of the monarchy in
the debate, see Duncan Bell, "The Idea of a Patriot Queen?" JICH, 34 (2006), 1–19.

[101] Curtis, *The Problem of Commonwealth* (London, 1916), 68.

The most common view among late Victorian imperial thinkers, however, was that the population of Greater Britain comprised one nationality. As I outlined above, Seeley argued for the "general proposition" that "Greater Britain is homogenous in nationality."[102] A leader article in *The Colonist* in 1874, highlighting the slippage of terms common at the time, stated that there "is no breach, no yawning gap in the Imperial State; it is one continuous expanse of a single nation."[103] De Labillière, hoping for "the permanent political unity of our race," proclaimed that the "spirit of national unity has been one of the most beneficent influences in the enlightened progress of modern times. It has made Italy; it has made Germany. . . . National magnetism, with the power of a loadstone [*sic*] is drawing together Great and Greater Britain in closer indissoluble union."[104] The historian Hugh Egerton talked of the "common nationhood" binding together the peoples of Greater Britain, while a pamphlet produced for the IFL argued that federation was "a means of securing the continued Union of our nation throughout the world."[105] The nation, in this sense, acted as a form of social cement connecting the scattered elements of the empire, and allowing it to be represented both as a natural outgrowth of England and as a cohesive whole.

[102] Seeley, *The Expansion of England*, 49 and 63. On 164 he notes that people did not at the moment see Canada as Kent. See also, Seeley, "Introduction," xxiv–v.

[103] [Anon.], "A Colony and Parliament," *The Colonist*, June 26, 1874, printed in *Imperial Federation of Great Britain and her Colonies*, ed. Young, 152.

[104] De Labillière, *Federal Britain*, 35–171. See also Samuel Wilson, "A Scheme for Imperial Federation," 590; and Young, *An Address on Imperial Federation*, 23.

[105] Egerton, *A Short History of British Colonial Policy*, 477; and "What Is Imperial Federation?" (1890), of which a copy can be found in the Minute Book of the General Committee of the Executive Committee of the IFL, British Library, Add MS, 62779, 256.

5

The Politics of the Constitution

All nations have their idols, the creatures of their
own hands, which having manufactured, they
bow down before as gods. . . . The Englishman
adores the British Constitution.
—Froude, "England's War" (1871)

HISTORIANS OF political theory frequently overlook the manner in which arguments are constructed and framed to resonate with particular groups of individuals and the way in which the prejudices and perspectives of those groups are reinforced, flattered, or contested by certain lines of thought. It is not simply the logical consistency or even the "rationality"—however that may be defined—of discrete arguments that counts most in motivating (or in attempting to motivate) political action, but rather their persuasive force when addressed to audiences that are already immersed in their own ideological universes. Political and conceptual transformation is more a matter of the potential "fit" between settled beliefs and proposed lines of adjustment than it is of logic, let alone "Truth." As a consequence, argues Quentin Skinner, "all revolutionaries are . . . obliged to walk backwards into battle." The key to such transformation—at least in the absence of violence—lies consequently in the "rhetorical re-inscription" of the existing modes of political discourse that shape the normative architecture of a society, in the ways in which political vocabularies can be remodeled to meet or accommodate specific goals.[1]

In order to gain widespread support visions of Greater Britain had to be promoted as compatible with the venerable traditions of British political thought and practice. The imperial advocates understood this, and they battled long and hard to establish the historical (and hence political) legitimacy of their cherished projects. The question of the necessity, and moreover the ethical status, of political innovation framed the debate. Was Greater Britain, and in particular an imperial federal structure, a

---

[1] Skinner, *Visions of Politics* (Cambridge, 2002), I, 149–50 (see also 175–88). For other discussions of this conception of political innovation and change, see Raymond Geuss, *History and Illusion in Politics* (Cambridge, 2001), 159–62; and Duncan Bell, "Language, Legitimacy, and the Project of Critique," *Alternatives*, 27 (2002), 327–50.

novel departure, or was it merely an extension or derivation of existing institutions? Was it necessary to escape the past, or to embrace it? Some imperialists celebrated novelty, demanding the construction of elaborate new political forms; others pleaded that only minor incremental adjustments were required. To put it schematically, the radicals were more likely to promote constitutional innovation, the conservatives to downplay or criticize it, and the liberals to vacillate uncomfortably. The opponents of federal schemes, meanwhile, condemned what they saw as utopian dreams, pointless, impractical, and even dangerous exercises in political speculation. Imperial discourse thus mirrored the divisions over the scope of political reform that preoccupied a generation of British thinkers.

It was a common Victorian belief that societal transformation, embodied most spectacularly in the rise of democracy, was inevitable; that history was unfolding in a specific direction, and that political action had to be accommodated to this ineliminable fact. It was this conception of preordination that underpinned the notion of progress, and although elements of it could be traced back to eighteenth-century "stadial" theories of the development of civil society, it was largely a nineteenth-century creed. Its most illustrious proponents were Alexis de Tocqueville, John Stuart Mill, and, in a very different vein, Karl Marx. As John Burrow has argued, this belief could be employed to justify both sweeping change and passivity, the former because transformation was viewed as immanent and therefore only needed encouragement, and possibly minor steering, the latter because it was better to follow the tide of history than to swim against it.[2] But was a federal Greater Britain inevitable? For some, this certainly seemed plausible: federation was the final, unavoidable evolution of the British constitution, the end of (British) history. It was a symptomatic response to what Dilke termed "a federal age."[3] The role of the political agent was simply to unveil the course of change. At times, this seemed to be the direction in which Seeley was gesturing. For the majority, though, this was far from the case, and federation had to be secured against heavy odds. The latter vision, of course, turned out to be more accurate. But even those who held this view tended to emphasize the world-historical diffusion of the English peoples (and therefore English manners, mores, and institutions) across the continents and oceans. They substituted one form of political predestination for another.

In examining the political theory of Greater Britain, then, it is important to focus on the idioms in which arguments were framed, and the plethora of strategies employed in order to help secure the support of public and (most importantly) elite opinion. In so doing, we observe one of

[2] Burrow, *Whigs and Liberals* (Oxford, 1988), ch. 2.
[3] Dilke, *Problems of Greater Britain* (London, 1890), I, 97.

the key reasons for their ultimate failure: the inability to convince a wider
audience that a global federal polity was compatible with the constitutional configuration of the United Kingdom. In this chapter I document
some of the arguments and rhetorical moves employed by (and also
against) the colonial unionists, highlighting the way in which the perceived nature of the constitution determined the *types* of arguments that
were considered legitimate. The next two sections analyze why numerous
imperialists encouraged vagueness about the future form of Greater
Britain as part of a deliberate political strategy, and how the constitution
became the main discursive battleground over which the future of the empire was fought. This is followed by an examination of the role performed
in the debates by long-standing civic humanist themes and vocabulary—
what I term the language of "civic imperialism." The final section inter-
prets J. A. Froude's views on the empire in this light.

The Virtues of Vagueness

In response to their fears about apathy (as outlined in chapter 2), imperialists repeatedly emphasized the need to educate the general population
about the value of the empire. What was required, wrote Frederick Young,
was a "universal awakening of the national mind." "The soil must be prepared for Federation," argued Seeley, "[t]he feelings must be roused, the
views and ways of thinking must be promoted, that would express themselves naturally in Federation."[4] Only through persuading an often cyni-
cal audience of the extant, though fragile, unity of the empire, as well as
the multifarious threats to which it was increasingly vulnerable, could the
advocates of Greater Britain even attempt to invoke specific policy proposals. The perceived need to shift the nature of public consciousness
helps to explain the mantra-like insistence that it was unnecessary to offer
detailed plans for the construction of a global imperial polity. The nation
first had to be woken. Vagueness was a deliberate, if perhaps ultimately
counterproductive, strategy.[5] But this was not simply a matter of identifying the most efficient sequence for embarking on institutional reforms,
for it was argued that introducing plans too early into the political process
might instead provoke a damaging backlash. "Our federation movement
is gaining great strength—the idea possesses men's minds," argued Forster, "but we might throw it back greatly by any premature plan." Labil-

---

[4] Young, *An Address on Imperial Federation* (London, 1885), 15; and Seeley, "Professor
Seeley at Cambridge," *IF*, 6/6 (1891), 176.

[5] For some general comments on the positive value of ambiguity in political thought, see
Michael Freeden, "What Should the 'Political' in Political Theory Explore?" *Journal of Political Philosophy*, 13 (2005), 117–24.

lière remarked that "it is possible to smother in its infancy a great principle by over-clothing it with details," while William Greswell contended
that enunciating precise plans, "would be to court annihilation at once."
For Lorne, meanwhile, it was "far too early to have cut-and-dried schemes
as to the best manner in which closer union may be effected. Any new
movement is only too likely at first to be misapprehended and misunderstood."[6] To engage with the finer points of constitutional design, of tariff and taxation policy, of the scope and powers of the judiciary, of the de-
limitation of sovereign spheres, and so forth, was to encourage a
self-defeating debate over procedures and mechanisms. Such issues should
be considered only after the general *idea* had been accepted widely in the
first place.

This was not simply unreflective ignorance or intellectual timidity, although it did sanction the evasion of difficult technical issues. Rather, it
was considered an unavoidable political and rhetorical strategy. Lord
Brassey encapsulated the reasoning behind this belief: "Agitation is too
often the necessary preliminary to all administrative or legislative action."[7] Joseph Chamberlain offered a more optimistic gloss: "I am told
on every hand that Imperial Federation is a vain and empty dream," he
declared in a speech in 1895, but, he continued, "[d]reams of that kind
which have so powerful an influence upon the imagination of men have
somehow or other an unaccountable way of being realised in their own
time." The most important step was to start people dreaming—and then
to channel the direction of those dreams. "[T]he greatest thing is—to use
a railway expression—to get the points right. If we do this we shall go on
parallel lines for the future. If we make any mistake we shall get wider
and wider apart till separation is complete."[8] In order to garner support
for their plans the colonial unionists needed to convince people not only

[6] Forster, letter to Sir George Bowen, 1886 [n.d.] in the *Life of the Right Hon. W. E.
Forster*, ed. Sir Thomas Wemyss Reid (London, 1888), II, 526; de Labillière, *Federal Britain*
(London, 1894), 189; Greswell, "The Imperial Federation League," *NR*, 14 (1889), 191;
and Lorne, *Imperial Federation* (London, 1885), 23. See also Samuel Wilson, "Imperial Federation," *NR*, 4 (1884), 383; J. W. Longley, "Canada and Imperial Federation," *FR*, 49
(1891), 466; George Parkin, *Imperial Federation*, (London, 1892), 297–99; and Forster, "A
Few More Words on Imperial Federation," *NC*, 17 (1885), 553.

[7] Brassey, "Address Delivered before the Bradford Chamber of Commerce, January 21,
1880" in, *Papers and Addresses by Lord Brassey*, ed. Arthur Loring and R. J. Beadon (London, 1894), 45; and also J. C. R. Colomb, *Imperial Federation* (London, 1886), 4. Thomas
Brassey, liberal MP for Hastings (1868–86), was a central figure in the IFL. He was the honorary treasurer, and he chaired the committee that produced the report presented to Gladstone. He also served as governor-general of Australia (1895–1900).

[8] Speech to celebrate the opening of the Natal railway, reprinted in *The Times*, November 7, 1895; and Chamberlain, letter to the Duke of Devonshire, July 4th, 1897, cited in J. L.
Garvin, *The Life of Joseph Chamberlain* (London, 1929–68), III, 193.

from across the political elite, but also from the middle and working classes. This desire was a reflection of the ever-increasing importance accorded to the power of public opinion. Such opinion had to be carefully nourished. In a typically patronizing manner, Seeley argued that the working classes were "childishly ignorant of larger political questions," and that consequently public opinion was "necessarily guided by a few large, plain simple ideas."[9] Proposals for imperial reform had to be easily digestible. But it was not only the content of the arguments that was important, so too was reaching the proper audience. The debate over Greater Britain heralded a transformation in understanding the scope of "the public." Articulating a long-standing idea, John Stuart Mill had argued in the early 1860s that one of the key reasons why a federation of the colonies would fail to satisfy the "rational principles of government" was that the colonists were "not part of the same public" as the British people.[10] A basic harmony of interests and sympathies was absent. For many of the advocates of Greater Britain, however, the public extended beyond the traditional boundaries of the (British) state, incorporating the settler communities of the colonial empire, increasingly wealthy, politically enfranchised, and linked via novel communications technologies to the "mother country." The public sphere had been stretched over the face of the earth.

Not only was deliberate vagueness a prerequisite for success, so too was patience. Lorne noted in his textbook on imperial federation that it was essential to proceed cautiously. It would take time to "permeate the colonies with ideas if they are able to carry them along with them to any happy result." But numerous federalists, so keen to push their ideas, were, one writer observed, simply too "impatient."[11] To act too soon, or to push too hard, would be fatal, undermining any chance of long-term success. As Charles Oman wrote: "The matter must, to a very large extent, be settled by sentiment; to thrust union on recalcitrant members would be fatal," and as a result "progress must inevitably be slow." But how slow? Lorne estimated that it would take twenty-five years to create an effective imperial advisory council. De Labillière claimed that it would be at least thirty or forty years before a proper global "Federal Britain" was feasible; another unionist wrote that federation was an ideal that "only our grandchildren may hope to see."[12]

---

[9] Seeley, "Political Somnambulism," *MM*, 43 (1880), 30 and 42; and also Seeley, *The Expansion of England* (London, 1883), 190.

[10] Mill, *Consideration on Representative Government*, CW, XIX, 564.

[11] Lorne, *Imperial Federation*, 20; and Anon., "The Integrity of the Empire," *FR*, 59 (1896), 739.

[12] Oman, *England in the Nineteenth Century* (London, 1899), 260; Lorne, "Our Relations with Canada and the Great Colonies," *PRCI*, 15 (1883–84), 51; Labillière, comments, *PRCI*, 8 (1876–77), 131; and Anon., "The Integrity of the Empire," 750.

As a result of the demand for patience, and for transgenerational com-
mitment to the cause, the education of the young was an issue of overriding importance. It was not only vital to shape the minds of the adult
population through teaching the value of Greater Britain, central as this
was, but also for molding future citizens. The unionists were keen to
spread the message around Britain and the colonies, to proselytize about
the past, present, and future of the empire. They encouraged and financially supported speaker tours, exhibitions, and the publication of historical texts, atlases, and guidebooks, all with the aim of propagating a positive image of the empire, while also stressing the necessity of change. Such
an education, it was frequently argued, had to begin at an early age; it was
essential to imbue children with the "imperial spirit." W. T. Stead even
proposed that Seeley be placed in charge of a college teaching the value
of the English global nation.[13] The ultimate aim was to instill an explicit
global national consciousness. But such arguments highlight a serious tension in the formulation of imperialist arguments, the conflict between the
repeated (and sometimes hysterical) exclamations about the urgency of
the problem and the equally common refrains (often emanating from the
same individuals) for a measured and long-term approach preparing the
ground for a reconfigured Greater Britain. It was rarely clear how the two
temporal logics could be reconciled.

Unfortunately for the proponents of a federal Greater Britain, while
they succeeded in sparking an extensive debate over the potential benefits
of imperial constitutional reform, the fact that they appeared so unwilling to come up with specific proposals meant that they opened themselves
up to powerful strains of criticism. They could be dismissed as blustering
amateurs, making it difficult for even sympathetic observers to judge their
ideas.[14] It led, moreover, to a situation in which the critics of a federal
Greater Britain, often having nothing in particular to sink their claws into,
resorted instead to constructing (and then dismembering) caricatured arguments, thus forcing the imperialists ever further onto the defensive. In
one of the most powerful broadsides against imperial federation, Edward
Freeman argued that in order to be consistent it implied either that all of
the empire—including the suspect "Hindoo"—had to be included, or, if

---

[13] H. F. Wilson, "The Public Schools and Imperial Federation," *IF*, 1/11 (1886), 304–
305; Stead, *The Life of W. T. Stead*, ed. Frederick Whyte (London, 1925), II, 209–10.
Bernard Porter, in *The Absent-Minded Imperialists* (Oxford, 2004), highlights the lack of
imperial education in many schools. George Parkin was probably the leading missionary of
the cause, embarking on various trans-imperial speaking tours funded by the IFL. See, for
example, George Parkin, *Round the Empire* (London, 1892). On Parkin's views, see T.
Cook, "George R. Parkin and the Concept of Britannic Idealism," *Journal of Canadian Studies*, 10 (1975), 15–31.

[14] A point made by Arthur Mills, "Imperial Federation," *ER*, 170 (1889), 247.

the key to deciphering which territories were to be encompassed lay in whether their inhabitants spoke English, that the United States must fall within the imperial embrace. "In either case," he complained in a letter to James Bryce, then serving as president of the Oxford branch of the IFL, the "kingdom of Great Britain and its Parliament will have to sink to the level of the State of Rhode Island and its Legislature."[15] Yet these were arguments that few imperialists had ever countenanced; the vast majority explicitly drew racial limits around their conception of Greater Britain, insisting on its Anglo-Saxon character. And while there were certainly a handful of individuals who sought a formal alliance with America, and no doubt many more who harbored it as a fantasy—as will be explored in more detail in chapter 9—this was a vision that the majority regarded as highly implausible. Greswell, most likely alluding to Freeman, dismissed the argument stipulating American inclusion as the "climax of absurdity," while an editorial in *Imperial Federation* in 1892 labeled Freeman's and Smith's claims about Indian incorporation "absurd."[16] The Australian politician Robert Stout proclaimed that "[l]earned historians and professors may define what federation means and what are necessary . . . of such unions. But mere names signify little. Is a union possible? Or is England to lose her Colonies? These are the questions the nation has to answer."[17] The type of reaction exemplified by Freeman, combined with impatience on behalf of many supporters of the federal ideal, generated a mounting chorus of voices demanding the development of detailed plans. The result was the disastrous presentation to Gladstone of a compromise plan that had been put together after a long consultation process and was rejected immediately.[18] It seemed as though the proponents of vagueness had been correct after all.

The notion of "practical" politics was central to Victorian imperial thought. It was an ideal of political action that the opponents of a federal Greater Britain employed as a battering ram, and that the advocates in turn—and often as a desperate response—tried to claim as a guiding feature of their vision. Practical politics was contrasted with mere theory,

[15] Freeman, "The Physical and Political Bases of National Unity" in Arthur S. White (ed.), *Britannic Confederation* (London, 1892), 33–56; letter to James Bryce, December 16, 1886, in W.R.W. Stephens, *The Life and Letters of Edward A. Freeman* (London, 1895), 356–57. Morley offered a similar argument: Morley, "The Expansion of England," *MM*, 49 (1884), 254.

[16] Greswell, "The Imperial Federation League," 186; and the Editorial, *IF*, 7/7 (1892), 86. See also F. P. de Labillière "Present Aspects of Imperial Federation," *IF* 1/1 (1886), 5–6. Freeman's argument was likewise targeted by [Urquhart Forbes], "Imperial Federation," *LQR*, 4 (1885), 325–26.

[17] Robert Stout, "A Colonial View of Imperial Federation," *NC*, 21 (1887), 356.

[18] Michael Burgess, "The Federal Plan of the Imperial Federation League, 1892" in Andrea Bosco (ed.), *The Federal Idea* (London, 1991), I, 139–53.

which was dismissed as an interesting intellectual pursuit, but one almost entirely irrelevant for the everyday business of government. Critics of federal schemes were quick to deride what they saw as the wild imaginings of people unable or unwilling to grasp the complexity of political life. A federal Greater Britain was not to be taken seriously as a *political* project; it was at best a stimulating intellectual game, pushpin for the educated classes. The idea of "practical" politics was linked, among other things, to a positive valuation of experience: that which was practical was that for which there was a successful precedent on which politicians and observers could draw. In so doing, they could compare and contrast ideas with the purported lessons of the past, and extract conclusions about the feasibility of any particular project. Abstraction needed to be tempered by, or even substitued for, the greater reliability of experiential understanding. This was yet another facet of the professedly "antitheoretical" mode of political theorizing that dominated late Victorian debates over the empire. It was also an example of a long-standing (and largely false) set of arguments that stressed the anti-intellectual and overwhelmingly pragmatic nature of the British "mind."[19] Federation lay, remarked Arthur Mills, "outside the domain of practical politics." For John Morley, Seeley's views, admirable though they might be as an exercise in "philosophical" speculation, were "tainted with vagueness and dreaminess." William Foster, a former governor of Victoria, observed haughtily that the issue of imperial federation "admits of a vast amount of abstract and even transcendental theorising, standing as it does, greatly outside the range of common political experience."[20] Citing Tocqueville, he argued that federation would lead to increasing political centralization, and that it was consequently to be resisted. For more circumspect federalists, therefore, certain rhetorical strategies—most conspicuously the celebration of constitutional innovation and upheaval—seemed to augur trouble. Whether they believed that their plans for Greater Britain were novel or not, to proclaim them as such was political suicide. The ambitions of unfettered modernity ran up against the barricades of political tradition.

The advocates of Greater Britain responded by insisting that their ideas fell within the domain of practical politics. The most obvious way to do so was to call for modest change, such as the creation of nonlegislating advisory councils. While it is probable that many of those supporting such plans did so because they thought them the best solution to the problems

---

[19] This view is neatly dissected in Stefan Collini, *Absent Minds* (Oxford, 2006).

[20] Mills, "Imperial Federation," *ER*, 170 (1889), 250; Morley, "The Expansion of England," 241 and 247; and Foster, "Fallacies of Federation," *PRCI*, 8 (1876–77), 79. See also Mills, *Colonial Constitutions*, 2nd ed. (London, 1891), 8; and Mills, "The Problem of Empire," *FR*, 37 (1885), 345–51.

besetting the empire, it is also highly likely that a number did so simply because they believed that other more sweeping suggestions were too unrealistic to be countenanced, at least in the foreseeable future. Numerous imperialists who were cautious about the present were optimists for the future, deferring the potential federation of Greater Britain to some unspecified date in the years to come. Another approach sought to transform the terms of debate. In 1888 Joseph Chamberlain argued that despite the fact that no plausible plans for federation had yet been offered, he nevertheless believed wholeheartedly in the ideal. "I do not think," he remarked cautiously, "that such a scheme is impossible." But within a decade he had modified his position, suggesting that as a result of the awesome changes wrought by the communications revolution ("we have annihilated space"), and because the "bonds" linking the colonies and the United Kingdom were rapidly "strengthening and multiplying," imperial federation fell within the scope of "practical politics."[21] Here technological and political developments had reshaped the compass of practicability. Another option, to which I now turn, consisted in arguing that whatever plans were proposed were compatible with the constitution.

IMPERIAL PATRIOTISM AND THE CONSTITUTION

The question is, can we glide into this position
of representation of the whole Empire
without any revolutionary breach of the
present Constitutional lines.
—William Westgarth, "The Unity of the Empire" (1884)

In his influential analysis of the constitution, A. V. Dicey argued that there were two categories of rules in English constitutional law. Firstly, there were the laws, both customary and statutory, that fell within the judicial domain of the courts. Secondly, there were the "conventions of the constitution," the unwritten practices and beliefs of the governing elite. The latter, more amorphous of these categories, represented the "political" or "constitutional morality" of the country. In a similar vein, John Stuart Mill argued that the "unwritten maxims" of the constitution, the widely

[21] Chamberlain, "Relations with the United States and the Colonies," Devonshire Club, April 9, 1888, in Charles W. Boyd (ed.), *Mr Chamberlain's Speeches* (London, 1914), I, 323; and Chamberlain, "Commercial Union of the Empire," Congress of the Chambers of Commerce of the Empire, London, June 9, 1896, in Boyd (ed.), *Mr Chamberlain's Speeches*, II, 366.

held assumptions about the sources and limits of power, comprised the "positive political morality of the country."[22] Discursive constructions of the (unwritten) constitution established the normative framework in which political arguments were propounded and judged. They shaped the acceptable limits of imperial theorizing. It was in this sphere that the advocates of a federal Greater Britain fought—and lost—their most important battles. For all but the least ambitious, it was imperative to try to (re)define the meaning of the constitution, and the main question revolved around how far it needed to be, or indeed could be, modified in order to account for shifting political circumstances. They portrayed the constitution as dynamic and elastic, always evolving and capable of adaptation, but never losing its anchor in the political wisdom accumulated throughout the ages. Their critics challenged this reading of constitutional flexibility.

If anxiety over the fate of the country catalyzed the demand for Greater Britain, so the question of the novelty of the proposals framed the rhetorical moves, and indeed guided the specific formulations, utilized by the protagonists in the debate. There were two parallel but conflicting streams of argumentation. One stressed the need for bold innovation under the auspices of necessity: Britain, and the empire as a whole, must transform or disintegrate. Drift, confusion, and sheer timidity, characterized British policy, and drastic change was required. This challenged the prevailing constitutional order. The other, perhaps more attuned to the whiggish sensitivities of the time, followed conflicting lines of attack. Its adherents suggested either pallid reforms or, more interestingly, tried to argue that the idea of a federal Greater Britain was not radical, that it was compatible with the existing constitution. Importantly, the distinction between the celebration of innovation and the insistence on caution did not map neatly onto the grid of those calling for minor changes, such as advisory councils, and those calling for federation proper. Some of the advocates of the latter argued that their proposals did not demand a fundamental shift in the "positive political morality" of the country, that they could be accommodated within the existing constitutional framework.

A common strategy was to insist that the question of empire should be elevated above the tumult of everyday political life. Colonial unionists argued that the future of the empire should transcend the vicissitudes of

---

[22] Dicey, *Lectures Introductory to the Study of the Law of the Constitution* (London, 1885), esp. ch. 1; and Mill, *Considerations on Representative Government*, CW, XIX, 422. On the importance of a "constitutionalist idiom" in the nineteenth century, see James Vernon, "Notes Towards an Introduction" in Vernon (ed.), *Re-Reading the Constitution* (Cambridge, 1996), 1; James Epstein, *Radical Expression* (Oxford, 1994), ch. 1; and J. P. Parry, *The Politics of Patriotism* (Cambridge, 2006), esp. pt. I.

party intrigue, squalid compromise, and the clash of competing interests, and they routinely assailed the party system itself, seeing it as the embodiment of self-interest and political myopia. Due to petty squabbling the truly important national questions, and especially the empire, were often sidelined.[23] They sought to make the empire coterminous with the public (national) good. It was for this reason that the presidency of the IFL alternated between Liberals and Tories. De Labillière summed up the position:

> It [imperial federation] ought never to be made a party question. . . . It is truly Conservative, for what is better worth conserving than our Empire from disintegration? It is liberal in the best sense of the term, for what can be more liberal and enlightened than the idea of maintaining the brotherhood of the British race—of keeping the people of England and the Colonies, of all creeds and classes, nationally united, never to be aliens to each other.[24]

In a sense, though, the colonial unionists wanted to have their cake and eat it: they sought to project the empire into a nonpartisan realm, but at the same time, they were desperate to keep it firmly within the bounds of practical politics during a period in which party machines were becoming increasingly effective and powerful. They found the two positions very hard to reconcile.

Noting the common refrain that the empire already represented a "shadowy" form of federation, Michael Burgess argues that the federalists were not demanding any sweeping constitutional upheaval.[25] This was certainly a frequently reiterated claim, albeit one that I sought to dispel in the previous chapter, but it was far from the only argumentative strategy, and it glosses over the manner in which debate over imperial innovation generated controversy over the constitution itself. For some, the novelty of their proposals was obvious, and it was to be celebrated as such. Just as the empire was unique in world history, so the federation of the empire could not draw on any example from the annals of Britain. A federal Greater Britain was to be either the culmination of the modern age, the end point of the developmental process of British state formation, as was the case for Seeley, or it was to represent, as it did in the eyes of assorted radicals, the inauguration of a new modernity, unencumbered by the ideas and institutions of the past.

The British political imagination was haunted by the specter of revolution, evoked most powerfully by the invective of Burke and Carlyle, and

[23] See, for example, Seeley, "The Impartial Study of Politics," CR, 54 (1888), 55–57; Seeley, "Ethics and Religion," FR, 45 (1889), 511–12; and the discussion of Froude below.
[24] De Labillière, Federal Britain, 171–72.
[25] Burgess, "Imperial Federation," Trivium, 13 (1978), 80.

indelibly associated with the violence of revolutionary France. This was a fire the flames of which were stoked heartily by the midcentury crises that traumatized Europe, and while a sense of British uniqueness was reinforced by the lack of corresponding strife at home, 1848 acted also as a warning of the dangers of serious political misjudgment, and of ignoring the embodied wisdom of the constitution.[26] This specter was one of the reasons that Greater Britain appealed to those of a more nervous political disposition, for it offered (as I explored in chapter 1) a means of ameliorating the social preconditions thought necessary for revolution. But it also meant that colonial unionists had to tread carefully in selling their plans, insisting that sweeping yet peaceful change was possible and that they were not endangering the stability of the country. In this endeavor they could draw on a notable precedent, for in the closing passages of volume two of his epic *History of England* (1848) Macaulay had characterized the glorious events surrounding 1688 as a "preserving revolution," as backward-looking and conservative as it was novel, and he had suggested that because of this relatively peaceful political transition Britain did not succumb to a "destroying revolution" in the nineteenth century.[27] The advocates of Greater Britain reiterated this argument by stressing the nonradical nature of their (often radical) plans. As de Labillière commented, "[t]here are revolutions *and* revolutions; there have been, in this country and many others, revolutions of the most conservative character," while Seeley wrote that "we have reduced revolution to a system and given it legal forms."[28] Young, after declaring that there "are revolutions and revolutions," argued that "revolution in its proper sense means simply a complete change effected without violence, and that in the course of time such complete changes may become necessary and can be adopted by constitutional methods." He wrote elsewhere that,

> The British Constitution has grown by slow degrees, through varying conditions of time, and of the temper of the people. Although viewed in certain

[26] Parry, "The Impact of Napoleon III on British Politics," *TRHS*, 6th series, 11 (2001), 147–75; Leslie Mitchell, "Britain's Reaction to the Revolutions," 83–99; and Robert Gildea, "1848 in European Collective Memory," 207–37, both in Richard J. Evans and Hartmut Pogge Von Strandmann (eds.), *The Revolutions in Europe, 1848–1849* (Oxford, 2000); and Miles Taylor, "The 1848 Revolutions and the British Empire," *P&P*, 166 (2000), 146–80.

[27] Macaulay, *The History of England from the Accession of James II*, ed. Peter Rowland (London, 1985 [1848]), II, 508. This passage was penned in November 1848, with events on the continent fresh in mind. The colonial empire is a notable absence in Macaulay's grand narrative, something that Seeley took as evidence of Macaulay's wrong-headed approach to history.

[28] De Labillière, comments, *PRCI*, 6 (1874–75), 83. Italics in original; Seeley, *Introduction to Political Science*, ed. Henry Sidgwick (London, 1896), 194–95.

logical lights, it may seem to be unwieldy and unworkable, it nevertheless
works well, on the whole. A Parliament which should make room within its
walls for the reception of the Colonies, would be quite in harmony with its
ancient traditions, and would be truly Imperial.[29]

Even the most blunt and ambitious of the federalists—and Young exhibited both characteristics—realized that they had to tread warily when discussing the constitution. It was, so they argued, evolving constantly and
was capable of accommodating and channeling change without losing its
essence (whatever that elusive quality might be).

The heroic vision of the future, of the building of a new world in order
to master the old, struck other advocates of Greater Britain not only as
bombastic, but as tactically inept. And in this they were surely correct, for
grandiloquent confidence in the necessity of transforming British political
institutions provoked a hostile reaction, and many of the harshest critics
of federation focused on the constitutional repercussions of such proposals. This issue plagued the movement from the outset. In 1870 William
Westgarth, in a critical riposte to a supraparliamentary scheme proposed
by the Liberal MP Robert Macfie, argued that, "[o]f a plan involving so
fundamental a change, whatever its merits as an abstract theory, one may
surely predict that it will never be realised. Such a change could hardly
occur except by revolution, and if we should have a revolution, it is not
likely to take a complex direction of this kind."[30] As an alternative, he
proposed colonial representation in Parliament. Similarly, C. W. Eddy, an
active member of the RCI and a prominent imperial campaigner, argued
that it was essential to "work along the lines of the ancient constitution,"
and to avoid "such startling proposals as are apt to unsettle men's minds,
to shock the timid and alarm the cautious, to disquiet men of business,
awake the fears of the taxpayer and," heaven forbid, "perhaps cause a
panic amongst the fundholders." It was possible, he continued, to secure
the unity of the empire without the "arduous and perilous and revolutionary process of drafting a constitution."[31] After noting that federation
would require a written constitution, Stout complained that this was
"opposed to any English precedent, and would form a new departure in

---

[29] Young, in a discussion following George Chesney's call for a reformation of the Privy
Council, "The British Empire," *PRCI*, 15 (1893–94), 178; and Young, *On the Political Relations of Mother Countries and Colonies*, 16. See also Young's comments in *Imperial Federation of Great Britain and Her Colonies*, 18–20.

[30] Westgarth, "Practical Views and Suggestions on Our Colonial Relations," *PRCI*, 3
(1870), 14. See also Westgarth, "Propositions for the Reform of our Relations with the
Colonies," *PRCI*, 3 (1871–72), 84–90.

[31] Eddy, "What Are the Best Means of Drawing Together the Interests of the United Kingdom and the Colonies?" *PRCI*, 3 (1875–76), 6. He suggested instead the extension of the
Privy Council.

the constitutional history of Britain," while another member of the RCI warned that supraparliamentary schemes were "wholly foreign to our instincts."[32] Writing anonymously, Graham Bower, a senior diplomat serving in South Africa, highlighted the limitations imposed by the demand for practicability, as well as the yearning for something more adventurous: "It would be easy to sit down and draw up the ideal Constitution of a poetic Anglo-Saxon Utopia; but such work, though pleasant as a dream, would be useless for practical purposes. The genius of the English nation is averse to sweeping changes or revolutionary measures."[33] In response to such attacks de Labillière argued that federation was hardly alien to the modern world: "[t]here is," he wrote in 1871, "clearly no need to formulate any more theoretical, detailed plans of union for our Empire, with such examples of Federation at work in the world. British Federation is no mere theory, no original idea. Its advocates are mere copyists, not speculative, but practical men, desiring the adoption, or *adaptation*, by our Empire of a well-proved system of government."[34]

In 1886 Lord Norton, a Tory ex–colonial secretary, noted with disdain the amount of "constitution-mongering" he had witnessed during the previous few years, defending instead the "national disinclination . . . to constitutional novelties."[35] Such arguments resonated widely, offering a serious challenge to the more audacious federalists. He mocked supraparliamentary schemes: "There is about as much chance of the English people turning their ancient Parliamentary system into such a constitution as of their deliberately restoring feudalism or the Heptarchy," and a "Minister coming down to the House with a proposal for abolishing Parliament, and issuing writs for a Federal Congress, would be immediately consigned to Bedlam." The "moral union" between the "mother country" and its colonies was strong enough. In an essay aptly entitled "Impossible Constitutions" (1886), and drawing explicitly on Dicey, he warned that "[t]o disintegrate an empire into a federal system is the reverse of the United States achievement—the union of states into a federal

[32] Stout, "A Colonial View of Imperial Federation," 355; and Trelawny Saunders, comments, PRCI, 11 (1879–80), 165. This comment was made in the course of a rather skeptical discussion about the supraparliamentary scheme propounded in A. Staveley Hill, "An Empire's Parliament," PRCI, 11 (1879–80), wherein Hill (a Tory MP) had insisted that his ideas could be accommodated due to the flexibility of the constitution (153). See also [Arthur Elliot] "Colonial and Imperial Federation," ER, 192 (1900), 264.
[33] "Centurion," *An Essay on Practical Federation* (London, 1887), 5. Instead he called for the creation of an advisory council and for colonial statesmen to attend relevant meetings of the Cabinet.
[34] Labillière, *Federal Britain*, 71. Italics in original. See also Robert Collier, Second Baron Monkswell, "State Colonization," FR, 43 (1888), 397.
[35] Norton, "Impossible Constitutions," NR, 7 (1886), 704. See also, C. R. Lowell, "English and American Federalism," FR, 43 (1888), 189–95.

system."[36] Conservatives in particular were desperate to stress the evolutionary nature of their proposals, however ambitious they were. Samuel Wilson, who proposed a fully representative federal chamber without bothering his readers with any details, maintained that this would simply require an "elastic extension" of the constitution, a constitution that he saw as malleable, not frozen in monolithic slumber.[37] A *National Review* stalwart wrote in response to Young's plan for an imperial senate that "it is really impossible to imagine the country, in cold blood, adopting the proposed scheme, or anything like it." And he resorted to emphasizing both the lack of novelty in his own plans for an advisory council, and the ability of the constitution to incorporate them without serious friction. After all, it would "take a great deal to make Englishmen listen to any plan which does not entirely fit into their present system of government." Another Tory, Frederick Wicks, was likewise critical of the lack of detail found in many of the plans, but he was also wary of sweeping change itself, suggesting that most schemes were "too drastic for immediate adoption." The House of Commons, he argued, was of central importance and its prestige must be upheld. "The value of the British constitution has always been shown in the ease with which it gives play to unexpected forces evolved from the community by the events of the hour. It is naturally artistic and capable of infinite variety."[38] He likewise advocated an advisory council.

John Morley, disciple of Mill and fierce opponent of imperial federation, focused on the constitutional question in his hostile review of Seeley's *The Expansion of England*. Like Freeman, he questioned the future status of the Palace of Westminster. Along with the constitution, the gothic revivalist edifice on the Thames acted as a symbolic marker of the greatness and stability of the country; it stood for many late Victorians as the physical embodiment of the spirit of liberty, balance, and order. To challenge it was to risk being committed to political oblivion. If imperial federation was to be a federation proper, argued Morley, it would demote the hallowed "mother of parliaments" to a mere "state legislature." This was politically unacceptable. Or, alternatively, if Britain was to secure its predominant role in the new world through framing a "federal" constitution that left the British fully in charge, the result could not be classified as a federation for it would merely replicate the existing mode of repressive

[36] Norton, "Imperial Federation—Its Impossibility," *NC*, 16 (1884), 512–13; and Norton, "Impossible Constitutions," 708.

[37] Wilson, "Imperial Federation," 382. Staveley Hill was another Tory supporter of supraparliamentary schemes: "An Empire's Parliament."

[38] Montagu Burrows, "Imperial Federation," *NR*, 4 (1884–85), 372–73; and Wicks, "The Confederation of the British Empire Practically Considered," *NR*, 8 (1886–7), 68 and 76.

governance under a different name. The "ideal," he concluded, "is as impracticable as it is puerile and retrograde."[39]

A further strategy adopted by some colonial unionists was to claim that the model of America was simply a mirror that the British political tradition held up to itself, that federalism was an extension (or even variant) of the British constitution. As such, the novelty of even supraparliamentary proposals was illusory. They were drawing on a common idiom: both Henry Maine and Freeman had pointed out the continuities, with the latter declaring that the "American constitution . . . is the English constitution with such changes—very great and important changes beyond doubt—as change of circumstances made needful." America was, Freeman declared, "the great English commonwealth beyond the Ocean."[40] In a similar vein, but with a very different goal, the imperial federalist J. N. Dalton presented the American constitution as a subtle reworking of existing British political forms, and even claimed that America was governed by the "Imperial Houses of Parliament in Congress."[41]

One of the most contentious moves was to link imperial federation to Irish Home Rule. Given the divisiveness of the issue, and the violent political passions that it aroused, this was something that the majority of colonial unionists were desperate to avoid. The editors of *Imperial Federation* disavowed any link between Home Rule and the empire, all too aware that this might cloud support for their own cause by tying it to an even more controversial one.[42] While the majority of unionists appear to have been opponents of Home Rule, there were, nevertheless, a number who tried to connect the issues.[43] For Bryce, Ireland was merely part of a

[39] Morley, "The Expansion of England," 254 and 258. See also Goldwin Smith, *Three English Statesmen* (London, 1867), 211; and, from a socialist critic, William Clarke, "An English Imperialist Bubble" (1885) in *William Clarke*, ed. H. Burrows and J. A. Hobson (London, 1908), 80. On Morley's political ideas, which fused Cobden and Mill, see D. A. Hamer, *John Morley* (Oxford, 1968). For criticisms of his position on federation, from a fellow liberal, see J. A. Murray Macdonald, "The Imperial Problem," *CR*, 80 (1901), 489–90.

[40] Freeman, "Some Impressions of the United States," *FR*, 32 (1882), II, 345; and Freeman, "The Growth of Commonwealths" [1873] reprinted in *Historical Essays*, 4th series (London, 1892), 375. See also [Henry Maine], "The Constitution of the United States," *QR*, 157 (1884), 1–32.

[41] Dalton, "The Federal States of the World," *NC*, 16 (1884), 109. Seeley, though, denied any such connection: *Introduction to Political Science*, 210.

[42] Editorial, *IF*, 3, (August 1888), 146–47. The danger they were trying to avoid is illustrated in Goldwin Smith, "Straining the Silken Thread," *MM*, 58 (1888), 241–46. George Boyce, in "Federalism and the Irish Question" in Bosco, *The Federal Idea*, I, 119, exaggerates in claiming that without the "Irish case," federalism would "hardly have merited serious political discussion in the British isles." The long-standing debate over federalism in relation to the colonies meant that it would have figured prominently anyway.

[43] See, for example, George Ferguson-Bowen, "The Federation of the British Empire," *PRCI*, 17 (1885–86), 288; Alexander Galt, "Relations of the Colonies to the British Em-

larger vision. Writing to Freeman, he argued that a federal solution in Ireland would lead to a federation of the empire, and then inexorably to a restoration of union with the United States.[44] A Tory barrister George Lancaster-Woodburne, stressing both the flexibility of the constitution and the threat posed to stability by Irish MPs, argued that Home Rule was an essential corrective. His phrasing, in offering support for a supra-parliamentary plan, is revealing: "In seeking the proper method of Imperial Federation, we must be prepared to accept some novelties—some constitutional changes—but, at the same time, we must endeavour, while adopting a thorough and successful measure, to maintain the Constitution of the country as much as possible in its present form."[45] At the turn of the century the journalist Edward Salmon suggested that India, in parallel with Ireland, could also be offered (limited) federal representation: "As federation should solve the Home Rule question—and solve it, moreover, on the lines of Colonial self-government so often held up for jealous admiration by the Nationalists themselves—so it might possibly solve the question of giving India a voice at Westminster."[46] Yoking together colonial unity and Irish politics was, however, a risky strategy and one that most imperial federalists shied away from, fearful that their own cause would be damaged by the failure of the Home Rule movement. Party political strife might contaminate their cross-party ideal. Added to this was the fact that most proponents of Greater Britain simply did not think that Ireland should be governed from Dublin; they ranged from those who wanted it to be independent, such as Charles Gavan Duffy, through to the far more numerous group who simply thought it an integral part of Britain. While the principle of (British) federation was prominent in the debates over Ireland, notably in the hands of Joseph Chamberlain, the association of the two issues damaged rather than aided the cause of Greater Britain. As Dilke wrote in 1890, the "discussions of Home Rule for Ireland have indeed, at a later period, somewhat weakened the influence of

pire," *PRCI*, 14 (1882–83), 391–409; Cunningham, *A Scheme for Imperial Federation*, 29; [Jenkins], "Imperial Federalism," 168; and M. Finch-Hatton, speech to the House of Commons, 12 April 1886, as recorded in *IF*, 1/9 (1886), 263. See, in general, Michael Burgess, "The Imperial Federation Debate in Great Britain, 1861–1893," unpublished PhD thesis, University of Leicester, 1976, ch. 6; and Eugenio Biagini, *Ireland and the British Nation* (Cambridge, 2007). In the Edwardian period, some of the members of the Round Table made an effort to combine Irish and imperial issues: J. E. Kendle, "The Round Table Movement and 'Home Rule All Round,'" *HJ*, 11 (1968), 332–53.

[44] Bryce, letter to Freeman, February 18, 1887, cited in Christopher Harvie, *The Lights of Liberalism* (London, 1976), 222.

[45] Lancaster-Woodbourne, "Imperial Federation and Home Rule," *NR*, 5 (1885), 612.

[46] Salmon, "Imperial Federation," *FR*, 58 (1900), 15. Salmon was a prolific imperial commentator who edited *Home News for India and Australia* (1889–99), the *Saturday Review* (1899–1913), and *United Empire* (1920–37).

the Imperial Federation League, although its speakers and its organ have been most careful to avoid committing themselves on the issue."[47]

The battle over the meaning of the constitution constrained the possibilities of political transformation by shaping the parameters of the debates over Greater Britain, rendering some arguments—namely those for mild reform—far more palatable to the majority than those advocating bold innovation. The idea of an imperial senate governing a globe-spanning polity was a novel idea that succeeded in catching the attention, if not the outright support, of a large number of individuals. But in advertising its novelty, often brazenly, its proponents undercut their chances of success by highlighting their divergence from the prevailing evolutionary and organic conventions of British political discourse. In this sense, Burke's shadow fell heavily across Victorian imperial thought. Those who stressed the novelty were often dismissed as reckless utopian dreamers; those who refrained from emphasizing innovation either resorted to schemes that were not really federal in any meaningful sense (and in so doing added further confusion to an already confused debate) or ended up making arguments about the almost limitless flexibility of the constitution, which failed to convince a cautious governing class. In its supra-parliamentary guise, Greater Britain was doomed from the very beginning. But its long and convoluted death throes offer a fascinating insight into the nature of Victorian political discourse, the ways in which agents must grapple with existing linguistic and moral conventions, and, consequently, into the nature of political argument itself.

CIVIC IMPERIALISM

Victorian political thought was infused with complaints about the atomism of modern commercial society. This was a criticism that reverberated throughout the century, emanating from, among others, liberal Anglicans, romantics, socialists, conservative organicists, philosophical idealists, and new liberals. The colonial unionists tended to concur, and they added a distinctive twist, arguing that the empire, and in particular Greater Britain, offered the best response. Although the role of republicanism (or civic humanism) in Victorian political thought has figured prominently in recent scholarship, the empire has been noticeable by its absence.[48] Yet re-

[47] Dilke, *Problems of Greater Britain* II, 481. See also H. E. Egerton, *A Short History of Colonial Policy* (London, 1897), 456; and Gavan Duffy, "Some Fruits of Federation," *IF*, 5/3 (1890), 68.

[48] See, for example, Burrow, *Whigs and Liberals;* Stefan Collini, *Public Moralists* (Oxford, 1991), 108–10; and Eugenio Biagini, "Neo-Roman Liberalism," *History of European Ideas*, 29 (2003), 313–39. In the historiography of European political thought, the terms

publican themes permeated debate over the future of the colonies, helping shape the thought of some of the leading imperial thinkers. Articulated most forcefully in Froude's Harringtonian *Oceana* (1886), they also
suffused the writings of figures as otherwise diverse as Dilke, Bryce, and,
as we shall see in the next chapter, Seeley.[49] Civic imperialism constituted
a late, partial, but nevertheless marked flowering of republicanism; indeed
in both its geographical reach and political ambition, if not its purity and
sophistication, it can be seen as the apotheosis of this enduring and ever
mutating political idiom. It placed duty, individual and communal virtue,
patriotism, disdain of luxury, and the privileging of the common good, at
the center of the political universe. Empire and liberty, it was argued, were
intimately connected. Fearful of the social, political, and moral dangers
heralded by the degradation and urban squalor of industrial capitalist society, many of the imperialists looked to the vast expanses of the colonial
empire to (re)shape a new breed of rugged imperial subjects. Greater
Britain was the stage upon which this vision of the morally and spiritually regenerative power of imperial patriotism was to be acted out.

Civic imperialism was not a discrete autonomous tradition, a position
separate from other modes of imperial ideology. Nor was it the antithesis
of "liberal imperialism." Such neat distinctions are misleading, missing
both the complexity of liberalism during the nineteenth century (and beyond) as well as the key point that republican language—which is to say
both the specific vocabulary employed by, and the key concerns that had
animated, previous generations of thinkers that we label republican—
were threaded through the tapestry of Victorian liberal thought and practice, although they were certainly not exclusive to it.[50] Republican themes
and language helped to structure certain forms of liberalism, while offering a powerful challenge to other varieties. Recent scholarship on the republican tradition produced by political philosophers and historians of
political theory has tended to focus on its purportedly distinctive conception of freedom.[51] It has, that is, concentrated on the relationship between

---

"civic humanism" and "civic republican" are often used interchangeably, as they will be
below.

[49] The art critic and social theorist John Ruskin is another example of a thinker (albeit a
self-described Tory) whose imperial thought is inflected with civic imperial themes, although
it is certainly not reducible to them. He exerted considerable influence over Froude's thinking. For one of the clearest articulations of his imperial vision, see his "Inaugural Lecture"
as Slade Professor at Oxford in 1870, reproduced in *The Works of John Ruskin*, ed. E. T.
Cook and Alexander Wedderburn (London, 1903–12), XX, esp. 42–43.

[50] I explore this issue further in Duncan Bell, "Virtue and Empire" in Bell and Quentin
Skinner (eds.), *Republicanism and Global Politics* (Cambridge, forthcoming).

[51] Most influentially in Quentin Skinner, *Liberty Before Liberalism* (Cambridge, 1998);
and Phillip Pettit, *Republicanism* (Oxford, 1997). For overviews of these debates, see Cécile

the individual and the state, often to the detriment of questions about how the inhabitants of "free states" should view foreign conquest and power politics. Yet republican thought, from its distant origins in ancient Greece and Rome, through its re-articulation in the Italian city-states of the Renaissance and onward into the Anglo-American world, had always been concerned with the dynamic relationship between empire and liberty. For many writers, the two were intimately linked: liberty at home was compatible with (and may even require) empire abroad—although empire itself, if understood and enacted improperly, could pose a threat to that very liberty.[52] Civic imperialism was an heir to this style of thinking, stressing as it did the necessary conditions for grandeur and greatness in the modern world.

Basking in the glory of the global British commonwealth, and cherishing the national traditions that furnished this greatness, civic imperialism was opposed to selfish individualism, emphasizing instead public duty, self-denying altruism, and the promotion of a virtuous patriotism, all on a global scale; its proponents worried about the corrupting powers of materialism, capitalism, and luxury; they stressed duty above rights, politics above economics, and the enchanted national above the unencumbered cosmopolitan. They counterposed the passive subject with the active imperial patriot. And they also repeatedly underlined the benefits bestowed by propertied independence, and especially the ownership of productive agricultural land in the colonies. This helps explain the deep suspicion expressed by many imperialists about the flight to the city and urban industrialism. This is not surprising given the deep historical roots, stretching back to Rome, of the connection between farming and the planting of people. After all, the Latin term *colonia*, derived from the verb *colere*, means to cultivate, or to farm.[53] This imaginative link has been a central theme in the history of Western imperial expansion.

Stefan Collini argues that eighteenth-century conceptions of virtue and Victorian notions of character shared a number of key features, most notably their asceticism and demanding political ethic. As such, Victorian thought was marked by "survivals and mutations" of the earlier language

---

Laborde and John Maynor (eds.), *Republicanism and Political Theory* (Oxford, forthcoming); and Daniel Weinstock and Christian Nadeau (eds.), *Republicanism* (London, 2004)

[52] Eric Nelson, *The Greek Tradition in Republican Thought* (Cambridge, 2004); Mikael Hörnqvist, *Machiavelli and Empire* (Cambridge, 2004); Hörnqvist, "The Two Myths of Civic Humanism" in James Hankins (ed.), *Renaissance Civic Humanism* (Cambridge, 2000), 105–43; David Armitage, *The Ideological Origins of the British Empire* (Cambridge, 2000), esp. ch. 5; and Bell and Skinner (eds.), *Republicanism and Global Politics*. I return to the dangers posed by empire to liberty in chapter 8.

[53] Moses Finley, "Colonies—An Attempt at a Typology," *TRHS*, 5th series, 6 (1976), 173.

of civic humanism, although he maintains that they differed in at least one important respect: their "sense of nemesis."[54] This difference resulted from divergent conceptions of historical time, for the eighteenth-century humanists feared corruption, grounded in a cyclical notion of rise and decline, while the Victorians feared stagnation as a threat to their open-ended notion of a progressive future. This was indeed a significant difference, the repercussions of which will be examined in chapter 8. For the civic imperialists, however, the sense of nemesis remained the same: the logic of imperial rise and decline threatened to swallow up the British, as it had all previous empires. To escape this fate, radical change was required. The dangers of imperial corruption, heralded by Sallust and Polybius, and rearticulated most famously by Edward Gibbon, infused the Victorian imagination, and the civic imperialists responded by insisting on the necessity of building a powerful Greater Britain.

The late Victorian debates were not a straightforward replay of the politics of ancient virtue, and nor did they witness an unmediated repeat of the eighteenth-century clash over the respective merits of the ancients and moderns. Rather, civic imperialism was a language adapted to and shaped by the late nineteenth-century imperial context.[55] Born of a modern industrial capitalist society, its proponents were simultaneously proud of the achievements of modern commerce and extremely wary of the dangers of the commercial spirit extending too far. Civic imperialism was defined as much by what it was opposed to as what it stood for. Among the main targets were liberals infected with the "virus of Manchesterism."[56] This strand of liberalism was characterized, it was claimed, by utilitarian reasoning, a narrow obsession with profit, and a debilitating individualism. Above all else, it was seen to underpin an attitude critical of empire: during the 1860s in particular, liberalism came to be associated with "indifference, if not hostility, towards the Colonies," and it was widely believed (as I expored in chapter 2) that the Liberal government was either planning to surrender important elements of the empire, or that it would simply let it fragment as a result of apathy.[57] It was against these forms of liberalism (or at least a crude caricature of them) that the civic imperial

[54] Collini, *Public Moralists*, 108–10.

[55] For an analysis of the wide-ranging eighteenth-century debates over luxury, see Istvan Hont, "Luxury and Commerce" in Mark Goldie and Robert Wokler (eds.), *The Cambridge History of Eighteenth-Century Political Thought* (Cambridge, 2006), 379–419. Hont notes elsewhere the "political synergies" between Renaissance claims about national grandeur and eighteenth-century debates on commercial modernity: Hont, *Jealousy of Trade* (Cambridge, Mass., 2005), 11. This was played out, I suggest, in a variety of imperial contexts over the course of the nineteenth century, flowering in the debates over Greater Britain.

[56] Edward Salmon, "The Colonial Empire of 1837," FR, 61 (1897), 863.

[57] The quotation is from Egerton, *A Short History of British Colonial Policy*, 455.

position was articulated. The enemy, in other words, was both an old and a new one—old in the sense that excessive wealth and the untrammeled commercial spirit had long been regarded as inimical to the republican vision, new in that the enemy was mainly a creature of the industrial capitalism of the nineteenth century, the political economists and their devotees in the business and political elites.

Materialism, it was thought, was destructive in three distinct ways, although they frequently overlapped. Firstly, it could corrupt individuals. The perfidious sensuality and vice of the East rebounding to undermine the polity from within was a long-standing (orientalist) concern, rising to prominence in the eighteenth century, where it was exemplified in Burke's dogged pursuit of Warren Hastings. It echoed throughout the nineteenth century.[58] The most common targets here were the "nabobs," the returning governing class of India. Modern luxury could also damage those not directly involved in the empire, either by entrenching social and economic conditions that debilitated the working classes, emasculating their virile energies, or through creating a rich but effete ruling class. Combined, this created a society unable to, and uninterested in, protecting and enlarging its strength and glory. The second dimension followed from this. Commercial society generated increasing economic inequality, triggering potentially destabilising political consequences as well as fueling fear of the blighted working classes rising to challenge their oppressors. A polarized society would be a weak one. Finally, there was a more indirect effect—the commercial spirit, it was often argued, corroded patriotism and the belief in a transcendent common good. Individuals became increasingly egotistical, placing self-interest above public duty.[59] Such people were perfectly happy to see the empire either fall into a state of disrepair, or, in some cases—most notably that of the self-proclaimed "last of the Manchester school," Goldwin Smith—to call the for the "emancipation" of the colonies. Julius Vogel, a former premier of New Zealand, warned of the dangers of Britain, stripped of its colonies, "sinking into a small money-loving State—a second Holland."[60]

These lines of thought came together in a re-articulation of the virtues (and not simply the economic benefits) of colonialism. Much of the debate over Greater Britain revolved around discussions about the type of character produced by and necessary for successful colonization. For

[58] See Miles Taylor, "Imperium et Libertas?" *JICH*, 19 (1991), 1–23; and on Hastings, Nicholas Dirks, *The Scandal of Empire* (Cambridge, Mass., 2006).

[59] Seeley's defense of classical notions of (merit-based) aristocracies, above party intrigue, noble, and acting in the name of the common good, can be seen as a response to this: *The Life and Times of Stein* (Cambridge, 1878), III, 564; and Seeley, *Introduction to Political Science*, 328–30.

[60] Vogel, "Greater of Lesser Britain," *NC*, 1 (1877), 831.

much of the nineteenth century, as argued in chapter 2, emigration was looked upon, on the one hand, as a safety valve for social problems, and on the other, as a means of escape for greedy and ambitious young men, and for the less talented sons of the aristocracy. While economists had repeatedly insisted on the value of colonies, the colonists themselves, despite the ardent efforts of many of the promoters of emigration, were frequently scorned, viewed as at best unlucky wretches, and often as rogues. E. G. Wakefield wrote in *A View on the Art of Colonization* (1849) that, "speaking generally, colonies and colonists are in fact, as well as in the estimation of the British gentry, inferior, low, unworthy of much respect, properly disliked and despised by people of honour here, who happen to be acquainted with the state of society in the colonies."[61] Although this was probably an exaggeration, it nevertheless reflected a common attitude. Throughout the century settlers were also routinely criticized for their brutality to indigenous populations, often by Britons who supported the empire but were worried about how some of its constituent elements were ruled.[62] The debates over Greater Britain witnessed a serious attempt to transform this negative image. The colonies were re-imagined as integral elements of the "mother country"; the existing colonists as loyal, hardy, rugged individuals, the descendents of the yeoman backbone of the nation in eighteenth-century country-party political thought. The colonies were seen as spaces for the transformation of character. Stark binaries abounded. The fresh air and uplifting lifestyle promised by the colonial propagandists was contrasted with the urban squalor of late Victorian Britain.[63] This vision was not simply the preserve of a few leading public intellectuals. It was widespread, though often diffused, in the popular languages of imperial Britain. An excellent summary of the idealized picture of the colonist can be found, for example, in a New Zealand school textbook, penned by a prominent scholar-imperialist, designed to teach the young about the empire:

> The successful colonist must be of sturdy character, persevering, unflinching
> in the face of difficulty, steady of nerve at those moments when he is exposed
> to terrible dangers, willing to endure hardship, and not too proud to labour

---

[61] Wakefield, *A View on the Art of Colonization* [1849] in *The Collected Works of Edmond Gibbon Wakefield*, ed. M. F. Lloyd-Prichard (Glasgow, 1968), 837. See also Arthur Mills, *Systematic Colonization* (London, 1847), 33–34. For later criticisms, see Dilke, *Problems of Greater Britain*, II, 244–46.

[62] See, for example, John Stuart Mill, *Considerations on Representative Government*, CW, XIX, 771–72.

[63] The representation of the colonies in publicity material often drew on classical images of the virtue (and purity) of femininity: Dominic David Alessio, "Domesticating 'The Heart of the Wild,'" *Women's History Review*, 6 (1997), 239–69. On the gendering of colonialism, see also Grant, *Representations of British Emigration, Colonisation, and Settlement*, ch. 8.

with his own hands; he must love the land, as the old Teuton forefathers of the English loved it; he must be active, enterprising, eager to take advantage of new opportunities for bettering his position in the world, moved by the trading as well as the farming spirit; he must delight in the sea, which is to bear him to his new home, and upon whose bosom he will entrust the fruits of his labour at home. All of these qualities are present in the national English character.[64]

Colonialism simultaneously demanded and fashioned a particular type of individual, the type that would help to foster and defend the glories of the British global community.

The pervasiveness of civic imperial themes in the debate over Greater Britain also helps explain the later infusion of imperial thought by philosophical idealism.[65] One of the reasons that idealism, emphasizing as it did the common good, duty, public service, and the mutual constitution of self and community, resonated so widely was that it proved compatible with extant patterns of thought, providing a new language and a new philosophical justification for some of the commonplaces of political discourse. The idealists, in other words, rather then simply importing Hegelian metaphysics into a largely hostile empiricist context, codified many of the moral and political assumptions of the time.[66] Idealism had a soft landing in imperial discourse, dovetailing with the civic imperial themes that had been prominent during the late Victorian era.

J. A. FROUDE AND THE "COMMONWEALTH OF OCEANA"

J. A. Froude was one of the foremost historians and political commentators of the age. The character of his thought has proved remarkably elusive—he has been labeled a radical Tory, a liberal Carlylean, and (rather more implausibly) a straightforward "great Liberal."[67] These interpreta-

[64] J. A. Hight, *The English as a Colonising Nation* (Wellington, 1903), 19. At this time Hight was a Lecturer in political economy and constitutional history at Canterbury University College.

[65] This has been a subject of recent scholarly interest; see for example, Jeanne Morefield, *Covenants Without Swords* (Princeton, 2005); E.H.H. Green, "Idealism, Conservatism, and Collectivism" in his *Ideologies of Conservatism* (Oxford, 2002), 42–72; and Daniel Gorman, "Lionel Curtis, Imperial Citizenship, and the Quest for Unity," *The Historian*, 66 (2004), 67–96.

[66] On the strong links between idealism and the liberal Anglicans, for example, see Jones, *Victorian Political Thought*, ch. 3; and James Allard, "Idealism in Britain and the United States" in Thomas Baldwin (ed.), *The Cambridge History of Philosophy, 1870–1945* (Cambridge, 2003), 43–59.

[67] Burrow, *A Liberal Descent* (Cambridge, 1981), Part III; Peter Mandler, *The English National Character* (London, 2006), 69; and Michael Bentley, *Lord Salisbury's World* (Cambridge, 2001), 225.

tions all catch aspects of his multifaceted intellectual persona, but they also miss some of the essential flavor of his thinking, especially in relation to the empire. Froude was certainly influenced by Carlyle, his mentor and friend, but he possessed an independent mind.[68] His spasm of religious doubt and the ferment of his spiritual life, his debts to Carlyle, even his articulation of political theory through the medium of historical writing, mark him as an example of *homo Victoriana*. Yet he was a man both of his time, and alienated from it. He sought desperately to escape, and to transcend, the evils that he thought were destroying his beloved England, and with it the modern world. Drawing deeply from the well of classical republican thought, he looked back to Harrington and further still to the ancients for the materials to help construct a better future.

For most of his career Froude was more concerned with religion than with foreign affairs. His vast, laudatory narrative of the reformation, the *History of England from the Fall of Wolsey to the Defeat of the Spanish Armada* (1856–70), did not emphasize Britain's imperial expansion.[69] Empire, though, became noticeably more pronounced in his writings from the early 1870s onward, coinciding with what John Burrow calls his increasingly "pessimistic and reactionary" tone.[70] This transition was directly linked to his grim diagnosis of the modern world, encapsulated in his declaration that "we are passing through a crisis in our national existence," and it was at this point that a civic dimension increasingly bolstered and supplemented his Carlylean vocabulary. His verdict on modern Britain was bleak: it had been systematically degraded by the creed of liberalism. Froude detested much about the society in which he lived. Obsessed with the "genius of English freedom," a genius he saw as largely consigned to the past, he believed that the only hope for the future lay in the unity of the empire. He saw corruption wherever he looked in the "mother country." The most obvious consequences of this blight were to be found in the cities. For Froude, excessive population growth was a manifest danger; it was as if the ghost of Malthus had returned. The country was overcrowded, the growing urban sprawls sites of moral decay, social and economic dislocation, and thus sources of political instability.

---

[68] On his debt to, and distance from, Carlyle, see A. F. Pollard, rev. William Thomas, "James Anthony Froude," *Oxford Dictionary of National Biography* (www.oxforddnb.com).

[69] Froude, *History of England from the Fall of Wolsey to the Defeat of the Spanish Armada*, 12 vols. (London, 1856–70). The most acute analysis of this work remains, Burrow, *A Liberal Descent*. For an early foray into imperial hagiography, albeit one that fails to make an explicit link to Victorian expansion, see Froude "England's Forgotten Worthies," *WR*, 2 (1852), 32–67.

[70] Burrow, *A Liberal Descent*, 281. Burrow also notes Froude's reliance on the "language of Bolingbroke and the eighteenth-century Country Party" (282), though he does not make enough of the civic elements of his imperialism.

Drawing on a passage from Horace, he noted the similarity between the causes of Roman decline and the perilous state of contemporary Britain: as people flocked from the fields to the cities they were exposed to ever increasing levels of vice. "Decay is busy at the heart of them, and all the fate of Rome seemed to me likely to be the fate of England if she became what the political economists desired to see her."[71]

One of the key ways Froude differed from the general tenor of the times (and from most of the other advocates of Greater Britain) was in his conception of historical time. Unlike the largely progressive cosmology of his peers, it drew from and modified the ideas of Carlyle. As Burrow has remarked, Carlyle combined a "Hebraic-Christian pattern of idolatry and retribution" with German idealist philosophy to provide a postromantic counterpart to the secular cyclical vision of the ancients.[72] For Carlyle history was a story of recurrent decline and fall, moving in cycles, destructive, vituperative, punitive. Froude's vision was less violent, but the temporal structure remained intact. Carlyle and Froude drew two lessons from the comparison with Rome: the first was that England was in danger of falling prey to the destructive internal dynamics that had claimed the glories of Rome; the second was a belief in the necessity of Britain picking up the imperial mantle thrown down by the Romans.[73] On the one hand, then, Rome offered the historical embodiment of the very pattern of history itself, of rise and decline. On the other, it presented a picture of a vigorous and powerful empire. The tension between the two visions—which are essentially slices taken at different times in a historical cycle—inflected the imperial writings of both.

The notion of character was central to Froude's historico-political thought. Character was not only a matter of personal development but a central concern of government policy: "all wise statesmen look first, in the ordering of their national affairs, to the effect which is being produced

[71] Froude, *Oceana*, 395, 2, 25, and 10. On his fear of Roman decline, see also Froude, *Caesar* (London, 1879), 5–7.

[72] Burrow, *A Liberal Descent*, 253. On Froude's challenge to the prevailing belief in progress, see for example, "On Progress," *FM*, 2 (1870), 671–91. On his indebtedness to Harrington, and eighteenth-century ideas about corruption, see also John Burrow, Stefan Collini, and Donald Winch, *That Noble Science of Politics* (Cambridge, 1983), 190. Froude was not consistent here, though, and he found it difficult to completely escape the belief in progress, occasionally lapsing into a Whiggishly optimistic defence of national development. As he wrote in 1864, "One lesson, and only one, history may be said to repeat with distinctness; that the world is built somehow on moral foundations; that, in the long run, it is well with the good; in the long run, it is ill with the wicked. But this is no science." Froude, "The Science of History" [1864], in his *Short Studies on Great Subjects* (London, 1877), III, 1–25.

[73] See, for example, Carlyle, *Chartism* in Carlyle, *Selected Writings*, ed. Alan Shelston (Harmondsworth, 1971), 202.

on character; and institutions, callings, occupations, habits, and methods
of life are measured and estimated first, and beyond, every other consideration, by this test." Because the state had failed in this task, the country was declining, but all was not lost—at least yet—as the essential English character, Froude cautioned, "is only sleeping." Awakening it,
dragging it from its current slumber, required strong political leadership
and a more vigorous conception of political life. The "wealth of a nation,"
he argued, "depends in the long run upon the conditions mental and bodily of the people of whom it consists, and the experience of all mankind
declares that a race of men sound in soul and limb can be bred and reared
only in the exercise of plough and spade, in the free air and sunshine, with
country enjoyments and amusements, never amidst fowl drains and
smoke blacks and the eternal clank of machinery."[74] But the tendencies
of modern society—and in particular those associated with liberal capitalism—precluded such a vision.

Liberalism exhibited three crippling vices, all of them lethal to British
stability and greatness: materialism, individualism, and a minimalist
("nightwatchman") conception of the state. Materialism was the popular
religion of the country; and luxury, understood as the excessive accumulation of personal wealth and its ostentatious display, was its progeny.
"Luxury," he lamented, was "no longer deprecated as an evil," but was
instead "encouraged as a stimulus to labour." In another essay he wrote
that the "modern creed [of liberalism] looks complacently on luxury as a
stimulus to trade. Fact says that luxury has disorganised society, severed
the bonds of goodwill which unite man to man, and class to class, and
generated distrust and hatred."[75] By polarizing society luxury was destabilizing the polity. It was allowed to do so because the modern liberal conception of the state failed to provide the necessary resources to deal with
the threat. In this broadly Spencerian rendering, the state was no more
than the uncoordinated aggregation of egoistic individuals, a hollow shell
lacking common purpose. This vision itself was premised on a rampant
individualism that, according to Froude, corroded the affective bonds necessary to unite communities, reconcile classes, and ensure greatness. "In
these modern times men govern themselves, and therefore their loyalty is
to themselves." He harked after an older understanding of self, society,
and state, praising the "ancient notion of a community," one that fostered
virtues "which Englishmen used most to desire," the virtues of "Patriotism, loyalty, fidelity, self-forgetfulness, a sense of duty." In such a society
the "sense of what is due to a man's self"—his rights, as he calls them—

[74] Froude, *Oceana*, 154, 109, 8, 246.
[75] Ibid. "Reciprocal Duties of State and Subject," *FM*, 81 (1870), 290; and ibid., "On
Progress," *FM*, 2 (1870), 687.

"is conspicuously absent."[76] Individuals should be bound by duty not seen as possessing inalienable rights; society was best understood as a co-operative hierarchical arrangement united by common purpose and interests; and the state should be regarded as a moral entity, the priorities of which were clear: "To repress needless luxury, to prevent capitalists from making fortunes at the cost of the poor, and to distribute in equitable proportions the profits of industry."[77] A "sound nation," he declared, "is a nation composed of sound human beings, healthy in body, strong of limb, true in word and deed—brave, sober, temperate, chaste, to whom morals are more important than wealth or knowledge—where duty is first and the rights of man are second—where, in short, men grow up and live and work hard, having in them what our ancestors called the 'fear of God.'" This "sound nation" was not necessarily democratic, for Froude believed that democracy fostered the dangers he was so desperate to avoid: it encouraged greed and hedonism.[78] His was instead a paternalistic vision in which a wise and beneficent elite governed a contented free people, bound together in loyalty to the nation and by the mutual reliance of all classes.

The diagnosis was clear; the cure lay in the wide-open spaces of Greater Britain. His dream, which was never specified with any great precision, was of a "united Oceana," a polity "united as closely as the American states are united." Although associated with the imperial federation movement, Froude did not advocate a formal federal structure, not only because he opposed specific plans for federation but because he was highly critical of written constitutions in general, prone as they were to rigidity.[79] He was also wary of forcing legislation on the colonies: "If the natural tie is not strong enough, no mechanical tie will hold," and the result would be that a "federation contrived by politicians would snap at the first strain." Pushing prematurely for federation, then, threatened the very success for which he strove, for "[c]onstitutions are made for the country, not the country for constitutions." Despite this skepticism he nevertheless foresaw the possibility of a formal federal constitution for the empire at

[76] Ibid., "Reciprocal Duties of State and Subject," 293 and 288; and ibid., "Party Politics," *FM*, 10 (1874), 11. See also Froude, "On Progress," 683. "As a member of society man parts with his natural rights, and society in turn incurs a debt to him which it is bound to discharge. Only then is he free." For his conception of liberty, see "On Progress," 682. For Seeley's assorted criticisms of "negative" conceptions of liberty, see his *Introduction to Political Science*, Lecture V.

[77] Froude, "Reciprocal Duties of State and Subject," 290. For criticisms of the increasing gap between rich and poor, see ibid., "On Progress," 685.

[78] Ibid., *Oceana*, 154; and ibid., "On Progress," 684; and also "Party Politics," 4.

[79] Ibid., *Oceana*, 91, 354–56. In 1870 he had called for an imperial council, with representatives from all the colonies in attendance. Froude, "England's War" [1871] reprinted in ibid., *Short Studies on Great Subjects* (London, 1907), III, 281.

some distant date, at least if the colonists demanded it. In the meantime, there was no need for further expansion as the contours of Oceana were discernible in the present structure of the empire—its material outline was "an achieved fact." The "English," spread throughout the world, were a "realised family," the population of the colonies "as much England as we are." A series of practical measures, including opening up the military and the civil service to talented colonists, and bestowing more honors on colonial worthies, would suffice to indicate that the separatist mood was a distant memory. Like Seeley, Froude believed that the major change required was a cultural and cognitive one—people simply needed to start thinking about the empire in a different way, to view it in an altered light. Once they did so, they would realize what might be lost. It was not too late, and nor was it an unworkable dream: "No great policy was carried through which did not once seem impossible."[80] But two main overlapping constituencies blocked this vision. The first, embracing materialism and self-interest, was the Manchester School and its legions of adherents. The second was the party system itself, an expression of the "factionalism" he detested, which challenged the articulation of the common good and made nonpartisan collective action extremely difficult to enact.[81]

Oceana would provide a destination for the waves of emigration Froude thought so necessary for Greater Britain. He was particularly worried about the flow of people to America, and he despaired of the perceived economic reasoning behind their choice of destination. There was, after all, more to life than money. In Oceana people would be able to live, he wrote, "under conditions the most favourable which the human condition can desire," spawning as a result, "fresh nations of Englishmen." It was to be a self-governing polity populated (largely) by individuals of the same race and nation, united by "common blood, common interest, and a common pride in the great position which unity can secure." The aim of British policy, then, should be to create a polity strong and "healthy" enough to "defy the storms of fate."[82] Oceana was to rule the waves: "Queen among the nations, from without invulnerable, and at peace and at health within . . . this was the alternative lying before Oceana: in every way more desirable than the economic." Froude dismissed the financial critique of federation in scathing terms.[83] "Neither the terms of the federation, the nature of the imperial council, the functions of the local legislatures, the present debates of the colonies, or the

---

[80] Ibid., *Oceana*, 103, 393, 300, 395, 15–16, 393–94.

[81] See especially ibid., "Party Politics"; and ibid., *Caesar*.

[82] Ibid., "England and Her Colonies," 15; and ibid., *Oceana*, 12 and 15.

[83] Ibid., *Oceana*, 11; and ibid., "England and Her Colonies," 14. See also Labillière, *Federal Britain*, 233–35; and Vogel, "Greater or Lesser Britain," 820.

apportionment of taxation, would be found problems hard of solution, if the apostles of *laissez faire* could believe for once that it was not the last word in political science."[84] Instead, the answer lay in returning to some of the first words of political science, drawing on the ancient resources of the republican tradition to map a glorious future for Greater Britain.

[84] Froude, "England and Her Colonies," 14; and also ibid., "Party Politics," 8.

6

The Apostle of Unity

[W]e think of Great Britain too much
and Greater Britain too little.
—Seeley, *The Expansion of England* (1883)

JOHN ROBERT SEELEY was not the most prolific advocate of a federal Greater Britain, nor was he the first to preach the creed. But due to his eloquence, perseverance, and intellectual authority—as well as his impeccable timing—he provided a substantial boost to the fortunes and credibility of those demanding a transformation in the relationship between the "mother country" and the colonial empire. Seeley played a notable role in a number of other significant debates in the late Victorian era: he was a notorious figure in the pervasive conflicts over the nature of religious belief, especially through his best-selling study of the moral example of Christ, *Ecce Homo* (1866); he was active in pushing for the reform of higher education, including the admission of women to the ancient universities; and he was a pioneer in the professionalization of the academic study of history, while also exerting a powerful influence on the development of political science as a distinct field of scholarly enquiry.[1] But he is remembered best as a panegyrist of the empire, most notably in *The Expansion of England* (1883), the bible of Greater Britain. Following Seeley's death, the historian H.A.L. Fisher wrote that this was both a "household book and a household phrase," its publication marking an "epoch in the popular education of the Anglo-Saxon race." "I question," he concluded, "whether any historical work has exercised so great an influence over the general political thinking of a nation."[2]

Seeley's ideal of history as a "school of statesmanship" demanded that the historian endeavor to shape public debate, to demonstrate the importance of the past and its relationship to the future. He was, in this sense,

[1] [Seeley], *Ecce Homo* (London, 1866); Seeley, "A Midlands University," *FR*, 42 (1887), 703–16; and ibid., *Introduction to Political Science*, ed. Henry Sidgwick (Cambridge, 1923 [1896]). See also, Peter Burroughs, "John Robert Seeley and British Imperial History," *JICH*, 1 (1973), 191–213; J. G. Greenlee, "A 'Succession of Seeleys,'" *JICH*, 4 (1976), 266–83; Reba N. Soffer, *Discipline and Power* (Stanford, 1994); and John Burrow, Stefan Collini, and Donald Winch, *That Noble Science of Politics* (Cambridge, 1983), ch. 6.

[2] Fisher, "Sir John Seeley," *FR*, 60 (1896), 191 and 193.

a self-proclaimed architect of political consciousness. In an essay on John Milton, one of his heroes, he argued that the author of *Paradise Lost* "was a politician, but he had also a religion and a faith; he was a religious man, but his religion did not make him into a political quietist." Above all, Seeley continued, Milton "felt the unity of national life."[3] This vision exemplified both Seeley's conception of his own role as an educator of the national mind and also his model of engaged statesmanship.

In Seeley's intellectual development we witness how a set of widely shared political goals—in this case, national glory and unity as manifested in a federal Greater Britain—can be reached by following an idiosyncratic route. Seeley's thought was shaped by an impressively eclectic range of sources. He mixed together Comtean positivism, Rankean historicism, German romanticism, civic republicanism, the doctrines of broad churchmanship derived ultimately from Coleridge and transmitted through Thomas Arnold and F. D. Maurice, and threw in, for good measure, a dose of the Oxbridge fetish for the "comparative method." They were reconciled in his mind, as a syncretic unity, with the same determination that he and the broad church theologians sought harmony in the conflict-ridden arena of modern commercial society. His intellectual persona was as multifaceted as that of any late nineteenth-century figure, and it cannot be generalized into a series of claims about the "intellectual foundations" of Greater Britain. To attempt to do so would be to miss a larger and more important point, namely that the conflicting visions of Greater Britain garnered support from people of often very different political persuasions. While Seeley was an intellectually distinctive figure, his ideas and sensibility were also fashioned by the anxieties outlined in chapter 2. He was fearful, especially from the early 1880s onward, about the deteriorating international situation, worrying constantly about how his beloved "England" would adapt to the turbulent dynamics of global politics. He was likewise deeply concerned about the potential for domestic unrest generated by the advent of democracy. The two were knotted together, in a manner usually underestimated by his modern interpreters.[4]

[3] Seeley, "Milton's Political Opinions," in ibid., *Lectures and Essays* (London, 1870), 102 and 103. Milton's republicanism is explored in David Armitage, Armand Himy, and Quentin Skinner (eds.), *Milton and Republicanism* (Cambridge, 1995).

[4] Useful accounts of Seeley can be found in: Deborah Wormell, *Sir John Seeley and the Uses of History* (Cambridge, 1980); Richard Shannon, "John Robert Seeley and the Idea of a National Church" in Robert Robson (ed.), *Ideas and Institutions of Victorian Britain* (London, 1967), 236–67; Burrow, Collini, and Winch, *That Noble Science of Politics*, ch. 7; Reba Soffer, "History and Religion" in R. W. Davis and R. J. Helmstadter (eds.), *Religion and Irreligion in Victorian Society* (London, 1992), 133–51; David Worsley, "Sir John Robert Seeley and His Intellectual Legacy"; and Krishan Kumar, *The Making of English National Identity* (Cambridge, 2003). None, however, stress sufficiently the interweaving of these concerns, or the theological inflection of his vision of Greater Britain.

Greater Britain was his solution to the multiple challenges ranged against
the foundations of British national destiny. And he relished the opportunity to spread the message: "I should like to be a working apostle of the
doctrine which interests me so much."[5] Seeley blended the impulse to
transform certain aspects of society with a Burkean gradualism and respect for tradition; he welcomed limited change but feared (violent) revolution, and was happy, ultimately, to support and nourish many of the
traditional social and political structures of British life. His thought was
also suffused with civic imperial themes.

In chapter 4 I outlined Seeley's conception of a global state. This chapter explores the general structure of his political thought, relating his
wider historical, moral, and theological commitments to his vision of the
empire. His understanding of the relationship between theology and public life serves as the key to unlocking his political thought, and it is this
topic to which I turn in the next section. This is followed by a discussion
of his "cosmopolitan nationalism." I then examine his views on the deterioration of British political life in the period leading up to the writing of
The Expansion of England; his previously (qualified) optimism gave way
to fears about the stability of the British polity. His interest in Greater
Britain should be located in this context. The penultimate section demonstrates how his focus on the "boundless spaces of Greater Britain" should
be seen in part as a solution to his concern about British political development.[6] I demonstrate how his understanding of the nature of political
change, the constitution, and British culture related to his conception of
the future of the "world-state." Finally, I analyze his views on India, show-
ing how he managed, in typical liberal fashion, to simultaneously advocate political self-determination as an ethical ideal as well as despotism in
Asia. In important respects this mirrored his views on Ireland.

The Love of Humanity: Toward a New "Political Religion"

In a letter written during the 1850s to the distinguished classical scholar
J. B. Mayor, Seeley voiced his concern about the "new orthodoxy" of
Comtean positivism. This creed, he argued, had gained its foothold not
as a consequence of any intrinsic merits, but rather due to the lack of con-
vincing alternatives. Hegel "will simply not do," he declared firmly, and
without substantive argument, but he could not yet provide any substitute. Two decades later he outlined a potential response in his "natural

---

[5] "Sir John Seeley and National Unity," letter quoted by H. F. Wilson, *Cambridge Review*, 16 (1895), 197.
[6] The quotation is from Seeley, *The Expansion of England*, 34.

religion," attempting to draw what he saw as the best features of positivism within the orbit of a more conventional Anglican theology.[7] In Seeley's attempt to reformulate religion—and in particular to re-establish the foundations necessary for a prescriptive ethical code—in terms absorbable by the modern, post-Darwin mind, we witness an instance of Nietzsche's characteristically insightful proclamation: "In England, in response to every little emancipation from theology one has to reassert one's position in a fear-inspiring manner as a moral fanatic."[8]

Seeley followed a trajectory typical of the son of "extreme" evangelicals.[9] Bypassing the early crisis of faith so common among his contemporaries, he glided from a youthful immersion in evangelicalism to a less unforgiving incarnationalism, from a harsh and apocryphal vision of the cosmos to a milder one in which the life of Jesus served as a noble example for human behavior. In particular, Seeley drew inspiration from the "broad church" theologians, A. P. Stanley, F. W. Robertson, and especially Thomas Arnold and F. D. Maurice.[10] The term "broad church" had been coined earlier in the century to encompass, albeit not with great accuracy, those sharing a more liberal theological sensibility in the face of the supernaturalism and biblical literalism that united the otherwise conflicting High (Anglo-Catholic, Tractarian-influenced) and Low (Evangelical) churches.[11] In the background hovered Samuel Taylor Coleridge, whose ideas on the relationship between Church and State influenced the

[7] Seeley to J. B. Mayor, March 2, 185?, Seeley Papers, University of London Library, MS903/1A/1. In this attempt to learn from but surpass Comte, Seeley was not alone among the liberal Anglicans; see also F. D. Maurice, *Social Morality* (London, 1869), 18–19 and Lecture XIX.

[8] Friedrich Nietzsche, *Twilight of the Idols* [1888] in Nietzsche, *Twilight of the Idols, and The Anti-Christ*, ed. Michael Tanner (Harmondsworth, 2003), 80. Although the degree to which Seeley "got rid" of the traditional deity, and the supernatural paraphernalia accompanying it, is far from clear—in *Ecce Homo* (1866) he gestured repeatedly to a belief in the transcendent realm, in *Natural Religion* (1882) his starting point was to disavow such a belief, and in the preface to the 3rd edition (1891) he restated his nontraditional Christianity, therein describing supernaturalism as "accidental" to the religion—this passage illustrates aptly the post-1860 currents of British moral thought in which he swam.

[9] Boyd Hilton, *The Age of Atonement* (Oxford, 1988), 334.

[10] By the late 1850s, in his correspondence with his family, Seeley was demonstrating his admiration for the broad church. See for example, J. R. Seeley to R. B. Seeley, September 29, 185?, Seeley Papers, MS903/2A/2 and J. R. Seeley to Mary Seeley, April 3, 1855, Seeley Papers, MS903/2B/1. See also Seeley, "The Church as a Teacher of Morality" in W. L. Clay (ed.), *Essays in Church Policy* (London, 1868).

[11] [W. J. Conybeare], "Church Parties," *ER*, 98 (1853), 273–342. Although Maurice himself was wary of the "Broad Church" label, preferring "Christian socialist," it was applied to him at the time, and is a common designation today. See Todd E. Jones, *The Broad Church* (Lanham, Md., 2003), ch. 3; Jeremy Morris, *F. D. Maurice and the Crisis of Christian Authority* (Oxford, 2005); and Bernard Reardon, *From Coleridge to Gore* (London, 1971).

broad church theologians, and whose notion of a "clerisy" Seeley also adopted, though, as we shall see, in a modified form.[12] Seeley's latitudinarianism seems to have been reinforced by the time he spent in London, where he mixed in liberal intellectual and political circles, although his religious views were never as radical as they might at first have appeared.[13] Indeed he can be seen as a fairly conventional follower of the broad church theologians, with their focus on the interrelationship between (the usually capitalized) Church and State, their quest to reconcile modernity and tradition and to cultivate the spiritual qualities of the people, and their concomitant desire for securing national unity through the eradication of interdenominational and class strife.[14] Seeley believed that the Church of England was failing in its appointed task of educating the nation morally, of providing a sense of concord and purpose for society.[15] In the last two decades of the century, he began to shift the burden of this task away from traditional religious institutions and onto the shoulders of what he hoped would become a reconfigured historical discipline, a new clerisy. Historians were to act not simply as literary chroniclers of past battles and monarchs, or indeed of the teleological unfolding of liberty, but as apostles of national destiny.

When not regarded as an imperialist propaganda tract, *The Expansion of England* has often been characterized as a case study of the "scientific" historiographical method that Seeley advocated. This was also how Seeley viewed it.[16] But his historiographical method and his understanding of science can only be comprehended adequately if viewed in a wider theological frame. Seeley was trying to combine a belief that the unity of the nation could be grasped systematically in light of its past with the harmonic moral instruction offered by the liberal Anglicans; he sought to animate through historical research the vague abstractions about commu-

[12] See Coleridge, *On the Idea of the Constitution of the Church and State* (London, 1830). The most explicit of Seeley's (published) references to Coleridge can be found in, "Milton's Political Opinions," *Lectures and Essays*, 99. For his vision of the clerisy, see Seeley, "Ethics and Religion," *FR*, 45 (1889), 507–58.

[13] On his time in London during the 1860s, see Wormell, *Sir John Seeley and the Uses of History*, ch. 1. His educational environment was also notably liberal: John Burrow, "The Age of Reform" in David Reynolds (ed.), *Christ's* (London, 2004), 111–43. He was appointed to the Reguis chair in Cambridge in 1869.

[14] For an excellent account of liberal Anglican theories of the state, see Matthew Grimley, *Citizenship, Community, and the Church of England* (Oxford, 2004), ch. 1.

[15] Seeley, *Natural Religion*, 43 and 135–37. See also, "The Church as a Teacher of Morality."

[16] See, for example, Henry Sidgwick, "Editor's Preface" to Seeley, *Introduction to Political Science*, xi. This view is endorsed in J. G. Greenlee, "A 'Succession of Seeleys,'" *JICH*, 4 (1976), 268. In 1880 Seeley wrote, "history belongs to science & not to literature at all." Draft letter to C. E. Maurice, April 8, 1880, Seeley Papers, MS903/1A/2.

nity, history, state, and nation articulated by the theologians. His lifelong obsession with improving the system of national education and his conception of the empire and world politics more generally, were all part of a unified moral-theological vision, a vision that formed the foundations of a "political religion." Propagating such a view was of the greatest importance, for "on religion," he argued, "depends the whole fabric of civilisation, all the future of mankind."[17]

Seeley was once pressed by a friend, the eminent classicist Richard Jebb, as to why he had not followed through on his promise, made in the preface to *Ecce Homo*, that he would write a sequel (*Ecce Deus*) focusing on the divine aspects of Christ. Much to Jebb's surprise, Seeley replied that he had written the promised book—the *Life and Times of Stein*.[18] This curious remark provides us with an insight into the profound relationship that Seeley envisaged between politics, history, and religion. His holistic vision was elaborated most illuminatingly in what he considered his two most important books, *Natural Religion* and *Stein*.[19] The former was an attempt to explore systematically the bases of belief and the purposes of faith in a world in which the naturalistic impulse, the will to science, was omnipresent. The latter was a detailed study of the career and ideas of a man whom Seeley regarded as one of the founding figures of modern Germany. They were conceived and written during the same period and should be viewed as two elements of a single intellectual compound, one the theoretical elaboration of his political theology, the other a case study of some of the most important aspects of this as put into practice by one of his heroes.

Like so many of his contemporaries, Seeley was obsessed with the challenge to reconcile science and religion. In *Natural Religion* he set out to analyze the relationship between modern forms of knowledge acquisition and the realm of religious belief, as manifested both in the individual consciousness and in society. This was an attempt to move beyond, while incorporating the most valuable aspects of, both eighteenth-century natural theology and nineteenth-century positivism. For Seeley there were two distinct but related forms of knowledge, the theoretical and the practical. In relation to the sacred—"in the realm of observing God"—the two corresponded to theology (theoretical) and religion (practical). "By theology the nature of God is ascertained and false views of it eradicated from

---

[17] Seeley, *Natural Religion*, 218.

[18] Caroline Jebb, *The Life and Letters of Sir Richard Claverhouse Jebb* (Cambridge, 1907), 85–86.

[19] *Natural Religion* was first published in serial form in *Macmillan's Magazine* between 1875 and 1878, during the period in which Seeley was researching and writing *Stein*. It was published as a book in 1882, the year during which the lectures on which the *Expansion of England* is based were being delivered.

the understanding; by religion the truths thus obtained are turned over in
the mind and assimilated by the imagination and the feelings." Theology
was concerned ultimately with the "attitude of Nature towards human
beings," where nature was defined as the "uniform laws of the Universe
as known in our experience." These included sociohistorical laws, such
as those governing the formation and growth of political communities.
(This was not to be confused with pantheism, however, for the focus
of veneration was not the concrete expressions of nature as manifested
in diverse and differentiated physical forms but nature considered as a
whole, an irreducible unity.) Theology examined metaethical and metaphysical issues such as the character of virtue, the nature of temptation,
and the role and limits of human conscience. "In one word," he inquired,
"is life worth having, and the Universe a habitable place for one in whom
the sense of duty has been awakened?" Since for Seeley the scientific
analysis of nature was an exploration of the laws of the universe, science
was "in the strictest sense Theology." And since history was an exploration of the laws of social development, it was also, in the "proper
sense," theological.[20]

Religion, on the other hand, was grounded on admiration, on the impulse to, and act of, worship. Whereas theology engaged reason and the
expressly cognitive functions of the human mind, religion was concerned
more with sensitivity, imagination, and empathy; it was as much about
emotion as rationality. Religion was constituted by three elements: "that
worship of visible things which leads to art, that worship of humanity
which leads to all moral disciplines, and principally the Christian, and
that worship of God which is the soul of all philosophy and science." The
third panel of this triptych focused on the worship of God-in-nature as
clarified by the theological disciplines of history, natural science, and philosophy. It was this aspect with which *Natural Religion* (if not natural religion) was concerned primarily. The aesthetic focus of the first panel
pointed toward Seeley's intense love of literature and poetry, and in particular the works, and the sensibility, of the great romantic writers. Like
Maurice, he admired Byron, Wordsworth, and above all Goethe, whom
he regarded as the model of modern cultivation, the human embodiment
of excellence in the simultaneous pursuit of art, science, and philosophy,
and hence as a "religious" thinker of the highest rank.[21] The middle panel

[20] Seeley, *Natural Religion*, 52–53, 66, 68, 56, and 257. Seeley's views can be seen as
part of what David Newsome has labeled the Broad Church understanding of the human
intellect as a tool for "progressive revelation." Newsome, *The Victorian World Picture* (London, 1997), 214–15.

[21] Seeley, *Natural Religion*, 131–32, 96–111; and also his, *Goethe Reviewed After Sixty
Years* (London, 1894). See also, *The Life of Frederick Denison Maurice* (London, 1884), II,
59. Aside from writing widely on literature, Seeley published, anonymously, some (bad) poetry of his own: [Seeley], *David and Samuel* (London, 1869).

of Seeley's triptych clarified his notion of morality: it was his understanding of religion as worship that underpinned his system of ethics. In
discussing Stein the lines of Seeley's own position again come into view:
"As religion without morality would be to him a monstrosity, so he cannot understand any morality without religion."[22]

In *The Methods of Ethics* (1874) Seeley's friend Henry Sidgwick had
delineated three "methods" for reaching ethical judgments: intuitionism
(roughly coeval with commonsense morality); rational egoism (directed
primarily at one's own happiness); and utilitarianism (aimed at universal
happiness). Sidgwick argued that because of the "dualism of practical reason," the inability to rationally decide between utilitarianism and egoism,
divine sanctions offered the ideal guide for ethical action. They would,
"of course, suffice to make it always in everyone's interest to promote universal happiness to the best of his [the individual's] knowledge."[23] Sidgwick, however, lamented his inability to believe fully in this vision, re-
quiring as it did concrete evidence for the existence of God that he was
unable to offer. Seeley dissented on different grounds, and he tendered a
further challenge, more political than philosophical. He was deeply critical of any system of morality derived from supernaturalism, the belief that
human behavior should be regulated by certainty in the eternal pleasures
or punishments of the afterlife. He labeled this form of reasoning the
"legal school in morals."[24] This was not only theologically indefensible,
but led inexorably to political inaction: "To hope even with enthusiastic
conviction for a future life is one thing; to be always brooding over it so
as to despise the present life in comparison with it is another." By the "side
of such a vision," he continued, "everything historical, all the destiny
of states and nations, fades away, and men become quietists if not
monks."[25] A supernatural mode of belief was likely to obstruct or deter
political action.

Rather than subscribing to what he considered this aberration of eigh-

---

[22] Seeley, *Life and Times of Stein*, III, 556.

[23] Sidgwick, *The Methods of Ethics* (London, 1874), 463–64. For the context, see Ross
Harrison, "Utilitarians and Idealists" in Tom Baldwin (ed.), *The Cambridge History of Philosophy, 1870–1945* (Cambridge, 2003), 255–66. John Maynard Keynes later commented
that Sidgwick "never did anything but wonder whether Christianity was true and prove it
wasn't and hope it was." Keynes, letter to Bernard Swithinbank, March 27, 1906 (Keynes
Papers, King's College, Cambridge), quoted in Bart Schultz, *Henry Sidgwick* (Cambridge,
2004), 4.

[24] Seeley, *Natural Religion*, 160 and 166. See also Seeley, *Introduction to Political Science*, 177–78.

[25] Ibid., *Natural Religion*, 254. He later offered another related criticism, suggesting that
it was best for adherents of diverse ethical positions (including utilitarianism and the "cat-
egorical imperative") to cooperate on effecting social and political change, rather than challenging competing fundamental meta-ethical commitments: Seeley, "Ethics and Religion,"
504–505.

teenth-century deism, Seeley suggested that his view of natural religion as the worship of nature (broadly defined) could sustain a system of morality based on the worship of humanity, of humans. People were to teach themselves to be generous and humane to one another and they would be guided in their understanding by the lessons offered by the historical clerisy—although he was never clear what exactly would motivate this benevolence, or what it would entail. Earlier, he had written to Sidgwick that utilitarian ethics were insufficient to guide action, for reason alone was incapable of identifying the "instinct for sympathy" that lay at the root of morality. Nor, he continued, could the "methodological" teachings of the philosophers help to inspire the "one law which is to be obeyed for itself, viz., love."[26] Here Seeley articulated, albeit in a rather different manner, the concern over the sources of motivation that plagued Sidgwick's own account of utilitarianism. He attempted to systematize this position in *Natural Religion*. The religion "that leads to virtue," he wrote, "must be a religion that worships men. It is worshipped under the form of a country, or of ancestors, or of heroes, or great men, or saints, or virgins, or in individual lives, under the form of a friend, or mother, or wife, or any object of admiration; who, once seizing the heart, made all humanity seem sacred, and turned all dealings with men into a religious service."[27] Here we see the direct link between Seeley's views on religion, morality, history, and politics. And the ordering he gives to the objects of worship is indicative, for he places the "country" at the top of his list. This was illustrative of his priorities: the country is the sphere within which the other objects either live or lived, and as such it takes precedence over them; the state subsumes society and all those in it. This simple insight lay at the heart of Seeley's political religion.

The Political Theology of Nationalist Cosmopolitanism

Unsurprisingly, Seeley was very critical of the "modern" secular liberal state, in which religion was pressed into a hermetically sealed private sphere. He viewed political developments in Britain through this prism. The situation was, he argued, an anomaly, for the panorama of human history was painted largely by the brushstrokes of religious ferment; religions, their institutions and patterns of belief, had played a fundamental role in social and political development, indeed in the origins and evolution of the modern state system itself. And the locus of religion in the mod-

[26] Ibid., letter to Sidgwick, July 2, 1867, Sidgwick Papers, Trinity College, Cambridge, Add Ms c95/64–73.
[27] Ibid., *Natural Religion*, 166, 168.

ern world was the nation-state. For Seeley, any human community could be labeled, almost interchangeably, "by the name State or Church." This claim was derived from his view of the Church as an institution constituting, the "atmosphere of thought, feeling and belief that surrounds the State; it is in fact its civilisation made more or less tangible and visible."[28] An ahistorical understanding of the interpenetration of politics and religion, one that failed to grasp this point, was inadequate for the contemporary age. A life without religion was mechanical and largely meaningless.

For Seeley, a momentous phase in modern history began with the completion of the state by the principle of nationality. The most important political development of the nineteenth century, the result of the "Anti-Napoleonic Revolution," was the increasing awareness and power of the "nationality doctrine." In a quasi-Hegelian spirit, the century had seen the emergent self-consciousness of the nation-state. This phenomenon was witnessed first in Spain, where the armies of Napoleon had crushed the institutions of the Spanish state but had then faced the onslaught of the Spanish nation, which after surviving the initial destruction had sought to reclaim its political destiny. When "the state fell to pieces," he wrote admiringly, "the nation held together and proceeded to put forth out of its own vitality a new form of state." It was in this period, so central to Seeley's understanding of history, that "a new idea took possession of the mind of Europe. That idea was not democracy or liberty . . . it was nationality."[29] From that time forward, he proclaimed, the doctrine of nationality began its triumphant march. Seeley's fascination with nationalism had two main intellectual sources: the ideas of the German romantics, especially as instantiated by Stein, and liberal Anglican theology, which through the work of Coleridge was also influenced by the currents of Germanic organic romanticism. Through his interpretation of the development of Stein's thought, Seeley drew inspiration from Fichte's "Addresses to the German Nation" (1807–1808).[30] Fichte had not only stressed the role of national education; he had also promulgated a holistic ideal of national unity and conceived of the state as a moral entity. "Here certainly is heard the tocsin of the anti–Napoleonic Revolution and of all the Nationality Wars that were to follow." In Fichte, Seeley discerned a foreshadowing of his distinction between the nation and the state. "Fichte proclaims the nation not only to be different from the state,

[28] Ibid., 183–85, 200.
[29] See also Seeley, *Life and Times of Stein*, II, 20 and 17; and ibid., "Georgian and Victorian Expansion," *FR*, 48 (1887), 126.
[30] See the extensive discussion in Seeley, *Life and Times of Stein*, II, 29–42; and Fichte, *Addresses to the German Nation*, ed. George A. Kelly (New York, 1968 [1807–1808]).

but to be something far higher and greater." Seeley's nationalism was ultimately a branch of his political religion, and the religiosity of his conception of nationality can be seen in his argument that, in Fichte's hands, the union of past and present in the doctrine of the nation "secures to the actions of man an earthly immortality."[31] It was the quest for the earthly immortality of the Anglo-Saxon race that ultimately shaped Seeley's vision of Greater Britain.

In assessing the political thought of any individual, the exact tracing of influence is often a difficult task. So it is with Seeley, especially in relation to the relative balance between the ideas of the often very different individuals from within the liberal Anglican constellation on whom he drew. I would argue, nevertheless, that Seeley's thought was marked deeply by the ideas of Coleridge, and Coleridge's admirer, F. D. Maurice. He identified Milton, Carlyle, Ruskin, and Coleridge, as "genius politicians," the prophetic seers of British politics, arguing that the key to their powers lay in their tenacious reiteration of one simple idea. For Coleridge, the "one conviction" that ran through his writings was "the hollowness of all hand-to-mouth statesmanship, and the necessity of grounding politics upon universal principles of philosophy and religion."[32] These were both ideas with which Seeley concurred wholeheartedly. Indeed, it is useful to view Seeley's dogged intellectual exertion on behalf of Greater Britain in this light. While he thought that of all the prophets Coleridge was the greatest philosopher, in formulating his conception of the state he drew more on Arnold and Maurice.[33] In *On the Idea of the Constitution of the Church and State* Coleridge had argued that the Church of England should be legally recognized as an intrinsic component of the constitution, as a balance to the great landed and commercial interests of the country; it was an essential but quasi-autonomous element of the political nation. Arnold went further, arguing that church and state were, in a sense "perfectly identical," and, in his *Postscript to Principles of Church Reform* (1833), that the "state in its highest perfection becomes the Church." Maurice, meanwhile, provided an extremely forceful exposition of the ideal of a spiritual nation in which church and state were mutually con-

[31] Seeley, *Life and Times of Stein*, II, 34 and 41.

[32] Ibid., "Milton's Political Opinions," 99.

[33] The claim about Coleridge can be found in Seeley, "Milton's Political Opinions," 98. He once wrote in a letter to his father that he was "more of an Arnoldite than a Mauriceite": Seeley to R. B. Seeley, n.d 185?, Seeley Papers, MS903/2A/2. The respectful distance was reciprocal, as Maurice wrote of *Ecce Homo*, which he admired greatly (Maurice to A. Macmillan, January 2, 1886, Seeley Papers, MS903/3A/1). Despite these proclamations, I would argue that while Seeley might have shared more theological ground with Arnold (at least in the 1850s), his political thought appears to owe considerably more to Maurice, although this might simply be because Maurice lived longer and thus wrote on questions that were also pressing to Seeley.

stitutive.[34] Seeley's conception of nationality, and his vision of Greater Britain, wove together the threads of Fichte's romantic nationalism and liberal Anglican theology. And it was frequently elaborated in a civic imperialist vocabulary.

Seeley's position can be characterized as "cosmopolitan nationalist." In his case—and indeed in the early and mid-Victorian era more broadly—this is not a paradoxical formulation, for his conception of international (and specifically European) politics was anchored in the idea of the ultimate, albeit only vaguely articulated, unity of humankind. The future, he wrote, "will witness national religions flourishing inside a grand universal religion."[35] And it was the idea of love, expressed through the worship of humans, and grounded in a nonexclusive, nonparochial, attachment to national-political communities that underpinned this complex (and probably unstable) admixture. For Seeley, there were two Churches: the universal church, accommodating all the species, believers and non-believers alike, and the national churches as institutionalized in the form of the modern state. The latter took priority, as the highest embodiment of human communal life, but it was embedded in the wider domain of the former. This neat binary was upset by Seeley's constant reference to a third (less clearly theorized) sphere; between the universal and the national he interposed an intermediary plane, namely Western Christendom, which he regarded as a form of transnational civilisation.[36] He argued, moreover, that the states of Europe constituted a "society" bound to a certain extent by common values and a common culture. "In the main," he continued, "I hold that it is healthy for a nation to live in society. Like an individual a nation should study its behaviour to its fellows, and for this purpose it should listen respectfully and anxiously to their opinion." In the *Introduction to Political Science* he asserted confidently that the "European brotherhood of nation-states" was responsible for the glories of modern civilization.[37] He also insisted that the United States, dynamic

---

[34] Arnold, "The Church and the State" [1839] and "National Church Establishments" [1840] in *The Miscellaneous Works of Thomas Arnold* [ed. Arthur P. Stanley] (London, 1845), 466–75 and 486–92; and Arnold, *Postscript to Principles of Church Reform* (London, 1833), 19. See also Maurice, *The Kingdom of Christ* (London, 1838); and Maurice, *Social Morality*.

[35] Seeley, *Natural Religion*, 207. On the universalism of the Church, see also Seeley, letter to Sidgwick, May 15, 1866, Sidgwick Papers. For the wider Victorian context, see Georgios Varouxakis, "'Patriotism,' 'Cosmopolitanism' and 'Humanity' in Victorian Political Thought," *EJPT*, 5 (2006), 100–18; and Tricia Lootens, "Victorian Poetry and Patriotism" in Joseph Bristow (ed.), *The Cambridge Companion to Victorian Poetry* (Cambridge, 2000), 255–80.

[36] See especially, Seeley, "The United States of Europe."

[37] Ibid., *Introduction to Political Science*, 88; and Seeley, "Our Insular Ignorance," 869. See also the comments in *The Expansion of England*, 225.

offspring of the Old World, should be included in this picture. Seeley thus adumbrated a multilayered and hierarchically arranged conception of global order, but one underwritten by a universal religious community.

Despite his constant avowal of the glories of the nation, Seeley was not an uncritical proponent of nationalism. He believed that the pure ideal that he so admired had often been corrupted, and that in practice it was usually "too narrow and provincial."[38] Like many liberal nationalists of our own time, Seeley's view of the positive characteristics of nationalism, as well as his belief that it could be controlled and kept within the limits he prescribed, displayed much naivete. He worried about the increasing militarization of Europe, fearing the great armies eyeing each other suspiciously from one end of the continent to the other.[39] He was wary of the dangers of revolution, and scathing of the Jacobite descent into terror. It was the association of the French Revolution with the thought of the *philosophes* that led Maurice to prefer the use of the term "humanity" to the otherwise equally appropriate "cosmopolitan" when outlining his own vision.[40] We can speculate—given his admiration for Maurice, his hatred of Revolutionary France, and the actual theological vocabulary that he adopted—that Seeley's view was similar. In *Ecce Homo* he was critical of "universal patriotism," which, without the instantiation of the state, was actually a form of "Jacobinism."[41] And in *Stein* he had sided with his hero's critique of the purportedly disembodied cosmopolitanism of Goethe and Herder, while, drawing on Coleridge, he defended instead the virtues of patriotism.[42] As we can see from an earlier essay, however, his use of the term was qualified,

> The abuse of patriotism is not to be cured by destroying patriotism itself; but patriotism is to be strengthened by being purified, by being deprived of its exclusiveness, and ultimateness. The Christian unity of mankind is to be taught as a final lesson, which will be easiest learnt, or rather will only be learnt, by those who have already realised the unity of the state.[43]

A nonexclusive form of patriotism, implausible as that may be, was for Seeley an ideal worth pursuing, and one demanded by his political reli-

---

[38] Ibid., *Natural Religion*, 200.

[39] Seeley, "The Eighty-Eights," *Good Words* (1888), 380.

[40] A point made explicit in Maurice, *Social Morality*, 19.

[41] Seeley, *Ecce Homo*, 121. He was here critical of the purported abstract "universal man" of Jacobinism, preferring to focus attention on individuals embedded in, and partly constituted by, their communities. See also the discussion in Shannon, "John Robert Seeley and the Idea of a National Church," 245–46; and Maurice, *Social Morality*, 122–23.

[42] Seeley, *Life and Times of Stein*, II, 384–88.

[43] Seeley, "The Church as a Teacher of Morality," 277. Coleridge had counterposed his conception of the national church (focusing on the Church of England in particular) with the universal church of Christ, which knew no legal or political borders. The two could coexist in the same space, but should not be confused.

gion. The nation was not an intolerant political order, the antithesis of wide human sympathies, it was instead an essential component of such sympathies. Nationalism was a constitutive element of his idiosyncratic cosmopolitanism. And in his formulation of the argument, he followed, once again, the broad church ideologues. Maurice had, after all, argued in a series of lectures delivered in Cambridge that "Christ's Kingdom of Peace" was "a Kingdom for all *nations*. Unless there are Nations, distinct Nations, this Kingdom loses its character; it becomes a world Empire." And world empires were associated with despotism and the eradication of national distinctions—"I have endeavored to shew [*sic*] you how much mischief has proceeded from every effort to constitute a Universal divine Society which shall swallow up . . . distinctions into itself."[44] It is little wonder that Seeley was so scathing about Napoleon's attempt to revive the ideal of a universal monarchy; or that he was so keen to avoid the term "empire" in relation to Greater Britain, preferring, as we saw in chapter 4, to call it a "world state." Empire, he wrote, "seems too military and despotic to suit the relation of mother-country to colonies," while imperialism connoted despotic governance, the provenance of both the hated Napoleon, and, in the annals of English history, the iron rule of Cromwell.[45] While he argued that despotism was not to be condemned automatically—that in certain circumstances, such as when a state was facing great external pressure or a war of survival, it could be justified—he remained very critical of its adoption in the "civilized" states of the modern Western world. India, as we shall see, was another matter.[46]

Seeley's cosmopolitanism was heavily circumscribed, as ultimately was that of Kant, the most philosophically astute enlightenment proponent of the old stoic philosophy.[47] For while Seeley's "purpose" was, like that of the great philosopher, to seek an ideal of national coexistence within a wider framework of progressive humanity, it simultaneously helped to defend, through its emphasis on the superiority of the Europeans, the ex-

[44] Maurice, *Social Morality*, 209 and 481. Italics in original.

[45] Seeley, *The Expansion of England*, 37. On Cromwell, see Seeley, *Introduction to Political Science*, 251; and on Napoleon, *A Short History of Napoleon the First* (London, 1886).

[46] Liberty, he wrote, "will appear to be a good or a bad thing according to circumstances": *Introduction to Political Science*, 127. For a general discussion of liberty, see Seeley, *Introduction to Political Science*, Part II, Lectures V and VI, and also, *The Expansion of England*, 237–38. The reason he thought the loss of liberty dangerous in modern Europe was, firstly, the lack of the relevant political conditions (especially external pressure), and, secondly, the fact that although despotism was sometimes necessary, it often lingered well beyond the time when it was required.

[47] See here, Immanuel Kant, "Idea for A Universal History with a Cosmopolitan Purpose" [1784] in Kant, *Political Writings*, ed. Hans Reiss (Cambridge, 1990), 41–54. Cf. James Tully, "The Kantian Idea of Europe" in Anthony Pagden (ed.), *The Idea of Europe* (Cambridge, 2002), 331–58.

isting power structures of international politics and the ethos of global hierarchy.

THE DARKENING OF AN ENGLISH MIND

During the 1870s and 1880s Seeley's interpretation of the world of "practical politics" became increasingly detached from his idealized vision of a global religious polity embracing the benign coexistence of diverse national churches. His interpretation of British politics, and of the relationship between Britain and the rest of the world, paralleled that of many liberals in the late Victorian age. In the 1860s and early 1870s he struck a note of confidence about the future. In 1870, for example, he appeared optimistic about the repercussions of democracy, suggesting that the English variant was but a "tame domestic animal" compared with the wilder continental beasts, and he declared that socialism had not made "much progress among us." Yet in 1881 Seeley wrote to his sister that, "[w]e are nearer to a Revolution than we have been since before I was born." "Radicalism," he fretted, "is triumphant everywhere."[48] He was by then considerably more nervous about the prospect of democracy, warning that the British were sleepwalking into a new era of mass politics, unprepared, unaware even, of the scope of the changes under way. Increasingly critical of what he saw around him, he had become, he remarked, "a great sceptic about the current political system." Seeley brooded on the condition of the British nation. It was badly educated and poorly led, and with the specter of democracy looming, it was about to embark on an unprecedented political transformation, heralding the possibility of further disunity, the darkest nightmare of a broad churchman. While he remained supportive of the need for franchise extension, Seeley thought that the country was inadequately prepared for the consequences. "The moment is very critical when such a nation as this enters for the first time on the path of speculative politics."[49]

The explanation for this lay partly in the deficient character of the people. The idea of individual and national character was a central explanatory and normative measure in Victorian political thought. It was explanatory in that it was invoked to demonstrate how nations and individuals developed over time, why some prospered and others did not, and why there existed hierarchies of both. It was normative in that par-

[48] Seeley, "The English Revolution of the Nineteenth Century," I, *MM*, 22 (1870), 251 and 246; and J. R. Seeley to Bessie Seeley, April 9, 1881, Seeley papers, MS903/2B/1.

[49] Seeley, "The Impartial Study of Politics," *CR*, 54 (1888), 59; and Seeley, "Political Somnambulism," *MM*, 43 (1880), 31; on the important role of Irish Home Rule in this switch, see Seeley, letter to Oscar Browning, April 6, 188[?], Browning Papers, Modern Archive Centre, King's College, Cambridge, OB/1/1455A.

ticular types of character were held up as exemplars, while others were to be scorned. Indeed, for many Victorian thinkers, their self-belief inflated by the arrogance of empire, the greatness of the national character explained the manifold successes of the country and its dominance not only over the "lesser races" but also over its European neighbors. At times Seeley expressed caution about the idea of character: "no explanation is so obvious, or suggests itself so easily. No explanation is so vague, cheap, and so difficult to verify."[50] But at other junctures it is clear that the idea was central to his thought. In 1889, for example, he bemoaned the "unprecedented perplexity and uncertainty" that was clouding the vision of his compatriots, and he warned that Britain was stumbling through a "moment of ethical famine." The people lacked the strength and the unity to act effectively in a world in rapid transition. "We have everything except decided views and steadfast purpose—everything in short except character! We have emotions, sentiment, thought, knowledge in abundance, only not character! And so to foreigners this nation seems degenerate—a nation in decay."[51]

Underpinning Seeley's fear about the deleterious effects of the modern educational system was the belief that teaching should be concerned with developing the "mind and character" of the people.[52] The building of character and the concurrent shaping of mind through a system of national education—a schooling in the glories of the nation—was an essential task of Seeley's historical clerisy. He argued that the people, and especially the working classes, were in many ways uncivilized, and he was scornful, in an Arnoldian vein, about their "philistinism." Like many of his peers, he feared the dilution of culture in a democratic age, "when the literary Emperors and Prime Ministers are chosen by universal suffrage." Cultivation of the (national) mind was essential in order to defeat the twin vices of secularism and materialism, that purely personal and selfish "Lower Life" characteristic of the modern world.[53] This was a longstanding liberal Anglican concern. Coleridge, in one of his *Lay Sermons* (1817), had spoken of the "need for a learned and philosophic public" to counteract the socially and morally dissolvent influence of the political economists and the inculcation of the detested commercial spirit.[54] This

---

[50] Seeley, *Introduction to Political Science*, 134.

[51] Ibid., "Ethics and Religion," 503 and 508. The question of character was also central to his discussions of India (*The Expansion of England*, 203, 242, and 276) and the United States (*The Expansion of England*, 156). See also Seeley, "Our Insular Ignorance," 869; and Maurice, *The Kingdom of Christ*, I, xxiii.

[52] Seeley, "Our Insular Ignorance," 862; and ibid., "Ethics and Religion."

[53] Ibid., *Natural Religion*, 91 and 107, and Part II.

[54] Coleridge, "A Lay Sermon" [1817] in *The Collected Works of Samuel Taylor Coleridge* (Princeton, 1972), VI, 170. As Reba Soffer has noted, moreover, there are continuities between Seeley's views on the degradations of materialism and the views of his father on the

was, after all, one of the reasons why the Sage of Hampstead argued that a clerisy detached from the great commercial and landed interests of society was indispensable. Seeley routinely castigated "money-worship," viewing it as a "morbid industry" defined by "insensibility to the highest interests and enjoyments."[55] Materialism was one of the major failings of the British character, especially as it precluded the pursuit of the "Higher Life," the animating principle of which was religion. This had not always been so, and at times Seeley waxed nostalgic, looking back to the days when his countrymen were more independent and rugged. Here we witness the intersection of liberal Anglican and civic humanist concerns—an intersection that also shaped many aspects of Coleridge's thought. Seeley's contemporaries, however, had developed for themselves a "kind of Deuteronomic religion" that provided them with great comfort, rendering their selfish behavior morally defensible. This perverse religion teaches us, he wrote, that "because we are honest and peaceable and industrious, therefore our Jehovah gives us wealth in abundance, and our exports and imports swell and our debt diminishes and our emigrants people half the globe." It was a mistake to fall under such a spell, for it represented the residue of a truly "primitive" creed.[56] An internal civilizing mission was a necessity.

The British educational system (and the Church) was to blame for the debasement of culture, for the divorce of the majority of the population from their glorious national heritage. "That bareness in ideas, that contempt for principles, that Philistinism which we hardly deny to be an English characteristic, was not always so," he lamented.[57] This was not simply the complaint of a cultural elitist (although it was that also), for as we have seen, Seeley's conception of culture was ultimately theological, and it underlay his notion of the "higher" life of the nation. To be uneducated was to lack the refinement and knowledge necessary to imagine oneself as part of a community; it was to be deficient in the necessary prerequisites of political agency. The "man" lacking a decent awareness of national literatures, suggested Seeley, "can have no link whatever with the past, he can have no citizenship, no country."[58] For Seeley, then, the lack of a proper education, including a wide schooling in English literature and history, as well as in the centrality of empire, was an important *political* problem, essential to confront.

Although this problem beset all classes, it affected the workers in par-

---

topic. Soffer, "History and Religion," 135–37. On Coleridge's thought, see Philip Connell, *Romanticism, Economics, and the Question of "Culture"* (Oxford, 1999).

[55] Seeley, "The Church as a Teacher of Morality," 270.

[56] Ibid., *Natural Religion*, 133.

[57] Ibid., "Liberal Education in Universities" [1867], *Lectures and Essays*, 215.

[58] Ibid., "English in Schools," *Lectures and Essays*, 238.

ticular for the majority of them were "childishly ignorant of larger political questions."[59] Their ignorance endangered the country: as well as lacking adequate national consciousness, they were still beholden to superstitions, including the belief in the possibility of a political "utopia," such as that promised by socialists. This was a potential harbinger of revolution. "In England the ideas of the multitude are perilously divergent from those of the thinking class."[60] Now, more than ever, it was essential for historians to fulfill their destiny as shapers of the national mind and as spiritual healers of the body politic. For Seeley, the ideal nation-state needed to strike a fine balance between democracy and aristocracy (understood in its classical sense as rule by the most suitably qualified).[61] Progress was fragile and in need of constant sustenance and supervision. This was a fairly common sentiment, expressed most famously in John Stuart Mill's anguished discussion of the need to balance expertise and inclusion in the *Considerations on Representative Government* (1861). For Seeley, the lack of national bonds of unity led to alienation between the individual and the state, and also between the different classes. Unrest loomed large in his mind.

The year 1887 was, declared Seeley, a time of "of depression, confusion, and anxiety."[62] Despite this, and many similar proclamations, Seeley was not an abject pessimist, and his views about the future were somewhat ambiguous. While at times he wrote in the vein of a doom-laden prophet, a latterday Carlyle, he also preserved a large measure of optimism. Increasingly apprehensive about the political life of the "mother country," he was also keen to stress that things had improved markedly since the first few decades of the century. And as he became ever more concerned about the international situation—warning of the "international danger, the gigantic discords, the gigantic armies!"—so he was also keen to stress the increasing strength and unity of the colonial empire. The continued expansion of England, and its consolidation since the troubled midcentury years, represented the "brightest side" of the Victorian age, and it gave him great hope for the future.[63] In Greater Britain lay a potential resolution to his fears about both the "mother country" and the wider world.

---

[59] Seeley, "Political Somnambulism," 42.

[60] Ibid., "The Political Education of the Working Classes," 145; and ibid., *Natural Religion*, 208.

[61] Ibid., *Introduction to Political Science*, 357. For his extended discussion on the nature of aristocracy, see 321–31.

[62] Ibid., "Georgian and Victorian Expansion," 124.

[63] Ibid., "The Eighty-Eights," 380; and ibid., "Georgian and Victorian Expansion," 127.

On the Necessity of Imperial Federation

In 1894 Seeley was knighted at the instigation of Lord Rosebery, the prime
minister and sometime president of the IFL. As Rosebury wrote to Seeley,
the award was not merely a testimony to "my admiration for yourself and
your work, but to my staunch adherence to the principles of empire that
you have so eloquently set forth."[64] In one sense, Seeley's reputation as
an ardent imperialist is rather ironic. He had not always been concerned
with empire; in fact the interest came to him quite late. In some of his earlier writings (as will be explored in the next section), he sketched a position on the fate of India, yet he failed therein to engage in any substantive
sense with the settler colonies. It has even been suggested that during the
early to mid-1860s he could be classified, alongside Goldwin Smith, as a
"separatist."[65] This was all to change, however, and by the early 1880s
he was preparing the lectures that were published as *The Expansion of
England*. An instant best seller, the book propelled him to the center of
debate.[66] Sensitive to the political and intellectual currents percolating
around him, Seeley's interest in the empire increased as his view of the
condition of British politics darkened.

The main argument of *The Expansion of England*—and of much of
Seeley's subsequent writing—was that the most important development
of modern British history was the remarkable global extension of the empire. The most significant period in this story had been victory over France
in the second "hundred years war" during the long eighteenth century.[67]
Both the public and the historians whose role it was to shape the popular
mind had missed the importance, and the ultimate meaning, of these
events. This monumental oversight was the result of an "insular" com-
prehension of British history, a form of parochial whiggery that focused
on the history of parliamentary debate—"tongue-fence"—and the post-
1688 evolution of liberty. Macaulay, above all, embodied this erroneous

[64] Rosebery to Seeley, March 5, 1894, Seeley Papers, MS903/1B/14.

[65] Worsley, "Sir John Robert Seeley and His Intellectual Legacy," 131; Wormell, *Sir John
Seeley and the Uses of History*, 163. Such a view is confirmed partially by Seeley, "The British
Race," [1872] *Education I* 4, (1881), 309–28, and also by a lecture on "The British Em-
pire" reproduced in the *Bradford Observer*, March 22, 1872. Worsley (148), following
Oscar Browning, suggests that Seeley only started working on the empire in 1879.

[66] For the impressive sales figures of the *Expansion*, see David Worsley, "Sir John Robert
Seeley and His Intellectual Legacy," 26; and also the general comments in John Gross, "Editor's Introduction" to Seeley, *The Expansion of England* (Chicago, 1971), xii–xiii. The
book remained in print until 1956, the year of the Suez fiasco.

[67] Seeley, *The Expansion of England*, 26, and Lecture II; and also, Seeley, "Georgian and
Victorian Expansion."

approach.[68] This was not only a historiographical critique, but (by definition) a political one also, for in losing sight of the importance of Greater
Britain, the people and the historians had forgotten the foundations as
well as the purpose of unity, and the colonies had nearly separated as a
result. The midcentury years had, as a consequence, seen the emergence
of a dangerous "system of indifference" that nearly led to a repeat of the
American fiasco: "We began to provoke and suggest secession."[69] Although things had changed since that time—in no small part, he might
have added, due to the efforts of the imperial federalists—it was still necessary to reconnect the people to their inheritance, and to their providential role.

Although the "system of indifference" had been successfully challenged, Seeley cautioned that much more work needed to be done. The
people had still not fundamentally modified their "imagination" or "ways
of thinking" about the empire; they understood it still as entirely separate
from the homeland, as fragments of foreign land scattered over the distant reaches of the planet. The full glory of Greater Britain "eminently
needs to be brought home to our imaginations." Despite the existence of
the necessary material foundations, "[w]e have not really then as yet a
Greater Britain."[70] It was therefore imperative to instruct the public mind
about the importance of the global nation-state. After all, as he had written in a different context, "the true moment of revolution is not so much
that in which the new legislation takes place as that in which the conviction becomes universal that a change must come." And so for Seeley education and political mobilization were interwoven, and in particular he
emphasized the increasing influence of public opinion—"what a power
has public opinion become"[71]—in shaping British politics. Political consciousness preceded legislative action; public opinion initiated parliamentary change. But public opinion needed to be organized and directed
in order to exert significant influence. The conditions for this appeared to
exist already, he argued, for through the agency of the many and varied
pressure groups established to shape opinion, great political changes had
transpired during the century. One of the most important forces guiding
the "English Revolution of the Nineteenth Century," in fact one of the

[68] Ibid., *Introduction to Political Science*, 236, 253, and 385; and Seeley, *The Growth of
British Policy* (Cambridge, 1895), 1–2. Seeley later upset the young G. M. Trevelyan by castigating his great uncle as a "charlatan." David Cannadine, *G. M. Trevelyan* (London,
1992), 27.

[69] Seeley, "Introduction," to *Her Majesty's Colonies* (London, 1886), xv.

[70] Ibid., "Introduction," vii; and ibid., *The Expansion of England*, 8 and 61.

[71] Ibid., "The English Revolution in the Nineteenth Century," Part I, 241, and Part II,
353. See also the comments on public opinion (in regard to India) in *The Expansion of England*, 190, and the discussion in chapter 5.

main reasons for the ending of the pervasive monopolies of the ancien régime, was the influence of the assorted "Leagues" that had demanded the repeal of the Corn Laws, and extensive parliamentary and religious reform. "These Leagues may be considered as a kind of occasional system of government set up for a particular purpose beside the permanent government of the country." It is in the context of his views on the efficacy of the "occasional systems of government" that Seeley's support for, and vision of, the IFL should be understood.[72] The power of political mobilization needed to be harnessed and directed toward the ends of national unity.

An important, and underappreciated, aspect of Seeley's critique of insular constitutionalism can be discerned in his outline of a theory of political development. For Seeley stagnation marked political death.[73] History did not, and could not be seen to, stand still: "It is impossible that the history of any state can be interesting unless it exhibits some sort of development. Political life that is uniform has no history, however prosperous it might be." Being "stationary," associated habitually with "Asiatic" modes of political order, was a characteristic liberal fear during this period.[74] Equally averse to violent revolution, and drawing on fashionable biological metaphors, Seeley suggested that political "organisms" demonstrated their health in perpetual change, in their active response to both internal and external pressures. "Surely we moderns do not believe much in cataclysms. Development is our word. The present grows out of the past."[75] In a revealing passage analyzing the development of the church, he argued that an "institution is healthy in proportion to its independence of its own past, to the confident freedom with which it alters itself to meet new conditions." Later, in the *Introduction to Political Science*, he wrote of the state that the "development of its institutions [were] the result of the effort which organisms make to adapt themselves to their environment."[76] To remain healthy, therefore, institutions needed to be

[72] Ibid., "The English Revolution of the Nineteenth Century," II, 353. For his support for the IFL, see ibid., "The Journal of the League," *IF*, 1/1 (1886), 4; ibid., "The Object to Be Gained by Imperial Federation," *IF*, 1/6 (1886), 206; and his Speech to the Imperial Federation League in Cambridge, May 29, 1891, reprinted in "Professor Seeley at Cambridge," *IF*, 6/6 (1891), 176.

[73] Ibid., *Natural Religion*, 61. See also ibid., "Roman Imperialism" [1869], II, in *Lectures and Essays*, 45.

[74] Ibid., *The Expansion of England*, 117. For Seeley's views on Asia, see "Roman Imperialism," III, 66–68; and, *Natural Religion*, 61. For examples of this position, see Matthew Arnold, "Democracy," 10 and 21; and, in reference to China, John Stuart Mill, *On Liberty* [1859], CW, XVIII, 273. On the influence of ideas about stagnation, see Stefan Collini, *Public Moralists* (Oxford, 1991), 108 and 274.

[75] Seeley, "Ethics and Religion," 514.

[76] Ibid., *Natural Religion*, 217; and ibid., *Introduction to Political Science*, 340.

ever adaptable, fitting comfortably into the evolving political environment in which they were embedded. Failure in this delicate process of adjustment and calibration would result in inexorable degeneration. Understanding this dynamic "environmentalist" conception of politics sheds light on the reason why Seeley considered imperial federation a necessity and also on his belief that it could be acheived, that it was not a utopian fantasy. The shifting—and increasingly threatening—geopolitical situation, combined with the febrile condition of the British polity, provided both the internal and external stimuli for change, and this in turn demanded constitutional revision and the realization of the imperatives of Greater Britain. To stand still, frozen, would be to court disaster. Once again, we witness Seeley attempting to divine the lessons of time.

Ultimately, then, Seeley focused on the necessity of shifting public consciousness, and he hoped that this could be initiated and then steered through the agency of the IFL, the latest in a long and successful line of pressure groups that had acted as the motor of the nineteenth-century "English Revolution." It was one more aspect of his notion of the clerisy, the sentinel of British political morality. It was necessary, first, to awaken the public to the dangers that confronted the empire, both from within and without, and, following this shift in political imagination, it was crucial to convince the people that the only adequate solution to the problems facing the country, and the world itself, was to make concrete the potential contained in Greater Britain. This was a monumental task; and it is one that Seeley, in his self-appointed role as apostle-historian, took upon himself with relish.

THE AMBIGUITIES OF UNITY: INDIA AND IRELAND

Viewing Greater Britain as a largely homogeneous "world-state" presented an obvious problem: what role should the rest of the empire play? For Seeley, as for many other late Victorian colonial unionists, Greater Britain was an imagined political community that failed to encompass many of the inhabitants of the existing British empire. One of the most noticeable things about Seeley's political writings, published at the very pinnacle of the European drive to carve up the world, was that he barely mentioned Africa. It did not even merit a brief discussion in his Rede Lecture on "Georgian and Victorian Expansion" (1887), where he declared that the greatest achievement of the Victorian age was the extension and consolidation of the empire. India, on the other hand, was a frequent point of reference throughout his writings.

Part II of *The Expansion of England* is dedicated to an analysis of the past, present, and future status of British rule in India. Seeley was far more ambiguous about the benefits of the British mission in South Asia than he was about Greater Britain. The two zones were simply not comparable. While Greater Britain was populated by transplanted British subjects bound loyally to the mother country, the Indians constituted an entirely separate category of political development. They lay well outside the scope of the English state. Drawing on the findings of contemporary philology, he argued that the Indians were an Aryan race, but that this was where the similarity with Europe ended. They were great once, but then they had fallen by the wayside of history. "The country has achieved nothing in modern times."[77] India was now static, displaying the unmistakable symptoms of a diseased body politic, deprived of the dynamism and "vigor" that Seeley considered so essential for a healthy political "organism."

In the *Introduction to Political Science* Seeley divided states into two broad classes, the organic and the inorganic, and while the book was mainly dedicated to classifying the varieties of organic states, he occasionally drew comparisons between the two types. Where organic states were generally vibrant and capable of progress, inorganic states were inert. They were polities that failed to meet the criteria of statehood (as explored in chapter 4), owing any real unity that they displayed to the interference of outside powers. They were largely the products of invasion and despotism. The inorganic state, he argued, "is the result of conquest, but has a similar appearance to the organic state, because it adopts and imitates the organisation of it." They were, as such, most accurately labeled "quasi states," the two defining features of which were low vitality and vast extent. Again with Seeley we find ambiguity on a key point. Given both his definitional discussion and his arguments in *The Expansion of England*, India could easily be regarded as an example—perhaps the prime example—of an inorganic state. It was, as he asserted repeatedly, composed of multiple peoples, it was immense, it lacked political consciousness, and it had been subjected to invasions and subjugation for centuries. It had never been "a conscious political whole" and a "homogeneous community does not exist there, out of which the State properly so called arises."[78] Yet Seeley appeared reticent to characterize it as an in-

---

[77] Ibid., *The Expansion of England*, 242 and 243. He here (242n) cites, for example, Max Müller's, *India, What Can It Teach Us?* (Oxford, 1883). Müller was a friend of Goldwin Smith's, and he also influenced his thinking on India (on which, see chapter 7). For the general context, see Tony Ballantyne, *Orientalism and Race* (Basingstoke, 2001).

[78] Seeley, *The Expansion of England*, 185–86, 202, and 204. This is why only a localized "village-patriotism" could be found (206). Henry Maine's *Village-Communities in the East and West* (London, 1871) was especially important for popularizing this type of argument. For context, see John Burrow, "The Village Community and the Uses of History" in Neil Mckendrick (ed.), *Historical Perspectives* (London, 1974), 255–85.

organic state. This is probably related to his harsh criticisms of the aggressive polities that fabricated such states, where "everything is founded on violence and conquest," and a grim despotism was the norm.[79] He did not want to associate the British with such horrors. This is also the most likely explanation for his determination to prove that the English had never actually "conquered" India in the first place. To conquer a country, Seeley argued, is to presuppose that it was a unified entity in the first place, and since India had "no sense whatever of nationality" there had been "no India" to defeat. As a result, the actions of the early British traders and later the East India Company, though perhaps disreputable, could not be classified as following from conquest. Rather, the spread of the British was due to the fortuitous circumstance of an "internal revolution."[80] It was as if they were sucked into a political vacuum, and both for their own good and that of the Indians, took control and brought stability and order.

Seeley saw India as an artificial country populated by a mix of races and religious creeds, devoid of the necessary and sufficient conditions of unity. It was thus disqualified from the sacred label "nation," and as a result the "fundamental postulate cannot be granted, upon which the whole political ethics of the West depend."[81] Self-determination meant nothing in such situations, for the "love of independence presupposes political consciousness," and the name India, he argued, "ought not to be classed with such names as England or France, which correspond to nationalities, but rather with such as Europe, marking a group of nationalities which have chanced to obtain a common name owing to some physical separation." As such, all the liberal maxims that Seeley applied to the states of Europe and North America were irrelevant. This was, as we shall see in the next chapter, exactly the type of argument employed by Goldwin Smith. If there was any unity to be divined, it had only trailed in the wake of British rule, for "a condition of anarchy seems almost to have been chronic in India since Mahmoud." On the whole, he concluded, "it may be said that India has never really been united so as to form one state except under the British" and even then, this was only really complete under the governorship of Lord Dalhousie in the mid-nineteenth century. This was not to suggest that India would remain forever in a servile position, for "Brahmanism" presented the "germ" of a potential nationality movement for the future. Seeley, a man with no direct experience of or knowledge about Indian culture or political life, could discern no signs of it at

[79] Seeley, *Introduction to Political Science*, 73–74, 76, 367–68, and 168.

[80] Ibid., *The Expansion of England*, 203, 207–208, and 228.

[81] Ibid., *The Expansion of England*, 205. While agreeing that India was not one country, Dilke nevertheless criticized Seeley's views. Dilke, *Problems of Greater Britain* (London, 1890), II, 94–95 and 98–99.

the time.[82] Two years after *The Expansion of England* was published the Indian National Congress was formed.

Seeley's views on Ireland exhibit a family resemblance to his understanding of India. Underpinning his assessment of the Irish question was his negative portrayal of Catholicism, yet another trait that he shared with Smith. The adherents of liberal Anglicanism were generally distrustful of Catholicism, perceiving it to stand for all that they were opposed to in religious life, most notably dogmatic and exclusive adherence to doctrine. Seeley regarded Catholicism as the least developed of the Christian denominations; it was, he suggested, bound by rigidity and prone to undermine the possibility of good government.[83] The mystical superstitions of the Indians and the feudal superstitions of the priests could be seen in a similar light, as obscuring the horizon of progress. In was in reference to nationality that Seeley was at his most explicit in linking the two countries. Neither was part of the British nation. And as with India, Seeley argued that the way in which the British had behaved toward the Irish was open to criticism.[84] The solution to the Irish question was not, however, to advocate separation, as a consistent liberal nationalism might seem to require, and nor was it to follow Gladstone down the rocky path to Home Rule. Seeley was, after all, a "very strong unionist," and he was highly critical of any plans that involved the devolution of power to Ireland, let alone emancipation. In a letter to his wife written in 1887, he was keen to talk about the continuing Home Rule tumult: "The public struggle goes pretty well. *The Times* is really tackling Parnell with some vigour."[85] Such vigor, Seeley would have thought, was energy well spent. Concerned with trying to improve relations between the English and the Irish, he believed that the ideal solution lay in the trends that had fermented and sustained the nineteenth-century "English Revolution," namely the ending of monopolies, which would include such practices as the closed labor market in the industrialized North.[86] In 1870 at least, he thought that this course of action might lead to a more just relationship. But his hopes, and his optimism, were soon dashed, and by 1885 he was writing that the Irish were "more hopelessly alienated than ever."[87] Within the confines of his political imagination, no solution appeared to be forthcoming. This was all the more reason to focus on a perceived British success story, to find in

[82] Seeley, *The Expansion of England*, 228, 221, 198, 224, 226–7.
[83] Ibid., *Natural Religion*, 168–69; and also, ibid., "The English Revolution of the Nineteenth Century," Part II, 450.
[84] Ibid., "The English Revolution of the Nineteenth Century," II, 446.
[85] Marquis of Lorne, "Report of the Proceedings," 58; and Seeley, letter to Mary Seeley, April 22 1887, Seeley Papers, MS903/2A/1. See also Harvie, *Lights of Liberalism*, 225–26.
[86] Seeley, "The English Revolution of the Nineteenth Century," II, 446–48.
[87] Ibid., "Our Insular Ignorance," *NC*, 18 (1885), 862.

Greater Britain a distraction from the more obviously problematic situation in Ireland.

While Seeley, like numerous other Victorian liberals, was critical of many facets of the history of British expansion, noting, for example, the "unjustifiable means" by which the early imperial pioneers acquired power, he also added the equally familiar qualifier that the behavior of the British was "not as bad as many others." And he stressed that such "crimes" as had been committed, "have been almost universal in colonisation."[88] He here employed what Cheryl Welch, in a discussion of de Tocqueville's views on Algeria, labels a "rhetoric of evasion," a rhetoric common to many Victorian commentators on India.[89] In particular, Seeley employed the argumentative strategy of "comparison as vindication," recognizing that the British had acted reprehensibly at times, but, rather than using such insights as the basis for a general critique of empire, resorting to comparing British behavior favourably to that of other imperial powers. In so doing he offered a justification of the imperial project. The simultaneous admission and relativization of imperial crimes exposed the uncomfortable tensions at the heart of liberal imperialism. The greatest crime of all, and one which Seeley was at great pains to criticize, was slavery. In the seventeenth century, he reminded his audience, Great Britain had taken the lead in this abominable practice: "From this date I am afraid we took the leading share, and stained ourselves beyond other nations in the monstrous and enormous atrocities of the slave trade." Even in the more enlightened Victorian age, he contended, there was "nothing to boast of" in the treatment of indigenous populations under British control.[90] Despite these qualifications, Seeley believed that it was still necessary to continue ruling India.

But why? Given the vast differences between Greater Britain and the Indian Empire, why not simply advocate the abandonment of the latter, perhaps (even especially) in order to strengthen the former? Seeley was, after all, skeptical of the advantages that were accrued by holding on to India: "it is not at once evident that we reap any benefit from it." While recognizing the economic importance of India to Britain, he stressed also the substantial noneconomic costs that occupation incurred. In particular, due to both its geopolitical position and the great extent of its borders, it increased the dangers of war with other great powers, and especially Russia.[91] Despite this complex of concerns, he did not espouse

---

[88]Ibid., *The Expansion of England*, 135–36.

[89] Welch, "Colonial Violence and the Rhetoric of Evasion," *PT*, 31 (2003), 235–64.

[90] Seeley, "Our Insular Ignorance," 135–36; and ibid., "Introduction," xiii.

[91] Ibid., *The Expansion of England*, 183; on the importance of Indian trade, see 191, 258–59, 263–64.

separation, and nor did many of the other colonial unionists, however much they preferred to talk about the great benefits of a federal Greater Britain. Indeed the debates over Greater Britain were frequently infused by a marked dissonance between skepticism about the benefits accrued by possession of the Indian empire and a fervent but often poorly explained desire to hold onto it anyway.

In future, argued Seeley, it may well be necessary to leave India; in the meantime, it "is obligatory to govern her as if we were to govern her forever." This was nothing to do with honoring the past, anointing the long line of British heroes who had subdued the Indian princes, for such groundless romanticism belonged to a "primitive and utterly obsolete class of ideas." Rather, Seeley presented two arguments for the maintenance of India. The first was that the British had a duty to remain; the second was the articulation of what we might call a disenchanted conception of the "civilizing mission." Withdrawal was impossible to imagine given the current political conditions: because they had incapacitated Indian governing institutions the British could not simply depart, leaving chaos in their wake. If political judgments were to be made purely on the grounds of national interests, the British would probably be better off withdrawing; however, it was imperative to place the interests of the Indians first. A "very moderately good Government," argued Seeley, "is incomparably better than none. The sudden withdrawal even of an oppressive government is a dangerous experiment." The British had a duty to remain, to finish the mission, "vast and almost intolerable responsibilities" to uphold.[92] This was as much a duty to themselves, to their idea of good character, as it was to the Indians, for self-denying conceptions of duty were a central tenet in the moral and political discourse of the Victorians, a core component in the formation of a virtuous people.

In discussing India Seeley drew on the experience of the classical world, as mediated by Victorian historical consciousness. In particular, he made a revealing comparison with the Roman empire (a theme to which I will return in chapter 8). He argued that a valuable lesson in the nature of good government and the priorities of fashioning a virtuous politics could be learned from the ancients. Liberty was not the only admirable quality in politics, nor was it always the most appropriate or the most useful. This was something that many of his countrymen, gripped by vague and illusory notions about the irreducibility of freedom, failed to grasp. Other great qualities included civilization and nationality. What distinguished, and also in a sense justified, the Roman and Greek empires—and the British in India—was that they were of a vastly superior level of civiliza-

[92] Ibid., 194–96, 183, and 195.

tion in comparison with those they were ruling.[93] They had huge reserves of knowledge to impart. In scattered passages in *Natural Religion*, Seeley was explicit about the kind of civilizing responsibilities that the British had in India, and he extended these comments in *The Expansion of England*. A "grand object of the modern Church," he proclaimed, "would be to teach and organise the outlying world, which for the first time in history now lies prostrate at the feet of Christian civilisation." For Seeley, as we have seen, civilization had an overtly sacred connotation; it was the "public aspect" of the religious impulse.[94] His vision of the "civilizing mission," however, was rather more muted, and certainly more pessimistic about the ease with which it could be achieved, than that of many of the earlier proponents, including most notably James and John Stuart Mill. As such it exemplified a strand of late Victorian thought that was less confident in the ability (if not the right) of the British to spread their version of civilization around the world.[95]

Western civilisation—and by this Seeley meant Western Christendom—was defined by three main features. Firstly, it facilitated and encouraged science and the set of attitudes toward truth and verification that accompanied it. Secondly, it presumed a cosmopolitan view of humanity, defined as the ability to think beyond the confines of the tribe or nation, and including such features as respect for women and the principle of liberty. And finally, it generated "delight and confidence" in nature, as opposed to the besetting superstition and mysticism of other, less sophisticated ways of life. Seeley thought it important to export these values and beliefs to "backward" regions, both at home and abroad. It was necessary, he argued, to teach both "the races outside it or the classes that have sunk below it."[96] India was one such target, a vast tissue of superstitious beliefs and torpid social and political institutions. It had been civilized once, and the British were not therefore dealing with a properly "backward" people, but rather with one stuck in time. The Indians corresponded to Europe in the medieval period, and it was England's sacred mission "to

---

[93] Ibid., 238–39. A few comments in Cicero aside, his claim about Greek and Roman views was historically problematic: Richard Tuck, "The Making and Unmaking of Boundaries from the Natural Law Perspective" in Allen Buchanan and Margaret Moore (eds.), *States, Nations, and Borders* (Cambridge, 2003), 145.

[94] Seeley, *Natural Religion*, 221 and 201. Rather surprisingly, Deborah Wormell asserts that Seeley disdained the civilizing mission, and criticized the moralizing vision of "helping" other races: Wormell, *Sir John Seeley and the Uses of History*, 159.

[95] On this general shift, see Karuna Mantena, "The Crisis of Liberal Imperialism" in Duncan Bell (ed.), *Victorian Visions of Global Order* (Cambridge, 2007); and Mantena, *Alibis of Empire* (Princeton, 2007).

[96] Seeley, *Natural Religion*, 201–202.

raise India out of the medieval and into the modern phase." It was ripe
for education. We "stand out boldly," he proclaimed, "as teachers and
civilisers," imparting the "superior enlightenment we know we ourselves
possess."[97] Seeley was fulsome in his praise of the possibilities that such
an education promised: "The true view of the universe must be opened to
the population of India, even though it should seem to blot out and can-
cel all the conceptions in which they have lived for three thousand
years."[98] Although India was in some ways a burden, the British had a
duty to instruct the indigenous population. Seeley was deeply chauvinis-
tic about India, displaying the cultural and racial arrogance, as well as the
ignorance, for which his age is notorious. He was likewise scathing about
the debased condition of many of his own compatriots. He thus managed
to combine a large dose of xenophobia with a wistful sense of melancholy
for the loss of British greatness. He sought refuge in the future of Greater
Britain.

[97] Ibid., *The Expansion of England*, 244–45, 248, 252, and 260.
[98] Ibid., *Natural Religion*, 243.

7

The Prophet of Righteousness

> If the institutions of the Colonies are directly opposed
> to those of the mother country in religion, in politics,
> and in trade; if, while we have a high electoral
> qualification, and an aristocratic Parliament, they have
> manhood suffrage and democratic assemblies; if, while
> we proclaim Free Trade as the principle of our
> commercial system, they pass measures of Protection,
> in what does "the unity of the Empire" consist?
> —Goldwin Smith, *The Empire* (1863)

GOLDWIN SMITH believed that the written word conveyed the power to persuade: "to command beautiful and forcible language," he declared in his inaugural lecture as Regius Professor of Modern History at Oxford, "is to have a key, with which no man who is to rule through opinion can dispense, to the heart and mind of man."[1] Over the course of half a century of provocative writing on the empire he attempted to put this maxim into practice. Smith was considered by his peers to be one of the main adversaries of the empire, a man renowned and reviled in equal measure for his clarion call to "emancipate" the colonies. According to the utilitarian politician Robert Lowe, he was a "masterly" imperial commentator; yet to others, his views were inflammatory and corrosive. There was, warned W. E. Forster, no "more able or more sincere representative of the policy of disunion."[2] The powerful echo of Smith's arguments was demonstrated by the fact that they were always treated with alarm, sometimes bordering on hysteria, by advocates of colonial unity. In his opening speech to the Royal Colonial Society, Lord Bury stated that in terms of style and verve Smith's writings "are unsurpassed within the range of modern literature" but that "in proportion as he is brilliant, he is dangerous." In-

---

[1] Smith, *An Inaugural Lecture* (Oxford, 1859), 25. On Smith's life and career, see Elisabeth Wallace, *Goldwin Smith* (Toronto, 1959); and Paul Phillips, *The Controversialist* (Westport, 2002).

[2] Lowe, "The Value to the United Kingdom of the Foreign Dominions of the Crown," *FR*, 22 (1877), 620; and Forster, *Our Colonial Empire* (Edinburgh, 1875), 28. See also Charles Nicholson, comments, *PRCI*, I, 66; and A. C. Cattanach, "On the Relations of the Colonies to the Parent State," *PRCI*, 2 (1870), 68.

deed, he continued, Smith's influence on his many young disciples was "immense" and needed to be counteracted; such work was to be one of the guiding aims of the new institute.[3]

Smith was one of main influences on the intellectual liberals who emerged as a prominent ideological force in the 1860s. In a popular satirial poem published in 1866 the young George Otto Trevelyan described this new generation as "On Bentham nursed, and fed on Goldwin Smith."[4] John Stuart Mill observed that Smith not only possessed "strong moral convictions which he is not afraid to act upon," but more importantly, a "decided power of leading others."[5] He was not a sophisticated political thinker, or a systematic one. A. V. Dicey summarized both the potency and the limitations of Smith's writings in proclaiming him "the last of our great pamphleteers," while Matthew Arnold, in *Culture and Anarchy* (1869), labeled him appositely "a writer of eloquence and power, although too prone to acerbity."[6] Smith was a master polemicist rather than a profound theorist, and his work reveals a mosaic of contending intellectual influences, the elements of which often enmesh awkwardly. He was also a man who embodied many of the contradictions of Victorian liberalism, his radicalism coexisting with an anti-Semitic streak, a deep cultural chauvinism (especially toward the Irish), and a fervent opposition to the enfranchisement of women.[7] Despite emigrating to the United States in 1868 (and then to Canada in 1871), he remained a formidable presence in British intellectual life, intervening repeatedly in imperial debates, and inspiring vociferous support and exasperated condemnation.

In this chapter I explore the manner in which Smith wielded his key, and in particular the connections between his own views on the future of world order and that of many of his critics. Despite his reputation, despite the deep hostility that his writings provoked, and despite his criticisms of plans for formal federation, Smith's views coincided with the proponents

---

[3] Bury, "Inaugural Speech" [March 15, 1869] *PRCI*, I (1869–70), 53 and 54.

[4] Trevelyan, "Ladies in Parliament" (1866), reprinted in *The Ladies in Parliament and Other Pieces* (Cambridge, 1869), 15.

[5] Mill, letter to Herbert Spencer (August 15 1860), in Mill, *CW*, XVI, 1192. But see also Mill's critical comments on *The Empire* in his letter to J. E. Cairnes, 8 November 1864, *CW*, XV, 195. On his impact on the university liberals, see Christopher Harvie, *The Lights of Liberalism* (London, 1976); J. P. Parry, *Democracy and Religion* (Cambridge, 1986), 249–57; Paolo Pombeni, "Starting in Reason, Ending in Passion," *HJ*, 37 (1994), 320–21; and R. T. Shannon, *Gladstone and the Bulgarian Agitation*, 1876 (London, 1963), 208 and 226.

[6] *Memorials of Albert Venn Dicey*, ed. Robert Rait (London, 1925), 182; and Matthew Arnold, *Culture and Anarchy and Other Essays*, ed. Stefan Collini (Cambridge, 1993), 229. This acerbity was on display in Smith, "Falkland and the Puritans," *CR*, 24 (1877), 925–42.

[7] Smith, "The Jews," *NC*, 13 (1887), 687–709; and Smith, "Female Suffrage," *MM*, 30 (1874), 139–50.

of a federal Greater Britain in a variety of ways. He sought a moral-cultural version of their political project, believing the former superior in terms of protecting British domestic stability and international status. The next section analyzes Smith's arguement that the formal ties of empire should be replaced by the global bonds of tradition and race. This is followed by two sections that examine, firstly, the elements out of which he constructed his conception of national and racial character, and secondly, the connections he drew between religion, morality, and political institutions. Finally, I explore some of the tensions in Smith's thought by investigating his views on India and Ireland.

Colonial Emancipation and the "Glorious Future" of the Anglo-Saxon Race

> [T]he greatness of England lies not
> in her Empire but in herself.
> —Goldwin Smith, *The Empire*

Smith began his public career as a Peelite, a man who worked amicably alongside Gladstone on the question of university reform in the 1850s.[8] After the American Civil War, he was driven into the intellectual orbit of Cobden and Bright, becoming a self-professed "Manchester Man," a position that he upheld consistently, indeed dogmatically, for the remainder of his long life; it was as if his politics and economics were frozen to ice during the 1860s, never to thaw, even during the most tumultuous political and philosophical transformations of the ensuing decades.[9]

While his arguments remained consistent, Smith's mood darkened perceptibly during Victoria's reign. His was an anxiety for the state of England and the world; it was also a fear for the position of England in the world. An aristocratic form of government, the degradations of party politics, low national morale, the predominance of crude commercial values, and a working class pursuing only its own material interests, plagued and ultimately threatened the country. It was a polity in crisis, hampered by the

---

[8] Harvie, *The Lights of Liberalism*, 108. See also, Smith, letter to Gladstone, May 2, 1855, in Arnold Haultain (ed.), *A Selection from Goldwin Smith's Correspondence* (London, 1910), 7. Smith finally lost all patience with Gladstone over Home Rule: *My Memory of Gladstone* (London, 1904), 58–78.

[9] The fundamental continuity of his thought on the empire can be seen by comparing *The Empire* (1863) with both "The Empire" in his *Essays on Questions of the Day*, 2nd ed. (New York, 1894 [1893]), 141–95, and his *Reminiscences* (New York, 1910), 221–22. For his views on America, see Smith, *Does the Bible Sanction American Slavery?* (Oxford, 1863); and ibid., *The Civil War in America* (London, 1866).

parasitic colonies and swiftly relinquishing its economic predominance.[10] "My notions of the state of England of course grow every day more dim."[11] Britain was in danger of forfeiting its greatness. The world, he thought, was turning away from the pacific Cobdenite path, toward aggressive competition, imperialism, jingoism, and war. The European powers (and potentially his beloved United States) were drawn increasingly into a brutal race to divide the world up between them. As with many of his liberal contemporaries, political life seemed to deteriorate significantly before Smith's eyes during the 1870s and 1880s, and this was to strengthen his calls for the defence of a re-invigorated global Anglo-Saxon community.

During 1862 and 1863 Smith penned a series of extended letters on the empire to the *Daily News*, which were then collected together into a best-selling book, *The Empire* (1863). He argued provocatively for "colonial emancipation," for severing the nearly "invisible filaments" that composed the political tie between the settlement colonies and England. True to form, Smith wrote that the empire "rests on unreflecting pride, ignorant of the true sources of English greatness," and that it was a burden on the country, serving only class interests: "the mere pride of empire, and the pleasure of indulging it, belong only to the imperial class."[12] The letters provoked a flurry of comment. In the House of Commons Disraeli launched a contemptuous attack, declaring that "Professors and rhetoricians find a system for every contingency, and a principle for every chance; but you are not going, I hope, to leave the destinies of the British empire to prigs and pedants." *The Times* was equally mocking, commenting on Smith's first letter that the author obviously possessed a "morbid mind" and stating regally that "it is almost an insult to our readers to repeat such stuff as all of this."[13] Yet Smith was simply following through the logic of the common refrain that sooner or later the colonies would seek independence after being granted limited self-government. For all the vitriol that was poured on him, there were others who praised Smith for confronting a difficult issue directly, even if they disagreed with the extent of his prescriptions.[14] While Smith's views remained consistent, the con-

[10] Letters to Max Müller, July 18, 1870; Mr Hutchins, May 6, 1886; and Mrs Hertz, September 17, 1879, in Smith, *Correspondence*, 27, 31, 188, and 82.

[11] Letter to Salisbury, January 31, 1870, *Correspondence*, 19.

[12] Smith, *The Empire*, xxi, 146 and 74–5. For another example of this argument, see Herbert Spencer, *The Proper Sphere of Government* (Indianapolis, 1982 [1843]), 220 and 261.

[13] Hansard, February 5, 1863, third series, vol. 169, 95; *The Times*, February 4, 1862, reprinted in Smith, *The Empire*, 11–18. See also B. Price, "England and Her Colonies," *FM*, 68 (1863), 454–70.

[14] See the anonymous contributions in *WM*, 24 (1863), 248–49; the *Saturday Review*, April 25, 1863, 545; and Smith, *Reminiscences*, 170.

tours of imperial discourse shifted around him, and the idea of separation became increasingly unpalatable. During the 1880s and 1890s he at times appeared a beleaguered voice. As one observer rejoiced in 1886, "the journalist of the school of Mr. Goldwin Smith is as extinct as the megatherium."[15]

Although he employed the term "British Empire" throughout his writings as convenient shorthand for all those territorial possessions administered from London, Smith was careful to indicate that technically "empire" signified a political form that was created by conquest. It was therefore crucial to understand the distinction between empire, colonies, and colonial dependencies. In this semantic division lies one of the keys to unlocking the nature of his imperial thought, as well as to the persistent misinterpretation of his intentions. About empire (in the limited sense) he was adamant: "Empire is the result of conquest, and conquest is the appetite of the savage man, who preys upon his fellows as the tiger preys upon the herd." For Smith, as for Seeley, the only true "empire" that Britain ruled over was in India.[16] Throughout the course of his career Smith was critical of commercial greed, glory-seeking, and the impulse to conquest, whether manifested in the establishment of the British Indian empire, in Disraeli's jingoistic imperialism—"how the country is deeply degraded by choosing him at its head"—or later in the South African War.[17]

Colonies, on the other hand, were an intrinsic aspect of human history: colonization was merely the inevitable diffusion of peoples and the consequent establishment of communities that maintained a sense of attachment to their place of origin. This link did not automatically entail any formal political relationship.[18] In response to later criticisms that he had advocated the severing of colonial ties, he responded indignantly that such a claim was absurd: "To get rid of the Colonies, as it would be highly criminal, is happily impossible, the relationship between Mother Country and a colony being one which can never be annulled."[19] Rather, he objected to the maintenance of imbalanced political relations between dependent colonies and the "mother country." "I am no more against Colonies than

[15] Anon., "The League and Its Journal," *IF*, 1/1 (1886), 18; and, for a similar verdict, F. P. de Labillière, *Federal Britain* (London, 1894), 204.

[16] Smith, *Commonwealth or Empire?* (London, 1902), 32; and ibid., *The Empire*, 8 and 257. See also ibid., "The Empire" and *The United Kingdom* (London, 1899), II, 384.

[17] Ibid., letter to Mrs. Winkworth, March 7, 1874; *Correspondence*, 47; letter to J. X. Merriman, December 1, 1899, *Correspondence*, 333.

[18] Compare with Seeley's (more standard) definition: Seeley, *The Expansion of England*, 38.

[19] Smith, "Manchester School," *CR*, 67 (1895), 381. For an early rehearsal of this argument, see ibid., *The Foundation of the American Colonies* (Oxford, 1861), 3.

I am against the solar system. I am against dependencies when nations are fit to be independent." It was the political and not the purportedly indestructible moral tie to which he objected, and it is this conception of the nature of colonies that allowed him to talk of "our independent colonies" in the United States.[20] In 1867 Smith wrote that the idea of political union "is a dream, and one from which we shall soon awake."[21] In light of the subsequent rise of the imperial federation movement, and indeed of late-Victorian imperialism, this was to prove a deeply inaccurate prophecy.

Smith was scathing about many of the romantic phrases applied to the empire. Among those that he viewed with disdain were Seeley's "Expansion of England," Froude's "Oceana," and Dilke's "Greater Britain." "Greater Britain," he complained, "seems to me, with the set of ideas and political speculations to which it belongs, to carry with it a fallacy something like the belief that the earth was the centre of the solar system."[22] He regarded such ideas as naive rhetoric, and as implying the unity and teleological development of the empire as a coherent political entity. Trying to impose order where there had been little, if any, they denoted a spurious view of global history, ignorant of the piecemeal and violent nature in which the empire was created and had evolved. But it would be a mistake to conclude, as was common, that Smith was repelled by the notion of Greater Britain, that he was a straightforward "Little Englander." Smith's vision of the future had much in common with the other proponents of Greater Britain. He thought that Britain was a force for good in global politics, and that consequently it needed to be protected from the stultifying decline that he feared was already under way. He was unafraid to declare himself a patriot.[23] In *The Empire*, he had proclaimed that "when our Colonies are nations, something in the nature of a great Anglo-Saxon federation may, in substance if not in form, spontaneously arise out of affinity and natural affection." "I am," he argued twenty years later, "a loyal and even ardent citizen of the Greater Britain, and most sincerely wish to see all children of England, including the people of the United States, linked to their parent by the bond of the heart."[24] And at the height

[20] Smith, *The Empire*, 122, 165, 196; and ibid., "The Empire," 163. For a similar claim, see George Cornewall Lewis, *An Essay on the Government of Dependencies* (London, 1841), 176.

[21] Smith, *Three English Statesmen* (London, 1867), 212; and ibid., "The Political History of Canada," NC, 20 (1886), 31.

[22] Ibid., "The Expansion of England," CR, 45 (1884), 531 and 524; and ibid., *Commonwealth or Empire?*, 81.

[23] Ibid., *The Empire*, vii; ibid., "Manchester School," 381; and ibid., *Dismemberment No Remedy* (London, 1886), 31.

[24] Smith, letter to Professor Tyndall, October 6, 1882; and Smith, *Correspondence*, 137. See also, Smith, "The Political History of Canada," 29; and, Smith, "Manchester School," 381–2. A similar view was expressed by E. A. Freeman, who suggested a "fellowship of civic

of the federalist campaign he stated that, "I have the greatest respect for the aspirations of the Imperial Federationists, and myself most earnestly desire the moral unity of our race and its partnership in achievement and grandeur."[25]

Dilke's arguments, or at least those regarding the nature of the settler colonies, were influenced by Smith. The "strongest of arguments in favour of separation," claimed Dilke, "is the somewhat paradoxical one that it would bring us a step nearer to the virtual confederation of the English race."[26] Smith believed that the most adventitious way to defend and extend the strength of Britain was through the fostering of the nonformal union of the "English" with their fellow racial kin spread throughout the colonies. Smith thus drew a clear distinction between artificial and natural unity. Artificial unity was that which relied on the establishment of a constitutional link, often against the wishes and interests of the colonies and the United Kingdom; it was pride, greed, and ignorance that prescribed this false unity. Such "unnatural" political unions were "sources of nothing but discord, unhappiness, and weakness," and they were "worse than worthless."[27] Natural unity, on the other hand, was simply the result of colonial diffusion, and was cemented by the bonds of race and culture. It was more powerful and durable than its artificial alternative.

Smith looked to "blood and sentiment" to connect the English-speaking peoples of the world. The elements necessary for fostering this sentiment were vague: "language, literature, intercourse, history, transmitted habits, institutions and forms of thought."[28] This was enough to form the core of a distinct Anglo-Saxon civilization. "That connexion with the Colonies, which is really a part of our greatness—the connexion of blood, sympathy, and ideas—will not be affected by political separation." As Smith's view of the world became gloomier, his belief that the moral unity of the race was essential as a bastion against the darkness strengthened. "Colo-

---

rights" between the Anglo-Saxons: *Life and Letters of Edward A. Freeman*, ed. W.R.W. Stephens (London, 1895), 384.

[25] Smith, "Straining the Silken Thread," *MM*, 58 (1888), 242; see also ibid., *Canada and the Canadian Question* (London, 1891), 265. For the claim that Smith was a "little Englander," see Wallace, *Goldwin Smith*, 19; and Harvie, *Lights of Liberalism*, 222. The fact that many saw him as a "Little Englander" is not however an accurate reflection of Smith's intentions or arguments, but rather a comment on the reception of his message. Indeed the sort of views expressed by Smith and Freeman—critical of formal connections with the settler colonies, but defenders of a global Anglo-Saxon cultural-moral union—highlight the inadequacy of the term "Little Englander."

[26] Dilke, *Greater Britain* (London, 1868), II, 157.

[27] Smith, *The Conduct of England to Ireland* (London, 1882), 28; and ibid., letter to Mr. Justice Longley, January 15, 1887, *Correspondence*, 195.

[28] Ibid., "The Expansion of England," 531. See also ibid., "The Political History of Canada," 31.

nial Emancipation, while the tie of affection still remains unbroken, is the only mode of securing that to which we all alike cling, that [to] which we all are alike proud."[29] This belief in Anglo-Saxon unity served also as the theoretical foundation for a federal Greater Britain. The basis of a strong relationship, and the manner in which it should be judged, was found, thought Smith, in the degree of "reciprocal advantage, not sentiment" that it afforded to the relevant parties, for political federations were not "religious communities." Echoing the modern theorists of commercial sociability, he continued that, "[n]one but a cynic would despise sentiment; none but a fool would build on it."[30] As a logical corollary of his argument about the extent of and limits to the boundaries of race, he included the United States within his sweeping vision.[31] The federalists in turn thought that Smith's ideas were visionary to the point of irrelevance. Frederick Young argued that racial "moral union" was a phrase as "utterly destitute of any practical significance as the equally vague, contemptuous talk against what are termed paper constitutions." Likewise, Francis de Labillière commented that Smith's idea of moral federation was "as yet too vast and visionary for practical imperial federationists."[32] Smith responded to the claim that his views were overly idealistic by insisting on the realistic nature of his prophecy, claiming that there was "nothing visionary in the hope of a moral reunion of the race."[33] Each side, in other words, resorted to accusing the other of proposing ideas that escaped the bounds of practical politics.

There was a double obligation contained in his argument for colonial independence: the colonies should be responsible for their own development, able to make their own mistakes and follow their own chosen path, while the imperial power had a duty to stand aside. "To play the gaoler of a people struggling for national existence is a part which can no longer be pressed on a great and generous nation."[34] Convinced of the need to sever the formal ties between London and the colonial dependencies, Smith was unsurprisingly critical of plans that sought to strengthen them, to transform the empire in order to save it. His analysis of the problems embodied in attaining political unity was acute, and a number of years before federal tracts began to pervade imperial discourse, he had already considered the issue and offered some telling criticisms of it.[35] The pro-

---

[29] Ibid., *The Empire*, 6; and ibid., *Three English Statesmen*, 212.

[30] Ibid., *The Empire*, 6, 35, and 36.

[31] Ibid., *Three English Statesmen*, 211–12; also, ibid., *The United Kingdom*, 385.

[32] Frederick Young, *An Address on Imperial Federation, at Cambridge* (London, 1885), 16; and Labillière, "Later Objections to Mr. Goldwin Smith," in *Federal Britain*, 211.

[33] Smith, "The Empire," 175.

[34] Ibid., *The Empire*, 233; and "The Empire," 173.

[35] Smith understood "federation" in a partial manner, akin to the notion of "confederation" in the theories of Mill and Freeman, whereby the political authority of the federal gov-

ponents of imperial federation were pursuing a "mere chimera" in their attempts to tighten the political bonds of empire: this was a policy guaranteed to fail. "To give a nation a Parliament of its own is to give it independence. Two Parliaments under the same crown never have produced, and never can produce, anything but clashing of interests, contradictions of policy, discord, and confusion; and, at last, angry separation, the grave of that glory which belongs to England, the mother of nations." He argued that the creation of a new imperial chamber was completely implausible given the selfish nature of national interests. And he also maintained that the strategy of federating colonial territories into larger political units constituted a move away from, rather than toward, the ideal of a federal Greater Britain. It was likely to strengthen the nationalist currents within each, thus challenging the very possibility of an empire-wide union. The idea of a formal imperial federation was, moreover, an anathema to his liberal nationalist sensibilities, for it smacked of continental European "schemes of 'universal empire' and a universal state."[36] Writing nearly thirty years later he remained critical, emphasizing the lack of concrete plans adumbrated by the federalists.[37]

Smith's condemnation of schemes for formal union combined two main elements. The first centered on his interweaving of morality and political economy. As he wrote, in symptomatic Manchester style, "a truly great policy is generally cheap, because it has the moral forces on its side."[38] In an age of free trade, the empire harvested no financial rewards, and through the cost of defending its far-flung lands it generated inexcusable expenses. The colonies were unwilling to help pay for their own defense, and Britain was exposed to the constant danger of war, most notably with the Americans over Canada.[39] The financial issue was not purely a matter of unnecessary expenditure abroad, but reflected also the lack of attention paid to the inhabitants of England. Smith was critical of the Kiplingesque notion of the "white man's burden" so central to the imperial ideology of the era.[40] The resources spent on the empire were being wasted and could be employed more judiciously on poverty alleviation at home. The second line of argument followed a Millian trajectory. Smith

---

ernment extends only to the constituent assemblies not the individuals governed by them (*The United States*, 123); See also, Smith's letter to J. X. Merriman, December 17, 1878, *Correspondence*, 75

[36] Smith, letter to Mr. Justice Longley, 195; ibid., *Three Statesmen*, 211; ibid., *Commonwealth or Empire?* 64; and ibid., *The Empire*, 86.

[37] Ibid., *Commonwealth or Empire*, 64.

[38] Ibid., *The Empire*, vii.

[39] This was a particularly acute worry during the American Civil War, but it was an issue to which Smith returned repeatedly throughout his writings. See Smith, "Manchester School," 381–82; ibid., *England and America*, viii; and ibid., *The Empire*, 8.

[40] Smith, letter to Mrs Hertz, November 9, 1899; Smith, *Correspondence*, 331. Although, for his hypocrisy on this matter, see the final section of this chapter.

claimed that constitutions, and political systems in general, could not simply be engineered and transposed onto communities, but rather that they grew organically and should be suited to local conditions. Like that of many of the imperial commentators of the time, Smith's work is saturated with metaphors of childhood and human development applied to the relationship between the colonies and Britain. In order "to be strong and respected," he maintained, "they must be developed by a nation itself out of the elements of its own character and circumstances," and as a result of their dependence, the colonies remained in a state of "political infancy," their growth stunted prematurely.[41] And in line with many of his fellow university liberals, he was supportive of the principle of national self-determination.[42] "The Sclav [sic] must be permitted to have his aspiration as well as the Anglo-Saxon."[43] He pictured a host of strong independent nations linked forever by common racial origin; nationality was to be grafted onto race (a theme I return to in the next section). But Smith diverged from the strict noninterventionist maxims of Cobden and Bright, arguing that military interference in the affairs of other states was sometimes a necessity, if only to support those fighting for national independence. This attitude was displayed in his dismay at the lack of substantive British support for the German cause in 1870.[44] Smith believed that Britain had a duty, assigned by history and character, to propagate and, when required, to defend by force the evolving sphere of international morality.

EMPIRE AND CHARACTER

[A] political unity is not a moral unity, nor will moral
grandeur be gained by stretching it till it bursts.
—Goldwin Smith, *The Empire*

Smith adumbrated a specific "civilizational" view of global politics, a view in which civilizations at different levels of moral and intellectual development coexisted, sometimes clashing, largely incommensurate with

[41] Ibid., *The Empire*, 3 and 13. He here makes explicit reference to Mill, nodding presumably to the recently published *Considerations on Representative Government* (London, 1861).

[42] Smith, *The Study of History* (Oxford, 1861), 34; and ibid., *Commonwealth or Empire*, 54. See also Harvie, *Lights of Liberalism*, ch. 5.

[43] Smith, "The Jews," 687. "No nation can live another's life": ibid., *The Empire*, 137.

[44] Ibid., "Mr. Cobden," *MM*, 67 (1865), 90. See also, ibid., *The Empire*, x; and ibid., "Manchester School," 133. On Germany, see his letters to Max Müller, July 18 and August 8, 1870, *Correspondence*, 26 and 27.

each other, but ultimately, if the correct political and economic institutions were adopted, capable of prosperous and peaceful cooperation. The key to unlocking the inner logic of his imperial thought lies in grasping his understanding of "character." Smith's advocacy of the "glorious future" of the Anglo-Saxon peoples was a position grounded in and shaped by a conception of racial and national character formed by an often extremely vague combination of environment, culture, religion, and political tradition. As with his views on politics and society, his understanding of race remained consistent throughout his life, while racial thinking itself shifted significantly. His most thorough discussion of race can be found in a pair of lectures published in 1878, the first on "The Greatness of the Romans," the second on "The Greatness of England."[45] Pervading both these sketches is an argument about the manner in which racial character is fundamental in political life. "Race," he declared, "when tribal peculiarities are once formed, is a most important feature in history."[46] He sought to tease out the reasons why the Romans had dominated their world, and how the English had assumed such a pivotal position in modern history. He argued that it was simplistic to claim that the Romans were great because they were a warlike race, for this was a circular argument: to state that race was the *explanans* was to beg the question rather than to answer it. It was essential, he asserted, to analyze the factors that shaped the racial character of the Romans, the English, or any other group.

The structure of his argument was grounded in an analogy between the development of individual personality and human aggregates (races or nations). The manner in which they developed was broadly comparable.[47] Although Smith often failed to clarify the differences between "character," "race," and "nation," it is possible to discern a distinctive understanding of racial identity in his thought. Like Seeley, he understood race in broadly cultural terms, as referring to people united by a shared language, religion, sensibility, and set of traditions and institutions. The nation (and "nationality") had race at its core, but in addition it implied a claim to sovereignty over a particular territory. "When there is a solid mass of people of one race inhabiting a compact territory, with a language, religion, character, laws, tendencies, aspirations, and sentiments of its own, there is a *de facto* nation."[48] This also implied a degree of collective purpose, connoting a distinct sense of communal identity that was shaped by local circumstance and could evolve over time. Thus communities of

[45] Ibid., "The Greatness of the Romans," *CR*, 32 (1878), 321–38; and "The Greatness of England," *CR*, 34 (1878), 1–19.

[46] Ibid., "The Greatness of England," 323.

[47] Ibid., *The Empire*, 3.

[48] Quoted in W. T. Stead, *The Americanization of the World* (New York, 1901), 105–106. I thank Katie-Louise Thomas for this reference.

"English" colonists living throughout the world would be expected to develop differentiated national characteristics. Smith posited, albeit unwittingly, a Lamarckian cultural inheritance argument whereby national traits were transmitted through habit and imitation between successive generations. While countries could have an identical racial basis—for example, the Anglo-Saxon foundations underlying the character of the Australian colonies—the national identity of the various countries could develop independently, to a degree at least. For Smith, attempting to combine liberal nationalist sympathies with his civilizational perspective, race was thus central to but also far wider than nationality. This was an equation riddled with tensions. For example, his thinking was torn by the clash between centripetal and centrifugal forces. He was interested primarily in the idea of unity, and yet this tended to fit uneasily with his support for national self-determination. Individual nations were likely to branch in different directions over time following his theory of race, and in so doing, their roots in Anglo-Saxon soil would wither, if not die. They would lose the tie of common experience and interests necessary for the development of community. Smith could not reconcile the divergent trajectories of independent states with his overarching thesis about the unity of race.

Smith's racial thinking drew on two distinct lines of Victorian thought, combining them in an unstable synthesis. Firstly, as with so much else in his intellectual constellation, it was pervaded by Millian ideas. Mill had argued in his *System of Logic* (1843) that the study of "national (or collective) character" was, of all the social sciences, "the most completely in its infancy." As such, a "political ethology," a "science of national character," was required.[49] For Mill, collective characteristics were the result of the flux of history, contingent and plastic. For Smith, as for Mill, racial character was, at least originally, determined primarily by the environment in which people lived, by the quality of the soil and the nature of the climate, for "man is mainly the creature of physical circumstance."[50] The term "race" thus denoted the sum of the cultural and behavioral characteristics of a people that had accreted over time, shaped by the vicissitudes of "physical circumstance," the nature of their religious and cosmological beliefs, and the type of political institutions that they had evolved and lived under. England was blessed with the advantages of fertile soil, a moderate climate, and an outstanding geographical position, all of which helped to determine the development of a superior racial profile.[51] But the difference between Smith and Mill was significant: whereas for Smith,

[49] Mill, *System of Logic*, CW, VIII, 904–905; and also the comments in, ibid., "Bentham" [1838], CW, V, 99. Mill defined character as "the opinions, feelings, and habits of the people" (905), a definition with which Smith would undoubtedly concur.

[50] Smith, "The Greatness of the Romans," 322 and 323; "The Ninety Years' Agony of France," *CR*, 31 (1877), 104; and "The Greatness of England," 9.

[51] Smith, "The Greatness of England," *Lectures and Essays*, 39.

racial characteristics had hardened over time, for Mill they remained more mutable.

Smith merged the first part of the Millian argument—that which focused on the initial environmental conditioning of character—with the then popular Teutonic theory of race.[52] Teutonists traced the roots of English political stability to a love of customs, and particularly liberty, which purportedly originated in the ancient village communities of Northern Germany.[53] One of the best-known purveyors of "democratic teutonism" was Smith's friend E. A. Freeman, and Smith's adoption of the Teutonic theory was similar to Freeman's. For both of them Greek and Roman ingredients were also vital in understanding the complex recipe of English liberty, whereas for Stubbs and Green the roots were almost entirely Teutonic.[54] Smith, though, was never as virulently racist as Freeman, nor, unlike his friend, did he trace the origins of race further back into an Indo-European Aryan unity.[55] Smith absorbed—but did not fully digest—the influences around him, and regurgitated them in a pallid synthetic form. While believing that there was a scale of racial comparison, with the Anglo-Saxons placed proudly at the peak, he assumed that all the other races could ascend the ladder given favorable circumstances, at least in principle. "That which is congenital is probably not indelible, so that the less favoured races, placed under happier circumstances, may in time be brought to the level of the more favoured, and nothing warrants inhuman pride in race."[56] There was no immutable essence to each race that precluded advancement, to hitching its star to the tail of Progress. The form of aggressive racism inflected with "scientific" credence by misapplied Darwinian notions of competition and survival played no role in his thought.[57] He believed in the idea (albeit not the actual practice) of human equality,

[52] On England as a "Teutonic Realm," see Smith, "The Greatness of England," 9; and also his letter to Müller, September 4, 1871, Correspondence, 40.

[53] Among the better known proponents of Teutonism were Kingsley, Froude, Freeman, and Stubbs. See Donald White, "Changing Views of the Adventus Saxonum in Nineteenth- and Twentieth-Century English Scholarship," JHI, 32 (1971), 585–94; and Mandler, The English National Character, ch. 3.

[54] Freeman, "Race and Language" [1877] reprinted in his Historical Essays, 3rd Series, 2nd ed. (London, 1892 [1879]), 176–230. See also Burrow, A Liberal Descent (Cambridge, 1981), Part III. The term "democratic Teutonism," referring to "advanced liberals" with Teutonist sympathies, is drawn from Peter Mandler, "'Race' and 'Nation' in Mid-Victorian Thought" in Stefan Collini, Richard Whatmore, and Brian Young (eds.), History, Religion and Culture (Cambridge, 2000), 239.

[55] On the circulation of ideas about Aryanism in the empire, see Tony Ballantyne, Orientalism and Race (Basingstoke, 2002).

[56] Smith, "The Greatness of England," 9.

[57] For some of his criticisms, see Smith, Commonwealth or Empire, 37. See also ibid., The Study of History, Lecture I, 26, and Lecture II, 45; ibid., "The Ascent of Man," MM, 35 (1877), 195; ibid., False Hopes (London, 1886), 72; ibid., An Inaugural Address, 27–33; and ibid., "The Treatment of History," AHR, 10 (1905), 511–20.

at least in the sense that each and every person had the capacity for moral development; here there were no natural racial gradations. "[M]an," Smith asserted, "is the same in his moral or intellectual essence" the world over, and he criticized theorists who reduced all explanations to race.[58] But his assessment of the potential for peaceful coexistence was shaken by the racial tension that he witnessed in the United States, a situation that highlighted (so he believed) the recalcitrant problems generated by races at different levels of development living side by side—the existence of and need for clear racial-cultural boundaries was, he thought, never clearer.[59]

Smith's awkward combination of Millian and Teutonic ideas led him to attempt a catalogue of English national characteristics. He argued that the British Isles were inhabited originally (and to some extent still) by two races, the Celts and the Teutons, the latter of which "are the dominant race, and have supplied the basis of the English character and institutions."[60] The Celts were now largely displaced, scattered around the fringes of the kingdom and concentrated mainly in Ireland; they were a weaker race, generally unreliable, prone to superstition, and not fit for self-government. The first step in explaining the superior character of the English was that they lived on an island, and as such they were settled originally by a "bold and enterprising race." The types of people capable of conquering the treacherous seas in order to establish themselves in England were equipped with the traits that Smith considered essential to the success of the Anglo-Saxons. "Not only is a race which comes by sea likely to be peculiarly vigorous, self-reliant, and inclined, when settled, to political liberty, but the very process of maritime migration can scarcely fail to intensify the spirit of freedom and independence." The beneficent physical characteristics of the island—its relative immunity from invasion, its moderate climate and excellent soil, its comparative isolation from the European mainland—all helped further shape the collective character. He identified five elements that could be traced initially to the Saxon conquest, when "Ethelbert and Augustine met on the coast of Kent." The king, symbolizing "Teutonism," was met by a representative embodying, "Judaism, Christianity, imperial and ecclesiastical Rome." In this eccentric mix lay the roots of the Anglo-Saxon racial character. A sixth element was added during the Reformation, when classical republicanism entered

---

[58] Ibid., *Two Lectures on History*, I, 29.

[59] Ibid., *The United States*, 408. See also the similar comments in ibid., *The Moral Crusader* (London, 1892), 190–92, and in a letter to Mrs. Winkworth, July 26, 1892, *Correspondence*, 247. It should be noted that much of Smith's attention here was focused on the Irish immigrant population in America, which Smith regarded with extreme hostility.

[60] Ibid., "The Greatness of England," 2. Cf. R. Barry O'Brien, "Mr Goldwin Smith," *FR*, 41 (1884), 202–207.

political discourse.[61] This pronounced strain in his thought was most evident in his repeated assaults on the dangers of standing armies and his praise for English free-holders and sturdy yeomen.[62] Furthermore, the insularity of the islands, combined with the industriousness and inventive flair of the inhabitants, led to a flourishing commercial spirit.[63] The greatness of the English could be attributed primarily to the intertwining of these elements. Smith did little more than simply list them, however, and he provided no detailed analysis of any of these ideas or the relations between them. This was typical of his work as a whole, based as it was on assertion rather than systematic argument. Nevertheless, the result was a strong, confident picture of the English, which meant that wherever in the world Smith's countrymen traveled—and he talked almost always of men—they would be able to master the conditions and prosper.[64] The very character that had made the English great explorers and conquerors, he argued, also meant that they could succeed without central political regulation, that they could thrive without formal empire, and that, ultimately, a moral and cultural vision of Greater Britain was sufficient.

Religion and Liberty

Smith had made his name originally in the movement to end religious tests in the University of Oxford.[65] As with race, so with religion: both were vital for his understanding of the nature, content, and purpose of politics. But while his political views remained unswerving throughout most of his adult life, his religious beliefs became steadily more idiosyncratic. Unusually for a university liberal, Smith was born to Broad Church parents and thus grew up in an environment skeptical of the claims of received scriptural authority; it was a temperament that remained with him always—although it often failed to translate into his attitude toward the sacred documents of classical political economy. His thought was free from the punitive doctrine of atonement central to the evangelical revival, or the meliorating incarnationalism that superseded it.[66] It was devoid also

---

[61] Smith, "The Greatness of England," 1, 3, and 5. Dilke expressed similar views on the character-shaping role of the sea: "All races that delight in the sea are equally certain to prosper, empirical philosophers will tell us." *Greater Britain*, I, 389.

[62] Smith, *Three English Statesmen*, 249.

[63] Ibid., "The Greatness of England," 6.

[64] Ibid., *The Empire*, 47.

[65] See, for example, ibid., *A Plea for the Abolition of Tests in the University of Oxford*, 2nd ed. (Oxford, 1864); and ibid., *The Reorganisation of the University of Oxford* (London, 1868).

[66] Letter to the Reverend Arthur G. Whatham, December 24, 1897, *Correspondence*, 313.

of tractarian mysticism. Nevertheless, as Christopher Harvie has argued, Smith, in common with the other university liberals, displayed the "secularization" of the evangelical mind, where "conviction now inspired the individual to realise himself in the service of the community."[67] In Smith's case, this was translated into a Millian obsession with open debate and a desire to educate the public, to tell the truth as he saw it, however contrary to conventional wisdom it might appear.[68]

Smith's and Seeley's views on religion sometimes differed greatly, and sometimes overlapped. For Smith religion was a private matter, and organized religion was something to be regarded with wariness, for its leaders and adherents were prone to conservative politics. Again in common with other university liberals, but unlike Seeley, he was critical of the connection between church and state, the problem of which he stated, at the very beginning of his career, was "to my mind the one thing worth caring for in English politics." Indeed this connection was a thoroughly dangerous one for political radicals as the Church was more often than not an "engine for evil."[69] Smith remained a critic of the Anglican—let alone the Catholic—Church throughout his life, and this reached its apex in his derisive comments on the role of the Church in the South African war.[70] But criticism of the Church did not signal a move into the ideal of personal communion with God that pervaded evangelicalism. After all, both the High and the Low Church, despite their many differences, shared a common orthodoxy orbiting around scriptural authority, a transcendental God, and a salvationist role for religion.[71] Smith could not follow them along this theological path, strewn as he saw it with superstition, and he retreated instead into ever greater religious skepticism, so much so that he was constantly assailed for being agnostic.[72] This was to mistake his position, for he remained a spiritual thinker; he was opposed not to faith, but to rigid and unreflective dogma. He cannot be interpreted as one of the "Victorian scientific naturalists," men who saw the world as a tissue of visible, mechanical phenomena open to investigation by experimental means; rather, he stands with his friend John Tyndall as a "transcendental materialist,"[73] a man who believed wholeheartedly in the claims of sci-

---

[67] Harvie, *Lights of Liberalism*, 27.

[68] Smith, *Guesses at the Riddle of Existence* (London, 1897), vi.

[69] Ibid., "The Ascent of Man," 203; and ibid., "The Manchester School," 383; ibid., letter to Roundell Palmer (later Earl of Selbourne), August 30, 1847, *Correspondence*, 2; and ibid., *Essays on Questions of the Day*, 96–97.

[70] Ibid., Letter to Mrs Hertz, October 29, 1900, *Correspondence*, 363: "The Anglicans, of course, have been the worst."

[71] Joseph Altholz, *Anatomy of a Controversy* (Aldershot, 1994), ch. 2.

[72] Smith, *Guesses at the Riddle of Existence*, iv–viii.

[73] On "scientific naturalism," see Frank Turner, *Between Science and Religion* (London, 1974). Turner includes, Morley, Huxley, Spencer, Galton, Frederic Harrison, and Leslie

ence and yet who continued to believe in (to need?) an underlying spirituality in the world.

The main purpose of religion, Smith believed, was to provide a cosmology that would guide the behavior of individuals in society. It was the foundation for a "political morality," an ethics of community living. This was the type of view that Seeley had dismissed as belonging to the "legal school in morals."[74] Without an eschatologically infused social cement, Smith believed, the national community would become morally and spiritually degraded as the incentives (both positive and negative) that a belief in religion dictated, and the role they played in shaping the character and behavior of individuals, would at one stroke be removed. "God and future retribution being out of the question, it is difficult to see what can restrain the selfishness of an ordinary man, and induce him, in the absence of actual coercion, to sacrifice his personal desires to the public good."[75] For an ardent liberal like Smith, this was a terrifying prospect: without a theological anchor for human action, coercion was necessary in order to restrain egoism, thus infringing sacrosanct personal liberties. Such an anchor was a precondition for living in an advanced, cohesive society.[76] The religion best suited to fortifying character was (it will come as little surprise) Protestant Christianity. "The moral aspiration—the striving after an ideal of character, personal and social, the former in and through the latter—seems to be the special note of the life, institutions, literature, and art of Christendom."[77] The Anglo-Saxon race derived a great deal of its strength from being Protestant to the core. Although he was keen to propagate religious freedom, he regarded such a foundation as essential to the character of the race, and he stressed repeatedly the superiority of Protestantism over other religions. While Islam was disquieting, it was peripheral in comparison with the insidious scourge of Catholicism. There could be no reconciliation, he argued, between the progressive mind, free from the shackles of mysticism and dogma and guided to a love of liberty by the light of reason, and the "absolute submission of the soul" intrinsic to Catholicism.[78] In his critical review of volumes five through eight of J. A. Froude's *History of England*, Smith was keen to contrast the brutal political regimes he associated with Catholicism and the "sounder morality"

Stephen in this broad category. On Tyndall, who was a leading scientist and served as superintendent of the Royal Institution, see Stephen Kim, *John Tyndall's Transcendental Materialism and the Conflict Between Religion and Science in Victorian England* (Lewiston, 1991).

[74] Seeley, *Natural Religion* (London, 1882), 166.

[75] Smith, "The Ascent of Man," 203.

[76] Ibid., letter to Professor Tyndall, October 18, 1878, *Correspondence*, 66 and 69.

[77] Ibid., "The Ascent of Man," 199.

[78] Ibid., *The Empire*, 244; and ibid., "The Defeat of the Liberal Party," *FR*, 26 (1877), 14. On the "political intolerance" of Islam, see ibid., "The Policy of Aggrandizement," *FR*, 22 (1877), 303.

that accompanied the Reformation, and the banishing of Rome from British political life.[79]

Pessimism stalked Smith's thought, and there was a serious tension between his adherence to a belief in progress and his mounting gloom about the state of England and the world.[80] For both Seeley and Smith it was essential to discover new foundations for morality. The increasing materialism of modern life left Smith worried: "We begin to perceive, looming through the mist, the lineaments of an epoch of selfishness compressed by a government of force."[81] Under the influence of German biblical criticism and the continuing advances of science, his religious beliefs seemed to retreat even further; and as he perceived religious belief in society to evaporate, he despaired, not so much for the sake of a lost God but for morality itself. Smith believed that religion had in the past acted as a bar to revolution, but now that it was, as he saw it, in rapid decline, the country was increasingly vulnerable. He even appeared to have surrendered faith in the role that religion could play in binding society together: "We must accept the results of science and criticism. Amidst all these perplexities our only salvation is steadfast adherence to the truth, wherever it may lead us." In vain, he searched for alternatives. This led him to try and imagine substitute sources of national unity; although never a positivist, he declared once that "I wish the Positivists could make haste and put a new foundation under the national character in place of the religious one, which is being very rapidly withdrawn."[82]

An environment in which political morality was firmly encoded, etched in the character of individual and collective alike, served as a necessary condition for the development and flourishing of progressive institutions. Smith believed above all and unwaveringly in the Anglo-Saxon "love of liberty."[83] His views on the nature and benefits of the Anglo-Saxon political tradition are best viewed through the prism of his attitude toward

[79] Ibid., "Froude's *History of England, Vols. V-VIII*," *ER*, 119 (1864), 243.

[80] His whole conception of human history was built around an immovable belief in progress, and key to this was the development of human character. His theory of history was, he declared, "in accordance with the doctrine of progress." Smith, *Two Lectures on History*, "Introduction," 3; and ibid., *On Some Supposed Consequences of the Doctrine of Historical Progress* (Oxford, 1861). He judged the progress of humanity according to advances in three areas: "virtue, science and industry." Ibid., *Two Lectures*, "Introduction," 3. This triad were elsewhere rendered as "moral, intellectual, and productive" (ibid., *On Some Supposed Consequences*, 9).

[81] Ibid., "The Ascent of Man," 204.

[82] Ibid., "The Organization of Democracy," 318–19; ibid., letter to Mrs Hutchins, May 26, 1897, *Correspondence*, 302; and ibid., letter to Mrs Hertz, January 1883, *Correspondence*, 103.

[83] Ibid., *The United States*, 60. See also ibid., letter to Professor J. K. Hosmer, October 25, 1890, *Correspondence*, 229.

the United States. Like many radicals Smith was an ardent admirer of America, considering it the politically advanced epitome of modernity, free from the dead weight of history that constantly beset English political life. In *Three English Statesmen* he argued—like Dilke had before him—that it was in the United States that English liberties had flourished most fruitfully.[84] Smith argued that the American colonies were actually part of the moral community of Greater Britain, and that it was only the folly of George III and his ministers that had led to the "great colony" being "accidentally and temporarily estranged from the mother country." It was love of liberty that joined them, grounded in their shared racial inheritance. "We are united by a common allegiance to the cause of freedom." Indeed this unity was so strong that Smith could proclaim, "Being in America, I am in England."[85] The intermixing of race, religion, and beneficent political tradition defined the character template of the Anglo-Saxons. This was a common radical refrain; as Dilke had proclaimed, "the map of the world will show that freedom exists only in the homes of the English race."[86] It was also a conception of the Anglo-Saxons with which many of the imperial federalists concurred, and indeed it underlay much of their advocacy of unity.

The war between the American colonists and the British government, Smith lamented, had brought a "great disaster on the English race."[87] It was not the split itself that was the cause of this "evil," but rather the fact that it was not accomplished peacefully; separation was inevitable, a war was not. Ultimately the division was beneficial for both countries, though, for it allowed them to follow their own national trajectories. Indeed, it offered unparalleled opportunities for national growth, and he regarded the establishment of the American "commonwealth" as "the great achievement of his race" and he looked forward to the "voluntary reunion of the American branches of the race within its pale."[88] Once again the problems with Smith's theory of racial identity are apparent, for as American nationality developed it would diverge ever further from the path trodden by the British, thus reducing any chance of fruitful reconciliation let alone unity between the two. Smith argued once that the United States had been founded originally on the noble principles of "freedom, self-help, and self-

[84] Ibid., *Three English Statesmen*, 143.

[85] Ibid., *Commonwealth or Empire?* 3 and 5; and ibid., *England and America*, "Introduction," iii. See also ibid., *Commonwealth or Empire?* 17.

[86] Dilke, *Greater Britain*, II, 382.

[87] Smith, *The Foundation of the American Colonies*, 30; and ibid., *The United States*, 74 and 57–63.

[88] Ibid., *The United States*, 60 and 5. Smith argued, to enormous controversy, that the United States and Canada should unite; see here ibid., "The Political History of Canada," and, *Canada and the Canadian Question*.

development under the necessary restraints of law."[89] This stands as a succinct digest of his own political creed. *Three English Statesmen*, moreover, acts as a portal through which to read his views on the nature of the ideal political tradition. In his moralizing and superficial analysis of Pym, Cromwell, and the younger Pitt, he returned constantly to themes close to his own heart.[90] Written to help fund the Jamaica Committee in their attempt to prosecute Governor Eyre, the book is not so much a work of history as a historical working-through of his own ideals, full of praise for the Anglo-Saxon love of liberty, of the collective good generated by the introduction of free trade, and of the dangers of adopting, or falling prey to, an alternative continental model of political and religious organization. Smith maintained this combination of respect for institutions and their mutually reinforcing effect on character throughout his life.

He remained highly critical of what he saw as the American fondness for protectionism.[91] As the nature of liberalism began to mutate during the 1880s and 1890s, Smith remained wedded to what he took to be the credo of the political economists and classical liberalism. "I stick to Adam Smith, and am relegated to Saturn in his company."[92] For Goldwin Smith, untrammeled free trade was the institution that would neutralize global instability; it was the pacifier of his civilizational conception of global politics. "We have embraced the principle of Free Trade, the most powerful principle perhaps, and the most fruitful of consequences, political and social as well as economical, that ever was introduced into the affairs of men."[93] Smith was not a close student of his namesake, and his reading of the *Wealth of Nations* was highly selective. He employed Smithian arguments against the economic viability of the colonial system, arguing that it led to wasteful profligacy and benefited only merchants and landowners, but he was highly critical of Smith's proposal (outlined in chap-

---

[89] Ibid., *Commonwealth or Empire?* 4.

[90] Smith, as was increasingly common in the middle and later decades of the nineteenth century, was an ardent admirer of Cromwell. This advocacy was beset by a double irony: firstly, as Blair Worden has argued, Thomas Carlyle, one of the main targets of Smith's acidic barbs, was the "galvanising force" behind Victorian Cromwellianism—a point also made by Seeley ("Milton's Political Opinions," *Lectures and Essays* [London, 1870], 89–90); and secondly, because one of the main reasons for his popularity was that Cromwell was seen as a staunch imperialist. Worden, *Roundhead Reputations* (London, 2001), chs. 9–10. On Smith's dislike of Carlylean "hero-worship," see *Three English Statesmen*, 80–82. Smith was the drafter of the original "Statement of the Jamaica Committee" (July 1866), although his indignation focused more on the dangers that aberrant militaristic behavior inflicted on Britain than on the suffering of the black Jamaicans. R. Kostal, *A Jurisprudence of Power* (Oxford, 2005), 157–59. For an overview, see Bernard Semmel, *The Governor Eyre Controversy* (London, 1962).

[91] Smith, "US Notes" in Haultain, *Life and Opinions*, 256. Smith, *Garrison*, 22. See also ibid., *The Empire*, 90.

[92] Smith, Letter to Lord Farrer, June 22, 1892: *Correspondence*, 246.

[93] Ibid., *The Empire*, 206. See also ibid., *The United States*, 186.

ter 3) for American representatives to sit in London.[94] In his claims to be a Smithian we can see some of the problems that occur when combining incommensurable theoretical systems. In adopting the Teutonic argument regarding the origins of Anglo-Saxon liberty, Goldwin Smith was directly contradicting—although apparently without realizing it—Adam Smith's theory of the development of liberty. For the great political economist, liberty had flourished coeval with commerce and could not be traced to misty forest clearings dotting medieval Germanic plains.[95]

What did Goldwin Smith mean by "liberty"? In his retrospective survey of the ideas of the Manchester School, he wrote that "[w]e were, and the survivors of us still are, for liberty. But liberty, in our conception, was not selfish and inhuman isolation." It meant instead the typical Victorian ideal of "self-exertion and self-reliance." It was not, that is, the atomistic, ultimately egotistical mode of conceiving the self that the increasingly popular "new liberals" argued, albeit inaccurately, was held by their intellectual predecessors. Nor was it the picture that the civic imperialists painted of their opponents. Smith continued that in his understanding, "self help is mutual help, because, constituted and related as we are, in a state of freedom, we all, at every moment of our lives, stand in need of each other's aid; whereas, under a paternal Government, be it that of an ordinary despot or a socialist committee, each man will look more to the government and less to his fellows."[96] Self-professed vanguards of the future often resort to maligning their own past, and the history of liberalism was rewritten by the emerging generation of thinkers. Midcentury liberalism, John Dewey later suggested, in a tone all too familiar to late Victorians, had failed to "hold its own" and it was condemned to a state of "unstable equilibrium," splitting off into either socialism, as he discerned in the work of the later Mill, or into conservatism, embodied with equal ambiguity in the trajectory of Henry Sidgwick's thought.[97] But Smith would not budge. He was aware that the world itself had moved on since he first put pen to paper, and that the prospects for world peace brought about through the moral agency of trade were diminishing steadily, but he argued that this simply meant that progress was being derailed, not that the arguments were obsolete. "To the taunt that the world had not continued to move in the direction of Cobden's policy, Free Trade and peace, Cobden could reply, so much the worse for the world."[98]

[94] Ibid., *The Empire*, 77.
[95] Smith, *An Inquiry into the Nature and Causes of the Wealth of Nations* [1776] ed. R. H. Campbell and A. S. Skinner (Oxford, 1976), Bk. III.
[96] Smith, "The Manchester School," 385–86.
[97] John Dewey, review of A. M. Sidgwick and E. M Sidgwick, *Henry Sidgwick* (London, 1906), in the *Political Science Quarterly*, 22 (1907), 135.
[98] Smith, "The Manchester School," 378. Smith was also keen to distance himself from socialism, claiming that all the radicals and socialists had in common was a broad desire for

    In order to illustrate the superiority of the English character, Smith con-
stantly highlighted what he perceived to be the striking political and moral
differences between England and France.[99] The Anglo-Saxon political
tradition was to be contrasted with the radically inferior French model,
which was plagued by a deadly cycle of barbarous revolutions. The
French, he argued, were generally servile and hence not steadfast in the
face of despotism, a system under which they spent a great deal of time.
Conjoined with his belief in the Teutonic theory of race, this helps to explain his initial support for Bismarck's fledgling German state in the
Franco-Prussian War (1870–1871).[100] Once again, a degree of geographical determinism was central to his argument: he claimed, for example, that as France had an extensive frontier, it required a large standing army, which was a common cause of despotic government. But
character was harder to change than institutions, and while the French
Revolution had transformed the former, it had failed in the more fundamental task of reworking the latter.[101] And for Smith, as we have seen,
the idea of a globe-spanning imperial polity—a "world-wide state"[102]—
was anathema, a continental European fantasy reminiscent of Napoleon.
In particular Smith hated the French revolution and its effects on the
French character. Revolution "[gave] birth to a race of intriguers, utterly
selfish, utterly unprincipled, trained to political infidelity in the school of
fortunate apostasy, steeped in perfidy by the violation of unnumbered
oaths, and at the same time familiar with the revolutionary use of violence."[103] The evils of revolution were something to which he returned
frequently in his writings. "The social organism, like the bodily frame, is
imperfect; you may help and beneficially direct its growth, but you cannot transform it."[104]

---

social justice (385). In a letter written to the positivist E. S. Beesly in the shadow of the South
African war (March 1900), when his views on the state of the world were darkening further, he stated, "I began to think that socialism is the only force capable of coping with Jingoism." Smith, *Correspondence*, 347. But this was only a momentary and speculative lapse
from a die-hard liberalism.

[99] This was a standard argumentative tactic: Georgios Varouxakis, *Victorian Political
Theory on France and the French* (London, 2002); J. P. Parry, "The Impact of Napoleon III
on British Politics, 1851–1880," *TRHS*, 6th series, 11 (2001), 147–75; and Burrow et al.,
That Noble Science, ch. 6.

[100] See the letters to Max Müller, on July 18, 1870, August 8, 1870, and January 8, 1871,
Correspondence, 24, 27, and 36.

[101] Smith, "The Ninety Years' Agony of the French," 103–104.

[102] Ibid., *The Empire*, 86.

[103] Ibid., "The Ninety Years' Agony of the French," 105; ibid., "The Organization of
Democracy," *CR*, 47 (1885), 320. On the nonrevolutionary nature of the Manchester creed,
see ibid., "The Manchester School," 383.

[104] Ibid., "Utopian Visions" in *Essays on Questions of the Day*, 53. For other comments
on the dangers of revolution, see ibid., *Three English Statesmen*, 2, 28, 40, 93, and 229; *England and America*, 14.

The English national character was riddled with internal tensions, and it was under constant threat. The sources of the peril, Smith claimed, lay simultaneously above, below, and around the fringes of the core. Firstly, it was challenged by the very policies that the government itself was pursuing. In adopting a "policy of aggrandizement," an aggressive quest for tracts of land throughout the world, there was a pressing danger that the governing elite would be infected by militarism and despotic aristocratic habits.[105] There was, moreover, the potentially destabilizing presence of the Celts, although they were mostly corralled in the highlands of Scotland, the South-West, and in Ireland. More ominously, the reactionary aristocracy, bent on preserving their undeserved privileges, were a constant danger to the development of progressive liberalism and heralded the eternal fear of a return to a feudal age. At the core of his argument lay a standard liberal interpretation of political development. As commerce grew, and as industry flourished, towns began to develop and replace the countryside as the focus of economic and political life. This transformation heralded a greater clamor for liberty. The bastions of liberalism, Smith proclaimed, consequently lay in the cities. But the countryside, ever conservative, remained a potent force in English political life, and this led to perpetual conflict between urban and agrarian interests. And yet with the growing specter of widespread participation in politics, dangers also lurked in the cities. Following from their (limited) victories in the franchise extensions of 1832 and 1867, the masses posed a danger to hard-won democracy. The perils for government, Smith argued, were "democratic passion, demagoguism, and factions."[106] England was losing its way under the fatal influence of party strife and corrupting mass politics, both of which encouraged populism and facilitated jingoism. The best of the Anglo-Saxon character and institutions was lost behind this lengthening shadow.[107] "I am afraid," Smith wrote in 1890, that "Anglo-Saxon institutions are now greatly imperilled in their native seat. Factory hands are bad material for a nation."[108] In his retrospect of the Manchester School, he wrote that they were perhaps "too trustful of the political intelligence of the masses, and too ready to concur in the sweeping extension of the suffrage."[109] Once again, Smith showed himself to be a man true to the conventions of his age.

---

[105] Ibid., "The Policy of Aggrandizement," 310–17.

[106] Ibid., *The United States*, 128.

[107] Ibid., letter to Mrs Hertz, January 1885, *Correspondence*, 163. In a letter to Salisbury (January 31, 1870) Smith suggested an alternative to party government; a return to "government by the Privy Council, or rather by the Council of State." *Correspondence*, 23. On a similar point, see ibid., "The Moral of the Late Crisis," 313.

[108] Ibid., letter to Hosmer, 229.

[109] Ibid., "Manchester School," 383; and ibid., "The Organization of Democracy."

India, Ireland, and the Necessity of Despotism

From war we have saved India.
—Goldwin Smith, "The Policy of
Aggrandizement" (1877)

Thus far I have outlined Smith's views on the future of the Anglo-Saxon race, and argued that despite his opposition to continued British rule over the settler colonies he was nevertheless concerned with erecting a defensive barrier—a moral-cultural Greater Britain—against the perceived dangers of an increasingly competitive world. Like Seeley and the other advocates of Greater Britain, he was deeply concerned with maintaining Britain's position of global dominance. But what was to be done with the hundreds of millions of Indians living under British rule? And what about the tumult over Home Rule in Ireland? These were problems that challenged the imperial theorists of the late nineteenth century, and the prescriptions offered by Smith and Seeley are here once again bound by as many similarities as differences.

In an essay written especially for inclusion in *The Empire*, Smith sketched the rudiments of his thinking on Indian affairs. The story started, as it finished, in an ambiguous manner. On one hand, he was critical of the original British conquest of India, of the motives of the individuals involved, and of their behavior once they were well established. A partial reading of Smith might lead one to conclude that he believed the genesis of the Indian empire was shrouded entirely in shame. In the annals of British political life, he wrote, there is "hardly a darker stain on the honour of England," and elsewhere he referred admonishingly to the "profligate rapacity of buccaneering Englishmen."[110] On the other hand, he defended the original conquest, and at times launched into rhapsodic praise for the "wonderful and romantic" spirit of the early imperial pioneers.[111] The subjugation could be defended, he argued, for at the time it was common practice to engage in such behavior, and the English were simply doing as others did. A further consideration, and yet another example of the strategy of "vindication by comparison" that Seeley also employed, was that it was better to be conquered by the British than the other European powers. "No one can justly impeach the morality of England in conquering India," he claimed, for "[i]f we had not conquered India, France would."[112] This mode of argument, which requires an action or

[110] Ibid., *The United Kingdom*, 414; and ibid., *The Empire*, 282. See also ibid., *Three English Statesmen*, 164.

[111] Ibid., *The United Kingdom*, 430.

[112] Ibid., *The Empire*, 258. See also ibid., "The Expansion of England," 526. On "vindication by comparison" see Cheryl B. Welch, "Colonial Violence and the Rhetoric of Evasion," *PT*, 31 (2003), 235–64; and the discussion in the previous chapter.

event to be ethically relativized, ran against the grain of Smith's regular (un)historical method: his writings were almost always pervaded by moralistic judgments of past actions and personalities from the perspective of the present. In order to defend the roots of empire, he had to change tack drastically.

The course of imperial conquest, although almost inevitable, Smith argued, was never planned as a means to destroy the civilization(s) of India.[113] The British had no grand imperial design, and India was overcome in a Seeleyan "fit of absence of mind." He argued that the original intention of conquest was to foster a trade monopoly, but this was no longer a valid reason for continued dominion, as the ports of the world were opening up. Neither side now benefited economically from the link. As a result, the prevailing assumption was that benevolence guided British policy, animated by the belief in the possibility of lifting the "backward" peoples of India into the modern world, of dragging them, kicking and screaming if necessary, to Enlightenment. "Never was an attempt made on so grand a scale or so much in earnest to wed conquest with beneficence."[114] Here Smith called for caution, noting that this was an easy conceit to adopt while sitting in the comfort of London. But not only was there little to be gained economically, potentially deleterious political consequences followed from continuing to govern such a vast expanse of land, for example in the corrupting influences of imperial rule on the aristocratic class.[115]

Despite the general trend of his thought, Smith nevertheless believed that it was imperative to retain control over India. It was not for reasons of profit that the British should remain, or for military or political advantage, but rather as a "duty" to the people who lived there.[116] This claim was based on an argument, not uncommon in liberal circles, that admitted British culpability in destroying India's indigenous political structures, and consequently burdened the British with a responsibility to govern.[117] It was also an argument that was commonly adduced by the advocates of a federal Greater Britain when trying to work through the consequences of their claims for communal self-determination on behalf of the settler empire.[118] He suggested that the British had backed themselves into a corner, left to administer an economically unproductive and politically divisive empire, which would be reduced to ruin by internal fighting if they withdrew. As with Seeley, so with Smith: emancipation

---

[113] Smith, *The Empire*, 261.
[114] Ibid., "The Expansion of England," 527.
[115] Ibid., *The Empire*, 276–77; and Smith, "The Policy of Aggrandizement," 310–17.
[116] Ibid., "The Empire," 158.
[117] Ibid., *The Empire*, 257. See also, Dilke, *Greater Britain*, II, 383.
[118] See, for example, Marquis of Lorne, *Imperial Federation* (London, 1885), 80–81.

simply did not apply to India. But the arguments for why it did not apply were different. Whereas for Seeley, the Indians had never been conquered, for Smith it was the very fact that they had been conquered that mattered. "The principle of Colonial Emancipation does not apply to India, because it is a conquered country, not a Colony; and to throw up the government without making any provision for the preservation of order when we are gone, would be to do a great wrong to the people in addition to those which have already been done."[119]

Returning to the subject of India in "The Empire" his views remained consistent, but the tone had changed, assuming a more pessimistic, defensive edge. He now wrote of the Indian Empire as the "noblest the world had ever seen." Once again, Smith justified the original conquest on moral grounds, claiming that at the time it was the correct course of action to take, despite the unfortunate repercussions. It was an improvement on what went before, and the "subject races" had benefited from British philanthropy. "Our title has been force, but it has not been rapine, which was the title of the chief native dynasties and powers." It is this that would be lost if the British withdrew, forcing the Indians back into a war of all against all. Stabilizing the inherent violence of the various Indian peoples was now the primary British reason for occupation. "[A]bout keeping India there is no question. England has a real duty there, she has undertaken a great work and stands pledged before the world to perform it. She has vast interests and investments. Her departure would consign Hindoostan to the sanguinary and plundering anarchy from which her advent rescued it."[120]

The key here lay—as it did with Seeley—in Smith's conception of nationality. Smith denied that there was any Indian nation that could act as the referent for his moral strictures about independence. Instead, there was "nothing but strata of race deposited by previous conquests and class." India, he argued, was split into separate, inchoate ethnic and religious units, all with long and brutal traditions of infighting.[121] As such, the original conquest and continued dominance could be defended, for no nationalities were being subjugated; indeed, the Indians were actually

---

[119] Smith, *The Empire*, 292.

[120] Ibid., "The Empire," 144–46; and also ibid., "The Policy of Aggrandizement," 307. Smith also, uncharacteristically, praised the potential of imperialism (not simply empire) to strengthen character ("The Empire," 159). His pessimism regarding British political decline appears here to have fostered a fanciful scheme more akin to that propounded by the "playing fields of Eton" school of imperial thought.

[121] Ibid., "The Expansion of England," 526; and ibid., "The Empire," 147. Note the similarity between Bryce's arguments about Indian political anarchy, the defense of British rule, and the climatic dangers faced by English settlers: Bryce, "The Roman Empire and the British Empire in India" in his *Studies in History and Jurisprudence* (Oxford, 1901), I, 1–84.

being assisted, in an altruistic move fit to warm the heart of social reformers everywhere. Smith could thus promulgate simultaneously a liberal nationalist program for the settler communities while denying the very foundations of such a project to the hundreds of millions of Indians living under British rule. As a result of the lack of national consciousness among the Indians, he was opposed to immediate withdrawal. Indeed, his paternalistic attitude was of a kind with the very "civilizing mission" ideology that he elsewhere criticized: "The subject race may be said, without fear of contradiction, to be governed more for its own good than ever before was the conquered by the conqueror." It is here that Smith falls back on the theoretical conventions of the liberals of his age, although (like Seeley) he was perhaps less optimistic than many regarding the possibility of success.[122]

Smith utilized a very similar argument in relation to Ireland. Once again, he declared that ideally Britain should never have become involved, and that the history of occupation had been disgraceful in many respects: "sickening are its annals."[123] Once established, though, the British had a duty to the people of Ireland and they could not simply withdraw. Indeed here Smith is at his clearest on the links between the two countries, for he argued in relation to the range of Indian policy options available to the government that "in granting the Hindoo independence they would be handing him over to a murderous anarchy, as they are to see that in granting the Irish Celt self-government they would be handing him over to political brigandage."[124] And Ireland, moreover, had never been politically united: "Ireland has a distinct boundary, but she can hardly be said to have any other element of a separate nationality."[125] The Celtic character was also, as we have seen, "politically weak," and as such liable to scorn the possibility of self-government and free institutions, instead falling under the spell of the priesthood and corrupt charismatic leaders. The civilizing mission was once again central to Smith's conception of governance; and again, this was an argument that drew him into the intellectual universe of many of the advocates of Greater Britain.

What then was to be done? How could India be governed more efficiently, given the destruction wrought previously by the British, and in light of the dangers that the empire bred for British political life? And what of the Celts in Ireland? The answer to the apparently endemic crisis across the Irish Sea lay in reform of the system of entailment and primo-

[122] Smith, "The Expansion of England," 527. For his pessimism, see ibid., "The Empire," 155.

[123] Ibid., *The Conduct of England to Ireland*, 3–5 and 9.

[124] Ibid., "The Moral of the Late Crisis," *NC*, 20 (1886), 311.

[125] Ibid., *The Conduct of England to Ireland*, 40; and also, *Dismemberment No Remedy*, 9.

geniture, the disestablishment of the Church, the creation of provincial councils, and the establishment of a Royal seat in Dublin. For Smith, as for Mill, the core of the Irish question was economic rather than political or religious; it lay with land not government or God.[126] The idea of Irish emancipation (or indeed Home Rule) was anathema to him. For India, he advocated reducing the responsibilities of the almost universally reviled Colonial Office, and assigning greater powers to the governor-general, the man on the spot.[127] Smith had elsewhere discussed the nature of despotism as a mode of political governance, and, drawing on an idiom articulated most famously by Mill in *On Liberty* (1859), he had argued that it was "an improvement on anarchy, and may lead to an ordered freedom."[128] "If you have an Empire," Smith went on to argue, "you must have an emperor; and only a Viceroy with absolute power, though responsible to British opinion, can possibly do justice to the subject race."[129] And so Smith, the purportedly radical enemy of empire, ended up advocating an amplification of "despotism" in the East and denying the claims of liberty made by Indian and Irish nationalists.

[126] Ibid., *Dismemberment no Remedy*, 19 and 5; and *The Conduct of England to Ireland*, 21, 26–27, and 10. See also Mill, "What Is to Be Done with Ireland" [1848] and "England and Ireland," Mill, CW, VI, 497–505 and 505–35; and Mill, *Considerations on Representative Government*, ch. 9.

[127] Smith, *The Empire*, 294–95.

[128] Ibid., *The Study of History*, Lecture I, 24. See Mill, *On Liberty*, CW, XVIII, 224–69; and also, Mill, *Considerations on Representative Government*, 394–95.

[129] Smith, "The Expansion of England," 528. Cf. J. N. Dalton, "The Federal States of the World," NC, 34 (1884), 109n.

8

From Ancient to Modern

The world has seen many vast and powerful empires,
history has recorded their decline, culmination,
and fall, but all past experience, varied and instructive
as it is, fails to throw much light on the unique
problem we are considering.
—Graham Berry, "The Colonies
in Relation to the Empire" (1886–87)

THIS CHAPTER explores some of the ways in which history was drawn
upon, and also the ways in which people tried to escape it, in the formulation of imperial political thought during the nineteenth century. In so
doing, it seeks to complicate current understandings of both imperial political theory and the character of Victorian historical consciousness. In a
political culture obsessed with precedent and the moral value of history
and tradition, many of the proponents of Greater Britain disavowed the
rich intellectual resources of the ancient world, a world that for centuries
had played a regulatory function in the imagining of empires. Instead they
sought inspiration in the present.

In much European political thought, it had since the Renaissance been
standard practice when justifying empire to draw moral and intellectual
authority from the writers and historical precedents of the ancient world,
either Greece or Rome or sometimes both. It is a historiographical commonplace, moreover, that the late nineteenth-century British empire was
conceived frequently, by both its advocates and opponents, in terms of a
new Rome.[1] Richard Jenkyns suggests that for the Victorians, when surveying their empire, "the usual, the inevitable comparison was with An-

---

[1] Raymond Betts, "The Allusion to Rome in British Imperialist Thought of the Late Nineteenth and Early Twentieth Centuries," *VS*, 15 (1971), 149–59; Richard Jenkyns, *The Victorians and Ancient Greece* (Oxford, 1980), 330–46; Andrew Thompson, *Imperial Britain*
(London, 2000), 18; Linda Colley, "What Is Imperial History Now?" in David Cannadine
(ed.), *What Is History Now?* (Basingstoke, 2002), 136; Richard Faber, *The Vision and the
Need* (London, 1966), ch. 1; Anthony Pagden, *Lords of all the World* (London, 1995), 8;
Pagden, *Peoples and Empires* (London, 2002), 28; Karma Nabulsi, *Traditions of War* (Oxford, 1999), 115–16; and, A. P. Thornton, *The Imperial Idea and Its Enemies* (London,
1966), 60–63.

cient Rome." "The parallel between imperial Rome and the British Empire," writes Richard Hingley, became "increasingly important in the late nineteenth century," and the "English often identified themselves with the classical Romans." After noting that Adam Smith began his famous chapter "Of Colonies" in the *Wealth of Nations* (1776) with an extended discussion of the classical empires, Richard Faber maintained that the "late Victorian imperialists were heirs to this classical tradition and the same comparisons came readily to mind."[2] "If," he argued, "the *Pax Britannica* was hailed in Latin it was because the *Pax Romana* served as a model for comparison and inspiration."[3]

This account is incomplete, and potentially misleading. In elaborating their visions of empire the proponents of Greater Britain almost overwhelmingly eschewed the models presented by both Rome and Greece. Instead they viewed America as a constructive template for the future. This was not simply a failure of historical imagination, nor was it a product of intellectual carelessness or political myopia. It represented a conscious break from previous modes of imperial argument. There are two different parts to this story. The first concerns the magnetic attractions of America—a theme that I explore in the next chapter. But there was another side to it: why did the advocates of Greater Britain so often exorcise the rich imaginative resources offered by the ancient world, especially in a culture in which the use of historical precedent was often considered a sine qua non of political argument, and in which the classics carried enormous intellectual authority? Underpinning the transition from the ancients to the moderns was a set of beliefs about the meaning and direction of history. Drawing on the different but complementary lessons inculcated by interpretations of Greece and Rome, many Victorians believed that empires were self-dissolving. This was a time-honored argument, but one that was out of step with prevailing conceptions of progress. By the mid-nineteenth century it was commonly believed that history was progressive, at least in the sense that the future was open and that society and polity were shaped by but not doomed to recapitulate the past. And Britain, it was confidently assumed, was in the vanguard of this future-oriented developmental trajectory.[4] There were still those who thought

[2] Jenkyns, *The Victorians and Ancient Greece*, 333; Hingley, *Roman Officers and English Gentlemen* (London, 2001), 26, 157; Faber, *The Vision and the Need*, 19 and 25; See here Adam Smith, *An Inquiry into the Nature and Causes of the Wealth of Nations*, ed. R. H. Campbell and A. S. Skinner, 2 vols. (Oxford, 1976), 556–58. Hingley correctly notes how multifaceted this comparison was, and how this "flexibility and complexity" (5) helped to ensure the wide popularity of the comparison. See also Norman Vance, *The Victorians and Ancient Rome* (Oxford, 1997), ch. 10.

[3] Faber, *The Vision and the Need*, 25.

[4] John Burrow, Stefan Collini, and Donald Winch, *That Noble Science of Politics* (Cambridge, 1983), 15–20, and Essay VI. See also Peter Bowler, *The Invention of Progress* (Oxford, 1989).

that history moved in cycles, including many of the followers of Thomas Arnold in the 1840s and 1850s, but they were exceptions to the rule.[5] Empires, however, exhibited a logic of recurrent rise and decline. After all, much of the earlier fascination with historical cycles, especially during the Augustan age, had been based on extrapolations of the political dynamics of the ancient world, and in particular the fall of Rome. In the nineteenth century the vision of cyclical movement was linked strongly with the polities from which it had originally been derived. Although the history of Europe could be relocated in a progressive narrative, that of the ancients continued to represent a spectacle of eternal return. Empires were found guilty by association.

Since the prevailing assumption underpinning much social and political thought was that "anything that does not progress is doomed to decline," and since empires stood in the political imagination as the most pertinent concrete examples of declension, Greater Britain had to be yoked to the idea of progress.[6] Its distance from all previous empires had to be established, its novelty affirmed. Given the desire to create a permanent Anglo-Saxon global union, the long-standing tradition of looking to the ancients to provide intellectual authority for the construction and maintenance of empires had to be overturned, or at least redirected. This is exactly what many of the theorists of Greater Britain attempted, and they did so by reorienting their gaze toward America, shifting the source of inspiration from the past to the present—all in the name of the future. America was to be a substitute, a modern exemplar, offering both a more apposite political structure on which to model Greater Britain, and also, and equally importantly, an imaginative means to escape the dangers heralded by the past. Claims about Britain as a New Rome, even a New Athens, exaggerate and oversimplify the legacy of the ancient world in nineteenth-century political thought.

This is not to suggest that Rome and Greece played insignificant roles in the intellectual life of the late Victorian era. Greece was employed occasionally to present alternative conceptions of empire, as had been common earlier in the century. Rome, meanwhile, was widely utilized as both a model for specific forms of imperial rule and as an antidote to what Benjamin Constant had once labeled the "spirit of conquest."[7] In assessing the imaginative resonance of Rome, however, it is essential to distinguish between claims made about the settler colonies and those made about other elements of the empire. The vast majority of references to Rome

---

[5] Duncan Forbes, *The Liberal Anglican Idea of History* (Cambridge, 1952).

[6] The quotation is from H. S. Jones, *Victorian Political Thought* (Basingstoke, 2000), 35.

[7] Constant, "The Spirit of Conquest and Usurpation and Their Relation to European Civilization" [1814] in Constant, *Political Writings*, ed. Biancamaria Fontana (Cambridge, 1988), 51–165.

concerned British imperial possessions in India.[8] In arguments about the importance of Greater Britain, on the other hand, the ancients retreated to the wings. The selective erasure of history, and the concomitant turn to America, marked an important break in the history of British imperial thought. It also constituted a significant moment in the Victorian debate over the relationship between past and present, tradition and modernity.

The following section sets the context for the late Victorian debate by exploring some of the different lessons purportedly taught by Rome and Greece throughout the century, and it highlights the way in which the popularity of the latter was supplanted in the imperial imagination by a resurgence of interest in the former during the closing decades of Victoria's reign. I then analyze some of the arguments made in favor of Greater Britain, demonstrating their explicit break from both the Greek model of settler colonial rule, which had been widespread earlier in the century, and the late Victorian fascination with the Roman empire. In particular, I outline the way in which they conceived of history and show how and why they emphasized the irrelevance, even the danger, of classical comparisons. The penultimate section argues that in order to construct a powerful set of arguments about a stable global polity, colonial unionists attempted to establish that the colonial empire was without precedent, at least until the emergence of the United States as an independent country. I conclude with some reflections on what the various attempts to escape the past can tell us about Victorian historical consciousness.

The Functions of the Ancients

> For a long time the greatness of the ancient
> world lay with an oppressive weight like
> an incubus upon the moderns.
> —J. R. Seeley, *Introduction to Political Science* (1896)

In the second of his *Untimely Meditations*, Nietzsche observed that the age in which he lived, and in so many ways loathed, was one beholden to the past—it was marked, he wrote, by "its cultivation of history." For

---

[8] Although this mode of comparison went back to the eighteenth century, it was perhaps most explicit during the Edwardian era. See, for example, James Bryce, *The Ancient Roman Empire and the British Empire in India* (Oxford, 1914/1902); Evelyn Baring, Earl of Cromer, *Ancient and Modern Imperialism* (London, 1910); and J. A. Cramb, *The Origins and Destiny of Imperial Britain* (London, 1915). See also the insightful discussions in Javeed Majeed, "Comparativism and References to Rome in British Imperial Attitudes to India" in Catherine Edwards (ed.), *Roman Presences* (Cambridge, 1999), 88–110; and Phiroze Vasunia, "Greater Rome and Greater Britain" in Barbara Goff (ed.), *Classics and Colonialism* (London, 2005), 34–68.

Nietzsche this was something of which to be "rightly proud" but simultaneously wary, for escaping history as much as for embracing it, for forgetting as much as for remembering, was a precondition of life.[9] While this fascination with the past was widespread in Germany, home to the emergence of the academic discipline of history, it was also pervasive in the country that Nietzsche frequently scorned: Great Britain.[10] One of the most significant manifestations of this historical (even historicized) culture was the way in which understandings of the past played a formative role in the construction, elaboration, and defense of political arguments. The "English," noted Seeley in 1880, "guide ourselves in the great political questions by great historical precedents."[11] History was regarded, in this sense, as inextricably linked to the empirical validation of experience, and thus to the ideal of "practical politics" explored in chapter 5. That which had been shown to work in the past, could do so once again; that for which there was no precedent demanded a much higher burden of proof. This understanding of the function of history was common throughout the nineteenth century, and well into the twentieth.

For centuries historical precedents had been employed in British political discourse to defend or dispute assorted ideological positions. Interpretations of the ancient world often played a central role. In the seventeenth century, "neo-roman" conceptions of liberty were recovered, reworked and deployed in the impassioned debates over the justified scope of monarchical power.[12] During the eighteenth century the multifaceted legacy of Rome, and in particular the ethical and economic messages conveyed by its decline and fall, served as a fertile intellectual resource for a number of otherwise varied developments: oppositional arguments propounded by the English country-party Whigs, the ideological architecture of the American founding, and nascent theories of commercial society, all relied to an extent on interpretations of the fate of the classical polities. In "Of the Study of History" (1741), David Hume observed that one of the several benefits of reading history, "a most improving part of knowledge," was to be able to "remark on the rise, progress, declension, and final extinction of the most flourishing of empires." Knowledge of British history, and the histories of Rome and Greece, was essential. Over a century later, in the opening passage of *On Liberty* (1859), Mill could still single out the histories of Greece, Rome, and "England," as those "with

---

[9] Nietzsche, "On the Uses and Disadvantages of History for Life" [1873] in his *Untimely Meditations*, ed. Daniel Breazeale (Cambridge, 1997), 60.

[10] For some typically critical comments about the "English," see Nietzsche, *On the Genealogy of Morality* [1887], ed. Keith Ansell-Pearson (Cambridge, 1994), 11–12.

[11] Seeley, "Political Somnambulism," *MM*, 43 (1880), 32. This point was still being rehearsed thirty years later: J. Howard Masterman, *A History of the British Constitution* (London, 1912), 1.

[12] Quentin Skinner, *Liberty before Liberalism* (Cambridge, 1998).

which we are earliest familiar."[13] According to Walter Bagehot, history
would be a "barren catalogue of isolated facts—life a discontinuous rush
of human events—if great, single, continuous nations did not bind the
whole together," and if, most importantly, one were to "[s]trike Greece
and Rome from ancient, or strike France and England from modern
times," people would soon "see how loose and aimless a secular history
would become."[14] In the nineteenth century, history was regarded as vital
for understanding the moral and political life of the nation, its long and
frequently painful evolution over time, and ultimately its fragility. Competing interpretations of critical historical movements and moments,
drawn both from the ancient world and from British history itself, inflected debates over the nature of democracy, the toleration of Catholicism and religious dissent, the function of the monarchy, the advancement
of liberty, and so forth.[15] Imbued with a heightened appreciation of the
unfolding of time—an appreciation derived from the complex interaction
between their conception of the direction of history and the latest developments in geology and later biology[16]—and the ethical instruction that
could be derived from it, the Victorians shaped their multiple pasts (and
were shaped by them in turn) to suit various ideological purposes. History, along with political economy, comprised the most influential mode
of political theorizing of the age.

Theories of empire had always been embedded in wider currents of
political thought. In particular, modern European imperialists exhibited
an "imaginative dependence" on Rome.[17] Humanism provided ideological support for justifying global exploration, conquest, and occupation.
The language of neo-Roman republicanism permeated early- and mid-
eighteenth-century defenses of the British empire, especially in the colonies. The most obvious manifestation of this dependence, though, resided
in the frequent reiteration of the classical debate, echoing through the cen-

[13] Hume, "Of the Study of History," in Hume, *Essays, Moral, Political, and Literary*, ed. Eugene F. Miller (Indianapolis, 1987), 566; and Mill, *On Liberty,* CW, XVIII, 217.

[14] Bagehot, "The Meaning and the Value of the Limits of the Principle of Nationalities" [1864] in *The Collected Works of Walter Bagehot*, ed. Norman St John-Stevas, 8 vols. (London, 1965–86), VIII, 150.

[15] On the role of Greece, see Frank M. Turner, *The Greek Heritage in Victorian Britain* (New Haven, 1981); Jenkyns, *The Victorians and Ancient Greece*; Fred Rosen, *Bentham, Byron, and Greece* (Oxford, 1992); and Kyriacos Demetriou, "In Defence of the British Constitution," *HPT*, 17 (1996), 280–97.

[16] John Burrow, *Evolution and Society* (Cambridge, 1966), 149–53; and Burrow, "Images of Time" in Stefan Collini, Richard Whatmore, and Brian Young (eds.), *History, Religion, and Culture* (Cambridge, 2000), 198–224.

[17] Pagden, *Lords of All the World*, 12. See also Richard Koebner, *Empire* (Cambridge, 1961).

turies, over the corrupting relationship between empire and liberty.[18] But nineteenth-century comparisons between the ancients and the moderns were always ambivalent and highly selective. There was simply too much distance—intellectual, technological, economic, and political—between them for direct replication and emulation. Rather than encouraging straightforward transposition, the imaginative resources generated by the ancient world fed a variety of often conflicting desires and demands: they provided inspirational templates for political institutions and, correspondingly, models for virtuous individual behaviour; embodied a long cherished purity of aesthetic forms; reinforced, through the self-conscious elitism of students and admirers of the classics, gender, racial, and class distinctions; and, ultimately, offered an alternative, even alien, world against and through which to measure the present.

For much of the century, Rome played second fiddle to Athens in the British political imagination.[19] Writing in the early 1880s, Seeley suggested that because for much of the century the British looked to the past "only for a kind of exalted pleasure," and because they sought this pleasure in a Whiggish love of the unfolding of liberty, the Roman empire was until then "thought uninteresting." "The Roman Republic was held in honour for its freedom; the earlier Roman Empire was studied for the traces of freedom still discernable in it. But we used to shut the book at the end of the second century, as if all that followed for some ten centuries were decay and ruin; and we did not take up the story again with any satisfaction until the traces of liberty began to reappear in England and in the Italian republics." It was only when people began to theorize more systematically about the British empire, and to develop arguments about how to administer it effectively in light of the lessons of the past, that Roman imperialism assumed a more prominent position.[20] This is not to suggest that it was entirely absent during the earlier period; Carlyle and Macaulay, for example, were keen to link Britain to the glories of the Roman empire

[18] David Armitage, "Empire and Liberty" in Martin van Geldren and Quentin Skinner (eds.), *Republicanism*, 2 vols. (Cambridge, 2002), II, 29–47; Pagden, *Lords of all the World*, chs. 1 and 7; Richard Tuck, *The Rights of War and Peace* (Oxford, 1999); and Andrew Fitzmaurice, *Humanism and America* (Cambridge, 2003).

[19] Hingley, *Roman Officers and English Gentlemen*, ch. 1; and Miles Taylor, "Imperium et Libertas?" *JICH*, 19 (1991), 4–5.

[20] Seeley, *The Expansion of England* (London, 1883), 237–38. Another reason for decreasing interest in Rome during the early and middle decades of the century was related to the impact of political reform in Britain. As arguments for the role of corruption and oligarchy resonated less, so Rome lost some of its centrality. See also Burrow, Collini, and Winch, *That Noble Science of Politics*, 188–89. Conversely, on the relationship between critiques of the liberal state and the increasing popularity of Ceasar in the late Victorian era, see Frank Turner, "British Politics and the Demise of the Roman Republic," *HJ*, 29 (1986), 577–99.

in a manner that, while often ambiguous, exerted considerable influence over the later Victorian habit of comparison.[21]

Admiration for aspects of the Greek empire can be seen as an important dimension of the general Hellenism of early- and mid-nineteenth-century Britain. Greece figured in at least two separate ways, and although they often overlapped, it is essential to distinguish them. The first was as an emblem of creativity and genius. A mythologized picture of the Greek polities as spaces for cultural ingenuity and individual freedom was widespread throughout the century. Popular especially among some of the romantics, this vision found its most powerful expression in poetry, notably in the preface to Shelley's *Prometheus Unbound* (1820). They were not alone in this admiration: French liberals displayed an "instinctive fondness" for the "cultural éclat" of Athens.[22] Understood in this manner, Greece offered inspiration but little in the way of detailed political prescription. The importance of this evocative picture led E. A. Freeman to claim that one of the great achievements of George Grote's monumental *History of Greece* (1846–56) was the way in which it illuminated the political (and especially institutional) genius of the Greeks, a topic that had long been cast under the shadow of their "literary" accomplishment.[23]

The second usage was more precise, and referred to specific political institutions. It focused mainly on democracy, but came increasingly to encompass empire. During the early years of the century, Athenian democracy had been employed in political argument as a byword for despotism, constituting a powerful weapon in the Tory intellectual armoury, until in the 1840s Grote's positive appraisal helped reshape the way in which the Greeks were imagined.[24] In this context, an increasing number of imperial commentators looked to Greece as an alternative to Rome. Arthur Mills wrote in 1856 that the "model of Colonial policy most frequently and prominently exhibited for the emulation of modern States is that of Greece." This model, he continued, pointed to a "union resting not on state contrivances and economical theories," like that of Rome, "but on religious sympathies and ancestral associations."[25] In particular, this idea appealed to political radicals, many of whom were influenced, like Grote

---

[21] Catherine Edwards, "Translating Empire?" in Edwards (ed.), *Roman Presences*, 70–87.

[22] Karen O'Brien, "Poetry Against Empire," *Proceedings of the British Academy*, 117 (2002), 282–83; and George Armstrong Kelly, *The Humane Comedy* (Cambridge, 1992), 58.

[23] Freeman, "Grote's *History of Greece*," *North British Review*, 25 (1856), 142. George Grote, *A History of Greece*, 12 vols. (London, 1846–56).

[24] See especially Kyriacos N. Demetrious, *George Grote on Plato and Athenian Democracy* (Berlin, 1999); and Turner, *The Greek Heritage*, 189–204.

[25] Mills, *Colonial Constitutions* (London, 1856), xix–xx. Mills, who was very critical of drawing direct analogies with the ancient world, also noted that Rome was a popular comparator.

himself, by utilitarianism. The Roman alternative was, argued James Mill in 1823, "so very defective."[26] The reason for this was that the "Few" dominated the "Many" to such an extent that expansion was pursued only in the interests of the aristocratic class. This was an exemplar, and a temptation, to be shunned in the modern world. Mill and a coterie of radical "reformers" in his wake argued that the Greek style of colonization, premised on peopling distant lands and establishing self-governing communities with strong emotional and cultural ties to the "mother country," offered a more suitable model to emulate—although they were generally loathe to demand immediate independence for the colonies.[27] In the 1840s John Stuart Mill eulogized the Greek colonies, praising them for "flourishing so rapidly and so wonderfully" and for guaranteeing freedom, order, and progress, and he argued that they served as an excellent template for British colonization.[28] For the reformers, it was still important to utilize the classics, even when making arguments that were essentially structured by the ultramodern doctrines of post-Smithian political economy. Admiration for the Greek alternative was also to be found across the political spectrum, notably in the works of W. E. Gladstone— secretary of state for war and the colonies (1845–46) and later, as prime minister, a staunch critic of imperial federation—whose thinking was influenced by Wakefield's notion of "systematic colonization" and the positive conception of Greek colonialism found in George Cornewall Lewis's *Essay on the Government of Dependencies* (1841).[29] While the Hellenistic vision circulated during the closing decades of the century, it was less widespread among defenders of the settlement empire, and it all but disappeared from the advocacy of Greater Britain.[30]

During the second half of the century, it became increasingly common to draw comparisons between the British empire and Rome. This was not only true of theoretical texts, it also assumed a central position in the na-

---

[26] James Mill, "Colony," *Essays from the Supplement to the Encyclopedia Britannica, Collected Works* (London, 1995), 4. Mill's views, though, were inconsistent, especially regarding India: Jennifer Pitts, *A Turn to Empire* (Princeton, 2005), ch. 5.

[27] Mill, "Colony," 5–9. On other positive comparisons with the Greeks, see also John Arthur Roebuck, *The Colonies of England* (London, 1849), 137–41; and, somewhat contrary to his later views, Arthur Mills, *Systematic Colonization* (London, 1847), 41–42.

[28] Mill, "Wakefield's 'The New British Province of South Australia'" in *The Examiner*, July 20, 1843, reprinted in Mill, CW, XXIII, 739. On his admiration for the "Greek empire" see also "Grote's *History of Greece*," II, [1853], CW, XI, esp. 321–24.

[29] W. E. Gladstone, *Our Colonies* (London, 1855), 11.

[30] For a rare example of the positive use of the Greeks by an imperial federalist, see Frederick Young, *On the Political Relations of Mother Countries and Colonies* (London, 1883), 3–4. Miles Taylor suggests that Dilke also adopted this view: Taylor, "Republics Versus Empires" in David Nash and Anthony Taylor (eds.), *Republicanism in Victorian Society* (Stroud, 2003), 32.

tional imagination, encoded in administrative practices and even city-scapes. Among the design mottoes submitted by hopeful candidates in the architectural competition for the new Foreign Office (later expanded to include the India Office) in the mid-1850s, were "Arcana Imperii," "Pro Regina et Patria semper," "Potentatus et Gloria," and "Rome was not built in a day." In India British officials were routinely artistically represented in classical poses and dress.[31] The lessons to be learned from the ancients, and especially the Romans, became a fixture in the entrance exams for the Indian civil service.[32] The Earl of Carnarvon, formerly a Tory secretary of state for the colonies, argued in 1878 that the only comparable precedent for the vast expanses of the British empire was Rome.[33] He was far from alone. For many individuals Britain was *Imperium Britannicum*, whether for good or ill. The proponents of Greater Britain tended not to follow this trend, for reasons that will be examined in the next section. There were nevertheless exceptions to this rule, the most prominent being J. A. Froude, whose cyclical view of history, which was central to his comparative gaze, was examined in chapter 5. But James Bryce expressed a more widely held sentiment when he wrote that the "movement of humanity is not, as the ancients fancied, in cycles, but shows a sustained, though often interrupted, progress."[34] This meant that the past could and should be transcended.

The historical narratives of imperial legitimacy generated during the nineteenth century were more complex and more contested than many recent commentators seem to allow. The manner in which classical models and illustrations were employed demonstrated both continuity and change. The ancients were still drawn upon in defending certain modes of expansive empire building and forms of despotic political rule, by both those who wanted to attack the policies of the government and those who sought to offer them support. In imagining the discrete elements of the

---

[31] G. Alex Bremner, "Nation and Empire in the Government Architecture of Mid-Victorian London," *HJ*, 48 (2005), 722; and Bernard Cohn, *Colonialism and Its Forms of Knowledge* (Princeton, 1996), 30. However, classical imperial architecture in India, dominant in the first half of the century, rapidly lost its appeal in the wake of 1857. Thomas Metcalf, *An Imperial Vision* (London, 1989), 1–18.

[32] Heather Ellis, "Proconsuls, Guardians, and Great Men," unpublished paper, University of Oxford, 2003; and Phiroze Vasunia, "Greek, Latin, and the Indian Civil Service," *Proceedings of the Cambridge Philological Society*, 51 (2005), 35–69.

[33] Henry Herbert, Earl of Carnarvon, "Imperial Administration," *FR*, 24 (1878), 759.

[34] Bryce, "An Age of Discontent," *CR*, 59 (1891), 29. See also Seeley, "Ethics and Religion," *FR*, 45 (1889), 514; and Seeley, "Georgian and Victorian Expansion," 124. While the view that ancient conceptions of history were cyclical was prominent in the nineteenth century, this was not actually the view held (at least in a straightforward sense) by any ancient writers. See Arnaldo Momigliano, "Time in Ancient Historiography" in his *Essays in Ancient and Modern Historiography* (Oxford, 1977), 179–205. They did not, however, have any conception of progress. I thank Oswyn Murray for this reference.

settler empire there was, however, a striking fracture in the foundations
of intellectual authority. Imperial federation was, the Marquis of Lorne
proclaimed, "a phrase representing an altogether new idea in the history
of nations," and there was "no precedent which may help us."[35] Displaying the pride in novelty common at the time, as well as the frequent
inability to escape entirely a highly connotative historical vocabulary, a
contributor to the *Westminster Review* wrote that "[h]istory affords no
parallel to the position of the British Empire. Great Britain stands *facile
princeps* among nations."[36] This attempted distancing from history—or
at least an aspect previously considered vital—was a remarkable course
to chart in a culture obsessed with heeding the purported lessons of the
past. The Victorian debate over Greater Britain signals an important
switch in the nature of British imperial political thought: the turn from
the ancients to the moderns as sources of intellectual, political, and moral
inspiration.

The End of Empire: Two Models

> There is no analogy in the condition of any nation
> in the past which can guide us in estimating the
> forces at work within our Empire.
> —Marquis of Lorne, *Imperial Federation* (1885)

Late Victorian imperial discourse was not brimming with detailed analyses of ancient history. Unlike those of Bruni and Machiavelli, Montesquieu or Beaufort, Smith or Hume, the historical writings of the imperial commentators were neither methodical nor particularly insightful.
Scholarly work on the ancient empires was being produced in the universities—ancient history was a burgeoning and increasingly professional
academic subject, although it still labored under the shadow of Theodor
Mommsen—but the popular notion of decline and fall, and the imagery
associated with the history of empires in general, was a vague trope.[37] It

---

[35] John Douglas Sutherland, Marquis of Lorne, *Imperial Federation* (London, 1885), 43
and 2; see also [Arthur Elliot], "Colonial and Imperial Federation," *ER*, 192 (1900), 270;
and [Urquhart Forbes], "Britannic Confederation and Colonisation," *LQR*, 19 (1893),
250–51.

[36] [Anon.], "The Federation of the British Empire," *WR*, 128 (1887), 484. The Latin
phrase "facile princeps" could mean simply, following Cicero, "indisputably first" or "leading" (or indeed, the leader of a state). However, it also had a more specific meaning, namely
the title under which Augustus Caesar and his successors exercised supreme authority in the
Roman Empire.

[37] At Oxford, the spiritual and intellectual home of classics in Britain, the second half of
the nineteenth century witnessed the "zenith of Greats," although ancient history only
achieved prominence in the teaching of Literae Humaniores in the last two decades of the

conveyed a stark, simple message: "The long annals of the world are but a record of the rise and fall of successive empires."[38] The combination of analytical ambiguity, narrative simplicity, and evocative emplotment helps explain its wide resonance among contemporaries. Indeed, the imagery of decline and fall played an important role in the "iconographic order" of Greater Britain, the imaginative system of symbols, stirring rituals, and nebulous (often poetic) imagery that provided a coherent and emotive picture of a shared past, a troubled present, and a glorious future.[39]

The political uses of imperial history came in two basic forms, one general, the other specific. The former sought to argue, using various examples of imperial rise and decline, that all empires followed the same trajectory; that they all eventually collapsed. This was the central theme of Viscount Bury's *Exodus of the Western Nations* (1865), a sprawling treatise cautioning that the British must urgently prepare to cede their colonies because fighting historical inevitability would be disastrous. The global spread of the Anglo-Saxons, and with them democracy itself, should not be inhibited by potentially counterproductive institutional fiddling. Counseling vigilance and critical of aggressive expansion, Goldwin Smith warned that the "decay of Empires is the theme of history."[40] The Tory MP C. E. Howard Vincent advised that "there is but too much ground to fear that unless within the course of the next few years a chain of connection can be forged, the fate of the great empires of Greece and Rome, of Portugal and Spain, no less than of Holland, will attend us, if we refuse to recognise the condition of things as they are to-day."[41] History taught, then, that empires followed a discernable pattern.

---

century, and even then little original and lasting scholarship was produced; it remained largely derivative of Mommsen, whose majestic *History of Rome* was translated into English in 1862–66 and soon became the standard text (this was followed in 1886 by his *Provinces of the Roman Empire*). The main focus of teaching and research in Roman history, following Mommsen's lead, lay in the study of the early empire and the late republic, and in the practices of imperial administration; only in 1903 was the study of the empire formally established as a period of instruction for undergraduates. The study of ancient Greek history was a poor relative to the study of the Roman world. See W. H. Walsh "The Zenith of Greats" and especially Oswyn Murray, "Ancient History, 1872–1914" in M. G. Brock and M. C. Curthoys (eds.), *The History of the University of Oxford* (Oxford, 2000), VII, 311–26 and 333–60.

[38] [John Robinson], "The Future of the British Empire," *WR*, 38 (1870), 74. Robinson, a keen imperial federalist, was a politician and journalist in Natal.

[39] See also Duncan Bell, "The Idea of a Patriot Queen?" *JICH*, 31 (2006), 1–19.

[40] William Keppel, Viscount Bury, *Exodus of the Western Nations*, 2 vols. (London, 1865); and Smith, "The Policy of Aggrandizement," *FR*, 22 (1877), 307. Bury was a colonial civil servant turned politician, as well as founder of the Colonial Society. His imperial thought, which was influenced by Tocqueville, is examined in Edward Beasley, *Empire as the Triumph of Theory* (London, 2005), ch. 6.

[41] Howard Vincent, "The British Empire To-Day," *PRCI*, 16 (1884–85), 323.

The second usage, which tended to draw on either Greece or Rome, looked instead at specific cases to illustrate the political dynamics that catalyzed the fall. The Romans and the Greeks presented the Victorians with two different models of self-dissolution, although they were rarely delineated clearly. The first, and probably the most powerful, was the belief that the drive for expansion inevitably led to disaster. This view had been formulated most powerfully, at least in modern European thought, by Machiavelli, who, drawing on the history of Rome as mediated by both Sallust and Polybius, had argued in Book II of his *Discourses on Livy* that states would inexorably seek to expand, but that in so doing would forfeit their liberty, collapsing under the moral and constitutional strain of the quest for *grandezza*.[42] This was to become a commonplace view in the following centuries, and many of the critics of bellicose empire-building, including Montesquieu, Hume, Kant, and Constant, pointed to the moral and physical collapse of Rome to warn of a comparable fate for those who pursued rapacious military policies. The reasons for, and consequences of, the collapse of Rome under the weight of its own expansive impulse had been imprinted further into British consciousness by the epic work of Edward Gibbon.[43] "I am amused at the people who call themselves Imperialists," wrote William Harcourt, a leading Liberal politician, for "I always remember the first pages in Gibbon on the 'moderation of Augustus,'" in which he shows how for the first two centuries of the greatest and wisest Empire that ever existed the cardinal principle was the nonextension of Empire, and whenever it was departed from they came to grief."[44] The trope of declension was also common in the literature and art of the nineteenth century, resulting in a fascination with what Karen O'Brien labels "proleptic nostalgia," the intimation of the future collapse of civilization, of Britain as a fragile and ultimately doomed empire, enunciated most eloquently in Tennyson's melancholy *Idylls of the King* (1859).[45] The art critic, social theorist, and ardent imperialist John Ruskin had struck a similar note in the opening lines of the first volume of his

[42] Machiavelli, *Discourses on Livy*, ed. Julia Conaway Bondanella and Peter Bondanella (Oxford, 1997), II. See also David Armitage, "Empire and Liberty," 29–45; and Mikael Hörnqvist, *Machiavelli and Empire* (Cambridge, 2004). For the general discursive context, see J.G.A. Pocock, *Barbarism and Religion, Vol. 3* (Cambridge, 2003), esp. Parts III–V.

[43] Gibbon, *The History of the Decline and Fall of the Roman Empire*, ed. David Womersley, 3 vols. (Harmondsworth, 1995 [1766–78]). On the popularity of the trope of decline and fall, see Vance, *The Victorians and Ancient Rome*, 234–35; Hingley, *Roman Officers and English Gentlemen*, ch. 3; and Jenkyns, *The Victorians and Ancient Greece*, 73–77.

[44] Harcourt, letter to Rosebery, September 27, 1892, in A. G. Gardiner, *Life of Sir William Harcourt* (London, 1923), II, 197. Harcourt was Chancellor of the Exchequer in 1886 and again in 1892–95.

[45] O'Brien, "Poetry Against Empire," 269–96; and also Matthew Reynolds, *The Realms of Verse, 1830–1870* (Oxford, 2001), ch. 9. For the general context, see Catherine Edwards and Michael Liversidge (eds.), *Imagining Rome* (London, 1996).

Stones of Venice (1850), where he talked of the historical greatness of the British, insisting that they stood proudly alongside Tyre and Venice in the ranks of those who had asserted "dominion . . . over the ocean," but he proceeded to warn that like the other two "thrones," Britain was in grave danger of decay. "Of the First of these great powers only the memory remains; of the Second, the ruin; the Third, which inherits their greatness, if it forget their example, may be led through prouder eminence to less pitied destruction."[46]

There were at least three analytically separable interpretations of the fall of Rome in widespread circulation, although they were often conflated. Firstly, as noted above, there were those who argued that Rome collapsed due to the corrupting power of luxury and the subsequent loss of virtue. This account was prominent especially among radical critics of empire who stressed the potential dangers of aristocratic nabobs returning from colonial service and threatening British political virtue with foreign-flavored vice. "Is it not just possible," asked Richard Cobden in 1860, "that we may become corrupted at home by the reaction of arbitrary political maxims in the East upon our domestic politics, just as Greece and Rome were demoralised by their contact with Asia."[47] Citing Gibbon, Herbert Spencer claimed that "in a conspicuous manner Rome shows how . . . a society which enslaves other societies enslaves itself."[48] This had been a theme in British debates over empire at least since Burke's dogged pursuit of Warren Hastings. A second account argued that overextension, war, and institutional paralysis were the primary causes. The critique of the consequences of adventurous militarism, and the usually conjoined deficit of commercial and productive spirit, could be found regularly in late Victorian political discourse. Seeley, for instance, was scathing about the failings of the Roman "military character." Greater Britain was commercial and productive, creative and vigorous, taming nature and generating wealth, whereas the Romans, despite their military prowess, did not know how to make constructive use of the lands they governed.[49] And finally, it was argued that the overcentralization of Ro-

---

[46] Ruskin, *The Stones of Venice, Vol. 1* [1851], in *The Works of John Ruskin*, ed. E. T. Cook and Alexander Wedderburn (London, 1903–12), IX, 17.

[47] Cobden, cited in Klaus Knorr, *British Colonial Theories, 1570–1850* (London, 1963 [1944]), 359. See also Frederic Seebohm, "Imperialism and Socialism," *NC*, 7 (1880), 726–36; Miles Taylor, "Imperium et Libertas"; and Burrow, Collini, and Winch, *That Noble Science of Politics*, 190.

[48] Spencer, "Imperialism and Slavery," in *Facts and Comments* (London, 1902), 115.

[49] Seeley, "Roman Imperialism, II," *MM*, 20 (1869), 54. Although he noted the role played by the "moral decay" generated by excess luxury in the fall of Rome, Seeley argued that the main problem was the lack of military manpower brought about by overambitious extension ("Roman Imperialism," II, 47–48). He was not, however, consistent on this point, for a decade later he was arguing that the "Empire of Rome was undermined by moral decay." Seeley, *Natural Religion* (London, 1882), 237.

---

man institutions, and the concentration of power in the hands of the few, led to eventual collapse. This was a central concern in Montesquieu's pathbreaking *Considerations on the Causes of the Greatness of the Romans and Their Decline* (1734).[50] Bernard Holland, in his evocatively titled *Imperium et Libertas* (1901), argued that small "nations" were perfectly suited for ingenuity, and that a decentralized federal empire could simultaneously exhibit great strength while ceding considerable autonomy to its constituent units. Rome, on the other hand, had been destroyed by the degeneration brought about through centralization. With an eye on the future, he concluded that the "failure of the Roman experiment does not prove that an empire which avoided this peril might not beneficially endure for a much longer period."[51]

History, however, was rarely transparent. John Bright once castigated the IFL for not heeding the obvious lessons of history, to which W. E. Forster, the president of the league, replied, "[y]es, but history teaches many lessons now-a-days, and they follow so fast one upon another that it is not always easy to learn from them."[52] For some, it taught that the empire would unavoidably come to an end. Critics of the empire seized upon the imagery of Roman decline, of vulnerability in the midst of apparent strength.[53] However, as long as the eventual end of empire was projected into an indeterminate but ideally distant future, it was not necessarily to be feared, as for many the empire was a tutelary and hence temporary structure: once the various elements were ready for "self-government" and had reached the requisite level of "civilization" the British parent could (in the common familial metaphor of the time) let the child loose upon the world. This was likely to happen first for the "settler" colonies, and over a more distant horizon for the "barbarous" elements; but the time would come nevertheless. For most of the proponents of a Greater British polity, such a view of the future, tied as it was to an understanding of the past, was unacceptable—at least for the settler colonies. Rather than emphasizing the invariable fate of the empire, Roman decline convinced them that Britain had to learn from and surpass the ancients in order to secure future greatness. They had to defy history, shape it to their political will. The Oxford historian Montagu Burrows warned

---

[50] In his later *L'Espirit des Lois* (1748) Montesquieu offered a resounding defense of the British model of maritime commercial empire, a counterpoint to the alternative territorial militaristic system that had ended in the collapse of liberty at Rome. Montesquieu, *The Sprit of the Laws*, trans. Anne Cohler, Carolyn Miller, and Harold Stone (Cambridge, 1989), ch. 27, Book xiii.

[51] Holland, *Imperium et Libertas* (London, 1901), 13–14. Morley also criticized the centralization of imperial federal plans: "The Expansion of England," *MM*, 49 (1884), 258.

[52] Forster, "A Few More Notes on Imperial Federation," 553.

[53] Goldwin Smith, "The Policy of Aggrandizement," 308. See also, Morley, "The Expansion of England," 258.

that the "danger of our not perceiving our real position is exactly the same as was experienced by the old Roman Empire. The decay of the centre gradually makes its way to the extremities; and these drop off, one by one, till the seat of the Empire itself, unprotected and forlorn, goes down in the general crash." "With the secession of the Colonies," argued Edward Salmon, "would begin the decline and fall of the British Empire." Without educating the British people (and especially the working classes) about the importance of the colonies, one Colonel Arbuthnot commented, "I fear it will not be long before some historian will have to undertake the melancholy duty of chronicling the Decline and Fall of the British Empire." Cautioning against the loss of empire, another ardent colonial unionist concluded that the "legend of Nero fiddling while Rome was burning, then, no longer will be the supreme instance of imperial folly and infatuation."[54] The grandeur of the present, he implied, would crumble to dust without radical action. It is not the least significant irony of the movement for imperial federation that Gibbon's centenary fell in 1894, the year after the IFL was dissolved.

An alternative conception of political termination was associated with the Greek model of colonization. "The ancient Greek city," explained Holland, "when its population became too large for its rocky island or edge of mainland shore, sent out a colony as a beehive sends out a swarm. The colonists took possession of a new territory and there built a city, maintaining a pious regard, except when interests clashed, for the Mother City, but not a true political connection." This system, noted Seeley, "gives complete independence to the colony, but binds it in perpetual alliance."[55] But was such a model relevant? Freeman, one of the most ferocious critics of imperial federation, argued that modern European colonies, including and perhaps especially the British, had much in common with their Greek predecessors, with one crucial exception: they were not ab initio independent. Under the Greek system, the "metropolis claimed at most a certain filial respect, a kind of religious reverence, which was for the most part freely given." As such, the colonial unionists had no precedent on which to draw. "Let us at least remember that what is proposed is unlike anything that ever happened in the world before."[56] Bryce observed in an obituary note that such reasoning underpinned Freeman's biting criticisms of imperial federation:

[54] Burrows, "Imperial Federation," NR, 4 (1884–85), 369; Salmon, "Imperial Federation," FR, 58 (1900), 1011; Arbuthnot, comments in, PRCI, 12 (1880–81), 370; and [Urquhart Forbes], "Imperial Federation," LQR, 64 (1885), 331–32.
[55] Holland, Imperium et Libertas, 13–14; and Seeley, The Expansion of England, 69.
[56] Freeman, "Imperial Federation," MM, 51 (1885), 436 and 437–38. See also Freeman, History of Federal Government (London, 1863), 5–26.

... [H]e disliked all schemes for drawing the colonies into closer relations with the United Kingdom, and even seemed to wish that they should sever themselves from it, as the United States had done. This view sprang partly from his feeling that they were very recent acquisitions, with which the old historic England had nothing to do, partly also from the impression made on him by the analogy of the Greek colonies. He appeared to think that the precedent of those settlements showed the true and proper relation between a "metropolis" and her colonies to be not one of political interdependence, but of cordial friendship and a disposition to render help, nothing more.[57]

The typical federalist riposte was equally adamant: as Forster wrote in his reply to Bright, "[t]his is not the time for alarm at novelties; the air is full of them. . . . Let us be as little enslaved by precedent in our colonial policy as in our domestic legislation."[58] Lord Rosebery also stressed the need to escape from the prison house of imperial history. In a speech delivered in Sydney in December 1883 he distanced the British empire from both Rome and Greece, and pleaded with his audience: "I will ask you only to remember one thing in your dealings with the old country, as I wish statesmen in the old country to remember it in their dealings with you. It is that neither you nor they should reason too much from precedent or from history. It has made its own history; it is creating its own precedent, it is steering its path into the future, where no chart and compass can guide it." This was a theme he reiterated in Adelaide in January 1884. The future of mankind, he told his audience, lay in the hands of the British "race" (including America); yet the future was sometimes shackled by perceptions of past failure. The empire should not be allowed to stagnate, for "let me remind this assemblage of the fact—that empires, and especially great empires, when they crumble at all, are apt to crumble exceedingly small."[59]

The "Greek model" was also invoked when another eighteenth-century image was employed, namely Turgot's metaphor of ripe colonial fruits falling from their parent tree. The argument here was that when colonies reached maturity, as they invariably would, separation was inevitable and should not be impeded. The conservative federalist Samuel Wilson, mixing his models, wrote that "[h]istory tells us that colonies are founded,

---

[57] Bryce, "Edward Augustus Freeman," *EHR*, 7 (1892), 502. On the sparring between Freeman and Bryce over federation, see Freeman's letters to Bryce, especially those on December 16, 1886, February 7, 1887, and November 11, 1889, all in *The Life and Letters of Edward A. Freeman*, ed. W.R.W. Stephens, 2 vols. (London, 1895), II, 256, 359, 411.

[58] Forster, "Imperial Federation," *NC*, 17 (1885), 217.

[59] Rosebery, speech in Sydney, December 10, 1883 and speech in Adelaide, January 18, 1884; reprinted in George Bennett (ed.), *The Concept of Empire* (London, 1953), 281–82 and 284.

grow, and mature, until, like ripe fruit, they fall from the parent tree, like the colonies of ancient Greece and Rome, or the American colonies of many European nations." But there was a way to circumvent this deadly sequence, he insisted, and that was to learn the lessons of the American debacle, and to federate in order to unite permanently.[60] Seeley considered it essential to refute Turgot's argument.[61] He stated that the secession of the American colonies had taught British statesmen and historians the wrong lesson about the nature of colonial empires, indeed that it had left a "faint and confused impression upon the national memory." It had taught them that the Turgotian refrain was an inviolable law of history. "I think then that we mistake the moral of the American Revolution when we infer from it that all colonies—and not merely colonies of religious refugees under a bad colonial system—fall off from the tree as soon as they ripen." The American colonies revolted for specific historical reasons, their secession the result of "temporary conditions, removable, and which have been removed." It was essential that misleading historical analogies not blind people to the novel form of Greater Britain.[62]

There is yet another reason why the ancients could offer little guidance. For the Greek and Roman philosophers, the moral and political universe was defined largely by the walls of the city or city-state (*polis, civitas*). These walls marked both the beginning, and in a sense, the end of political association; in so doing they sorted the inhabitants of the world into citizen and noncitizen, civilized and barbarian. This understanding of the ideal spatial configuration of ethico-political life was translated into the modern world by the Renaissance retrieval of ancient learning and it was reiterated, albeit often obliquely, in the political theories that emerged from the Italian city-states. It formed a central element of the intellectual heritage of Europe. But once again, such an understanding of the ideal nature of political life could not be accommodated to the geographical realities of Greater Britain. Rome offered little direct inspiration or consolation. Not only did it demonstrate that empire and liberty were irreconcilable, it also seemed to suggest that political life was pursued best in

---

[60] Wilson, "Imperial Federation," 380. For the metaphor of ripe fruits, see also Dalton, "The Federal States of the World," *NC*, 16 (1884), 116–17; Morley, "The Expansion of England," *MM*, 49 (1884), 258; and J. H. Muirhead, "What Imperialism Means" [1900] reprinted in *The British Idealists*, ed. David Boucher (Cambridge, 1997), 240.

[61] Turgot used the phrase repeatedly. Seeley may well have picked it up from his "Tableau Philosophique des Progres Successifs de L'Esprit Humain" [1750], which was published in an edition by Dupont de Nemours in the early nineteenth century. See *Oeuvres de Turgot*, ed. Gustave Schelle (Paris, 1913), I, 222: "Les colonies sont comme des fruits qui ne tiennent a l'arbre que jusqu'a leur maturite; devenues suffisantes a elles-meme, elle firent ce que fit depuis Carthage, ce que fera un jour l'Amerique." I thank Emma Rothschild for this pointer.

[62] Seeley, *The Expansion of England*, 15, 256, 17, 155, 16, 297.

confined spaces, indeed that this was the only possible locus of civilization. Such an understanding was certainly compatible with the imperial
conquests in India and Africa, for not only did many of the British governing elite live in Anglicized urban enclaves but their mission, and their
conception of the ends of empire, were often very different. For those intent on securing a permanent Greater Britain, it was entirely inappropriate. The colonial outposts of Greater Britain, while studded with emerging towns and even some large metropolitan areas, were still largely rural,
and oceans separated the territorial elements of the empire, its lands
stretched out over continental expanses. The ancients seemed to teach little, except insofar as they suggested that the political order of which the
(British) moderns were so proud was unsuitable, even flawed fundamentally. It is little wonder that the colonial unionists looked instead across
the Atlantic, and that the emotive archetype of the rugged American frontier replaced the restricted space of the *urbis* as the site of political desire.
Moral regeneration—modern *virtú*—was to be found, or at least sought,
in the vast open spaces of the empire.[63] Combined with a character discourse that stressed the elevating properties of colonialism, this understanding of the settler empire as a politically and morally transformative
association underpinned the theoretical arguments for Greater Britain.

   The widely held conceptions of the meaning of history help to explain
the degree of anxiety that the future status of the empire generated during the 1860s, and throughout the years of the agitation for colonial
union. Proponents of Greater Britain were convinced from the outset that
they were racing against time itself. The ancients, and in particular Rome,
offered a series of perturbing lessons, providing them with a compelling
reason to distance themselves from the past. Their ambition was to create a *permanent* Greater British polity. "The essential thing," William Gisborne stressed, "is to weld together the constitutional parts of the Empire
into one harmonious whole, so as to render their separation, humanly
speaking, impossible."[64] The empire had to escape the clutches of time
that Polybius and Sallust had illuminated two millennia previously, and
that Gibbon and Macaulay, among others, had re-injected into the political imagination. It also had to avoid the calls of inevitable independence
heralded by the ancient Greeks. Its fate had somehow to be brought under

---

[63] On the importance of the frontier in the ideology of the settlers, see Alan Lester,
"British Settler Discourse and the Circuits of Empire," *HWJ*, 54 (2002), 25–48; and, for
the European context, R. K. Betts, "Immense Dimensions," *Western Historical Quarterly*,
10 (1979), 149–66.
   [64] Gisborne, "Colonisation," *PRCI*, 20 (1888–89), 58. See also [John Edward Jenkins],
"An Imperial Confederation," *CR*, 17 (1871), 66–67; Forster, "Imperial Federation," 553;
Seeley, "Georgian and Victorian Expansion," 139; and Francis De Labillière, *Federal Britain*
(London, 1894), vi.

control, steered back within the province of human agency. As the historian and imperial federalist Hugh Egerton cautioned, "[i]t is at once the glory and the responsibility of nations that in their case, no ceaseless law of change is operating, to make dissolution and decay inevitable. To each generation, in its turn, is given the privilege and power to shape its own destinies."[65] It was therefore necessary to conceive of alternative ways of thinking about the empire.

ON NOVELTY

This re-imagining was attempted by emphasizing the historical distinctiveness of Greater Britain. Other empires, whether ancient or modern, had been motivated by profit and retained through brute force, but the British, while militarily powerful and perhaps guilty of past excesses, were driven by more lofty ideals. Or so it was claimed. Bryce suggested that the British empire was unique due to the fact that its colonies were so scattered. Given this geographical spread, not even his beloved America offered a straightforward comparison, although Bryce, typically, considered it the most useful example from which to learn. For Francis de Labillière the United States and the Victorian empire were exceptions to the patterns of history because their "very existence" was not based on the employment of force.[66] They were not empires in any traditional sense, he continued, and consequently they did not fall under the embrace of the same historical logic. Drawing on one of the most powerful arguments used to highlight the radical novelty of the Victorian era—a theme I explored in chapter 3—the honorary secretary of the RCI observed that the "oceanus dissociabilis" objection to governing political communities across expanses of water, drawn originally from antiquity and pervasive well into the nineteenth century, "is a Roman, not an English idea." The "ocean steamship and the submarine cable have," he boasted, "annihilated distance."[67] A new world had dawned, and the ancient models were no longer pertinent.

For Seeley, the former professor of Latin and editor of Livy, the ancients offered no lessons for the "boundless expanses" of Greater Britain. He was a great admirer of the classical world, arguing that much could be learned from it. "I feel more at home at Rome in the times of Cicero," he

---

[65] H. E. Egerton, *A Short History of Colonial Policy* (London, 1897), 478.
[66] Bryce, comments in the *PRCI*, 24 (1892–93), 124; and De Labillière, *Federal Britain*, 199.
[67] C. W. Eddy, "What Are the Best Means of Drawing Together the Interests of the United Kingdom and the Colonies," *PRCI*, 3 (1875–76), 9.

wrote, "than at Paris in the disturbances of the Fronde."[68] Historical analogies, however, had to be appropriate. While the Greeks and the Romans offered contrasting models of imperialism, neither was relevant for mapping the future of Greater Britain. Seeley warned that viewing Britain as an heir to Rome, a tendency he detected among many of his compatriots, was a serious error. It is thus a mistake to claim that his imperial vision was inspired by, or modeled on, the history of Rome.[69] In *The Expansion of England* he argued that "[o]ur colonies do not resemble the colonies which classical students meet with in Greek and Roman history, and our Empire is not an Empire at all in the ordinary sense of the word."[70] There were various reasons for this difference, including the "ethnological unity" of the Greater British population and the development of new communications technologies facilitating global concord. This did not mean, however, that the classical world failed to offer Seeley any insights into the patterns of contemporary international politics, for the Roman archetype, he argued, bore some resemblance to the British mode of rule in India. While the analogy was far from exact—a key difference was indicated by the geographical fact that India was not contiguous with Britain, and thus the territorial transmission belts that had led to the corruption of metropolitan Rome were absent—they did share the status of "superior races" intent not only on ruling, but on "civilizing" those under their control.[71] As the Roman empire in the West was "the empire of civilisation over barbarism," so the British empire in India was "the empire of the modern world over the medieval."[72] In their civilizational superiority over the conquered, the two empires were, he suggested, of the same "type," despite considerable practical differences.

---

[68] Seeley, *The Expansion of England*, 38–43; and ibid., "The Teaching of Politics" in his, *Lectures and Essays* (London, 1870), 301.

[69] Ibid., "Introduction" to *Her Majesty's Colonies* (London, 1886), xviii. For the argument that Seeley saw the British as heirs to Rome, see Reba Soffer, "History and Religion" in R. W. Davis and R. J. Helmstadter (eds.), *Religion and Irreligion in Victorian Society* (London, 1992), 142–43; and Hingley, *Roman Officers and English Gentlemen*, 24–5. Both of these interpretations are incorrect, at least when referring to his (far more influential) writings from the early 1880s onward. Note, however, that Seeley's view on the identity of the empire had changed from his more ambivalent position in the early 1870s. If "we should at some future time cease be its Rome," he suggested in 1872, it would be best if the British could ideally "remain its Athens." Seeley, "The British Race" [1872] *Education I*, 4, (1881), quoted in Deborah Wormell, *Sir John Seeley and the Uses of History* (Cambridge, 1980), 163.

[70] Seeley, *The Expansion of England*, 51.

[71] See for example, the comments in ibid., 193; there is, he proclaimed, "no analogy in history" for the Indian empire. This unqualified claim does not sit easily with his latter comments about the relationship between the Roman and Indian Empires (239).

[72] Ibid., 304, 239, 261, 244.

Nevertheless, such comparisons had nothing to do with the settlement colonies.

Another key difference between past and present, and one of the primary reasons to avoid deriving lessons from the former in order to analyze the latter, concerned the status and limits of freedom. This had been a recurrent theme in the history of modern European political thought. Once again, this was an issue raised by Seeley. History taught, he argued, that empire and liberty could not be reconciled.

> Every historical student knows that it was the incubus of the Empire which destroyed liberty at Rome. Those old civic institutions, which had nursed Roman greatness and to which Rome owed all the civilisation which she had to transmit to the countries of the West, had to be given up as a condition of transmitting it. She had to adopt an organisation of, comparatively, a low type. Her civilisation, when she transmitted it, was already in decay.[73]

Greater Britain, a "state" rather than an empire, was not subject to such a predicament. William Greswell, formerly a professor of classics in South Africa, likewise accentuated the fundamental differences between the ancient empires and the modern British and he emphasized, echoing an argument made famous by Constant, the superiority of modern freedom. "The Britannica *civitas* is a far wider, and we may be allowed to believe a far more honoured, privilege. It is a *civitas* built upon freedom not despotism, upon tolerance rather than upon force, upon voluntary effort and individual enterprise rather than upon bureaucratic orders and state diplomacy." Greswell demanded a "confederacy of the British race," but added the qualifier that it was foolhardy to "refer for guidance to ancient or modern confederacies." It was instructive instead to look to the inspiring example set by United States.[74] "The British Empire of to-day, it cannot be too often repeated," intoned Egerton, "is without precedent in the past. Even this, indeed, hardly expresses the truth." The reason for this novelty, he maintained, lay in the fact that the colonies had been granted "responsible government";[75] its uniqueness resided in the degree of political freedom accorded its inhabitants. The concern with the nature of freedom, however vaguely articulated, was one of the reasons America figured so prominently in imperial debate.

---

[73] Ibid., 246.

[74] Greswell, "Imperial Federation" in *England and Her Colonies* (London, 1887), 7. See also Benjamin Constant, "The Liberty of the Ancients Compared with That of the Moderns" [1819], in Constant, *Political Writings*, 307–28. Constant was, however, a vehement critic of empires, as they challenged liberty both at home and abroad.

[75] Egerton, *A Short History of British Colonial Policy*, 455.

BACK TO THE FUTURE

During the late nineteenth century, when the British empire straddled the globe, many of the defenders and critics of this massive but fragmented political system drew frequently on the past in order to construct their clashing visions of the future. The pasts to which they looked were different, however, and so were the lessons they drew from them. As I have argued in this chapter, a prominent group of imperial thinkers deliberately eschewed mining the richest seam of historical precedent, thus defying centuries of imperial political thought and the historicizing trends of the time. Rather than simply ignoring the ancient empires, they actively dismissed them. Imaginatively leaping across time and space, over two thousand years and the vast breadth of the Atlantic Ocean, many of the advocates of Greater Britain instead sought authority in the image of America. This move was the result of the perceived consequences of understanding empires as transient, temporary, and above all, self-dissolving. In order to defend a permanent global Anglo-Saxon polity, they tried to escape this trajectory, to anchor their vision in secure temporal foundations. Greater Britain was to be located in a progressive narrative, open to the future not condemned by the past. The selective erasure of ancient learning and the corresponding turn toward America was indicative of the persistence in Victorian political discourse of claims (as well as unease) about unrepentant novelty and innovation. It was, that is, both a symptom and a result of the fragile consciousness of modernity. And it pointed simultaneously to the tension in this complex of sensibility and beliefs, to the necessity—at least in terms of staying within the semi-articulated parameters of mainstream political discourse—of tempering an aggressive sense of being modern with a Burkean conception of the moral value of history, tradition, and experience.

But the magnetic pull exerted by the ancient world was hard to resist. During the following generation some of the leading advocates of colonial unity returned to the Greeks as an inspiration for the idea of a global British commonwealth. In particular Lionel Curtis, drawing on the work of the classicist Alfred Zimmern, sought to model a future imperial polity on a highly modernist interpretation of Athens.[76] The Victorians were ultimately no more successful in escaping the orbit of the ancients: by focusing on the United States, itself so much the product, at least in the heated moment of founding, of the ancient writers, the proponents of a Greater British polity ended up taking an indirect route back to Greece

---

[76] Curtis, *The Commonwealth of Nations* (London, 1916), 26. See Jeanne Morefield, "'An Education to Greece': The Round Table, Imperial Theory, and the Uses of History," *HPT* (2007).

and Rome, to the very point of their departure. Forged in the ideological cauldron of the late eighteenth century, the intellectual roots of the independent United States were to be found in the works of the pagan ancients, the "resolve" of the founders "fortified by the sturdy civic virtue of Cato and Brutus, their idea of republican self-government indebted to Greco-Roman models."[77] America was rooted in the ancient soil that the advocates of Greater Britain sought so desperately to evade.

[77] Colin Kidd, "Damnable Deficient," *London Review of Books*, 27 (2005), 30. See also J.G.A. Pocock, *The Machiavellian Moment* (Princeton, 1975); Carl J. Richard, *The Founders and the Classics* (Cambridge, Mass., 1994); M.N.S. Sellers, *American Republicanism* (Basingstoke, 1994); and Caroline Winterer, "From Royal to Republican," *Journal of American History*, 91 (2005), 1264–90.

9

Envisioning America

> Will the English race, which is divided by so many
> oceans, making a full use of modern scientific
> inventions, devise some organisation like that
> of the United States, under which full liberty
> and solid union may be reconciled with
> unbounded territorial expansion?
> —J. R. Seeley, *The Expansion of England* (1883)

ACCOUNTS OF divergent historical trajectories, alternative institutional structures, and contending ways of governing society, have provided the fodder for much theoretical reflection on politics, inspiring new ideas and shaping accounts of how best to live. Reaching backward in time and across geographical space, the comparative gaze played a fundamental role in the political theory of empire during the nineteenth century. As I argued in the previous chapter, many Victorians sought insight in studying the long history charting the rise and fall of empires. But they also looked outward at their competitors and potential challengers, searching for successful models of political association and drawing lessons about what to avoid as well as how to proceed.[1]

The debate over Greater Britain illustrates the importance of this comparative gaze. It was catalyzed and structured to a large degree by (often conflicting) perceptions—of the standing of Britain relative to other great powers, and of the roots of economic, cultural, and political vitality in a world in rapid transition. Representations of America served as a constant referent, offering thinkers from across the political spectrum an imposing but indeterminate source of argument. For centuries America, North and South alike, had played a vivid role in the European imperial imagination, serving as the focal point for arguments over the compass of civilization, religion, and political economy, and, ultimately, the nature of humanity itself.[2] British political theorists had grappled repeatedly with topics in-

---

[1] For further examples, see Duncan Bell, "Empire and Imperialism" in Gregory Claeys and Gareth Stedman Jones (eds.), *The Cambridge History of Nineteenth Century Political Thought* (Cambridge, 2008).

[2] See, inter alia, Tzetvan Todorov, *The Conquest of America*, trans. Richard Howard (New York, 1984); Anthony Pagden, *Spanish Imperialism and the Political Imagination*

spired by the discovery and colonization of the great landmass across the
Atlantic, culminating in the fiery debates in the years preceding the War
of Independence (1775–83). This chapter traverses less well-charted ter-
rain, investigating some of the ways in which representations of "America" ordered Victorian imperial thought.

America played a fluctuating role in British political discourse throughout the "long" nineteenth century. Perceptions of the country derived
from a combination of factors, including the dynamics of British domestic politics, the often fraught state of Anglo-American diplomatic relations, and the political persuasion and sensibilities of the individuals
involved. Generalizations across a century are thus often less than instructive. Some broad patterns can nevertheless be discerned. Deep into
the first half of the nineteenth century, America was commonly regarded
with a mixture of unease and disdain.[3] Not only had the Americans re-
belled against the Crown, against the very country from which they had
originated, they had also initiated a potentially dangerous experiment with
democracy, a mode of political organization that, following the French
revolution and the terror, was regarded with considerable skepticism (and
often abject fear) in British elite circles. It was the harbinger of a new form
of mass politics, enacted on a grand scale. The strident Anglophobia frequently exhibited by leading American journalists and politicians reinforced this disapproval. Views of America, though, were never homogeneous. Until the 1880s, Tories were mostly sneering about the country and
its inhabitants, while Whigs, and then later liberals, were usually more
sympathetic. For radicals in particular the development, indeed the mere
existence, of America seemed to offer assurances that their desire for the
deepening of democracy in the United Kingdom was not misplaced, and
that it could be met without falling prey to the cataclysms predicted by
nervous critics. (This optimism began to wane during the closing years of
the century as the failings of the American political system became more
obvious, and as it began to embark on its own global imperial mission in
the 1890s, first in Hawaii and then in the Philippines.) As the reform movement in Britain gathered momentum, the example of the United States,

(New Haven, 1990); Pagden, *Lords of All the World* (New Haven, 1995); Karen Ordahl
Kupperman (ed.), *America in European Consciousness, 1493–1750* (Chapel Hill, 1995).

[3] For example, see Paul Langford, "Manners and Character in Anglo-American Perceptions, 1750–1850" in Fred Leventhal and Roland Quinault (eds.), *Anglo-American Attitudes* (Aldershot, 2000), 76–90. James Mill, "Colonies," reprinted in Mill, *Essays from the
Supplement to the Encyclopedia Britannica, Collected Works* (London, 1995 [1828]), 1–2;
and also, John Stuart Mill, "State of Society in America" [1836], CW, XVIII, 91–117. Later
in the century, Matthew Arnold expressed a variation on this theme, arguing that Britain
was in danger of becoming "*Americanised*," and as such pervaded by low ideals and "want
of culture." Arnold, "Democracy" [1861], in *Culture and Anarchy and Other Writings*, ed.
Stefan Collini (Cambridge, 1993), 13 and 15 (italics in original).

often mediated to the educated public by Alexis de Tocqueville's *Democracy in America* (1835 and 1840), was utilized across the political spectrum. John Stuart Mill commented in 1835 that "[a]ll who write or speak on either side of the dispute . . . are prompt enough in pressing America into their service."[4] This indeterminacy was one of the reasons for Tocqueville's popularity: his arguments pointed to the strengths as well as the inevitability of democracy, while also offering an incisive analysis of its weaknesses. Anxiety about democracy helped intensify the crises and confrontations that punctuated relations between the two countries. But despite these concerns, the importance of America oscillated in British political consciousness during the early decades of the century, and it often remained in the background due to its relative lack of weight in global power politics and also its great distance from Europe. It was as much an object of curiosity as of outright admiration or dread.

The Civil War (1860–65) intensified interest in America, so much so that during the period 1860–74 it "burst into the mainstream of British political life."[5] And there it remained—a site of both powerful desire and nightmarish visions of the future. Critics and advocates of a federal Greater Britain drew divergent lessons from the conflict: it either proved that federalism was robust enough to survive a crisis, or it demonstrated that it was the very weakness of federalism that led to war in the first place. A series of other highly visible issues, including the protracted Alabama Case, the Geneva negotiations, and Irish-American agitation, ensured that America retained a crucial place in British minds from the 1860s onward. This was partly a result of the apparent shrinkage of the world (as explored in chapter 3), for the re-envisaging of the limits of nature had the effect of drawing America "closer" to Europe. And the same technologies that appeared to render venerable ideas about scale redundant also facilitated easier travel across the Atlantic, leading to an increase in personal and political interaction.[6] These developments formed an important backdrop to debates over the future of the British empire.

Just as "America" functioned in a Janus-faced manner in the impassioned struggle over democracy, so it served as an indefinite referent in debates over Greater Britain. It provided the raw material for multiple fan-

[4] Mill, "De Tocqueville on America" [I, 1835], CW, XVIII, 49–50. On the impact of Tocqueville on debates over empire, especially in the second half of the century, see Edward Beasley, *Empire as the Triumph of Theory* (London, 2005), ch. 6; and Beasley, *Mid-Victorian Imperialists* (London, 2005).

[5] Murney Gerlach, *British Liberalism and the United States* (Basingstoke, 2001), 5.

[6] On transatlantic issues and interactions, see Gerlach, *British Liberalism and the United States;* Hugh Tulloch, "Changing British Attitudes Towards the United States in the 1880's," *HJ*, 20 (1977), 825–40; and Christopher Mulvey, *Transatlantic Manners* (Cambridge, 1990).

tasies of the future, of places and spaces yet to come. Even those historians who identify the centrality of America in Victorian imperial discourse tend not to specify adequately the various roles that it played. For example, although Ged Martin stresses the importance of America throughout nineteenth-century debate, he places too much emphasis on continuity and not enough on the considerable shifts in the perception of America over time.[7] While America was indeed a common referent in imperial discourse from the 1820s onward, the frequency with which it was drawn upon increased strikingly in the closing three decades of the century, and the sense of anxiety that it generated intensified in the wake of the Civil War. America was a more potent, more disquieting presence in the later period. Earlier in the century it had been viewed as a distinct but local threat (especially to Canada) and as a significant *potential* competitor, a possible future pretender to the global throne. In the later debates it was seen as a pressing challenger to British supremacy. The tense of alarm had altered, from future to present, from possible to actual. This was accompanied by a significant transformation in the way in which the doctors of the British body politic diagnosed (and potentially prescribed) American political institutions.

This chapter analyzes how ideas about America shaped visions of Greater Britain. The next section demonstrates how America offered the most pertinent example of a working federal state, a vast and dynamic country governed by effective representative institutions. It was the obvious practical template for a federal Greater British polity. But the country was also regarded as a threat to British economic and sometimes even geopolitical superiority, and it acted, therefore, as one of the original catalysts for the eruption of debate over colonial unity. Respect was interwoven with apprehension. This is the subject of the second section. The third section documents the role of ideas about scale and competition. This is followed by an examination of the idea that a giant polity could act as a guarantor of peace and justice in a turbulent world. I then turn to the ways in which the past acted as a regulatory mechanism shaping ideas about Greater Britain, for the purported lessons of the War of Independence were burned deeply into British political consciousness. In the conclusion I sketch some of the claims made about global Anglo-Saxon unity and the need for a future alliance between Britain and America, as well as pointing to tensions that emerged between the transatlantic and imperial visions.

[7] Martin, "Empire Federalism and Imperial Parliamentary Union, 1820–1870," *HJ*, 16 (1973), 73–14. For other accounts that stress the important role of America, see Ronald Hyam, *Britain's Imperial Century, 1815–1914* (Basingstoke, 2002 [1976]); Paul Kennedy, "The Theory and Practice of Imperialism," *HJ*, 20 (1977), 761–69; and D. George Boyce, *Decolonisation and the British Empire, 1775–1997* (London, 1999), ch. 2.

The Model of the Future: America as Template

See the United States—how they expand,
how they refuse to be divided.
—J. R. Seeley, "The Objects to be
Gained by Imperial Federation" (1886)

During the 1830s, Hegel proclaimed that "America is . . . the country of the future, and its world historical importance has yet to be revealed in the ages ahead." It was the precursor of a new type of political order. The widespread belief in American preordination generated a wide array of expectations, and it influenced colonial thought throughout the century. Tocqueville, one of the leading ideological architects of French imperialism, saw America as an archetype for the society he hoped would emerge in Algeria, while in 1852 Gladstone argued that America served as the "great source of experimental instruction, so far as colonial institutions are concerned." A quarter of a century later, Gladstone pushed Charles Darwin on whether the theory of evolution pointed to the decline of the Eastern civilizations and the triumphant emergence of America as the world's leading power. Darwin responded with a positive answer. As America grew in strength, so too did the imaginative pull it exerted. The late Victorian age was, proclaimed Dicey, one of "Americomania."[8]

The advocates of Greater Britain looked across the Atlantic and saw the future of the empire. Writing in 1900 the philosopher J. H. Muirhead observed that during the 1880s the "argument from America is turned. America is no longer an argument for separation, but for retention." While in the past it had provided a model of a flourishing postcolonial independent state, it could now be used to help defend a permanent colonial connection. This was because it had "shown how political union has been maintained over an immense territory."[9] This "turn" to America, which was a common theme of imperial debate in the last three decades of the century, did not meet with universal approval. The Marquis of Lorne, for example, complained in 1885 that it had become standard practice to anchor arguments about the practicability of an imperial sen-

---

[8] Hegel, *Lectures on the Philosophy of World History*, trans. H. B. Nisbet (Cambridge, 1980 [1822–31]), 170; Tocqueville, "Notes on the Voyage to Algeria in 1841" in Tocqueville, *Writings on Empire and Slavery*, ed. Jennifer Pitts (Baltimore, 2001), 56; Gladstone, Hansard, 3, CLXII, 962 (May 21, 1852); Adrian Desmond and James Moore, *Darwin* (London, 1991), 626; and Dicey, "Americomania in English Politics," *The Nation*, January 21, 1886, xlii.

[9] Muirhead, "What Imperialism Means" [1900] reprinted in *The British Idealists*, ed. David Boucher (Cambridge, 1997), 244.

ate (which he opposed) by pointing to the United States.[10] America was
regarded as a political laboratory, a testing ground for modes of politics,
democracy and federalism especially, that were likely, and perhaps even
inevitably, to be replicated in other states around the world. This vision
was underpinned by an interpretation—one that was often greatly sim-
plified, and subject to disorienting amnesia—of the American past and
present. Not only was the course of the Civil War often dismissed as a
minor blip in an otherwise linear march of progress, but the actual analysis of America frequently verged on the eulogistic. Seeley's veneration of
the United States was typical of federalist attitudes. He believed that it was
perhaps the happiest polity recorded in the annals of human history, the
fortuitous result of the complex interaction of individual character and
political institutions:

> If a philosopher were asked for a recipe to produce the greatest amount of
> pure happiness in a community he would say, take a number of men whose
> characters have been formed during many generations by rational liberty, se-
> rious religion, and strenuous labour. Place these men in a wide territory,
> where no painful pressure shall reach them, and where prosperity shall be
> within the reach of all. Adversity gives wisdom and strength, but with pain;
> prosperity gives pleasure, but relaxes the character. Adversity followed after
> a time by prosperity, this is the recipe for healthy happiness, for it gives plea-
> sure without speedily relaxing energy.

Formed in a "temperate zone, by Teutonic liberty and Protestant religion," and combining the best of the old world and the new, America offered a shining example to the world.[11] And although it was in danger of
forfeiting political paradise by becoming overly assertive, he argued that
it was nevertheless at the apex of its greatness. The British had much to
learn from it. We can discern in this encomium a picture of Seeley's ideal
Greater Britain, and also a hint of apprehension about the dynamics of
competition between the two powers.

But America was great not only because of what it was, but because of

---

[10] Lorne, *Imperial Federation* (London, 1885), 26–27; see also C. R Lowell, "English
and American Federalism," *FR*, 43 (1888), 189–95; and George Parkin, *Imperial Federation* (London, 1892), 49. For a later attempt to employ America as a template for Greater
Britain, this time through a tendentious reading of the American founding, see F. S. Oliver,
Alexander Hamilton (London, 1906). Among other key imperial thinkers, this book influenced Lionel Curtis and Philip Kerr (Lord Lothian).

[11] Seeley, *The Expansion of England*, 155–56. For some other positive accounts of America, see Greswell, "Imperial Federation" in *England and Her Colonies* (London, 1887), 8;
Francis de Labillière, *Federal Britain* (London, 1894), 178; C. E. Howard Vincent, "The
British Empire To-Day," *PRCI*, 16 (1884–85), 324; and William S. Harris, "The Commercial Advantages of Federation," *PRCI*, 13 (1881–82), 210.

the obstacles it had overcome. Swimming against the current of centuries of political thought, the Americans had succeeded in creating a territorially extensive republic. This offered a practical challenge to a long-standing argument that insisted on the impossibility of establishing a stable and nondespotic polity on such a scale. The increasing political and economic vitality of the country seemed to demonstrate that federalism could work, and work well, indeed that it could be seen as a solution to the problem of ruling massive countries under the auspices of representative institutions.[12] The Canadian imperial federalist George Parkin—described by Dilke as the "orator of the League"—observed that "the growth of the United States had widened political horizons." It had "proved," he wrote in a revealing passage, "that immense territorial extent is not incompatible, under modern conditions, with that representative system of government which had its birth and development in England, and its most notable adaptation in America."[13] From the apparent triumph of America, the proponents of a federal Greater Britain divined the possibility of success for their global schemes. No longer did federation connote weakness, or size despotism. "Libertas et Imperium"—Disraeli's artful misquotation of Tacitus[14]—could be reconciled after all.

America had succeeded in two different senses. Firstly, it had shown that federal arrangements were robust enough to govern a large country, that the intrinsic weakness traditionally associated with them could be circumvented by clever constitutional design. "The type of future state," announced Seeley, "is shown in the United States, which has spanned a whole mighty continent from east to west, and has emphatically refused to submit to disintegration."[15] Discussing long-standing views about the impossibility of representation over great distances—a theme explored in chapter 3—he claimed that a new era had dawned: "Those very colonies, which then broke off from us, have since given the example of a federal organisation, in which vast territories, some of them thinly peopled and newly settled, are held easily in union with older communities." This was

---

[12] On the way in which the American founders reshaped the meaning of federation, extending it beyond the older idea of confederation and Montesquieu's *république fédérative*, see J.G.A. Pocock, "States, Republics, and Empires" in Terence Ball and Pocock (eds.), *Conceptual Change and the Constitution* (Lawrence, Kans., 1988), 55–78. For a useful survey of the debates over size, see Jacob Levy, "Beyond Publius," *HPT*, 27 (2006), 50–90.

[13] Parkin, *Imperial Federation*, 33; and Dilke, *Problems of Greater Britain* (London, 1890), II, 466.

[14] Disraeli coined the phrase in 1851: Richard Jenkyns, *The Victorians and Ancient Greece* (Oxford, 1980), 333. Freeman also employed the phraseology, albeit in a critical manner: "'Imperium' and 'libertas' after all do not get on well as yoke-fellows" ("Imperial Federation," *MM*, 51 [1885], 444). See also the criticisms in Herbert Spencer, "Imperialism and Slavery," *Facts and Comments* (London, 1902), 117.

[15] Seeley, "Introduction" to *Her Majesty's Colonies* (London, 1886), xi.

an argument about political feasibility. And secondly, it had demonstrated that liberty could flourish in such a polity. "[T]he whole enjoys in the fullest degree parliamentary freedom."[16] Whereas it was thought that the ancient empires had demonstrated the incompatibility of empire and liberty, and that empires were incapable of sustaining themselves over time, the United States proved that it was possible to achieve both goals. This was a normative argument suggesting that federalism established the conditions necessary for the sustenance of freedom. Conceived as a global polity based around a single system of representation, and having its legislative powers divided along federal lines, Greater Britain had a successful precedent to draw upon.

SIZE MATTERS: AMERICA AS COMPETITOR

America also presented the advocates of Greater Britain with a daunting challenge. It was, a radical federalist wrote, "our most formidable rival."[17] The late Victorian era was saturated by a sense of faltering confidence, sometimes bordering on crisis, about the role of Britain in the world. Externally powerful and assured, there were inward signs of decline—in production, in power, even in morals and national character. The rise of Germany was eyed warily, while France, as ever, remained the subject of habitual suspicion. Russia loomed broodingly farther to the east, a threat to the integrity of the Indian empire and beyond. From across the Atlantic, the post–Civil War revival of the United States heralded the rise of a potent Anglo-Saxon competitor. This was one of the principal driving forces behind the injunction to build Greater Britain.

The United States had featured prominently in discussions over political economy and imperial strategy throughout the century. As Froude commented in 1870, "[w]e have no present quarrel with the Americans; we trust most heartily that we may never be involved in any quarrel with them, but undoubtedly from the day they became independent of us, they became our rivals." As its power increased, America came to figure much more prominently in British elite consciousness. Whereas Britain appeared to either slow down, or even go into reverse, America seemed to be accelerating. This was added to fear about the swelling wave of emigration to the United States, a theme I discussed in chapter 2. "They con-

[16] Ibid., *The Expansion of England*, 74.

[17] Anon., "Imperium et Libertas," WR, 57 (1880), 92. From a nonfederalist perspective, see also James Keith, "Our Great Competitor," NC, 21 (1887), 792–79; and Disraeli's speech, "Conservative Principles" delivered at Manchester, April 3, 1872, in T. E. Kebbel (ed.), *Selected Speeches of the Late Right Honourable the Earl of Beaconsfield* (London, 1882), II, 522.

stitute," warned Froude, "the one great Power whose interests and whose pretensions compete with our own, and in so far as the strength of nations depends on the number of thriving men and women composing them, the United States have been made stronger, the English empire weaker, to the extent of those millions and the children growing of them."[18] This picture was further complicated by the fact that one of the main catalysts of the agricultural depression that burdened Britain in the closing decades of the century was the opening up of the vast North American prairies. While Germany, Russia, and to a lesser degree, France, were considered strategic and military threats close to home, the image of America hovered menacingly before the eyes of the British, its enormous potential clear for all to see.

There are two elements of this threat—or at least the perception of it— that are frequently overlooked. Firstly, although America was viewed primarily as an economic competitor, geopolitical concerns also intruded. And secondly, it was seen to challenge British leadership of the Anglo-Saxon "race." Washington was no longer widely regarded as a direct military threat to Canada, although there were those who continued to believe that it was. Goldwin Smith's vociferous advocacy of the American incorporation of Canada fanned the dimming flames of such a view.[19] Rather, the challenge was global. In an address to the Royal Colonial Institute in 1869, William Westgarth argued that the British empire presented the "greatest spectacle of its kind in history." There was, however, an imminent danger that this position would be forfeited if the colonies were surrendered, and America, he suggested, would usurp Britain as the anointed political leader of the world.[20] Two main lines of argument predominated. One stated that if the colonies were given a chance to develop as independent countries, the end result would be a series of dynamic new states, and an old one, Britain, bereft of one of the main sources of its strength. Without colonies, it was simply another medium-sized European state; Samson shorn of his locks. Following colonial independence, argued Alexander Galt, "we would become an insignificant independent country," like one of the "minor nations" that were "the very playthings of the powerful nations of the earth." "The fact is," another federalist warned,

---

[18] Froude, "England and Her Colonies," *FM*, 1 (1870), 1.

[19] Smith, *Canada and the Canadian Question* (London, 1891). Critical ripostes to Smith's position from colonial unionists include Parkin, *Imperial Federation*, ch. VII; and De Labillière, *Federal Britain*, ch. 11. This had been a common theme among radicals and French-Canadians throughout the century: George Lillibridge, *Beacon of Freedom* (Philadelphia, 1955), 40; and Miles Taylor, "The 1848 Revolutions and the British Empire," *P&P*, 116 (2000), 162–63.

[20] Westgarth, "The Relation of the Colonies to the Mother Country," *PRCI*, 1 (1869), 84–85.

"unless we are prepared to share our sovereignty with our fellow subjects beyond the seas, as fast as they are fitted for that sovereignty, and unless we are content to live with them beneath one sceptre, and on equal terms, we shall be depressed into a second or third-rate power, and they will rise into separate, mighty, and perhaps antagonistic States." The British empire, Parkin insisted, must keep "abreast of the spirit of the age." If this spirit, the spirit of expansion and consolidation, was ignored, the British would forfeit their hegemonic status. "If England wishes to maintain the position she has hitherto occupied amongst the nations of the world, she must endeavour to bind together the far-distant portions of her Empire."[21] America, warned de Labillière, was "all-powerful and preponderating." Stretching around the globe, Greater Britain was the only adequate response.

> For England to be separated from the rest of her Empire, will be to remain stationary or comparatively so, while new countries grow up to and outstrip her in population, wealth, and power. . . . United in a great British Imperial Union, we shall in the future stand in a position of equality beside the American Union, or any other great power; divided, neither England nor any of the Colonies, for generations, will be able to do so, and we must, at no distant date, resign the leadership of the Anglo-Saxon race to our American cousins.[22]

In order to rebuff this double challenge, the British colonial empire had to undergo a constitutional transformation. The other line of argument contended that if they were so careless as to let their invaluable colonies secede, sooner or later the leaders of the embryonic states would realize the impossibility of prospering in a world dominated by massive political units and they would seek union with a different great power, the obvious choice being America. They would be incorporated into an expanding Greater America. Even more worryingly, some imperialists discerned the threat of a military confrontation over the colonies with an increasingly aggressive American empire.[23]

Tocqueville had prophesied in the closing lines of *Democracy in Amer-*

---

[21] Galt, "The Relations of the Colonies to the Empire," reprinted in *PRCI*, 14 (1882–83), 395; [Urquhart Forbes], "Imperial Federation," *LQR*, 4 (1885), 332; Parkin, *Imperial Federation*, 25; and Wilson, "A Scheme for Imperial Federation," 597–98.

[22] De Labillière, *Federal Britain*, 213 and 46. The employment of the term "stationary" is here revealing, fitting into a common idiom that dichotomized "stationariness" (usually associated with China) with dynamism (usually associated with Britain). See Stefan Collini, *Public Moralists* (Oxford, 1991), 108 and 274.

[23] For concern about American incorporation, see Froude, "England and Her Colonies," 1–3 and 15; and Seeley, *The Expansion of England*, 15. Jenkins saw as much of a threat from America as Germany or Russia in the Southern hemisphere: [Jenkins], "An Imperial Confederation," *CR*, 17 (1871), 66.

ica that the future belonged to Russia and America. Seeley, forty years later, saw this divination materializing before his eyes. America, he warned, was growing powerful in the west, while on the "other side of Europe, Russia is giving in very different circumstances another proof of the capacity of the modern world for political combination over vast spaces." Such countries, he continued, "have shown that in the present age of the world political unions may exist on a vaster scale than was possible in former times."[24] Urgent action was required to counter these giants. "The present growth of the United States and Russia threatens to dwarf the old states of Europe," warned another federalist, "and wisdom counsels union to the English nation."[25] Such a union would maintain Britain's rightful position of global supremacy. Dilke was similarly concerned, arguing in *Greater Britain* that the leading powers of the future would all be continental in size: the United States and Russia were already so, although the former would also absorb Canada and Mexico. All of Europe except Britain would fall to Germany. Greater Britain, a fragmented global polity minus Canada, would also join this exclusive club. Later, in *Problems of Greater Britain*, he argued that the "future mastery of the world" would be shared between four powers: Russia, China, the United States, and Greater Britain. The Americans and the British, conceived as one racial group, would gradually pull away from the other two, assuming that Greater Britain (now with Canada forming an integral part) remained united and strong.[26] The fear of being dwarfed was not new. In 1828 William Huskisson had declared that "England cannot afford to be small," and that it was the colonies that made her great.[27] This had been an important theme in the writings of the colonial reform movement. But it reached a crescendo later in the century. The ideologues of Greater Britain were determined to prove that Tocqueville's vision of the future was not preordained, that the British would play a pivotal role in governing the world.

Their arguments alternated between two competing responses. Sometimes they seemed to suggest that the primary purpose of Greater Britain was to balance the power of Russia, Germany, and the United States. This was the traditional European mechanism for restraining great power ambitions, albeit this time promoted on a global scale. But the most common

[24] Tocqueville, *Democracy in America*, II, 456–57; Seeley, "Introduction," xi–xii; and Seeley, *The Expansion of England*, 159.

[25] Samuel Wilson, "Imperial Federation," *NR*, 4 (1884), 386.

[26] Dilke, *Greater Britain*, I, 104–105; and Dilke, *Problems of Greater Britain*, II, 583, 384. He envisaged an alliance with China, which would bring peace and stability to the East (II, 86, 160, 492).

[27] Huskisson, speech on May 2, 1828, in the *Speeches of the Right Honourable William Huskisson* (London, 1831), II, 287.

line of argument, as we shall see in the next section, recommended that Greater Britain should assume the responsibility of global leadership. It would be so powerful that substantive competition was unlikely, and perhaps inconceivable. Therefore, by definition, it would escape the logic of balancing. As was so common in imperial political thought, questions were posed, occasional answers sketched, but the details and the consequences were left unexplored. Part of the reason for this lack of clarity was that the advocates of Greater Britain rarely distinguished between three dimensions of power: military, economic, and, more vaguely, moral. Balancing required the first, and, in order to finance increasing military expenditure, it presupposed the second. Global leadership, on the other hand, was anchored in a claim about moral superiority, but it was premised on the possession of both economic and military might. Sliding between the idea of balance and that of hegemonic domination, and failing to properly delineate the sources of British power, followed from uncertainty over the ultimate rationale of Greater Britain.

The British position was beset by irony. For much of the nineteenth century, political commentators on the European mainland, and especially those in France and Germany, had felt overshadowed, trapped even, by Russia and Britain, the two great empires to their east and west. This fueled their desire for territorial empires, for a place in the sun, cravings that when satisfied in the closing decades of the century led to intense concern in London and yet further calls for the expansion of England. The British fear of Russia and the United States thus mirrored the French and German fear of encirclement, and it can be seen as one more indicator of the beginning of the end of the western European dominance of international politics. Tocqueville's prophecy was, of course, amply confirmed in the twentieth century.

The fear of being overtaken as a great power fed into another set of concerns. Not only would the British lose their position as the leading political and economic force in the world, they would lose it to a country composed largely of people of the same race.[28] This revolt signified a double blow, for as well as catalyzing fears about the composition of geopolitical power, it generated consternation that the "leadership" of the Anglo-Saxon world would be lost forever. This issue had figured occasionally in debates during the Revolutionary era—in the context of a possible switch in the location of legislative authority within Anglo-Saxondom due to inexorable demographic trends[29]—but by the closing decades of the nineteenth century it had become a source of widespread trepidation. To draw

---

[28] Froude, "England and Her Colonies," 15; and De Labillière, *Federal Britain*, 46.

[29] Smith, *An Inquiry into the Nature and Causes of the Wealth of Nations*, Book IV, 625–26; and Benjamin Franklin, *The Interest of Great Britain Considered* (London, 1760).

on a then common familial idiom, it appeared as though the offspring had returned to wrestle responsibilities from the parent. But the loss of leadership could be read in a more positive light. Since the peoples of America and Britain were "essentially one," argued Dilke, the British were merely continuing their global advance, except this time utilizing a different political vehicle. Conceived of as a racial community, not a strictly political one, the British were not confined to the limits of Crown sovereignty. They were slowly dispersing throughout the world, taking their customs, culture, and political habits with them. In the creation of America, he wrote, the world witnessed the "rise of a new English country," a country that was now at the forefront of the globalization of the British people. America, he continued,

> ... is becoming, not English merely, but world-embracing in the variety of its type; and as the English element has given language and history to that land, America offers the English race the moral directorship of the globe, by ruling mankind through Saxon institutions and the English tongue. Through America, England is speaking to the world.[30]

The apparent transfer of power and prestige from the United Kingdom to the United States also represented the passing on of the baton of modernity. From the 1760s onward the English had seen themselves, and had been seen by foreign visitors, as the country most illustrative of the trends likely to shape the trajectory of the modern world.[31] Commercial, constitutional, and industrial innovation combined to produce a picture of vitality and relentless progress, dragging the image of the country from the insular feudal past and projecting it into an expansive global future. A monumental uprooting of traditional national self-understanding, this caesura in part helps to explain the late nineteenth-century British obsession with the recovery and veneration of its heritage; radical change needed to be balanced with (and made more palatable by) a recognition of the glories of the past.[32] It also helps explain the combination of apprehension and admiration felt toward the United States, for during the closing decades of the century the role of pioneer of modernity was rapidly slipping across the Atlantic.

Visions of America were anchored in an array of widely shared assumptions about the importance of scale in determining the structure of world order. It was commonly thought that large states bred confidence and a sweeping sense of possibility in their people; they could not be in-

---

[30] Dilke, *Problems of Greater Britain*, I, 5; and Dilke, *Greater Britain*, I, 226 and 318.

[31] Paul Langford, *Englishness Identified* (Oxford, 2000), 5–7.

[32] The idea of an ancient English "heritage" to be preserved and cherished was an invention of the late nineteenth century: Peter Mandler, "Against 'Englishness,'" *TRHS*, 6th series, 7 (1997), 155–76.

timidated. This was as much a question of political self-consciousness as brute material power. In a book that was standard reading in British universities, the Swiss-born legal philosopher J. K. Bluntschli wrote that the "extent" of the state has a "great influence on its political character and development."[33] The advocates of Greater Britain concurred. It was the obsession with size that led the liberal critic of imperialism J. M. Robertson to castigate "our megalophiles," among whom he singled out Seeley, and L. T. Hobhouse to argue that the "genuine pride of patriotism is surely lost when littleness of geographical extent can be construed into a term of reproach."[34] It was believed that large political units were better equipped to deal with the practical exigencies of international affairs, that size could be equated with both capability and prestige. Although the power of a country was assessed principally through the size of its population—which indicated its potential "rifle strength"—this in turn depended on a series of factors including the vulnerability of its frontiers, its natural resource base, the geographic density of its population and industrial facilities, and so forth. These demanded capacious physical dimensions. Such concerns paralleled the emerging field of "geopolitics." Awareness of the political significance of geography was ubiquitous.[35] This was reflected not only in the theoretical writings of the imperialists, but also in their support for the expansion of geographical education in schools and universities—an expansion that was itself inflected with, and sometimes shaped by, imperial concerns. Halford Mackinder, the leading British proponent of geopolitics, was an early advocate of imperial federation. He argued that human history had reached a critical juncture: the world had finally "closed," as the "Columbian era" of Western imperial expansion came to an end due to lack of further space to conquer. Political and economic competition would now intensify, its previous outlets removed, and the British colonial empire, constituted by a "league of democracies," had to unify to secure its position against two growing "Eurasian" powers (Russia and Germany) that threatened to control the "Heartland," a zone he later famously termed "the geographical pivot of history."[36] Lorne, who served as the president of the Royal Geographical

---

[33] Bluntschli, *Theory of the State*, trans. D. G. Ritchie, P. E. Matheson, and R. Lodge (Oxford, 1885), 222.

[34] Robertson, *An Introduction to English Politics* (London, 1900), 257; and Hobhouse, *Democracy and Reaction* (London, 1904), 17.

[35] See the early hints about the importance of "political geography" in Dilke, *Greater Britain*, I, 106–107. On geopolitics, see Jonathan Haslam, *No Virtue Like Necessity* (New Haven, 2002), ch. 4; and Robert Strausz Hupe, *Geopolitics* (New York, 1942). See also the discussion of Seeley and geopolitics in David Worsley, "Sir John Robert Seeley and His Intellectual Legacy," unpublished PhD thesis, University of Manchester, 2001, 206–20.

[36] Initially a liberal and a free trader, he later became a key supporter of Chamberlain's abortive campaign for Tariff Reform and an ardent Tory. See Mackinder, "The Geographical Pivot of History," *Geographical Journal*, 23 (1904), 421–37. On his conception of im-

Society, argued that the accumulation of systematic geographical knowledge was indispensable in a world defined by competition between empires. It was also vital for strengthening Greater Britain. "Knowledge and sympathy are essential to the consolidation of empire," he argued, for such knowledge (and the sympathy it inculcated) provided a "fresh anchor for the greatness, and therefore for the unity of the empire." It was especially important for emigrants, who needed accurate information about the lands that they would be populating.[37] The political dimensions of space, the moral and psychological effects induced by diverse physical and cultural environments, and the relationship between character (both individual and collective) and landscape—all were central to Victorian imperial thought.[38] And so too was a concern with the creation and dissemination of geographical knowledge, with understanding the world as a precursor to controlling it.

In an increasingly interdependent world, states could no longer even attempt to isolate themselves from the actions and interests of others. In one of the most important passages in *The Expansion of England*, Seeley wrote that "[t]hese new conditions make it necessary to reconsider the whole colonial problem. They make it in the first place possible actually to realise the old utopia of a Greater Britain, and at the same time they make it almost necessary to do so." There are two interwoven arguments that need disentangling here. The first related to the fact that, following the revolution in communications technologies, it was finally possible to envisage a true Greater Britain. What had once been considered utopian was now rendered plausible. The second relates to Seeley's enigmatic statement that it is as a result "almost necessary to do so." While the first argument referred to possibilities, this one points to some of the dangers stalking (and brought into sharp relief by) this re-imagined world. As the planet appeared to shrink, so competition seemed more intense, as if projected through a magnifying glass. The "same inventions which make vast political unions possible," he claimed, "tend to make states which are on the old scale of magnitude unsafe, insignificant, second-rate."[39] Anxiety about America needs to be understood in this light. It was certainly not a

---

perialism, see Brian W. Blouet, *Halford Mackinder* (London, 1987), ch. 9; W. H. Parker, *Mackinder* (Oxford, 1982), ch. 3; and Gerry Kearns, "*Fin de Siècle* Geopolitics" in Peter Taylor (ed.), *Political Geography of the Twentieth Century* (London, 1993), 9–25. On the entanglement of geography and empire, see David Livingstone, *The Geographical Tradition* (Oxford, 1992), ch. 7; and Felix Driver, *Geography Militant* (Oxford, 1999).

[37] Lorne, "The Annual Address on the Progress of Geography, 1885–86," *Proceedings of the Royal Geographical Society*, 8 (1886), 420–22.

[38] Uday Singh Mehta's argument that there was no serious reflection on territoriality by liberal (imperial) thinkers in nineteenth-century Britain is contradicted by the debates over Greater Britain. Mehta, *Liberalism and Empire* (Chicago, 1999), ch. 4.

[39] Seeley, *The Expansion of England*, 74 and 75. See also, Seeley, *Introduction to Political Science*, 81–82; and his "Georgian and Victorian Expansion," *FR*, 48 (1887), 137.

novel departure to argue for political and economic interdependence; after all, Hume, Smith, and Kant, a century beforehand, had perceived clearly that cross-cutting patterns of interaction defined the logic of international politics.[40] This reciprocal sensitivity was now heightened. As Stephen Kern has observed, "[t]he new technology changed the dimensions of experience so rapidly that the future seemed to rush towards the present at a tempo as hurried and irregular as Stravinsky's music."[41] This future was "rushing" in what suddenly appeared a far smaller world, a confined space whose dimensions made it difficult to imagine peaceful coexistence. From this followed the belief in the necessity of large, aggregate states. Although Darwin, and quasi-scientific social theorizing more generally, made few inroads into the debates over Greater Britain, the outlines of a doctrine of "survival of the fittest" can be discerned in the obsession with fierce competition. The perception that the world was shrinking induced the paranoia and a heightened awareness of interconnection and dangerous proximity, the political repercussions of which were played out on the killing fields of Flanders only a generation later.

Added to the arguments about the value of immense political units was the belief that history was moving toward an age dominated by an ever decreasing number of mammoth omnicompetent polities. The examples most commonly adduced were Germany, Russia, and, of course, the United States. Superlatives abounded. "This is," declared Greswell, the "age of large states and colossal armaments." "In the world's future," one federalist predicted, "great empires seem fated to take the place of the small states of to-day."[42] For Froude, warning of the possibility that the colonists might seek to link up with the United States if they were surrendered by London, the lessons were clear. "These are not the days for small states: the natural boundaries are broken down which once divided kingdom from kingdom; and with the interests of nations so much intertwined as they are now becoming, every one feels the benefit of belong-

[40] Smith, *An Inquiry into the Nature and Causes of the Wealth of Nations*, especially Books III and IV; Hume, "Of the Jealousy of Trade" in Hume, *Essays, Moral, Political, and Literary*, ed. Eugene F. Miller (Indianapolis, 1987), 327–32; and Immanuel Kant, "Perpetual Peace" [1795] in Kant, *Political Writings*, ed. Hans Reiss, 2nd ed. (Cambridge, 1991), 93–125. This had been a common theme since political thinkers had begun to grapple with the problems engendered by international trade in the seventeenth century. See the essays in Hont, *Jealousy of Trade*. For a particularly clear mid-nineteenth century example, see Karl Marx and Friedrich Engels, *The Communist Manifesto* [1848], ed. Gareth Stedman Jones (Harmondsworth, 2002), 223.

[41] Kern, *The Culture of Time and Space, 1880–1914* (Cambridge, Mass., 1983), 88.

[42] Greswell, "The Imperial Federation League," 196; and Wilson, "A Scheme for Imperial Federation," *NC*, 17 (1885), 592. See also Seeley, *The Expansion of England*, 283; [Jenkins], "Imperial Federalism," 175; and Frederick Young, *On the Political Relations of Mother Countries and Colonies* (London, 1883), 15.

ing to a first-rate Power."[43] Nationalism and state consolidation were
conjoined in a new world order. Dilke predicated that "[i]t is small powers, not great ones, that have become impossible: the unification of Germany is in this respect but the dawn of a new era." As a result America
was, he wrote, "in many points, the master country of the globe."[44] The
belief in inevitability leads to a final point. As I outlined above, the example of the United States was thought to have proved that large states
could be reconciled with liberty. But if the world was moving inexorably
in the direction of great states, then this implied that such a state was essential in order to secure the hallowed conditions of liberty, that it was
vital to embed them in an institutional shell robust enough to ride the
waves of the turbulent future. Only "enormous" polities could foster and
protect freedom. Once again, Greater Britain provided the answer.

PEACE AND JUSTICE: THE BENEFITS OF HEGEMONY

And in the time to come, the time that must come,
when these colonies of ours have grown in stature, in
population, and in strength, this league of kindred
nations, this federation of Greater Britain, will not only
provide for its own security, but will be a potent factor
in maintaining the peace of the world.
—Joseph Chamberlain, "Splendid Isolation" (1896)

A strong and confident Greater Britain would, so it was claimed, benefit
the entire planet. It was to be the indispensable nation. The idea of a federal global order had long played a part in imagining a more peaceful future. Herbert Spencer, probably the most widely read British philosopher
of the century, had argued repeatedly from the 1840s onward that a federation of the major states was the best way to escape the barbaric cycle
of interstate conflict perpetuated by the residue of the "militant" ethos.
In Part V of *The Principles of Sociology* (1882), he argued that "in time
to come, a federation of the highest nations, exercising supreme authority (already foreshadowed by occasional agreements among 'the Powers'),
may, by forbidding wars between any of its constituent nations, put an

---

[43] Froude, "England and Her Colonies," 15.

[44] Dilke, *Greater Britain*, I, 274 and 48;. Chamberlain repeated the phrase in 1902, declaring that "The days are for great Empires and not for little States." Speech at Birmingham, May 16, 1902, in J. L. Garvin and J. Amery, *The Life of Joseph Chamberlain* (London, 1929–68), IV, 177. See also Froude, "England's War" [1871] reprinted in Froude,
Short Studies on Great Subjects (London, 1907), III, 276.

end to the rebarbarization which is continually undoing civilisation."[45]
This was a common theme in late Victorian political thought.[46] But it did
not follow from this long-standing dream that the federation of the British
colonial empire was the answer, or even a step in the right direction.
Spencer was highly critical of imperial federation, writing in response to
an invitation to sit on a committee propagating the "Pan-Britannic Idea"
that a "federation of Great Britain with her colonies would in my opinion
have the effect of encouraging aggressive action on the part of the colonies,
with a still more active appropriation of territories than is at present going
on, and there would be continued demands upon the mother country for
military and financial aid." But for others, including J. A. Hobson, a federal Greater Britain was an important institutional foundation in the quest
for a more pacific global order.[47]

The proponents of Greater Britain usually insisted that their vision was
a guarantor of both international justice and security—indeed they implied that security was the precondition of justice, the necessary if not sufficient condition for creating a more harmonious world. "To no class of
persons," proclaimed Julius Vogel, "should confederation more appeal
than to those who desire to abolish the horrors of war." An imperial federation, wrote another advocate, would be of "untold value to the whole
world." Jenkins, in his early federalist manifesto, concurred: "We cannot
overstate the advantages to the world's peace and progress of large states
or confederations. They reduce the possibilities of war between smaller
communities which compose them, by creating the bond of common citizenship, and subjecting all to a permanent and superior arbitration in
cases of dispute."[48] This was a vision of a benign, paternalistic hegemon.
Greater Britain was to be a gift to humanity, expressing the British "genius" for political organization. "The fruits of political union will . . . be
found," argued Frederick Young at a meeting of the IFL in Cambridge,
"in the progress of an intelligent and prosperous people, marching in the
van of civilisation, for the benefit not only of themselves, but of mankind,
bound together in one nationality, though widely scattered over the broad

[45] Spencer, *Principles of Sociology* (London, 1876–96), III, 600. For his earlier views on
the matter, see Spencer, *Social Statics* (London, 1851), 272–73. On his international thought,
see Casper Sylvest, "Liberal International Thought in Britain, 1880–1918," unpublished
PhD thesis, University of Cambridge, 2006, ch. 3.

[46] See also Duncan Bell and Casper Sylvest, "International Society in Victorian Political
Thought," *MIH*, 3 (2006), 1–32; David Weinstein, "Consequentialist Cosmopolitanism"
in Duncan Bell (ed.), *Victorian Visions of Global Order* (Cambridge, 2007); as well as the
discussion in chapter 4.

[47] Spencer to J. Astley Cooper, 20 June 1893 in D. Duncan, *The Life and Letters of Herbert Spencer* (London, 1908), 328; and Hobson, *Imperialism* (London, 1902), 332.

[48] Vogel, "Greater or Lesser Britain," *NC*, 1 (1877), 828; Anon., "The Federation of the
British Empire," *WR*, 128 (1887), 485; [Jenkins], "An Imperial Confederation," 79. See also
Greswell, "Imperial Federation. Prize Essay," 38; and de Labillière, *Federal Britain*, 166.

surface of the globe." Such a beneficent development, at least if enacted on this scale, was unique in world history: "beside it Rome's range of influence sinks into comparative insignificance."[49] Moreover, such a strong and stable polity was the best platform from which to help govern the rest of the empire. Stressing that it was essential for Britain to "extend the reign of law and justice upon earth," James Hight, a leading imperialist from New Zealand, proclaimed that,

> Britain is at the head of the most progressive and most just of modern nations. It is therefore fitting that she should guide and control the destiny of new and infant countries; to her and no other should be committed the fate of the lower races of mankind, who are, many of them, engaged in an unequal struggle for very life with powers whose rule is not so merciful.[50]

This conceited belief in the moral superiority of the British did not convince everybody. Frederic Rogers, a former permanent undersecretary of state for the colonies and an advocate of colonial independence, argued that imperial federation was an "unattainable phantom." He also challenged the complacency of Anglo-Saxon self-belief: "To contend for such an alliance on the ground that Anglo-Saxons—the great exterminators of aborigines in the temperate zone—would, when confederated, set a new and exceptional example of justice and humanity, seems to me a somewhat transcendental expectation."[51] This was, however, very much a minority position.

In their hubristic belief the imperialists were following in the footsteps of John Stuart Mill. The colonial empire, he had suggested in the early 1860s, "is a step, as far as it goes, towards universal peace and general friendly cooperation between nations."

> It renders war impossible among a large number of otherwise independent communities; and moreover hinders any of them from becoming absorbed into a foreign state, and becoming a source of additional aggressive strength to some rival power, either more despotic or closer at hand, which might not always be so unambitious or so pacific as Great Britain. It at least keeps the markets of the different countries open to one another, and prevents that mutual exclusion by hostile tariffs, which none of the great communities of mankind, except England, have yet completely outgrown. And in the case of the British possessions it has the advantage, specially valuable at the present time, of adding to the moral influence, and weight in the councils of the

---

[49] Young, *An Address on Imperial Federation* (London, 1885), 23. See also Parkin, *Imperial Federation*, 46.

[50] Hight, *The English as a Colonising Nation* (Wellington, 1903), 11–12.

[51] Rogers, *Pall Mall Gazette*, January 19, 1885, reprinted in George Bennett (ed.), *The Concept of Empire* (London, 1953), 293. He had been convinced since the 1860s that the colonies were heading for independence. For more on Rogers, see Beasley, *Mid-Victorian Imperialists*, ch. 4.

world, of the Power which, in all existence, best understands liberty—and whatever may have been its errors in the past, has attained to more of conscience and moral principle in its dealings with foreigners, than any other great nation seems either to conceive as possible, or recognise as desirable.[52]

Mill here identified a number of points that were to be reiterated constantly by the advocates of Greater Britain. Firstly, he combined strategic and economic factors in defending the advantages of colonial unity. Secondly, he claimed that a preponderance of large political units reduced the probability of war by limiting the number of antagonistic sovereign communities in the international system. Thirdly, he suggested that retaining the colonies neutralized the danger of their being "absorbed" by another power, a fate that would simultaneously debilitate Britain while bolstering a competitor. And finally, and perhaps most importantly, he assumed that the British were morally superior to other people, and that they therefore deserved the crown of global leadership. Not only would they handle it with greater restraint and conscientiousness than any other contender, but in so doing they would offer an example for other states to follow in their quest for liberty and progress.

The demand for Greater Britain can be read as an echo of the time-honored argument that a virtuous hegemonic power, the "Friend of Mankind," was the ideal solution to the problems of a world beset by contentious and often violent relations between states. A strong, commercial, progressive state would act as a disciplinary presence in international affairs, offering both a beneficent example and the threat of punishment for transgressors of the global order. It wielded both carrot and stick. Such an argument, focusing on the European state system, had been proposed frequently in the eighteenth century by, among others, Fénelon and Mirabeau in France and Fichte in Germany. Working with the same basic idea, the colonial unionists expanded the scale and ambition of the project, from Europe to the globe.

Through a Glass, Darkly: America as Lesson

> We learnt our lesson in 1776, and have
> most certainly benefited from it.
> —Frederick Young, *An Address
> on Imperial Federation* (1885)

The past haunted the imperialists. History taught lessons and supplied a guide to successful imperial statecraft: it was the supreme source of ad-

---

[52] Mill, *Considerations on Representative Government,* CW, XIX, 565.

vice to modern princes. And the United States instilled one of the most primitive but vital lessons, namely that it was necessary to respect the desires of the colonists, for unless they were placated, they would turn against their sovereign. "The memory of the American war," Seeley lamented, "is humiliating to us." The revolution had created a "schism in Greater Britain," a tear in the political fabric. The British needed to recognize this and grab hold of their "second chance."[53] This message played a crucial role in shaping the ways in which Victorian thinkers conceived of the link between the "mother country" and its colonial territories. What followed from the fear of repeating the mistakes of the past was both a sense of urgency and a belief that it was essential to bind the elements of the empire together more tightly, to weave its diverse elements into a single vast tapestry, without alienating the colonists so much that they would be driven to demanding independence.

Underlying concern about the future was a narrative of the way in which the British empire had been torn asunder by the disastrous policies of George III and his ministers. There could be no repeat of the eighteenth-century fiasco. For Frederick Young, the lesson was direct and resonant: "Taxation without representation is impossible." It was essential that the increasingly confident and prosperous colonists were incorporated in the legislative structure of a global polity. It was far from clear, however, that learning properly from past mistakes boded well for the success of imperial federation. Hobson argued that the direction of colonial policy in the closing decades of the century had been strongly influenced by the trauma of American independence. Great Britain had, he argued, "in the main learned well the lesson of the American Revolution; she has not only permitted but favoured [the] growing independence of her Australian and American colonies." This policy was simultaneously a political necessity and an impediment, the former because without it the empire would have been placed under severe strain, and history may well have repeated itself, the latter because it meant that federation was increasingly unlikely.[54] Others remained optimistic, suggesting that if learned properly the lessons of history could guide effective political action and bolster colonial unity.

Fear of repeating past mistakes also shaped the tactics that the colonial unionists adopted in attempting to persuade the colonists to join their quest for global concord. It limited the types of arguments that could be made: change was required, but it could not be forced on what were, after

---

[53] Seeley, *The Expansion of England*, Lecture VIII; Seeley, "Introduction," xvi; and ["A Colonist"], "A Proposed Reform of the English Constitution," *FM*, 8 (1873), 603. For similar sentiments, see also, Arthur Cooper Key, "Naval Defence of the Colonies," *NC*, 20 (1886), 285; Andrew Robert Macfie, "On the Crisis of the Empire," *PRCI* 3 (1871–72), 3; Daniel Cooper, *A Federal British Empire* (London, 1880), 3; and John Clifford, *God's Greater Britain* (London, 1899), 13.

[54] Hobson, *Imperialism*, 348.

all, British subjects. The proponents of Greater Britain had to convince rather than cajole the often reluctant colonists to accept their audacious plans. And since the granting of "responsible government," it was believed, whether accurately or not, that the empire was held together by the bare minimum of administrative links.[55] The ties were, as Goldwin Smith had scoffed, mere "filaments," part of a weak and "airy fabric."[56] Mill had likewise noted the voluntarist dimension of the link between Britain and its more powerful settler colonies.

> It is now a fixed principle of the policy of Great Britain, professed in theory and faithfully adhered to in practice, that her colonies of European race, equally with the parent country, posses the fullest measure of internal self-government. They have been allowed to make their own free representative constitutions, by altering in any manner they sought fit, the already very popular constitutions which we had given them. Each is governed by its own legislature and executive, constituted on highly democratic principles.[57]

Not only was the political connection feeble, but the bonds of the "heart" were frail also, and it was thought that the American Revolution had illustrated clearly the limits of colonial patriotism. As Seeley observed, "the loss suffered in the secession of the American colonies has left in the English mind a doubt, a misgiving, which affects our whole forecast of the future of England."[58] This was another lesson that had been learned the hard way. Apprehension about the strength and vigor of patriotism generated repeated calls for engaging the colonists in debate. Successful pedagogy was essential in persuading the colonists that the British were not trying to impose an alien, centralized government: *Imperial Federation* and other proselytizing organs, pamphlets, and books, combined with the work of the colonial branches of the IFL, were thus central to the vision as well as the campaigning tactics of the imperial advocates.[59] We can read the constant affirmations of the indestructible loyalty of the global British nation (or race) as a sign of anxiety as much as of anodyne self-confidence; of hope as much as candid assessment.

The critics of federation drew their own lessons from the revolutionary

---

[55] For an antipathetic picture of British treatment of the colonists, see Charles Gavan Duffy, "How British Colonies Got Responsible Government," I, *CR*, 57 (1890), 617–43 and II, *CR*, 58 (1890), 153–81. These pieces call for the colonists to have a greater say in their own decision-making, and they end with qualified support for imperial federation. See also Duffy, "Some Fruits of Federation," *IF*, 5/3 (1890), 68.

[56] Smith, *The Empire* (Oxford, 1863), xxi; and Smith, *Canada and the Canadian Question* (London, 1891), 206. See also [John Martineau], "New Zealand and our Colonial Empire," *QR*, 128 (1870), 135. Seeley agreed: *The Expansion of England*, 73.

[57] Mill, *Considerations on Representative Government*, CW, XIX, 563.

[58] Seeley, *The Expansion of England*, 14.

[59] See also the discussion of education in chapter 5.

era. John Morley argued that the extraordinary success of America in the nineteenth century was a consequence of independence from Britain; if it had remained part of the empire it would never have flourished. "Independence," he argued, "not only put the Americans on their mettle, but it left them with fresh views, with a temper of unbounded adaptability, with an infinite readiness to try experiments, and free room to indulge as largely as ever they pleased." It conditioned the very qualities that made them great. Morley condemned Seeley's use of the United States as a precedent for imperial federation, suggesting that the historian was inadvertently pointing to an example that disproved his own argument. Institutional centralization, regarded by Morley as the core characteristic of empires past and present, stifled creativity and dulled the political senses. This was the "real significance" of the revolution.[60] Even if imperial federation fell within the range of "practical politics," which he doubted, it would be catastrophic for the progressive development of the colonies.

Dilke sought to avoid both abject anxiety about colonial attitudes and a complacent belief in the indissolubility of the patriotic bond. He argued that some parts of the colonial empire were more loyal than others, which in turn explained why some were more open to the ideas of the imperial federalists. Among Australians, for example, he saw the colonists of New South Wales as highly nationalist and those residing in Victoria as largely pro-British. On balance, however, he believed that the bond was too fragile, too tenuous, to be endangered by forcing the colonies into a formal federal structure. It would be counterproductive to impose new institutions on them. "The best friends of the mother-country in the colonies hold that the attempt to create a common imperial Parliament would of itself destroy the empire; and I agree with them that if we are ever to have a council of the empire it will have to be very unlike a Parliament."[61] Such ambitions pushed too hard against the limits of "practical politics."

But the history of the United States did not only instill negative lessons. Numerous federalists, as I have shown, claimed that the progressive grand narrative of American development confirmed the possibility of reconciling expansion and liberty. George Parkin, meanwhile, argued that there was much to be learned from the period immediately following the colonial revolt, from the initial difficulties and eventual success of the founding itself. Drawing on James Bryce's influential analysis of *The American Commonwealth* (1888), he argued that the detractors of imperial federation, and especially those who focused on its purported lack of feasibil-

[60] Morley, "The Expansion of England," *MM*, 49 (1884), 245–45. He cites C. J. Rowe, *Bonds of Disunion* (London, 1883), as evidence of the dangers of centralized rule in the colonies. For further criticism of the American analogy, see J. W. Cross, "The New World," *NC*, 29 (1891), 470.

[61] Dilke, *Problems of Greater Britain*, I, 260, 313, and 458.

ity, could learn much from the American example.[62] Noting that it was common during the latter decades of the nineteenth century to praise American federalism, to point to its bravura political achievements, he then reminded his readers, again relying on Bryce, how fraught the founding had been originally. The proponents of imperial federation as well as their critics should, he proposed, reflect on this when they pointed to the number of people opposed to such audacious plans, or the obstacles involved. All great political experiments were plagued with problems; in this respect at least there was nothing new about imperial federation. History could implant an understanding of the complexity, contingency, and practical difficulties that stood in the way of any great reforming effort. And it could also demonstrate how such complexity was not necessarily a bar to success. To acknowledge this fact, he suggested, was an essential starting point for serious discussion.

AMERICA, EMPIRE, AND RACIAL UNITY

For British imperialists the postrevolutionary history of Anglo-American relations was a bittersweet one. On the one hand, many saw the nineteenth century as a lost opportunity, for after the catastrophic "schism," the two main branches of the Anglo-Saxon world had followed radically different trajectories, and the chance to act in unison had been forfeited. But on the other, the growth of the United States pointed the way into the future, offering a usable template for a global polity. And at some stage, perhaps soon, but more likely in decades to come, a substantive reunion, even re-unification, might occur. The possibilities were tantalizing, but there existed little agreement over how best to calibrate relations with the United States. This was a pressing question for virtually all late-Victorian imperial thinkers. As Seeley argued, there was "no topic so pregnant as this of the mutual influence of the branches of the English race. The whole future of the planet depends on it."[63]

Most advocates of Greater Britain hoped for some sort of alliance with the United States, although they differed over whether this was to be informal, and anchored in a shared culture, history, and interests, or whether it was to be institutionalized in a federal structure of some kind. This mirrored the general divisions over the nature of Greater Britain. The former was the most common position, and it was of course the most realistic. It finds its modern expression in the asymmetric "special relation-

[62] Parkin, *Imperial Federation*, 49–51. Parkin was following the analysis in Bryce, *The American Commonwealth* (London, 1888), I, especially Parts I and V.
[63] Seeley, *The Expansion of England*, 150.

ship." This was an ideal that attracted many adherents, ranging from enthusiastic colonial unionists to some of their most vociferous critics, including Goldwin Smith and Edward Freeman.[64] Indeed in 1891 Smith
criticized the imperial federalists for failing to recognize the true significance of America.

> There is a Federation which is feasible, and to those who do not measure
> grandeur by physical force or extension, at least as grand as that which the
> Imperialist dreams. It is the moral federation of the whole English-speaking
> race throughout the world, including those millions of men speaking the En-
> glish language in the United States, and parted from the rest only a century
> ago by a wretched quarrel, whom Imperial Federation would leave out of its
> pale.[65]

For Dilke, the United States was already an integral element of Greater
Britain—at least in one of his more capacious definitions of the term—
and he was always at pains to emphasize the significance of the British-
American connection. This was largely because he regarded the Americans, avatars of modernity, as the vehicle for Anglo-Saxon (and hence
English) greatness. The "true moral of America," he wrote in 1868, "is
the vigour of the English race." Although twenty years later he was much
more confident about the prospects for the colonial empire, he was still
keen to reiterate the prime importance of the United States. Indeed he
went as far as criticizing Seeley for not giving enough prominence to the
founding of America in *The Expansion of England*, and for seeking to
clearly distinguish Greater Britain from the United States. For Dilke, this
distinction was pernicious and misleading, for the Americans were an
integral element of the glorious whole.[66] Such a position found some support on the other side of the Atlantic. A *New York Times* editorial cele-
brating Queen Victoria's Diamond Jubilee (in 1897), for example, proclaimed that "[w]e are a part, and a great part, of the Greater Britain
which seems so plainly destined to dominate the planet."[67]

For some, Greater Britain would not be complete without the political
union, even the federation, of the two Anglo-Saxon great powers. Cecil
Rhodes, a man who once boasted that he would annex the stars if it were

[64] Freeman, "Imperial Federation," 455; and Freeman, letter to Goldwin Smith, August
19, 1888, in *The Life and Letters of Edward A. Freeman*, ed. W.R.W. Stephens (London,
1895), II, 384. For Smith's views, see chapter 7.
[65] Smith, *Canada and the Canadian Question*, 205.
[66] Dilke, *Greater Britain*, I, 308; and ibid., *Problems of Greater Britain*, II, 171. However, Dilke did change his mind on whether America should fall under the label of Greater
Britain; in his early work it did, but by the late 1890s he was arguing that this was an error:
Dilke, *The British Empire* (London, 1899), 9.
[67] The editorial is cited in Jan Morris, *Pax Britannia* (London, 1968), 28.

possible, believed that the United States should and could be absorbed back into a united Anglo-Saxon empire.[68] The leading nonconformist minister and social reformer John Clifford thought that a federation of the colonial empire was compatible with a transatlantic union, a vision that he preached on both sides of the ocean. In *God's Greater Britain* (1899), he argued that providence had bestowed a mission on the English peoples, equipping them for the exercise of beneficent empire. "It is the Lord's doing, and it is marvellous in our eyes that we should be the first colonising people of the world, and that at present we are as indispensable to the process of filling and replenishing the earth as we are supreme." Despite the many faults that the British, like all people, exhibited, he insisted that that they were the "greatest depository of altruistic sentiments upon the globe at this time." Citing the work of the French historian Ernest Renan, he proceeded to argue that the populations of the United States and Britain composed a single nation, and that they should be formally united, although he also maintained that the details of how exactly this was to happen should be left to the politicians to decide.

> There is a feeling that there ought to be, and that there must be, a close alliance between the Anglican and American folk. As to the form of it, this must be left to our politicians to determine, but that it must be really based on principles of truth, righteousness, and justice, and directed to the redemption of mankind from evil, on this, I think, we are all agreed. Nay, more; we are feeling that the very next step, the necessary and inevitable step in the higher progress of mankind is the alliance of the English and American people.[69]

The Canadian journalist John Dougall, meanwhile, argued that the Americans, "those other sons of our Viking race," were an essential component of a true global polity: "no federation of the empire will be complete which does not make room for the whole of Greater Britain."

> To England the alliance is desirable, as the future of the race seems undoubtedly as much connected with America as with England; to the United States it is desirable, as the past of the race belongs inalienably to England, as England possesses an expansive elasticity which the United States envies, and as the alliance of the two countries would bring all the waste places of

---

[68] See especially Rhodes, "Confession of Faith" [1877], reprinted as an appendix in John Flint, *Cecil Rhodes* (London, 1976), 248–52. On the way in which some American imperialists looked to Britain for lessons in empire, see Paul Kramer, "Empires, Exceptions, and Anglo-Saxons," *Journal of American History*, 88 (2002), 1315–53.

[69] Clifford, *God's Greater Britain*, 174, 185. This sermon was preached at Tremont Temple, Boston, in 1898.

the earth under the aegis of a joint Power, whose common flag would be a messenger of peace to the world.

For these reasons, a "Pan-Saxon alliance is not only desirable, but possibly an early necessity." "If, as we now confidently hope, they [America and Britain] hold together and combine in some more or less definite federal scheme," predicted the historian Charles Oman, "the future of the whole world lies in the hands of the Anglo-Saxon race."[70]

It was as if the incessant arguments about the definitive meaning of America had come full circle. America was not to be regarded simply as a potential or actual competitor but rather as a partner in the quest for global progress. Indeed, it is noticeable that the obsession with Anglo-American rapprochement and racial concord reached its peak in the late 1890s, just as the movement for imperial federation was beginning to run out of steam.[71] But while race underpinned the idea of Greater Britain, there were numerous advocates of Anglo-Saxon unity who were skeptical about the primacy of the colonial empire, believing that it distracted attention from, or even blocked, their ambition to fully reconcile the United Kingdom with its American offspring. For Andrew Carnegie, ruthless industrialist and leading light in the American anti-imperial movement, the union between Britain and the United States, anchored in an inviolable "race alliance," was more important than the future of the settler colonies. From his perspective, the empire was acting as a barrier to a proper transatlantic alliance, and as such he was very critical of plans for imperial federation.[72] A number of the critics of imperial federation even foresaw, and welcomed, some form of globe-spanning union emerging *after* the colonies had secured independence. These new Anglo-Saxon states could then join, with Britain and possibly the United States, in a grand racial alliance of sovereign polities. This would allow accession and participation on more equal terms, and as such it would neutralize many

[70] Dougall, "An Anglo-Saxon Alliance," *CR*, 48 (1885), 706 and 700; and Oman, *England in the Nineteenth Century* (London, 1899), 261. See also John Fiske, "Why the American Colonies Separated from Great Britain," *FR*, 28 (1880), 163, and, for an argument for the federation of the "English-speaking" world, John Robinson, "The Colonies and the Century," *PRCI*, 30 (1898–99), 325–54.

[71] On how ideas about Anglo-Saxon kinship helped smooth some tricky diplomatic issues (notably, the Vernezuela dispute, the Alaskan boundary controversy, and the revision to the Clayton-Bulwer treaty), see Alexander Campbell, *Great Britain and the United States, 1895–1903* (London, 1960); and also Stuart Anderson, *Race and Rapprochement* (London, 1981).

[72] Carnegie, *The Reunion of Britain and America* (Edinburgh, 1898); and Carnegie, "Imperial Federation," *NC*, 30 (1891), 490–508. His position was criticized strongly in George Parkin, *Imperial Federation*, ch. 11.

of the theoretical and practical problems identified by Freeman and Dilke. For William Lobban, such a federation would represent a fruitful movement toward the ideal of "an all-embracing cosmopolitical institution."[73]

In looking to America the advocates of Greater Britain sought imaginative refuge in an archetype suitable for the tumultuous modern world, an apposite model for an expanded republic in the wake of Montesquieu. Hegel wrote in his *Lectures on the Philosophy of World History* (1822–30) that America was "a land of desire for all those who are weary of the historical arsenal of old Europe. . . . It is up to America to abandon the ground on which world history has hitherto been enacted."[74] This vision was shared by many radicals (and even liberals), who saw the United States as a promised land embodying the democratic political telos toward which the United Kingdom was moving intermittently but relentlessly.[75] Cobden, Bright, and John Stuart Mill were only the most prominent of nineteenth-century British thinkers to view the United States as the prototype for a democratic world. To others, perhaps less romantically inclined, America was simply a dynamic industrial competitor and nascent great power, peopled by the descendants of the British. It was therefore to be emulated in its best practices and regarded with fraternal (if not paternal) affection. Whatever underlay the various blends of admiration and anxiety that shaped individual perceptions of America, it was impossible to ignore the country.

America—the idea as much as the protean reality—played a central but ambiguous role in shaping political thought, assuming multiple and often conflicting roles in the Victorian imperial imagination. As I have argued in this chapter, it served as a lesson, albeit an indeterminate one, about how to act in the modern world, and by offering a formidable challenge to British interests and self-identity it provided the impetus for much of the debate over Greater Britain. It fanned the flames of angst and self-doubt. Could Britain remain "great" while America seemed to be angling for this mantle? By its very success it offered a constitutional model to imitate. Imperial discourse was pervaded by an uneasy combination of envy and disdain, fortified by an insidious sense of anxiety. The United States exhibited great social and political dynamism, expanding industrial strength, and a growing geopolitical presence, but its vitality was not simply reducible to a series of statistical indicators of size, wealth, and productivity. It seemed to represent, even to embody, a set of attitudes—a

---

[73] Lobban, "Is Imperial Federation a Chimera?" *WR*, 136 (1891), 54–58. See also J. W. Longley, "Canada and Imperial Federation," *FR*, 49 (1891), 466–79; and Hobson, *Imperialism*, 351.

[74] Hegel, *Lectures on the Philosophy of World History*, 170–71.

[75] On America as a "site of the modern," see James Epstein, ""America" in the Victorian Cultural Imagination" in Leventhal and Quinault, *Anglo-American Attitudes*, 107.

striving to conquer the natural and, later perhaps, the political world—as much as anything else. Apparently unfettered by the weight of historical tradition, it appeared to be charging into the future, leaving its elderly relative trailing behind. It was the epitome of modernity. This was the image that many British observers were simultaneously drawn to and troubled by. They held up a mirror to themselves, and to their country, and were found wanting. The Anglo-Saxon race appeared divided by a "schism"—a schism not only between Britain and America, but between the past and the future. It was this divide that the ideologues of Greater Britain tried so hard to bridge. Although they failed to achieve many of their immediate (and most ambitious) goals, in helping to propel the question of Anglo-American relations to the forefront of political debate, and in insisting on the importance of both the multifarious ties and the common dangers uniting the two countries, they played a significant role in laying the intellectual foundations of the "special relationship" that was to shape so much of the political landscape of the twentieth century and beyond.

10

Conclusion: Lineages of Greater Britain

> It is begging the question to assume that the ties of
> common race and language make nations better
> inclined to enter into active political alliance or
> better suited for harmonic acting.
> —Walter Bagehot, "An Anglo-Saxon Alliance" (1875)

IN 1900 THE IDEALIST philosopher J. H. Muirhead tried to capture the nature of the imperial age in which he lived. British attitudes toward the empire from the mid-eighteenth to the dawn of the twentieth century had followed, he suggested, a chaotic trajectory: "enthusiasm" prevailed in the turbulent era of George III, "passing into indifference" following the loss of the thirteen colonies, and then subsequently "into hostility . . . to the very idea of Empire" during the early years of Victoria's long reign. Finally, during the remaining three decades of the century, the empire returned as a "consuming passion" in British political debate.[1] *The Idea of Greater Britain* has focused on the last of these perceived transitions, on the period in which ambitious visions of colonial unity became a commonplace of imperial discourse, and in so doing, it has sought to excavate and interrogate some of the languages employed in theorizing the future of world politics. In this brief conclusion I summarize some of the key arguments propounded by the colonial unionists and highlight a number of ways in which ideas about imperial federation and "global Britishness" reverberated throughout the subsequent decades.

GLOBAL CONSCIOUSNESS AND THE IMPERIAL IMAGINATION

The advocates of a federal Greater Britain—and in particular the theorists of a supraparliamentary polity—demanded the transformation of existing political structures to confront a new world and to shape the future.

---

[1] Muirhead, "What Imperialism Means" [1900] in *The British Idealists*, ed. David Boucher (Cambridge, 1997), 239. For Muirhead, there existed multiple causes for these shifts, but the key to understanding the final transition was, unsurprisingly for an idealist, the "Spirit of the Century," a spirit that bred civilization, organization, and industry in Europe and projected it overseas; this was the spirit of "unity."

The construction of an extended transcontinental composite polity was the most ambitious answer to the anxieties of the age. It was one of the most elaborate (and perhaps most desperate) rejoinders to a multitude of apparent threats, both domestic and international. Proposals for colonial unity tended to mix originality and conformity to the zeitgeist. Their conformity lay in the obsession with scale, in the belief that size and global reach were the essential determinants for securing stability, power, and prestige. This was a core element of the contemporary geopolitical imagination. Their originality lay in believing that it was possible to create a noncontiguous representative polity that straddled the planet. The former of these beliefs thrived in the twentieth century, and in an age of American "unipolarity" and "full-spectrum dominance," it continues to this day; the latter, despite occasional outbursts, especially during the interwar period, has rarely been advanced with as much passion as during the late nineteenth century.

Imperial imaginaries comprise a key element in the history of globalization. Today globalization appears omnipresent: it envelops us, dominating media, academic, and policy discourses. It is the most prominent area of research in the social sciences; its processes, impact, future trajectory, and normative status are the subject of intense scrutiny and bitter contestation. A foreboding sense that the world is undergoing a historic transformation has permeated both academic reflection and public debate for much of the post–Cold War era. Yet this sense of novelty betrays the fact that the dynamics of global competition have been the subject of extensive theoretical debate for centuries.[2] Although historians have recently started exploring past modes of globalization, searching for patterns of continuity and change, much works remains to be done.[3] The history of globalization is not only a history of the spread of capitalism across the face of the planet (whether through the agency of empire or not), and of increasing social, political, and economic interdependence, central as they are. It is also a history of the multiple ways in which the world came to be imagined as integrated, as interconnected, and finally, as a "global village." The transformation of perception, then, is an inte-

---

[2] The best illustration of this is Istvan Hont, *Jealousy of Trade* (Cambridge, Mass., 2005).

[3] For historical accounts of globalization, see A. G. Hopkins (ed.), *Globalization in World History* (London, 2002); Michael Geyer and Charles Bright, "World History in a Global Age," *AHR*, 100 (1995), 1034–60; C. A. Bayly, *The Making of the Modern World, 1780–1914* (Oxford, 2003); and, for a useful overview, Patrick O'Brien, "Historiographical Traditions and Modern Imperatives for the Restoration of Global History," *Journal of Global History*, 1 (2006), 3–39. See also, Duncan Bell, "History and Globalisation," *International Affairs*, 4 (2003), 801–15. For some criticisms of the concept of "globalization" from the perspective of a historian, see Frederick Cooper, *Colonialism in Question* (Berkeley, 2005), ch. 4.

gral component of the history of global consciousness. The late nineteenth
century was a foundational moment in this process. As distance was dissolved in the minds of observers, so understandings of temporality mutated; as space was "annihilated," so time was apparently compressed.
This reframed political possibilities. The language and some of the ideas
utilized by the proponents of Greater Britain—including the apparent
"shrinking" of the world and the belief in the power of technology to ameliorate social and political problems—bear a remarkable similarity to
those employed by many contemporary observers, spellbound by the purported uniqueness of the times in which we live. The argument that technological prowess and instantaneous communication engender a powerful sense of integration, even community, is far from novel. It was as naive
then as it is now.

Rather than heralding the end of the state, as both Marx and many
modern neoliberals suggest, and as visionaries of "cosmopolitan democracy" and a postsovereign global order point toward, many of the advocates of a federal Greater Britain insisted on reinforcing it, extending it
over previously unimaginable distances while simultaneously attempting
to reconfigure the bases of national self-consciousness.[4] They envisioned
a new form of state, unprecedented in scale and power. But others, either
less ambitious or less enamored of the notion of a global state, sought to
create novel forms of political association, hybrid colonial-state architec-
tures. Imperialists of all but the palest stripes demanded the transformation of the way in which both Britain and the empire were conceived—
through a reconsideration of the relationship between the two—and in so
doing they challenged the boundaries, language, and traditions of British
political thought. This novelty helps to explain their interest to the modern historian and political theorist, and ultimately their failure to convince
the public and the governing elites of the desirability of their cause.

In articulating their visions of the future, the supporters of Greater
Britain, often unwittingly it seems, proposed the creation of institutional
forms that challenged arguments central to the evolution of European political theorizing. For example, in the eighteenth century, thinkers such as
St. Pierre had argued that federation was antithetical to empire, while the
tension between liberty and empire had been a key feature of both ancient
and modern thought.[5] So too had the fraught relationship between liberty and democracy, a theme that assumed a heightened sense of urgency

---

[4] On the idea of a "post-Westphalian" order, see Andrew Linklater, *The Transformation
of Political Community* (Cambridge, 1998); and David Held, *Global Covenant* (Cambridge,
2004).

[5] Anthony Pagden, *Lords of All the World* (New Haven, 1995), chs. 1 and 7; and David
Armitage, "Empire and Liberty" in Martin van Geldren and Quentin Skinner (eds.), *Republicanism* (Cambridge, 2002), II, 29–47.

in the nineteenth century. Greater Britain could, it was believed, square the circle: just as it was possible to reconcile liberty with empire, so democracy could be combined with both freedom and constitutional stability. This comprised an intriguing, if ultimately doomed, attempt to fuse a number of political concepts that have often been considered in agonistic opposition, and even as antithetical, in post-Renaissance thought: empire, state, federation, democracy, and freedom. This was a massive undertaking, and in light of the great theoretical and practical difficulties it presented, its eventual failure is unsurprising.

During the late Victorian age Britain's preeminent global status seemed increasingly precarious. Not only did British economic, military, and political might appear fragile, but the regime of domestic stability—premised on constitutional strength and flexibility, the ultimate harmony of classes and economic interests, and the superiority of the national character, all underpinned by substantive yet fragile material and moral progress—was also apparently threatened. In response, Greater Britain promised the ability to maintain and even strengthen global dominance through the development of a massive, militarily powerful and economically productive polity. It also offered an outlet for the masses, a convenient safety valve to defuse the potentially explosive impact of franchise extension: the frontiers of the empire would serve not only as the formidable borders of a world-shaping polity but as breeding grounds for a newly invigorated nation of imperial patriots, their characters molded by the shift in environment. Modernity fused with tradition as an ancient language of glory and political virtue was adapted to and reconfigured by the dynamics of an emerging industrial capitalist demos.

As I have argued throughout this book, then, the drive for Greater Britain, and the movement for imperial federation in particular, was a response to the perception that the world had reached a monumental turning point, a point at which Britain's international supremacy was imperiled, and where the rise of democracy, both at home and abroad, threatened to reshape the very nature of politics. Fears of global competition and domestic disquiet fed into each other, sustaining imperial debate. But anxiety was not the only reaction: for some people, albeit a minority, this welcome confluence of trends offered the possibility of accelerating and extending the democratization of both the British state and the international system.

I have also sought to illustrate, through juxtaposing the intellectual trajectories of Smith and Seeley, that concern over the future of Greater Britain united figures who so often stood apart from each other: the passionate imperialist (who was wary of imperialism) and the "Little Englander" (who was no such thing). While their styles and sensibilities may have differed, the fears that animated their political thought and the ultimate ends that they sought were far closer than many of their contemporaries, as well as their later interpreters, recognized. Their assumptions—about the paramount role that Britain should play in shaping the world and the general superiority of the Anglo-Saxons—were shared widely, even if there existed considerable divisions over the best institutional prescriptions for defending them. Although a concern with the future of Greater Britain was far from universal among the members of the intellectual and political elite, it attracted widespread interest. The debates also witnessed a number of innovations. The most radical of these was the idea of a global supraparliamentary nation-state. This vision, along with many other less ambitious ones, rested on a number of other theoretical innovations, including the shift from the ancients to the moderns as sources of intellectual legitimacy, and the focus on the "shrinking" of the globe as the precondition for global unity. The role of communications technologies symbolized the political opportunities of modernity as well as the dangers that this brave new world portended. Such developments allowed many imperialists to argue that there now existed, for the first time, a powerful global British national identity. It was on these foundations that they hoped to erect an enduring Greater Britain.

The debates over Greater Britain constituted a key moment in reconfiguring the relationship between Britain and its colonial empire. In the Edwardian period, demands for colonial unity tended to assume a more explicitly economic focus, and it was often argued that the creation of an intra-imperial trading system was the best way to hold the empire together in a world of increasingly protectionist states. This was partly the result of the limitations of "practical politics," for by the late 1890s it had become apparent to most advocates of federation that, whatever their own individual preferences, there was virtually no chance of a major shift in the constitutional structure of the empire. So they redirected their energies. This was one of the reasons that Joseph Chamberlain's ultimately abortive tariff-reform campaign took the form it did. But even in these later debates, questions of individual and collective virtue, glory, and honor were pervasive, shaping and helping to motivate the economic arguments.[6] And ambitious visions of political federation did not disappear: the themes that preoccupied the early imperialist federalists prefigured, and indeed fed directly into, those promulgated by some of the most vocal early-twentieth-century federalist thinkers, including Lionel Curtis and Philip Kerr (Lord Lothian), a point I return to in the next section.

The Victorian colonial unionists frequently combined political ambition and theoretical novelty with hubristic arrogance, leading numerous

---

[6] Peter Cain, "Empire and the Language of Character and Virtue in Later Victorian and Edwardian Britain," *MIH*, 4 (2007), 1–25.

critics to dismiss them as utopian, and even as dangerous. Whether realistic or not, in the minds of many unionists, federation presented itself as a practical scheme of political action. But the fact that a fully fledged Greater Britain was conceivable was certainly no guarantee that it could be (or was ever likely to be) realized. The unionists critically underestimated the indifference of the settler communities, exaggerating, or at least misunderstanding, the political and emotional links between the distant and increasingly politically conscious colonies and the "mother country." Furthermore, they failed to persuade a pragmatic British governing class of the necessity of such radical political plans. Most of the unionists went out of their way to emphasize the nonrevolutionary manner of their proposals, however radical they were, arguing that visions of a transcontinental polity were merely extrapolations of existing ideas about federalism. They tried to bolster their case by arguing that the unfolding of history pointed toward the increasing role of federalism in structuring the organization of human communities, that it would define the politics of the future. And they also claimed to draw on the practical lessons taught by existing federations, most commonly the United States, but also Switzerland and the nascent German union. But the proponents of Greater Britain confronted a governing discourse the boundaries of which, although relatively flexible, prescribed limits to political ambition. In a predominantly whiggish political culture, they faced an epic task. The normative boundaries that marked the limits of these discursive conventions—including skepticism about sweeping change, suspicion of written constitutions, and a belief in the territorial contiguity of major political units—were all too often ignored or pushed beyond stretching point by the colonial unionists. In so doing they consigned themselves to inevitable disappointment. This relates to what Quentin Skinner has termed the "rhetorical re-inscription" of ethico-political vocabularies.[7] Political agents need to successfully legitimate their actions through wresting control over the dominant evaluative concepts and languages structuring political discourse within a community (at least, the qualifier should be added, in the absence of violence). This was surely the case with the proponents of Greater Britain. Many of them realized that in order to stand any chance of success, they had to persuade the British governing elite of two things: firstly, that drastic change was required; and secondly, that their suggested responses could be accommodated within the prevailing conventions of political debate. This meant that they had to be able to reconcile their ideas with the dominant interpretation(s) of the "constitutional morality" of the country. This morality centered on incremental evolution, and was grounded in a firm belief in the value of balance,

---

[7] Skinner, *Visions of Politics* (Cambridge, 2002), I, esp. ch. 8.

order, and stability. The unionists needed to redefine the meaning of the constitution; in this they failed. And with this failure died their dream of a global polity. It is not only the content and style of the arguments over Greater Britain that are of interest, then, but also the reasons for their ultimate failure to translate into reality.

REVERBERATIONS: SOME AFTERLIVES OF GREATER BRITAIN

The debates over the future of Greater Britain brought together, and projected to the forefront of political consciousness, two things that had previously been downplayed or sidelined in metropolitan discourse, namely the colonial empire and the principles of federation. There they would remain for much of the following century, often tracing divergent paths through the sprawling maze of British political argument, but also sometimes intersecting, reunited initially in discussions over the future of the empire during the first four decades of the century, and finally, following the Second World War, in the tortured debates over how best to dissolve it. At the beginning of a new millennium, both the empire and the question of political federation remain central in British intellectual life, but at least for the moment they appear to have been decoupled, the former the reserve of disputes over the legacy of conquest and decolonization in a multicultural society, as well as the direction of contemporary foreign policy, the latter over the tendentious question of British relations with continental Europe. And the relationship between Britain and the United States, empire past and empire present, is once again a prominent topic of debate, though often generating more rhetorical heat than historical or analytical light.[8]

What of the term "Greater Britain"? Its late nineteenth-century vogue lasted into the early years of the twentieth century, but it then died out, only to resurface, in its most malevolently intoxicating appearance, when Oswald Mosley, the leader of the British fascist movement, published *The Greater Britain* in 1932.[9] It is little surprise that it then dropped below the horizon. It has recently experienced a minor renaissance as an analytical device for exploring the multifarious flows and interconnections linking the "British world" since the early modern period.[10]

A number of the ideas and issues associated with the debates over the

[8] See in particular Niall Ferguson's encomiums for the British empire, and its role as a model for American hegemony: *Empire* (London, 2003); and *Colossus* (London, 2004).

[9] Mosley, *The Greater Britain* (London, 1932).

[10] David Armitage, *Greater Britain, 1556–1776* (Aldershot, 2004); and Eliga Gould, "A Virtual Nation?" *AHR*, 104 (1999), 476–89. For a different usage, see John Wolffe, *God and Greater Britain* (London, 1994).

future of the empire reverberated widely. One of the most interesting, albeit indirect, lines of influence ran from the imperial federalists and into early twentieth century pluralism—a broad label that encompasses F. W. Maitland, J. N. Figgis, and, slightly later, Harold Laski, G.D.H. Cole, and Ernest Barker, as well as fellow travelers such as Bertrand Russell and A. D. Lindsay.[11] Although the pluralists drew on many sources, perhaps most notably the work of the German historian Otto Gierke, imperial federation can be seen as a significant background feature. Pluralists argued that federal arrangements were necessary in order to effectively coordinate the multiple associations of modern life (primarily but not solely within the state), while simultaneously defending the autonomy of communities and the liberty of individuals. The thirty-year debate over possible federal arrangements for Greater Britain provided fertile ground for the pluralist seed to flower. A further development, which again can be traced in part to the popularity of ideas about colonial unity, was the increasing popularity of imperialism among liberals. While there had always been liberal supporters of the empire, and while many of those figures that liberals claimed as their intellectual progenitors (including John Locke) were deeply implicated in the justification of foreign conquests, empire had played a deeply ambivalent role in the evolution of liberalism.[12] Although they attracted individuals of all political stripes the debates over Greater Britain served an important role in persuading many liberals—and even some socialists—that the empire, and especially the settler territories, did not herald an atavistic throwback but instead a potentially beneficent force. Federation can be seen, then, as helping to facilitate the emergence of fin de siècle "social" imperialism, and once again, and unsurprisingly, there was continuity in personnel between the two movements with, for example, Lord Rosebery playing a significant role in both.[13] This is not to suggest that liberalism contains an inherent imperial logic.[14] Rather, the point is that the empire provided an issue—and a

[11] On the pluralists, see Marc Stears, *Progressives, Pluralists, and the Problems of the State* (Oxford, 2002); Cécile Laborde, *Pluralist Thought and the State in Britain and France, 1900–1925* (Basingstoke, 2000); and David Runciman, *Pluralism and the Personality of the State* (Cambridge, 1997).

[12] See also the discussion in Bell, "Empire and International Relations in Victorian Political Thought"; and Duncan Bell, "Empire and Imperialism" in Gregory Claeys and Gareth Stedman Jones (eds.), *The Cambridge History of Nineteenth Century Political Thought* (Cambridge, 2008).

[13] On Edwardian liberal imperialism, including the role of Rosebery, see H.C.G Matthew, *The Liberal Imperialists* (Oxford, 1973); and Bernard Semmel, *Imperialism and Social Reform* (London, 1960). But on the general weakness of the "liberal imperialists" in parliament, see George L. Bernstein, "Sir Henry Campbell-Bannerman and the Liberal Imperialists," *JBS*, 23 (1983), 105–24.

[14] The charge is leveled in Uday Singh Mehta, *Liberalism and Empire* (Chicago, 1999);

vision—around which a large number of liberals could coalesce, often for different, and sometimes conflicting, reasons. It was also the case that heated opposition to imperialism (although rarely to all facets of the empire) continued to emanate from within the liberal ranks, perhaps most stingingly from the pen of Herbert Spencer.[15] Liberal attitudes toward the empire remained complex and heterogeneous.

The failure of the late Victorian federalists also changed the nature of imperial campaigning. The broad church of imperial federation had served to raise political consciousness about the destiny of the colonies, but the ideological incoherence and organizational disarray of the movement—combined with the practical implausibility of many of the proposals that emerged from it—meant that it was never a truly successful political force. This was a failing that many contemporaries recognized and were determined not to repeat. During the Edwardian period, the lines of advocacy were drawn more clearly, and a number of prominent organizations, such as the Tariff Reform League and the Navy League emerged, often staffed by individuals associated previously with imperial federation. Campaigning on more strictly defined issues, they were often able to mobilize support and direct their political activities in a more effective fashion.[16] These organizations tended to divide along the lines that had split the IFL, between the promotion of an economic or a political-military vision of the empire; this was an ideological battle fought out over the next few decades, without an ultimate victor. Other imperialists preferred to move further away from the model of the IFL and its successors, instead joining informal groups, including the "co-efficients" or the "compatriots," which acted as forums for discussion among like-minded and influential individuals, and which often provided high-level political access. Probably the most effective of these was the so-called Pollock committee, named after its chairman, Frederick Pollock, the Corpus Professor of Jurisprudence at Oxford. Pollock was a supporter of supraparliamen-

---

and Bikhu Parekh, "Decolonizing Liberalism" in Aleksandras Shtromas (ed.), *The End of "Isms"?* (Oxford, 1994), 85–103. This mode of argument is usually premised on the (false) belief that a tradition of thought can be comprehended through an interpretation of one or two canonical writers (usually John Locke and John Stuart Mill).

[15] See, for example, Spencer, "Imperialism and Slavery" in Spencer, *Facts and Comments* (London, 1902), 112–21. See, in general, Duncan Bell and Casper Sylvest, "International Society in Victorian Political Thought," *MIH*, 3 (2006), 1–32; Bernard Porter, *Critics of Empire* (London, 1968); Nicholas Owen, "Critics of Empire," *OHBE*, IV, 188–212; and Gregory Claeys, "The 'Left' and the Critique of Empire, c.1865–1900" in Duncan Bell (ed.), *Victorian Visions of Global Order* (Cambridge, 2007).

[16] A useful analysis of their organization and methods is provided in Andrew Thompson, *Imperial Britain* (London, 2000). On the theoretical aspects of tariff reform, see Peter Cain, "The Economic Philosophy of Constructive Imperialism" in Cornelia Navari (ed.), *British Politics and the Spirit of the Age* (Keele, 1996), 41–65.

tary federalism, but (like Chamberlain) he recognized that this position was dead in the water, and the committee stuck to more moderate goals relating to imperial reorganization.[17]

Another significant progeny of imperial federation was the Round Table movement. Emerging out of Alfred Milner's notorious South African "kindergarten," and centered on a group of Oxford-educated friends, most notably Philip Kerr and Lionel Curtis, the members of the kindergarten played a significant role in the creation of the Union of South Africa (1910) before turning their attention to the empire as a whole.[18] Established in 1909–10, its leaders initially focused on the need to bring the colonies into the chambers of imperial decision-making and they argued that the only way for this to work in practice was through the formation of a representative imperial parliament.[19] Despite internal differences, the group was far more homogeneous ideologically than the imperial federalists had ever been.[20] They had learned from some of the failings of the amorphous Victorian campaigns. But the imperial conference of 1911 and then the First World War derailed their initial plans, making the prospects of a formal constitutional federation almost inconceivable, and during the 1920s a new set of questions arose, most notably over the future of India.

The Round Table's repetitive advocacy of federation as the answer to virtually every political problem fed into the development of the British Federal Union (formed in 1938), which in turn, through the considerable influence of Lothian, Lionel Robbins, and R.W.G. Mackay, helped shape the thinking of some of the leading architects of the post-1945 political integration of Europe.[21] The British federalists secured a receptive audi-

[17] On the Committee, see the overview by Pollock, "Imperial Organization," *PRCI*, 36 (1905), 287–319; and the discussion in J. E. Kendle, *The Colonial and Imperial Conferences, 1887–1911* (London, 1967), ch. 4.

[18] On the Kindergarten, see Walter Nimocks, *Milner's Young Men* (London, 1970). On the Round Table, see especially, J. E. Kendle, *The Round Table Movement and Imperial Union* (Toronto, 1975); Kendle, *Federal Britain* (London, 1997), ch. 5; and Michael Burgess, *The British Tradition of Federalism* (Leicester, 1995), 70–76. On the foreign policy impact of the Round Table, see Andrea Bosco and Alex May (eds.), *The Round Table* (London, 1997).

[19] For one of the most comprehensive statements, see Lionel Curtis, *The Problem of the Commonwealth* (London, 1915). On Curtis, see Deborah Lavin, *From Empire to International Commonwealth* (Oxford, 1995).

[20] As well as direct links with the British government (both through regular contact with officials and ministers and through serving themselves, most prominently in the case of Curtis and Lothian), Round Tablers were prominent in establishing the Royal Institute of International Affairs, in drafting aspects of the Treaty of Versailles, and, finally, in pushing appeasement as a policy option during the 1930s.

[21] Kendle, *Federal Britain*, 103–104 and ch. 6; Andrea Bosco, "Lothian, Curtis, Kimber and the Federal Union Movement (1938–40)," *Journal of Contemporary History*, 23 (1988), 465–502; and Burgess, *The British Tradition of Federalism*, Part III. On the impact

ence on the continent, fitting comfortably into an interwar period in which the "cult of federalism" was widespread.[22] The irony would not have been lost on Seeley, whose 1870 essay "The United States of Europe" argued both that federalism was necessary to maintain peace and prosperity in Europe and that such an institution was a practical impossibility.[23] None of this is to suggest that the imperial federalists were solely responsible for any and every position adopted by later advocates of federalism, but rather that the debates they spawned acted as early catalysts for the development and transmission of British federal thinking, which over the ensuing decades was to play a considerable role in international affairs.

While Curtis, Kerr, and their associates made significant contributions to debates over world order during the first few decades of the twentieth century, their ideas proved less enduring than Goldwin Smith's conception of the moral and cultural unity of the "Anglo-Saxon" peoples. Smith's rendition of this story was regarded as utopian by the federalists— the bonds seemed too weak and too diffuse. Yet the intimate relations between the former settler colonies and Britain helped shape the history of the twentieth century (and beyond), while extravagant visions of a global racial polity never came close to fruition. The course of two world wars and a variety of other conflicts, numerous economic and military treaties, defense and intelligence cooperation, and dense webs of cultural exchange all bear out the complex intertwining, and continuing salience, of colonial and postcolonial histories.[24] This is not to claim that tensions have

---

of Lothian, see Andrea Bosco, "National Sovereignty and Peace"; and John Pinder, "Prophet Not Without Honor," both in John Turner (ed.), *The Larger Idea* (London, 1988), 108–23 and 137–53.

[22] The term is from David Thompson, E. Meyer, and Asa Briggs, *Patterns of Peacemaking* (London, 1998 [1945]), 162–63. See also Martin Ceadel, "Pacifism and *Pacificism*" in Terence Ball and Richard Bellamy (eds.), *The Cambridge History of Twentieth Century Political Thought* (Cambridge, 2003), 480; and Hidemi Suganami, *The Domestic Analogy and World Order Proposals* (Cambridge, 1989), chs. 5–6.

[23] Seeley, "The United States of Europe," *MM*, 23 (1871), 436–48.

[24] A recent example of this can be seen in the controversy over the secret "Echelon" intelligence-gathering network, which allegedly links the United States, the United Kingdom, Australia, Canada, and New Zealand. This came to a head with the publication of a critical report in 2001, commissioned by the European Parliament, which concluded that the network breached various European laws. *Report on the Existence of a Global System for the Interception of Private and Commercial Communications (Echelon Interception System)*, 2001/2098 INI. "That a global system for intercepting communications exists, operating by means of cooperation proportionate to their capabilities among the USA, the UK, Canada, Australia, and New Zealand under the UKUSA Agreement, is no longer in doubt" (133). The report argues that the main target is private and commercial (not military) intelligence. It can be accessed on the website of the Federation of American Scientists: www.fas .org/irp/program/process/rapport—echelon—en.pdf.

been absent, or that clashes of interest and opinion have not occurred; nor is it to defend a vision of Anglo-Saxondom. Rather, it is important to recognize the strong sense of identification and affinity exhibited by many inhabitants (and especially the political elites) of the countries once settled by the British, and the considerable impact that this has had on creating the politics of our own world, for good or ill. But ironies abound. Many colonists flocked to the flag during the First World War, dying alongside the British (and other imperial troops) in appalling numbers. However, the war was not simply evidence of colonial "unity," for it was also a formative moment in the evolution of national self-consciousness in Australia, New Zealand, and Canada, and this served to undermine any possibility of the emergence of a substantive imperial federation. At the very moment at which some of the federalist goals appeared to have been met, especially with the creation of an Imperial War Cabinet in 1916–19, the idea dissolved in the face of the implacable opposition to political centralization evinced by the leaders of the colonies, who sought instead greater national autonomy.[25]

Plans for the formal union of the former settler colonies of Great Britain were nevertheless propounded throughout the twentieth century, the dream never dying, even as it receded ever further from the realm of plausibility. They persist to this day, and although marginal they identify a powerful impulse: a desire to build on the legacy, and the purported lost glory, of empire. In the 1930s and 1940s the idea of a transatlantic federal alliance—occasionally focusing simply on the British colonial empire and America, at other times on the "democracies of the North Atlantic"— garnered some support in America under the banner of "Union Now."[26] Today it is the United States that stands at the heart of such visions. The notion of an "Anglosphere," the vast imagined community of Anglo-Saxon states, has surfaced in American political debate.[27] At the dawn of

[25] The War Cabinet incorporated the assorted prime ministers of the dominions. For conflicting assessments of the prospects of formal federation in light of the War Cabinet and the conference, see J.A.R. Marriott, "British Federalism?" *NC*, 82 (1917), 389–403; Frederick Pollock, "Imperial Unity," *QR*, 229 (1918), 1–27; Sidney Low, "The Imperial Contribution," *The Nineteenth Century and After*, 82 (1917), 234–50; and R. L. Schuyler, "The British War Cabinet," *Political Science Quarterly*, 33 (1918), 378–95. On the role of the imperial war conference, see John Turner and Michael Dockrill, "Philip Kerr at 10 Downing Street, 1916–1921" in Turner (ed.), *The Larger Idea*, 36.

[26] For the federation of the "Atlantic" democracies, see Clarence K. Streit, *Union Now* (New York, 1938). During WWII Streit suggested, in *Union Now With Britain* (New York, 1941), that a more limited federation of the British "commonwealth" and the United States would help end the war. Meanwhile George Caitlin, a British academic, proposed a less ambitious form of integration, starting with closer cultural and economic ties and resulting ultimately in a formal federation. Caitlin, *One Anglo-American Nation* (London, 1941).

[27] See, for example, James C. Bennett, *The Anglosphere Challenge* (Lanham, Md., 2004).

the twenty-first century the conservative poet and historian Robert Conquest called for the "English-speaking" countries of the world to join together in a "flexibly conceived Association," something "weaker than a federation, but stronger than an alliance." This would encompass a core group comprising Britain, the United States, Canada, Australia, and New Zealand, in addition ("it is hoped") to Ireland and some of the formerly British imperial territories in the Caribbean and the Pacific. The continuities with the debates over Greater Britain are striking, although this passes unrecorded by Conquest. Dominating the earth, this vast "Anglo-Oceanic" polity, a "[n]atural rather than artificial" association, would combine "grandeur with modesty," offering the world a benign hegemon, and the British a way of escaping the clutches of an increasingly integrated Europe. "We face what is still a dangerous period," he warned. Sharing the same legal, political, and cultural traditions, this great arc of territories would, if united, form a "viable hyperpower." This demanded, though, the conversion to the cause of the diverse national publics and political elites. Because this presents a monumental challenge, providing detailed institutional plans would be "premature." But as the problems generated by distance have been transcended by new communications technologies—"the argument by distance fails"—a shift in political consciousness is possible, albeit difficult to foster. "Imagination will be needed, as it always is, to effect such a great political transformation. Against it will be ranged, not merely opposition of various sorts but also forces of apathy, and even more of established habit and interest."[28] Grandiose fantasies of Anglo-Saxon unity and superiority continue to exert their mesmeric power, shaping visions of a future world order, and drawing people back into the dangerous orbit of empire.

[28] Robert Conquest, *Reflections on a Ravaged Century* (London, 2000), 267–81. For a triumphalist account of the value of the "English-speaking" world, see Andrew Roberts, *A History of the English-Speaking Peoples Since 1900* (London, 2006).

Select Bibliography

The bibliography is limited to texts cited in the book. For the sake of concision, I have maintained the system of abbreviations employed throughout. Names placed in square brackets indicate that the book or article was originally published anonymously, and attributions for published articles are taken from Walter E. Houghton, Esther Rhoads Houghton, and Jean Slingerland (eds.), *The Wellesley Index to Victorian Periodicals, 1824–1900*, 5 vols. (Toronto: University of Toronto Press, 1965–1988), and the updates accessible on the *Wellesley* CD-Rom (London: Routledge, 1999).

PRIMARY SOURCES

1. Private Papers

John Robert Seeley papers, University of London Library (Senate House).
Imperial Federation League papers, British Library, London.
Oscar Browning papers, Modern Archive Centre, King's College, Cambridge.
Sidgwick papers, Trinity College, Cambridge.
Royal Commonwealth Society papers, University of Cambridge Library.
Frederick Young papers, University of Cambridge Library.

2. Books and Pamphlets

Abbott, Edwin, and Seeley, John, *English Lessons for English People* (London: Seeley, 1871).

Adderley, Charles Boyer, Lord Norton, *Imperial Fellowship of Self-Governing British Colonies* (London: Rivington, 1903).

Adorno, Theodor, and Horkheimer, Max, *Dialectic of Enlightenment* (London: Verso, 1997 [1944]).

Ambler, Benjamin George, *Ballads of Greater Britain and Songs of an Anglo-Saxon* (London: Elliot Stock, 1900).

Amery, Leo, *Union and Strength: A Series of Papers on Imperial Questions* (London: Arnold, 1912).

Amos, Sheldon, *The Science of Politics* (London: Kegan Paul, 1883).

Arnold, Matthew, *Culture and Anarchy and Other Writings*, ed. Stefan Collini (Cambridge: Cambridge University Press, 1993).

Arnold, Thomas, *The Miscellaneous Works of Thomas Arnold*, ed. Arthur P. Stanley (London: B. Fellowes, 1845).

Austin, John, *The Province of Jurisprudence Determined, An Outline of a Course of Lectures of General Jurisprudence or the Philosophy of Positive Law* (London: John Murray, 1832).

Bagehot, Walter, *The Collected Works of Walter Bagehot*, ed. Norman St John-Stevas, 8 vols. (London: The Economist, 1965–86).

——, *Physics and Politics, Or Thoughts on the Application of the Principles of Natural Selection and Inheritance to Political Society* (London: Kegan Paul Trench Trubner and Co., 1896 [1872]).

———, *The English Constitution*, ed. Paul Smith (Cambridge: Cambridge University Press, 2001 [1867]).

Baring, Evelyn, Earl of Cromer, *Ancient and Modern Imperialism* (London: John Murray, 1910).

Beddoe, John, *The Races of Britain: A Contribution to the Anthropology of Western Europe* (London: Trubner and Co., 1885).

Bentham, Jeremy, "Emancipate Your Colonies!" (1793/1830) in ibid., *Nonsense upon Stilts and Other Writings on the French Revolution*, ed. Philip Schofield, Catherine Pease-Watkin, and Cyprian Blamires (Oxford: Oxford University Press, 2002), 289–314.

———, "Rid Yourselves of Ultramaria!" (1820–22) in Bentham, *Colonies, Commerce, and Constitutional Law: Rid Yourselves of Ultramaria and Other Writings on Spain and Spanish America*, ed. Philip Schofield (Oxford: Oxford University Press, 1995), 3–190.

———, "Memoirs of Bentham" in *The Works of Jeremy Bentham*, vol. 10., ed. John Bowring (Edinburgh: William Tait, 1843).

Bluntschli, Johan Kaspar, *The Theory of the State*, trans D. G. Ritchie, P. E. Matheson, and R. Lodge (Oxford: Oxford University Press, 1885).

Boyd, Charles W. (ed.), *Mr Chamberlain's Speeches* (London: Constable and Co., 1914).

Brassey, Thomas, Lord Brassey, *Papers and Addresses by Lord Brassey: Imperial Federation and Colonisation*, ed. Arthur Loring and R. J. Beadon (London: Longman, Green, 1894).

Browning, Robert, *Poetical Works*, ed. Ian Jack (Oxford: Oxford University Press, 1970).

Bryce, James, *The American Commonwealth*, 3 vols. (London: Macmillan, 1888).

———, *The Ancient Roman Empire and the British Empire in India: The Diffusion of Roman and English Law Throughout the World, etc.* (Oxford: Oxford University Press, 1914).

Burt, A. L., *Imperial Architects, Being an Account of Proposals in the Direction of a Closer Imperial Union, Made Previous to the Opening of the First Imperial Conference of 1887* (Oxford: Blackwell, 1913).

Caitlin, George, *One Anglo-American Nation* (London: Dakers, 1941).

Carlyle, Thomas, *Past and Present* (London: Dent, 1915 [1843]).

———, *Chartism*, in *Selected Writings*, ed. Alan Shelston (Harmondsworth: Penguin, 1971).

Carnegie, Andrew, *The Reunion of Britain and America: A Look Ahead* (Edinburgh: Darien Press, 1898).

"Centurion" [Sir Graham Bower], *An Essay on Practical Federation* (London: Hatchards, 1887).

Clay, W. L. (ed.), *Essays in Church Policy* (London: Macmillan, 1868).

Clifford, John, *God's Greater Britain, Letters and Addresses* (London: J. Clarke and Co., 1899).

Coleridge, Samuel Taylor, *On the Idea of the Constitution of the Church and State, According to the Idea of Each* (London: Hurst, Chance, and Co., 1830).

Colomb, J.C.R., *Imperial Federation: Naval and Military* (London: Hawson and Sons, 1886).

Cooper, Daniel, *A Federal British Empire, The Best Defence of the Mother-Country and Her Colonies* (London: William Ridgway, 1880).

Cornewall Lewis, Sir George, *An Essay on the Government of Dependencies* (London: J. Murray, 1841).

Cramb, J. A., *The Origins and Destiny of Imperial Britain, Nineteenth-Century Europe* (London: John Murray, 1915).

Cunningham, Granville, *A Scheme for Imperial Federation: A Senate for the Empire* (London: Longmans, 1895).

Curtis, Lionel, *The Problem of the Commonwealth* (London: Macmillan, 1915).

Denison, Colonel George T., *The Struggle for Imperial Unity: Recollections and Experiences* (London: Macmillan, 1909).

Dicey, Albert Venn, *Lectures Introductory to the Study of the Law of the Constitution* (London: Macmillan, 1885).

———, *Lectures on the Relation between Law and Public Opinion in England During the Nineteenth Century*, 2nd ed. (London: Macmillan, 1914 [1905]).

———, *Introduction to the Study of the Law of the Constitution*, 8th ed. (London: Macmillan, 1915 [1885]).

———, *Memorials of Albert Venn Dicey, Being Chiefly Letters and Diaries*, ed. Robert Rait (London: Macmillan, 1925).

Dilke, Charles, *Greater Britain, A Record of Travel in the English-Speaking Countries During 1866 and 1867*, 2 vols. (London: Macmillan, 1868).

———, *Problems of Greater Britain*, 2 vols. (London: Macmillan, 1890).

———, *The British Empire* (London: Chatto and Windus, 1899).

Egerton, H. E., *A Short History of British Colonial Policy* (London: Methuen and Co., 1897).

Farrer, Thomas Henry, *Free Trade versus Fair Trade* (London: Cassell, Peter, and Galpin, 1882).

Fichte, Johann Gottlieb, *Addresses to the German Nation*, trans. R. F. Jones and G. H. Turnbull, ed. George A. Kelly (New York: Harper Torch Books, 1968 [1807–1808]).

Forster, William E., *Our Colonial Empire; An Address Delivered Before the Philosophical Institution of Edinburgh on Friday, November 5, 1875* (Edinburgh: Edmonston and Douglas, 1875).

———, *Life of the Right Hon. W. E. Forster*, ed. Sir Thomas Wemyss Reid, 2 vols. (London: Chapman and Hall, 1888).

Franklin, Benjamin, *The Interest of Great Britain Considered, with Regard to Her Colonies, and the Acquisitions of Canada and Guadaloupe* (London: T. Becket, 1760).

Franklyn, H. Mortimer, *The Unit of Imperial Federation* (London: Sonnenschein and Co., 1887).

Freeman, E. A., *History of Federal Government, from the Foundation of the Achaean League to the Disruption of the United States* (London: Macmillan, 1863).

———, *History of the Norman Conquest, Its Causes and Its Results*, 6 vols. (Oxford: Clarendon, 1877–79).

———, *The Methods of Historical Study* (London: Macmillan, 1886).

———, *Greater Greece and Greater Britain, and, George Washington the Expander of England* (London: Edward Augustus, 1886).

————, *The Life and Letters of Edward A. Freeman*, ed. W.R.W. Stephens (London: Macmillan, 1895).

Frere, Sir Bartle, *The Life and Correspondence of the Rt. Hon. Sir Bartle Frere*, ed. John Martineau (London: J. Murray, 1895).

Froude, James Anthony, *History of England from the Fall of Wolsey to the Defeat of the Spanish Armada*, 12 vols. (London: Longman's, Green, and Co., 1856–70).

————, *Caesar: A Sketch* (London: Longman's, Green, and Co., 1879).

————, *Oceana, or England and Her Colonies* (London: Longmans, Green and Co., 1886).

Garran, Robert Randolph, *The Coming Commonwealth: An Australian Handbook of Federal Government* (London: Simpkin and Marshall, 1897).

Gibbon, Edward, *The History of the Decline and Fall of the Roman Empire*, ed. David Womersley, 3 vols. (Harmondsworth: Penguin, 1995).

Gladstone, William Ewart, *Our Colonies: An Address Delivered to the Members of the Mechanics' Institute, Chester, on Monday, the 12th November 1855* (London: W. Parker, 1855).

Goldman, Charles Sydney (ed.), *The Empire and the Century, A Series of Essays on Imperial Problems and Possibilities* (London: John Murray, 1905).

Grant, Daniel, *Home Politics, or the Growth of Trade Considered in Its Relation to Labour, Pauperism, and Emigration* (London: Longman's, Green, and Co., 1870).

Green, Thomas Hill, *Lectures on the Principles of Political Obligation and Other Writings*, ed. Paul Harris and John Morrow (Cambridge: Cambridge University Press, 1986 [1882]).

Greswell, William Parr, *Outlines of British Colonisation* (London: Percival and Co., 1893).

Grey, Charles, Earl Grey, *The Colonial Policy of Lord John Russell's Administration* (London: R. Bentley, 1853).

Grote, George, *A History of Greece*, 12. vols (London: J. Murray, 1846–56).

Harrington, James, *The Commonwealth of Oceana, and, A System of Government*, ed. J.G.A. Pocock (Cambridge: Cambridge University Press, 1992 [1656]).

Hegel, Georg Wilhelm Friedrich, *Lectures on the Philosophy of World History, Introduction: Reason in History*, trans. H. B. Nisbet (Cambridge: Cambridge University Press, 1980 [1822–31]).

Her Majesty's Colonies, A Series of Original Papers Issued under the Authority of the Royal Commission, Colonial and Indian Exhibition, 1886 (London: William Clowes and Sons, 1886).

Hight, Sir James, *The English as a Colonising Nation* (Wellington: Whitcome and Tombs, 1903).

Hobhouse, Leonard Trelawney, *Democracy and Reaction*, ed. Peter Clarke (Brighton: Harvester, 1972 [1904])

————, *Liberalism and Other Writings*, ed. James Meadowcroft (Cambridge: Cambridge University Press, 1994 [1911]).

Hobson, J. A., *Imperialism: A Study* (London: James Nisbet and Co., 1902).

————, *The Crisis of Liberalism: New Issues of Democracy* (London: P. S. King, 1909).

Hume, David, *Essays, Moral, Political, and Literary*, ed. Eugene F. Miller (Indianapolis: Liberty Fund, 1987)

————, *An Enquiry into the Principles of Morals*, in Hume, *Enquiries*, ed. P. H. Nidditch (Oxford: Oxford University Press, 1975 [1777]).

Huskisson, William, *Speeches of the Right Honourable William Huskisson* (London: Murray, 1831).

Imperial Federation League, *Imperial Federation, Report of the Conference Held July 29, 1884, at the Westminster Palace Hotel* (London: Cassell and Co., 1884).

Jebb, Caroline, *The Life and Letters of Sir Richard Claverhouse Jebb* (Cambridge: Cambridge University Press, 1907).

Jebb, Richard, *Studies in Colonial Nationalism* (London: Edward Arnold, 1905).

————, *The Britannic Question: A Survey of Alternatives* (London: Longmans, 1913).

[Jenkins, John Edward], *Ginx's Baby, His Birth and Other Misfortunes* (London: Strahan and Co., 1871).

Kant, Immanuel, *Political Writings*, ed. Hans Reiss (Cambridge: Cambridge University Press, 1990).

Keppel, William, Viscount Bury, *Exodus of the Western Nations*, 2 vols. (London: R. Bentley, 1865).

Labillière, Francis P. de, *Federal Britain; Or the Unity and Federation of the Empire* (London: Simpson Low, Marston and Company, 1894).

Lambton, John George, Earl of Durham, *Lord Durham's Report on the Affairs of the British North American Colonies*, ed. C. P. Lucas (Oxford: Oxford University Press, 1912).

London Chamber of Commerce, *England and Her Colonies: The Five Best Essays on Imperial Federation Submitted to the London Chamber of Commerce for Their Prize Competition* (London: S. Sonnenschein, Lowrey, 1887).

Lord, Walter Frewen, *The Lost Empires of the Modern World: Essays in Imperial History* (London: Richard Bentley, 1897).

Macaulay, Thomas Babington, *The History of England from the Accession of James II*, ed. Peter Rowland (London: Folio Press, 1985 [1848]).

Machiavelli, Niccolo, *Discourses on Livy*, ed. Julia Conaway Bondanella and Peter Bondanella (Oxford: Oxford University Press, 1997).

Macnaught, William, *Federation of the Empire . . . Especially Written for the Working Classes* (Liverpool: James Gage, 1887).

Maine, Henry, *Village-Communities in the East and West* (London: John Murray, 1871)

————, *International Law, A Series of Lectures Delivered before the University of Cambridge 1887* (London: John Murray, 1888).

Marx, Karl, and Engels, Friedrich, *The Communist Manifesto* [1848], ed. Gareth Stedman Jones (Harmondsworth: Penguin, 2002).

————, *Capital, A Critical Analysis of Capitalist Production, Volume I* (Moscow: Foreign Languages Publishing House, 1954 [1887]).

Masterman, J. Howard, *A History of the British Constitution* (London: Macmillan, 1912).

Matthews, Jehu, *A Colonist on the Colonial Question* (London: Longmans, 1872).

Maurice, John Frederick Denison, *The Kingdom of Christ: Or, Hints on the Principles, Ordinances, and Constitution of the Catholic Church*, 3 vols. (London: Darnton and Clark, 1838).

———, *Social Morality: Twenty-One Lectures Delivered in the University of Cambridge* (London: Macmillan, 1869).

———, *The Life of Frederick Denison Maurice, Chiefly Told in His Own Letters* (London: Macmillan, 1884).

Merivale, Herman, *Introduction to a Course of Lectures on Colonies and Colonization* (London: Longman, Orme, Brown, Green, and Longmans, 1839).

———, *Lectures on Colonies and Colonization*, 2 vols. (London: Longman, Orme, Brown, Green, and Longmans, 1841).

Mill, James, *Collected Works*, 4 vols. (London: Routledge/Thoemmes Press, 1995).

Mill, John Stuart, *The Collected Works of John Stuart Mill*, ed. John M. Robson, 33 vols. (Toronto: University of Toronto Press, 1963–91).

Mills, Arthur, *Systematic Colonization* (London: John Murray, 1847).

———, *Colonial Constitutions: An Outline of the Constitutional History and Existing Government of the British Dependencies* (London: John Murray, 1856).

———, *Colonial Constitutions: An Outline of the Existing Forms of Government in the British Dependencies* (London: Edward Standford, 1891).

Mommsen, Theodor, *History of Rome*, trans. W. P. Dickinson, 4. vols. (London: Richard Bentley, 1862–75).

Montesquieu, Charles de Secondat, Baron de, *The Spirit of the Laws*, ed. Anne M. Cohler, Basia C. Miller, Harold Stone (Cambridge: Cambridge University Press, 1989 [1748]).

Morley, John, *On Compromise*, 2nd ed. (London: Macmillan, 1886 [1874]).

Mosley, Oswald, *The Greater Britain* (London: British Union of Fascists, 1932).

Müller, Max, *India, What Can It Teach Us? A Course of Lectures Delivered before the University of Cambridge* (Oxford: Longman's, 1883).

Nietzsche, Friederich *On the Genealogy of Morality*, ed. Keith Ansell-Pearson (Cambridge: Cambridge University Press, 1994 [1887]).

———, *Twilight of the Idols and The Anti-Christ*, ed. Michael Tanner (Harmondsworth: Penguin, 2003).

Oliver, Frederick Scott, *Alexander Hamilton: An Essay on American Union* (London: Archibald Constable and Co., 1906).

Oman, Charles, *England in the Nineteenth Century* (London: Edward Arnold, 1899).

Ostrogorski, Mosei, *Democracy and the Organisation of Political Parties* (London: Macmillan, 1902).

Paine, Thomas, *Common Sense*, ed. Isaac Kramnick (Harmondsworth: Penguin, 1982 [1776]).

Parkin, George, *Imperial Federation* (London: Macmillan, 1892).

————, *Round the Empire: For the Use of Schools* (London: Cassells, 1892).

Pearson, Charles, *National Life and Character*, 2nd ed. (London: Macmillan, 1894 [1893]).

Pownall, Thomas, *A Letter from Governor Pownall to Adam Smith* [1776] in *The Correspondence of Adam Smith*, 337–77.

————, *A Memorial Most Humbly Addressed to the Sovereigns of Europe: On the Present State of Affairs between the Old and New World* (London: J. Almon, 1780).

Price, Richard, *Political Writings*, ed. D. O. Thomas (Cambridge: Cambridge University Press, 1991).

Rawson, Rawson W., *Sequel to Synopsis of the Tariffs and Trade of the British Empire, Prepared and Presented to the Commercial Committee of the Imperial Federation League* (London: Office of the Imperial Federation League, 1889).

Rein, Gustav Adolf, *Sir John Robert Seeley*, trans. J. L. Herkless (Wolfeboro, N.H.: Longwood Academic, 1987 [1912]).

Robertson, J. M., *An Introduction to English Politics* (London: Grant Richards, 1900).

Roebuck, John Arthur, *The Colonies of England, A Plan for the Government of Some Portion of Our Colonial Possessions* (London: John W. Parker, 1849).

Ross, Patrick H. W., *Federation and the British Colonies* (London: Sampson, Low, and Co., 1887).

Rowe, Charles James, *Bonds of Disunion, or English Misrule in the Colonies* (London: Longman's and Co., 1883).

Ruskin, John, *The Stones of Venice, Vol. 1* [1851] in *The Works of John Ruskin*, ed. E. T. Cook and Alexander Wedderburn (London: G. Allen, 1903–12), vol. 9.

Seeley, Ada, *In the Light: Brief Memorials of Elizabeth Phebe Seeley, by Her Sister* (London: Seeley and Co., 1884).

[Seeley, John Robert], *Ecce Homo: A Survey of the Life and Work of Jesus Christ* (London: Macmillan, 1866).

[Seeley, John Robert], *David and Samuel; With Other Poems, Original and Translated* (London: Seeley, 1869).

Seeley, John Robert, *Lectures and Essays* (London: Macmillan, 1870).

————. *The Life and Times of Stein, or Germany and Prussia in the Napoleonic Age*, 3 vols. (Cambridge: Cambridge University Press, 1878).

————, *Natural Religion* (London: Macmillan, 1882).

————, *The Expansion of England: Two Courses of Lectures* (London: Macmillan, 1883).

————, *The Expansion of England: Two Courses of Lectures*, ed. John Gross (Chicago: University of Chicago Press, 1971).

————, *Goethe Reviewed after Sixty Years* (London: Seeley, 1894).

————, *Introduction to Political Science: Two Series of Lectures*, ed. Henry Sidgwick (London: Macmillan, 1923 [1896]).

————, *The Growth of British Policy: An Historical Essay* (Cambridge: Cambridge University Press, 1895).

[Seeley, Robert], *Essays on the Church; by, a Layman* (London: R. B. Seeley and W. Burnside, 1836).

Senior, Nassau, *Remarks on Emigration* (London: R. Clay, 1831).

——, *An Outline of a Science of Political Economy* (London: W. Clowes, 1836).

Sidgwick, Henry, *The Methods of Ethics* (London: Macmillan, 1874).

——, *The Elements of Politics*, 4th ed. (London: Macmillan, 1919 [1891]).

——, *The Development of European Polity*, ed. Eleanor Sidgwick (London: Macmillan, 1903).

Smith, Adam, *An Inquiry into the Nature and Causes of the Wealth of Nations*, general editors R. H. Campbell and A. S. Skinner; textual editor W. B. Todd (Oxford: Oxford University Press, 1976).

——, *The Correspondence of Adam Smith*, ed. E. C. Mossner, and I. S. Ross (Oxford: Oxford University Press, 1977).

Smith, Goldwin, *An Inaugural Lecture Delivered November 1859* (Oxford: J. H. and J. Parker, 1859).

——, *On Some Supposed Consequences of the Doctrine of Historical Progress: A Lecture* (Oxford: J. H. and J. Parker, 1861).

——, *The Study of History: Two lectures* (Oxford: J. Henry and J. Parker, 1861).

——, *The Foundation of the American Colonies: A Lecture Delivered before the University of Oxford, June 12, 1860* (Oxford: J. Henry and J. Parker, 1861).

——, *Does the Bible Sanction American Slavery?* (Oxford: J. Henry and J. Parker, 1863).

——, *The Empire, A Series of Letters Published in "The Daily News," 1862, 1863* (London: J. Henry and J. Parker. 1863).

——, *A Plea for the Abolition of Tests in the University of Oxford*, 2nd ed. (Oxford: Wheeler and Day, 1864).

——, *England and America: A Lecture Delivered by Goldwin Smith before the Boston Fraternity during His Recent Visit to the United States* (Manchester: Ireland, 1865).

——, *The Civil War in America: An Address Read at the Last Meeting of the Manchester Union and Emancipation Society* (London: Simpkin and Marshall, 1866).

——, *Three English Statesmen, A Course of Lectures on the Political History of England* (London: Macmillan, 1867).

——, *The Reorganization of the University of Oxford* (Oxford: J. Parker and Co., 1868).

——, *Lectures and Essays* (Toronto: Hunter and Rose, 1881).

——, *The Conduct of England to Ireland: An Address Delivered at Brighton, Jan. 30, 1882* (London: Macmillan, 1882).

——, *False Hopes, or, Fallacies, Socialistic and Semi-Socialistic, Briefly Answered* (London: Cassell, 1886).

——, *Canada and the Canadian Question* (London: Macmillan, 1891).

——, *The Moral Crusader, William Lloyd Garrison: A Biographical Essay* (London: Funk and Wagnalls Co., 1892).

——, *The United States: An Outline of Political History, 1492–1871* (New York: Macmillan 1893).

———, *Guesses at the Riddle of Existence: And Other Essays on Kindred Subjects* (London: Macmillan, 1897).

———, *The United Kingdom: A Political History* (London: Macmillan, 1899).

———, *Commonwealth or Empire? A Bystander's View of the Question* (London: Macmillan, 1902).

———, *My Memory of Gladstone* (London: T. Fisher Unwin, 1904).

———, *A Selection from Goldwin Smith's Correspondence*, ed. Arnold Haultain (London: T. W. Laurie, 1910).

———, *Reminiscences*, ed. Arnold Haultain (New York: Macmillan, 1910).

———, *Goldwin Smith, His Life and Opinions*, ed. Arnold Haultain (London: T. Werner Laurie, 1913).

Sorel, Georges, *Reflections on Violence*, ed. Jeremy Jennings (Cambridge: Cambridge University Press, 1999 [1908]).

Spencer, Herbert, *The Proper Sphere of Government* (1843) in *The Man Versus the State, with Six Essays on Government, Society, and Freedom*, ed. Albert Jay Nock (Indianapolis: Liberty Fund, 1982), 181–265.

———, *Social Statics; Or, the Conditions Essential to Human Happiness Specified, and the First of Them Developed* (London: Chapman, 1851).

———, *Principles of Sociology*, 3 vols. (London: Williams and Norgate, 1876–96).

Stead, W. T., *The Life of W. T. Stead*, ed. Frederick Whyte, 2 vols. (London: Jonathan Cape, 1925).

Streit, Clarence K., *Union Now: A Proposal for a Federal Union of the Democracies of the North Atlantic* (New York: Harper, 1940).

———, *Union Now with Britain* (London: Jonathan Cape, 1941).

Sutherland, John Douglas, Marquis of Lorne, *Imperial Federation* (London: Swan Sonnenschein, 1885).

Tocqueville, Alexis de, *Democracy in America*, trans. Henry Reeve, 2 vols. (London: Longman, 1862).

———, *Writings on Empire and Slavery*, ed. Jennifer Pitts (Baltimore: Johns Hopkins University Press, 2001).

Todd, Alpheus, *Parliamentary Government in the British Colonies* (London: Longman, Green, and Co., 1880).

Torrens, Robert, *Colonisation of South Australia* (London: n.p., 1835).

———, *Self-Supporting Colonization: Ireland Saved Without Cost to the Imperial Treasury* (London: Ridgeway, 1847).

Wakefield, Edward Gibbon, *The Collected Works of Edward Gibbon Wakefield*, ed. M. F. Lloyd Prichard (Glasgow: Collins, 1968).

———, *England and America: A Comparison of the Social and Political State of Both Nations* (London: Richard Bentley, 1833).

White, Arthur S. (ed.), *Britannic Confederation* (London: G. Philip and Son 1892).

Young, Arthur, *Political Essays Concerning the Present State of the British Empire* (London: W. Strahan and T. Cadell, 1772).

Young, Frederick (ed.), *Imperial Federation of Great Britain and Her Colonies; in Letters Edited by Frederick Young* (London: S. W. Silver, 1876).

———, *On the Political Relations of Mother Countries and Colonies, A Paper*

Read at the "Conference et Congrés Scientifiques" of the Exposition Internationale Coloniale et d'Exportation Générale, at Amsterdam, September 19, 1883 (London: Edward Stanford, 1883).

———, *An Address on Imperial Federation, at Cambridge, June 4, 1885* (London: Edward Stanford, 1885).

———, *A Pioneer of Imperial Federation in Canada* (London: George Allen, 1902).

3. Essays and Speeches

Anon., "The Federation of the British Empire: Thoughts for the Queen's Jubilee on Imperial Federation," WR, 128 (1887), 484–94.

Anon., "Home Rule and Imperial Federation," WR, 132 (1889), 225–30.

Anon., "*Imperium et Libertas,*" WR, 57 (1880), 91–111.

Anon., "The Integrity of the Empire," FR, 59 (1896), 738–50.

Anon., "The League and Its Journal," IF, 1/1 (1886), 16–18.

Anon., "State-Directed Colonization," WR, 128 (1887), 71–82.

Anon., "What We Offer to the Working Classes; Part 1," IF, 1/2 (1886) 50–51.

Anon., "What We Offer to the Working Classes; Part 2," IF, Vol. 1/3 (1886), 77–78.

Anon., "What We Offer to the Working Classes; Part 3," IF, Vol. 1/4 (1886), 105–106.

Anon., "Working Men Federationists," IF, 2/9 (1887), 205–206.

Adderley, Charles Boyer, Lord Norton, "Imperial Federation—Its Impossibility," NC, 16 (1884), 505–16.

———, "Imperial Federation: Impossible Constitutions," NR, 7 (1886), 704–11.

Amery, L. S., "Imperial Defence and Naval Policy" in Goldman (ed.), *The Empire and the Century*, 174–97.

Andrews, Charles M., review of Goldwin Smith, *The United Kingdom: A Political History, AHR*, 5 (1900), 738–42.

Arnold, Matthew, "Democracy" [1861] in Arnold, *Culture and Anarchy and Other Writings*, 1–26.

Arnold, Thomas, "The Church and the State" [1839] in *The Miscellaneous Works of Thomas Arnold*, 466–75.

———, "National Church Establishments" [1840] in *The Miscellaneous Works of Thomas Arnold*, 486–92.

Baden-Powell, George, "National Unity," PRCI, 16 (1884–85), 43–72.

Bagehot, Walter, "Responsible Government" [1856] in *The Collected Works of Walter Bagehot*, IV, 99–104.

———, "George Cornewall Lewis" [1863] in Bagehot, *Biographical Studies*, ed. R. H. Hutton (London, 1889), 206–47.

———, "The Meaning and the Value of the Limits of the Principle of Nationalities" [1864], *Collected Works*, VIII, 149–53.

———, "An Anglo-Saxon Alliance" [1875] *Collected Works*, VIII, 335–39.

Beadon, Robert, "Why the Imperial Federation League Was Dissolved," NR, 22 (1893–94), 814–22.

Berry, Sir Graham, "The Colonies in Relation to the Empire," PRCI, 18 (1886–87), 4–26.

Bourne, Stephen, "Extended Colonisation a Necessity to the Mother Country," *PRCI*, 11 (1879–80), 8–36.

Brabazon, Reginald, 12th Earl of Meath, "State-Directed Emigration: Its Necessity," *NC*, 16 (1884), 764–87.

——, "State-Directed Colonization," *NR*, 9 (1887), 525–37.

Bradshaw, W. J., "Imperial Federation" in, London Chamber of Commerce, *England and Her Colonies*, 73–89.

Brassey, Thomas, "Address Delivered before the Bradford Chamber of Commerce, January 21, 1880," *Papers and Addresses of Lord Brassey*, 30–46.

——, "On Work and Wages in Australia, Paper Read at the Royal Colonial Institute, February 14, 1888," *Papers and Addresses*, 235–37.

——, "Imperial Federation as Recently Debated," *NC*, 30 (1891), *Papers and Addresses*, 156–69.

Bruce, R. Bryce, "English Evils and Imperial Remedies," *IF*, 1/9 (1886), 248–51.

Bryce, James, "The Roman Empire and the British Empire in India" in *Studies in History and Jurisprudence* (Oxford: Clarendon, 1901), I, 1–84.

——, "An Age of Discontent," *CR*, 49 (1891), 14–30.

Burke, Edmund, "Observations on a Late Publication Intituled 'The Present State of the Nation'" [1769] in *The Writings and Speeches of Edmund Burke, Volume 2: Party, Parliament, and the American Crisis*, ed. Paul Langford (Oxford: Oxford University Press, 1981), 102–219.

——, "Speech on Conciliation with America" (March 22, 1775), in *The Writings and Speeches of Edmund Burke, Vol.3: Party, Parliament, and the American War, 1774–1780*, ed. W. M. Elofson with John A. Woods (Oxford: Oxford University Press, 1996), 102–69.

——, "Address to the Colonists" (January 1777), in *The Writings and Speeches of Edmund Burke*, III, 277–86.

——, "Speech at Bristol Previous to Election" [1780] in *The Writings and Speeches of Edmund Burke*, III, 623–63.

Burrows, Montagu, "Imperial Federation," *NR*, 4 (1884–85), 365–80.

Campbell, John Douglas Sutherland, Marquis of Lorne, "Our Relations with Canada and the Great Colonies," *PRCI*, 15 (1883–84), 41–51.

——, "Unity of Empire," *NC*, 17 (1885), 397–404.

——, "The Annual Address on the Progress of Geography: 1885–6," *Proceedings of the Royal Geographical Society*, 8 (1886), 417–36.

Carlyle, Thomas, "Signs of the Times" [1829] in *The Collected Works of Thomas Carlyle*, 16 vols. (London: Chapman and Hall, 1857), II, 98–119.

Carnegie, Andrew, "Imperial Federation: An American View," *NC*, 30 (1891), 490–508.

Cattanach, A. C., "On the Relations of the Colonies to the Parent State," *PRCI*, 2 (1870), 68–74.

Cecil, Robert Arthur Talbot Gascoyne, Marquis of Salisbury, "The Confederate Struggle and Recognition," *QR*, 112 (1862), 538–70.

——, "Speech at the Inaugural Dinner of the Institution of Electrical Engineers, Nov. 1889," printed in *The Electrician*, November 8, 1889, 13.

Chesney, Charles Cornwallis, "Our Panics and their Remedy," *MM*, 23 (1871), 448–57.

Chesney, George, "The British Empire," *PRCI*, 15 (1893–94), 167–74.

Clarke, William, "An English Imperialist Bubble" (1885), in *William Clarke, A Collection of his Writings*, ed. H. Burrows and J. A. Hobson (London: S. Sonnenschein, 1908), 76–90.

Coleridge, Samuel Taylor, "A Lay Sermon" [1817] in *The Collected Works of Samuel Taylor Coleridge, Vol. 6, Lay Sermons*, ed. R. J. White (Princeton: Princeton university Press, 1972), 117–233.

Collier, Robert, 2nd Baron Monkswell, "State Colonization," *FR*, 43 (1888), 387–98.

Colomb, Sir John, "A Survey of Existing Conditions," in White (ed.) *Britannic Confederation*, 3–33.

Constant, Benjamin, "The Liberty of the Ancients Compared with That of the Moderns" [1819], in Constant, *Political Writings*, ed. Biancamaria Fontana (Cambridge: Cambridge University Press, 1988), 307–28.

——, "The Spirit of Conquest and Usurpation and Their Relation to European Civilization" [1814] in Constant, *Political Writings*, 51–165.

[Conybeare, W. J.], "Church Parties," *ER*, 98 (1853), 273–342.

[Courthope, W. J.], "Problems of Greater Britain," *NR*, 15 (1890), 433–45.

Coutts, William, Viscount Bury, "Inaugural Speech" [March 15, 1869] *PRCI*, I (1869–70), 51–62.

——, "The Unity of the Empire," *NC*, 17 (1885), 381–96.

Cross, J. W., "The New World," *NC*, 29 (1891), 468–76.

Dahlberg-Acton, John Emerich Edward, Lord Acton, "Nationality" in *Selected Writings of Lord Acton, Vol. I: Essays on the History of Liberty*, ed. J. Rufus Fears (Indianapolis: Liberty Fund, 1985), 409–39.

Dalton, J. N., "The Federal States of the World," *NC*, 16 (1884), 96–118.

——, "What is Meant by Imperial Federation," *IF*, 1/2 (1882), 37–39.

Dewey, John, review of A. M. Sidgwick and E. M Sidgwick, *Henry Sidgwick, A Memoir* (London: Macmillan, 1906), *Political Science Quarterly*, 22 (1907), 133–35.

Dicey, Albert Venn, "Home Rule from an English Point of View," *CR*, 42 (1882), 66–86.

——, "Americomania in English Politics," *The Nation*, January 21, 1886, xlii.

——, "Alexis de Tocqueville," *NR*, 21 (1893), 771–84.

——, "A Common Citizenship for the English Race," *CR*, 71 (1897), 457–77.

Disraeli, Benjamin, "Conservative Principles" delivered at Manchester, April 3, 1872, in *Selected Speeches of the Late Right Honourable the Earl of Beaconsfield*, ed. T. E. Kebbel (London: Longmans, Green, and Co., 1882), II, 500–24.

Dougall, John Redpath, "An Anglo-Saxon Alliance," *CR*, 48 (1885), 693–706.

Douglas, John, "Imperial Federation from an Australian Point of View," *NC*, 16 (1884), 840–53.

Duffy, Sir Charles Gavan, "How British Colonies Got Responsible Government," I, *CR*, 57 (1890), 617–43.

——, "How British Colonies Got Responsible Government," II, *CR*, 58 (1890), 153–81.

——, "Some Fruits of Federation," *IF*, 5/3 (1890), 68.

Eddy, C. W., "What Are the Best Means of Drawing Together the Interests of the

United Kingdom and the Colonies, and of Strengthening the Bonds of Union," *PRCI*, 3 (1875–76), 3–23.

Editorial, *IF*, 3/6 (1888), 146–47.

[Elliot, Arthur] "Colonial and Imperial Federation," *ER*, 192 (1900), 247–70.

Farrar, J. M., "The Rise and Decline of the Confederate Government," *CR*, 40 (1881), 229–45.

Farrer, J. A., "The Integrity of the Empire," *FR*, 43 (1885), 338–44.

Farrer, Thomas Henry, "The Strength of England," *FR*, 23 (1878), 384–403.

Ferguson-Bowen, George, "The Federation of the British Empire," *PRCI*, 17 (1885–86), 282–96.

Fielding, William, "Imperial Migration and Settlement," *NR*, 8 (1886–87), 777–95.

Fisher, H.A.L., "Sir John Seeley," *FR*, 60 (1896), 183–89.

Fiske, John, "Why the American Colonies Separated from Great Britain," *FR*, 28 (1880), 147–63.

[Forbes, Urquhart], "Imperial Federation," *LQR*, 4 (1885), 320–35.

Forster, W. E., "Our Colonial Empire," the *Times*, Monday, November 6, 1875, 9.

———, "Imperial Federation," *NC*, 17 (1885), 201–18.

———, "A Few More Words on Imperial Federation," *NC*, 17 (1885), 552–56.

Foster, William, "Fallacies of Federation," *PRCI*, 8 (1875–76), 79–101.

Freeman, E. A., "Grote's *History of Greece*," *North British Review*, 25 (1856), 141–72.

———, "The Growth of Commonwealths" [1873] reprinted in Freeman, *Historical Essays*, 4th series (London, 1892), 353–88.

———, "Federation and Home Rule," *FR*, 16 (1874), 204–15.

———, "Race and Language" [1877], reprinted in his *Historical Essays*, 3rd Series, 2nd ed. (London: Macmillan, 1892 [1879]), 176–230.

———, "Some Impressions of the United States," *FR*, 32 (1882), I and II, 133–55 and 323–46.

———, "The Physical and Political Bases of National Unity" in White (ed.), *Britannic Confederation*, 33–56.

———, "Imperial Federation," *MM*, 51 (1885), 430–35.

Froude, J. A., "England's Forgotten Worthies," *WR*, 2 (1852), 32–67.

———, "The Science of History" [1864], *Short Studies on Great Subjects* (London: Longman's, Green, and Co., 1877), III, 1–25.

———, "England and Her Colonies," *FM*, 1 (1870), 1–16.

———, "Reciprocal Duties of State and Subject," *FM*, 81 (1870), 285–301.

———, "On Progress," *FM*, 2 (1870), 671–91.

———, "England's War," *FM*, 3 (1871), 135–50.

———, "Party Politics," *FM*, 10 (1874), 1–18.

Galt, Sir Alexander, "The Future Destiny of the Dominion of Canada," *PRCI*, 12 (1880–1), 88–109.

———, "The Relations of the Colonies to the Empire, Past and Future: Two Addresses Delivered in Edinburgh and Greenock," *PRCI*, 14 (1882–3), 391–409.

Gardiner, A. G., *The Life of Sir William Harcourt*, 2 vols. (London: Constable and Co., 1923).

Gisbourne, William, "Colonisation," *PRCI*, 20 (1889–90), 53–69.

Grant Duff, Sir Mountstuart Elphinstone, "The Pulse of Europe," CR, 28 (1876), 338–64.

[Greswell, William], "England and Her Second Colonial Empire," QR, 158 (1884), 131–61.

———, "Imperial Federation: Prize Essay" in London Chamber of Commerce, England and Her Colonies, 1–42.

———, "Colonization and the Friendly Societies," NR, 11 (1888), 685–700.

———, "The Imperial Federation League," NR, 14 (1889), 184–89.

Harris, William, "The Commercial Advantages of Federation," PRCI, 13 (1881–2), 209–225.

Harrison, Frederic, "Empire and Humanity," FR, 27 (1880), 288–308.

Hazell, Walter, "Practical Means of Extending Emigration," PRCI, 19 (1887–88), 48–64.

Henniker-Heaton, John, "The Postal and Telegraphic Communication of the Empire," PRCI, 19 (1887–88), 171–96.

———, "An Imperial Telegraph System," NC, 45 (1899), 906–14.

Hobson, J. A., "The Inner Meaning of Protectionism," CR, 84 (1903), 365–74.

Howard Vincent, C. E., "The British Empire To-day," PRCI, 16 (1884–85), 308–25.

———, "Inter-British Trade and its Influence on the Unity of the Empire," PRCI, 22 (1891–92), 265–88.

Hume, David, "Of Civil Liberty" in Hume, Essays, Moral, Political, and Literary, 87–97.

———, "Of the Balance of Power," Essays, 332–42.

———, "The Idea of a Perfect Commonwealth," Essays, 512–33.

———, "Of the Study of History," Essays, 563–69.

Jebb, Richard "Imperial Organization" in Goldman (ed.), The Empire and the Century, 332–48.

[Jenkins, John Edward], "Imperial Federalism," CR, 16 (1871), 165–88.

———, "An Imperial Confederation," CR, 17 (1871), 60–79.

[Jennings, L. J.], "Travels in the British Empire," QR, 162 (1886), 443–67.

Kant, Immanuel, "Idea for A Universal History with a Cosmopolitan Purpose" [1784] in Kant, Political Writings, 41–54.

———, "Perpetual Peace: A Philosophical Sketch" [1795] in Kant, Political Writings, 93–125.

Keith, James, "Our Great Competitor," NC, 21 (1887), 792–99.

Key, Sir A. Cooper, "Naval Defence of the Colonies," NC, 20 (1886), 284–93.

Kipling, Rudyard, "Deep-Sea Cables" in Rudyard Kipling's Verse, 1885–1932 (London: Hodder and Stoughton, 1932).

Labillière, F. P. de "The Permanent Unity of the Empire," PRCI, 6 (1874–75), 36–48.

———, "Present Aspects of Imperial Federation," IF, 1/1 (1886), 5–6.

———, "British Federalism: Its Rise and Progress," PRCI, 24 (1892–93), 95–120.

Laveleye, Emile de, "The European Situation," FR, 18 (1875), 1–21.

———, "The Progress of Socialism," CR, 43 (1883), 561–82.

Lobban, William, "Is Imperial Federation a Chimera?" *WR*, 136 (1891), 54–58.

Longley, J. W., "Canada and Imperial Federation," *FR*, 49 (1891), 466–79.

Low, Sidney, "The Imperial Contribution: The New Phase," *The Nineteenth Century and After*, 82 (1917), 234–50.

Lowe, Robert, "The Value to the United Kingdom of the Foreign Dominions of the Crown," *FR*, 22 (1877), 618–30.

Lowell, Frances Cabot, "English and American Federalism," *FR*, 43 (1888), 188–95.

Lucas, C. P., "Introduction" to Sir George Cornewall Lewis, *An Essay on the Government of Dependencies* (Oxford: Clarendon Press, 1891), vii–lxvii.

Ludlow, John Malcolm, "Europe and the War," *CR*, 15 (1870), 648–67.

———"Principles and Issues of the War," *CR*, 15 (1870), 348–63.

Macfie, Andrew Robert, "On the Crisis of the Empire: Imperial Federation," *PRCI*, 3 (1871–72), 2–12.

Mackinder, Halford, "The Geographical Pivot of History," *Geographical Journal*, 23 (1904), 421–37.

[Maine, Henry Sumner], "The Constitution of the United States," *QR*, 157 (1884), 1–32.

Mallet, Bernard, "The Whigs and Imperial Federation," *MM*, 61 (1890), 214–20.

Marriott, J.A.R., "British Federalism: A Vanished Dream?" *The Nineteenth Century and After*, 82 (1917), 389–403.

[Martineau, John], "New Zealand and Our Colonial Empire," *QR*, 128 (1870), 134–62.

Matthews, Jehu, "Nature and Need of Imperial Federation," *IF*, 1/4 (1886), 94–96.

Merivale, Herman, "The Colonial Question in 1870," *FR*, 7 (1870), 152–75.

Mill, James, "Colonies" in Mill, *Essays from the Supplement to the Encyclopedia Britannica, Collected Works*, 3–33.

Mill, John Stuart, "De Tocqueville on America," I and II [1835], *CW*, XVIII, 47–91 and 153–205.

———, "State of Society in America," [1836] *CW*, XVIII, 91–117.

———, "Bentham," [1838] *CW*, X, 75–117.

———, "Wakefield's 'The New British Province of South Australia,'" [1843], *CW*, XXIII, 738–42.

———, "Grote's "History of Greece," I [1846], *CW*, XI, 271–307.

———, "What is to be Done with Ireland" [1848], *CW*, VI, 497–505.

———, "Grote's "History of Greece," IV [1859], *CW*, XXV, 1128–34.

———, "A Few Words on Non-Intervention" [1859], *CW*, XXI, 109–25.

———, "England and Ireland" [1868], *CW*, VI, 505–35.

Mills, Arthur, "Our Colonial Policy," *CR*, 11 (1869), 216–39.

———, "The Problem of Empire: The Imperial Federation League," *FR*, 37 (1885), 345–51.

———, "Imperial Federation," *ER*, 170 (1889), 247–57.

Molyneux, Henry Howard, 4th Earl of Carnarvon, "Imperial Administration, Address to the Edinburgh Philosophical Institute, November 1878," *FR*, 24 (1878), 751–64.

Monypenney, W. F., "The Imperial Ideal" in C. S. Goldman (ed.), *The Empire and the Century*, 5–29.

Morley, John, "The Expansion of England," *MM*, 49 (1884), 241–58.

Muirhead, J. H., "What Imperialism Means" [1900] reprinted in *The British Idealists*, ed. David Boucher (Cambridge: Cambridge University Press, 1997), 257–53.

Murray Macdonald, J. A., "The Imperial Problem," *CR*, 80 (1901), 489–90.

Nicholls, H. R., "The Prophetic Objections to Federation," *IF*, 1/9 (1886), 273–74.

Nicholson, J. Shield, "Tariffs and International Commerce" in White (ed.), *Britannic Confederation*, 93–123.

Nietzsche, Friedrich, "On the Uses and Disadvantages of History for Life" [1873] in Nietzsche, *Untimely Meditations*, ed. Daniel Breazeale (Cambridge: Cambridge University Press, 1997), 57–125.

O'Brien, Barry, "Mr Goldwin Smith: Past and Present," *FR*, 41 (1884), 202–207.

Parkes, Sir Henry, "Australia and the Imperial Connection," *NC*, 15 (1884), 867–73.

Parkin, George, "Report of the Proceedings at the Meeting for the Promoting of a Memorial to the late Sir John R. Seeley, June 13, 1895," *Cambridge University Reporter*, no. 1088 (October 11, 1895), 54–72.

Peel, George, "The Nerves of Empire" in Goldman (ed.), *The Empire and the Century*, 249–88.

Pollock, Sir Frederick, "Imperial Organization," *PRCI*, 36 (1905), 287–319.

———, "Imperial Unity: The Practical Conditions," *QR*, 229 (1918), 1–27.

Potter, George, "Imperial Emigration," *NR*, 1 (1883), 193–207.

Price, B., "England and Her Colonies," *FM*, 68 (1863), 454–70.

Price, Richard, "Observations on the Nature of Civil Liberty, the Principles of Government, and the Justice and Policy of the War with America" [1776] in *Two Tracts on Civil Liberty, the War with America, and the Debts and Finances of the Kingdom*, in Price, *Political Writings*, 14–101.

Rainbow Circle, *Minutes of the Rainbow Circle, 1894–1924*, ed. Michael Freeden (London: Royal Historical Society, 1989).

Renan, Ernest, "Qu'est-ce qu'une nation?" [1882] in Geoff Eley and Ronald Grigor Suny (eds.), *Becoming National: A Reader* (Oxford: Oxford University Press, 1996).

Robinson, John, "The Social Aspect of Colonisation," *PRCI*, 1 (1869), 135–54.

[Robinson, John], "The Future of the British Empire," *WR*, 38 (1870), 47–74.

———, "The Colonies and the Century," *PRCI*, 30 (1898–99), 325–54.

Rogers, J. E. Thorold, "Contemporary Socialism," *CR*, 47 (1884), 51–64.

Royal Colonial Institute, "Account of the Dinner Held at the Canon Street Hotel, on Friday, 15th, November, 1872, to celebrate the completion of Telegraphic Communications with the Australian Colonies," published as a supplement to, *PRCI*, 3 (1871–72), 1–43.

Ruskin, John, "Inaugural" [1870] in *The Works of John Ruskin*, ed. Cook and Wedderburn, 18–44.

Salmon, Edward, "Imperial Federation: The Condition of Progress," *FR*, 68 (1900), 1009–19.

Schuyler, R. L., "The British War Cabinet," *Political Science Quarterly*, 33 (1918), 378–95.

Seebohm, Frederic, "Imperialism and Socialism," *NC*, 7 (1880), 726–36.

Seeley, John Robert, "Liberal Education in Universities" in F. W. Farrar (ed.), *Essays on a Liberal Education* (London: Macmillan, 1867), 145–78.

———, "Milton's Political Opinions," *Lectures and Essays* (London: Macmillan, 1870).

———, "Roman Imperialism, I: The Great Roman Revolution," *MM*, 20 (1869), 185–97.

———, "Roman Imperialism, II: The Fall of the Roman Empire," *MM*, 20 (1869), 281–91.

———, "Roman Imperialism, III: The First and Last Parts of Roman Imperialism Compared," *MM*, 20 (1869), 473–84.

———, "The Church as a Teacher of Morality" in W. L. Clay (ed.), *Essays on Church Policy* (London: Macmillan, 1868).

———, "The English Revolution of the Nineteenth Century," Parts I–III, *MM*, 22 (1870), 241–51, 347–58, and 441–51.

———, "The United States of Europe: A Lecture Delivered before the Peace Society," *MM*, 23 (1871), 436–48.

———, "The British Empire," *Bradford Observer*, March 22, 1872.

———, "Political Education of the Working Classes," *MM*, 36 (1877), 143–45.

———, "History and Politics," I–III, *MM*, 40 (1879), 289–99, 369–78, and 449–58.

———, "History and Politics," IV, *MM*, 41 (1879), 23–32.

———, "Political Somnambulism," *MM*, 43 (1880), 28–44.

———, "The British Race," [1872] *Education I* 4 (1881), 309–28.

———, "Our Insular Ignorance," *NC*, 18 (1885), 861–73.

———, "Introduction" to *Her Majesty's Colonies, A Series of Original Papers Issued under the Authority of the Royal Commission, Colonial and Indian Exhibition, 1886* (London: William Clowes and Sons, 1886), ix–xxvi.

———, "The Journal of the League," *IF*, 1/1 (1886), 4–5.

———, "The Object to Be Gained by Imperial Federation," *IF*, 1/8 (1886), 205–206.

———, "Georgian and Victorian Expansion: The Rede Lecture, 1887," *FR*, 42 (1887), 23–39.

———, "A Midlands University—Presidential Address to the Midlands Institute," *FR*, 42 (1887), 703–16.

———, "The Eighty-Eights," *Good Words* (1888), 272–360.

———, "The Impartial Study of Politics: Inaugural Address to the Cardiff Society for the Impartial Discussion of Politics and Other Questions, October 18th 1886," *CR*, 54 (1888), 52–65.

———, "Ethics and Religion: An Address before the Ethical Society of Cambridge," *FR*, 45 (1889), 501–14; reprinted in The Society of Ethical Propagandists (ed.), *Ethics and Religion, A Collection of Essays by Sir J. Seeley, Dr. F. Adler, Mr. W. M. Salter, Prof. H. Sidgwick, Prof. G. von Gizycki, Dr. B. Bosanquet, Mr. Leslie Stephen, Dr. S. Coit, and Prof. J. H. Muirhead* (London: Sonnenschein, 1900).

————, "Professor Seeley at Cambridge," *IF*, 6/6 (1891), 176.

————, "Sir John Seeley and National Unity," *Cambridge Review*, 16 (1895), 197.

Sidgwick, Henry, "Editor's Preface" to Seeley, *Introduction to Political Science*, v–xi.

Smith, Adam, "Smith's Thoughts on the State of the Contest with America, February 1778," ed. David Stevens, in *The Correspondence of Adam Smith*, 377–85.

Smith, Goldwin, "Froude's *History of England, Vols. V–VIII*," *ER*, 119 (1864), 243–79.

————, "Richard Cobden," *MM*, 67 (1865), 90–92.

————, "Female Suffrage," *MM*, 30 (1874), 139–50.

————, "The Ascent of Man," *MM*, 35 (1877), 194–204.

————, "The Defeat of the Liberal Party," *FR*, 26 (1877), 1–24.

————, "The Ninety Years' Agony of France," *CR*, 31 (1877), 103–23.

————, "The Policy of Aggrandizement," *FR*, 22 (1877), 303–24.

————, "Falkland and the Puritans: A Reply to Matthew Arnold," *CR*, 24 (1877), 925–42.

————, "The Greatness of England," *CR*, 34 (1878), 1–19.

————, "The Greatness of the Romans," *CR*, 32 (1878), 321–38.

————, "The Expansion of England," *CR*, 45 (1884), 524–40.

————, "The Organization of Democracy," *CR*, 47 (1885), 315–33.

————, "The Political History of Canada," *NC*, 20 (1886), 14–33.

————, "The Moral of the Late Crisis," *NC*, 20 (1886), 305–21.

————, "The Jews: A Deferred Rejoinder," *NC*, 13 (1887), 687–709.

————, "Straining the Silken Thread," *MM*, 58 (1888), 241–46.

————, "The Empire" in his *Essays on Questions of the Day*, 2nd ed. (New York: Macmillan, 1894 [1893]), 141–95.

————, "The Impending Revolution: Political England Revisited," *NC*, 35 (1894), 353–66.

————, "The Manchester School," *CR*, 67 (1895), 377–90.

————, "Burke, an Anniversary Study," *Cornhill Magazine*, 1 (1896), 17–29.

————, "Imperialism in the United States," *CR*, 75 (1899), 620–29.

————, "The Treatment of History, The Presidents Address to the American Historical Association, December 28, 1904" *AHR*, 10 (1905), 511–20.

————, "Burke on Party," *AHR*, 11 (1905), 36–41.

————, "The Experience of the American Commonwealth" [1867] in W. L. Guttsman (ed.), *A Plea for Democracy, an Edited Selection from the 1867 Essays on Reform and Questions for a Reformed Parliament* (London: MacGibbon and Kee, 1967), 140–50.

Smith, William Roy, "British Imperial Federation," *Political Science Quarterly*, 36 (1921), 274–97.

Spencer, Herbert, "From Freedom to Bondage" [1891] in Spencer, *The Man Versus the State*, ed. Albert Jay Nock, 487–518.

————, "Imperialism and Slavery" in Spencer, *Facts and Comments* (London: Williams and Norgate, 1902), 112–21.

Staveley Hill, A., "An Empire's Parliament," *PRCI*, 11 (1879–80), 136–54.

Stephen, J., "The Atlantic Telegraph and Its Lessons" *FR*, 5 (1866), 442–61.

Stout, Sir Robert, "A Colonial View of Imperial Federation," *NC*, 21 (1887), 351–62.

Tanner, J. R., "Sir John Seeley," *EHR*, 10 (1895), 1–8.

Taylor, Henry D'Esterre, "The Advantages of Imperial Federation," *IF*, 3/7 (1888), 129–30.

Thring, Sir Henry, "The Consolidation of the British Empire," in White (ed.), *Britannic Confederation*, 151–73.

——, "The Fallacy of Imperial Federation," *NC*, 19 (1886), 22–34.

Torrens, William, "Imperial and Colonial Partnership in Emigration," *PRCI*, 12 (1880–81), 175–96.

——, "Transplanting to the Colonies," *NC*, 9 (1881), 536–56.

Trevelyan, George Otto, "Ladies in Parliament" (1866), reprinted in *The Ladies in Parliament and Other Pieces* (Cambridge: Deighton, Bell, and Co., 1869), 3–33.

Tupper, C. Lewis, "India and Imperial Federation," *IF*, 7/7 (1892), 77–78.

Tupper, Charles, "Federating the Empire, A Colonial Plan," *NC*, 30 (1891), 509–20.

——, "How to Federate the Empire," *NC*, 31 (1892), 525–37.

Turgot, Anne Robert Jacques, "Tableau Philosophique des Progres Successifs de L'esprit Humain" [1750] in *Oeuvres de Turgot*, ed. Gustave Schelle (Paris, 1913–23), 214–35.

Vogel, Julius, "Greater or Lesser Britain," *NC*, 1 (1877), 809–31.

——, "The British Empire: Mr Lowe and Lord Blachford," *NC*, 3 (1878), 617–36.

Wakefield, E. G., "Outline of a System of Colonization" [1829], *The Collected Works of Edmond Gibbon Wakefield*, 178–87.

——, "A View of the Art of Colonization: With Present Reference to the British Empire; In Letters Between a Statesman and a Colonist" [1849], *The Collected Works of Edmond Gibbon Wakefield*, 758–1040.

Westgarth, William, "The Relation of the Colonies to the Mother Country," *PRCI*, 1 (1869), 74–85.

——, "On the Colonial Question," *PRCI*, 2 (1870), 58–64.

——, "Practical Views and Suggestions on Our Colonial Relations," *PRCI*, 3 (1871–72), 13–18.

——, "Propositions for the Reform of Our Relations with the Colonies," *PRCI*, 3 (1871–72), 84–90.

——, "The Unity of the Empire: Federation, Intercolonial and Imperial," *NR*, 4 (1884), 504–11.

White, Arthur Silva, "Introduction" in Silva (ed.), *Britannic Confederation*, ix–xv.

Wicks, Frederick, "The Confederation of the British Empire Practically Considered," *NR*, 8 (1886–87), 66–76.

Wilson, H. F., "The Public Schools and Imperial Federation," *IF*, 1/11 (1886), 304–305.

Wilson, Samuel "A Scheme for Imperial Federation," *NC*, 17 (1885), 590–98.

——, "Imperial Federation," *NR*, 4 (1884), 380–86.

Winton, Frances W. de, "Practical Colonisation," *PRCI*, 18 (1886–87), 297–312.
———, "Address," *Proceedings of the Royal Geographical Society*, 11 (1889), 613–22.
Woodburne, G. B. Lancaster, "Imperial Federation and Home Rule: A Conservative Solution," *NR*, 5 (1885), 608–15.
Young, Frederick, "Emigration to the Colonies," *PRCI*, 17 (1885–86), 368–74.
———, "Schemes and Suggestions for Imperial Federation," *IF*, 1/3 (1886), 71–72.
Young, G. A., "The Canadas," *The British and Foreign Review*, 8 (1839), 286–330.

SECONDARY SOURCES

1. Unpublished Theses

Burgess, Michael, "The Imperial Federation Movement in Great Britain, 1861–1893," Unpublished PhD thesis, University of Leicester, 1976.
Sylvest, Casper, "Liberal International Thought in Britain, 1880–1918," Unpublished PhD thesis, University of Cambridge, 2006.
Worsley, David, "Sir John Robert Seeley and His Intellectual Legacy: Religion, Imperialism, and Nationalism in Victorian and Post-Victorian Britain," Unpublished PhD thesis, University of Manchester, 2001.

2. Books

Adas, Michael, *Machines as the Measure of Men: Science, Technology, and Ideologies of Western Dominance* (Ithaca: Cornell University Press, 1989).
Altholz, Josef, *Anatomy of a Controversy: The Debate Over "Essays and Reviews," 1860–1864* (Aldershot: Scolar Press, 1994).
Anderson, Stuart, *Race and Rapprochement: Anglo-Saxonism and Anglo-American Relations, 1895–1904* (London: Associated University Presses, 1981).
Armitage, David, *The Ideological Origins of the British Empire* (Cambridge: Cambridge University Press, 2000).
———, *Greater Britain, 1516–1776: Essays in Atlantic History* (Aldershot: Ashgate, 2004).
Armitage, David, Armand Himy, and Quentin Skinner (eds.), *Milton and Republicanism* (Cambridge: Cambridge University Press, 1995).
Baldwin, Thomas (ed.), *The Cambridge History of Philosophy, 1870–1945* (Cambridge: Cambridge University Press, 2003).
Ballantyne, Tony, *Orientalism and Race: Aryanism in the British Empire* (Basingstoke: Palgrave, 2002).
Bayly, C. A., *Imperial Meridian: The British Empire and the World, 1780–1830* (London: Longman, 1989).
———, *The Making of the Modern World, 1789–1914: Global Connections and Comparisons* (Oxford: Blackwell, 2003).
Beasley, Edward, *Empire as the Triumph of Theory: Imperialism, Information, and the Colonial Society of 1868* (London: Routledge, 2005).

———, *Mid-Victorian Imperialists: British Gentlemen and the Empire of the Mind* (London: Routledge, 2005).

Bell, Duncan (ed.), *Victorian Visions of Global Order: Empire and International Relations in Nineteenth-Century Political Thought* (Cambridge: Cambridge University Press, 2007).

Benians, E. A., Butler, Sir James and Carrington, C. E. (eds.), *The Cambridge History of the British Empire: Volume 3: The Empire-Commonwealth, 1870–1919* (Cambridge: Cambridge University Press, 1959).

Bennett, George (ed.), *The Concept of Empire, Burke to Attlee, 1774–1947*, 2nd ed. (London: Adam and Charles Black, 1962).

Bennett, James C., *The Anglosphere Challenge: Why the English-Speaking Nations Will Lead the Way in the Twenty-first Century* (Lanham, Md.: Rowman and Littlefield, 2004).

Bentley, Michael, *Politics Without Democracy: Great Britain, 1815–1914: Perception and Preoccupation in British Government*, 2nd ed. (Oxford: Blackwells, 1999).

———, *Lord Salisbury's World: Conservative Environments in Late-Victorian Britain* (Cambridge: Cambridge University Press, 2001).

Biagini, Euginio (ed.), *Citizenship and Community: Liberals, Radicals and Collective Identities in the British Isles, 1865–1931* (Cambridge: Cambridge University Press, 1996).

———, *Ireland and the British Nation: Passion, Populism and the Radical Tradition in the British Isles, 1876–1906* (Cambridge: Cambridge University Press, 2007).

Blouet, Brian W., *Halford Mackinder: A Biography* (College Station, Tex.: Texas A&M University Press, 1987).

Bodelsen, C. A., *Studies in Mid-Victorian Imperialism* (London: Heinemann, 1960 [1924]).

Bosco, Andrea (ed.), *The Federal Idea*, 2 vols. (London: Lothian Foundation, 1991).

Bosco, Andrea, and May, Alex (eds.), *The Round Table: The Empire/Commonwealth and British Foreign Policy* (London: Lothian Foundation, 1997).

Boyce, George, *Decolonisation and the British Empire, 1775–1997* (London: Macmillan, 1999).

Bowler, Peter, *The Invention of Progress: The Victorians and the Past* (Oxford: Blackwell, 1989).

Brantlinger, Patrick, *Dark Vanishings: Discourse on the Extinction of Primitive Races, 1800–1930* (Ithaca: Cornell University Press, 2003).

Briggs, Asa, David Thompson, and E. Meyer, *Patterns of Peacemaking* (London: Routledge, 1998 [1945]).

Brock, M. G., and Curthoys, M. C. (eds.), *The History of the University of Oxford, Vol. VII* (Oxford: Oxford University Press, 2000).

Burgess, Michael, *The British Tradition of Federalism* (Leicester: Leicester University Press, 1995).

Burrow, J. W., *Evolution and Society: A Study in Victorian Social Theory* (Cambridge: Cambridge University Press, 1966).

———, *A Liberal Descent: Victorian Historians and the English Past* (Cambridge: Cambridge University Press, 1981).

———, *Whigs and Liberals: Continuity and Change in English Political Thought* (Oxford: Clarendon, 1988).

———, *The Crisis of Reason: European Thought, 1848–1914* (London: Yale University Press, 2000).

Burrow, J. W., Stefan Collini, and Donald Winch, *That Noble Science of Politics: A Study in Nineteenth-Century Intellectual History* (Cambridge: Cambridge University Press, 1983).

Burton, Antoinette (ed.), *After the Imperial Turn: Thinking With and Through the Nation* (Durham, N.C.: Duke University Press, 2003).

Cain, Peter, *Hobson and Imperialism: Radicalism, New Liberalism, and Finance 1887–1938* (Oxford: Oxford University Press, 2002).

Cain, P. J., and Hopkins, A. G., *British Imperialism, 1688–2000* (Harlow: Longman, 2002).

Campbell, Alexander, *Great Britain and the United States, 1895–1903* (London: Longmans, Green, 1960).

Cannadine, David, *G. M. Trevelyan: A Life in History* (London: HarperCollins, 1992).

———, *Ornamentalism: How the British Saw Their Empire* (London: Penguin, 2001).

———, *In Churchill's Shadow: Confronting the Past in Modern Britain* (London: Allen Lane, 2002).

Cheng, Seymour, *Schemes for the Federation of the British Empire* (New York: Columbia University Press, 1931).

Chew, Kenneth, and Wilson, Anthony, *Victorian Science and Engineering Portrayed in the Illustrated London News* (Stroud: Sutton, 1993).

Claeys, Gregory, and Gareth Stedman Jones (eds.), *The Cambridge History of Nineteenth Century Political Thought* (Cambridge: Cambridge University Press, 2008).

Clarke, I. F., *Voices Prophesizing War: Future Wars, 1763–3749*, 2nd ed. (Oxford: Oxford University Press, 1992).

———, (ed.), *The Tale of the Next Great War, 1871–1914: Fictions of Future Warfare and of Battles Still-to-Come* (Liverpool: Liverpool University Press, 1995).

———, (ed.), *The Great War with Germany, 1890–1914: Fictions and Fantasies of the War to Come* (Liverpool: Liverpool University Press, 1997).

Clarke, Peter, *Liberals and Social Democrats* (Cambridge: Cambridge University Press, 1978).

Cohn, Bernard, *Colonialism and Its Forms of Knowledge: The British in India* (Princeton: Princeton University Press, 1996).

Colley, Linda, *Britons: Forging the Nation, 1707–1837* (New Haven: Yale University Press, 1992).

Collini, Stefan, *Liberalism and Sociology: L. T. Hobhouse and Political Argument in England, 1880–1914* (Cambridge: Cambridge University Press, 1979).

———, *Public Moralists: Political Thought and Intellectual Life in Britain 1850–1930* (Oxford: Clarendon, 1991).

————, *Absent Minds: Intellectuals in Britain* (Oxford: Oxford University Press, 2006).

Collini, Stefan, Whatmore, Richard, and Young, Brian (eds.), *History, Religion, and Culture: British Intellectual History, 1750–1950* (Cambridge: Cambridge University Press, 2000).

Connell, Philip, *Romanticism, Economics, and the Question of "Culture"* (Oxford: Oxford University Press, 1999).

Conquest, Robert, *Reflections on a Ravaged Century* (London: W. W. Norton, 2000).

Cooper, Frederick, *Colonialism in Question: Theory, Knowledge, History* (Berkeley: University of California Press, 2005).

Daly, Nicholas, *Literature, Technology, and Modernity, 1860–2000* (Cambridge: Cambridge University Press, 2004).

Demetrious, Kyriacos N., *George Grote on Plato and Athenian Democracy: A Study in Classical Reception* (Berlin: Peter Lang, 1999).

Desmond, Adrian, and Moore, James, *Darwin* (London: Michael Joseph, 1991).

Dickinson, H. T., (ed.), *Britain and the American Revolution* (London: Longman, 1998).

Dirks, Nicholas, *The Scandal of Empire: India and the Creation of Imperial Britain* (Cambridge, Mass.: Harvard University Press, 2006).

Drayton, Richard, *Nature's Government: Science, Imperial Britain, and the "Improvement" of the World* (New Haven: Yale University Press, 2000).

Driver, Felix, *Geography Militant: Cultures of Exploration in the Age of Empire* (Oxford: Blackwell, 1999).

Eddy, John, and Schreuder, D. M. (eds.), *The Rise of Colonial Nationalism: Australia, New Zealand, Canada and South Africa First Assert Their Nationalities, 1880–1914* (London: Allen and Unwin, 1988).

Edwards, Catherine (ed.), *Roman Presences: Receptions of Rome in European Culture, 1789–1945* (Cambridge: Cambridge University Press, 1999).

Edwards, Catherine, and Liversidge, Michael (eds.), *Imagining Rome: British Artists and Rome in the Nineteenth Century* (London: Merrell Holberton, 1996).

Eldridge, C. C., *England's Mission: The Imperial Idea in the Age of Gladstone and Disraeli, 1868–1880* (London: Macmillan, 1973).

————, *Disraeli and the Rise of a New Imperialism* (Cardiff: University of Wales Press, 1996).

Elliott, J. H., *Empires of the Atlantic World: Britain and Spain in America, 1492–1830* (London: Yale University Press, 2006).

Epstein, James, *Radical Expression: Political Language, Ritual, and Symbol in England, 1790–1850* (Oxford: Oxford University Press, 1994).

Evans, Julie, Grimshaw, Patricia, Phillips, David, and Swain, Shurlee, *Equal Subjects, Unequal Rights: Indigenous People's in British Settler Colonies, 1830–1910* (Manchester: Manchester University Press, 2003).

Evans, Richard J., and Pogge Von Strandmann, Hartmut (eds.), *The Revolutions in Europe, 1848–1849: From Reform to Reaction* (Oxford: Oxford University Press, 2000).

Faber, Richard, *The Vision and the Need: Late Victorian Imperialist Aims* (London: Faber and Faber, 1966).

Farnsworth, Susan, *The Evolution of British Imperial Policy During the Mid-Nineteenth Century* (New York: Garland, 1992).

Feenberg, Andrew, *Critical Theory of Technology* (Oxford: Oxford University Press, 1991).

Ferguson, Niall, *Empire: How Britain Made the Modern World* (New York: Basic Books, 2003).

———, *Colossus: The Price of America's Empire* (London: Allen Lane, 2004).

Field, H. John, *Towards a Programme for an Imperial Life: The British Empire at the Turn of the Century* (Westport, Conn.: Greenwood Press, 1982).

Fitzmaurice, Andrew, *Humanism and America: An Intellectual History of English Colonisation, 1500–1625* (Cambridge: Cambridge University Press, 2003).

Floud, Roderick, and McCloskey, Donald (eds.), *The Economic History of Britain Since 1700*, 2nd ed. (Cambridge: Cambridge University Press, 1994).

Forbes, Duncan, *The Liberal Anglican Idea of History* (Cambridge: Cambridge University Press, 1952).

Forsyth, Murray, *Unions of States: The Theory and Practice of Confederation* (Leicester: Leicester University Press, 1981).

Francis, Mark, *Governors and Settlers: Images of Authority in the British Colonies, 1820–60* (London: Macmillan, 1992).

Freeden, Michael, *The New Liberalism: An Ideology of Social Reform* (Oxford: Clarendon, 1978).

Freeman, Michael, *Railways and the Victorian Imagination* (London: Yale University Press, 1999).

Gannon, Michael, *Rumors of War and Infernal Machines: Technomilitary Agenda-Setting in American and British Speculative Fiction* (Liverpool: Liverpool University Press, 2005).

Garvin, J. L., with J. Amery, *The Life of Joseph Chamberlain*, (London: Macmillan, 1929–68).

Gerlach, Murney, *British Liberalism and the United States: Political and Social Thought in the Late Victorian Age* (Basingstoke: Palgrave, 2001).

Geuss, Raymond, *History and Illusion in Politics* (Cambridge: Cambridge University Press, 2001).

Goldman, Lawrence, *Science, Reform and Politics in Mid-Victorian Britain: The Social Science Association, 1857–1886* (Cambridge: Cambridge University Press, 2002).

Gould, Eliga, *The Persistence of Empire: British Political Culture in the Age of the American Revolution* (Chapel Hill: University of North Carolina Press, 2000).

Green, E.H.H., *The Crisis of Conservatism: The Politics, Economics, and Ideology of the Conservative Party, 1880–1914* (London: Routledge, 1995).

———, *Ideologies of Conservatism: Conservative Political Ideas in the Twentieth Century* (Oxford: Oxford University Press, 2002).

Grimley, Matthew, *Citizenship, Community, and the Church of England: Liberal Anglican Theories of the State Between the Wars* (Oxford: Oxford University Press, 2004).

Hall, Catherine, *Civilising Subjects: Metropole and Colony in the English Imagination, 1830–1867* (Cambridge: Polity, 2002).

Hamer, D. A., *John Morley: A Liberal Intellectual in Politics* (Oxford: Clarendon, 1968).

Hardt, Michael, and Negri, Antonio, *Empire* (Cambridge, Mass.: Harvard University Press, 2000).

Harris, Jose, *Unemployment and Politics: A Study in English Social Policy, 1886–1914* (Oxford: Clarendon, 1972).

——, *Private Lives, Public Spirit: A Social History of Britain, 1870–1914* (Harmondsworth: Penguin, 1994).

Harvey, David, *The Condition of Postmodernity: An Enquiry Into the Origins of Cultural Change* (Oxford: Blackwell, 1989).

Harvie, Christopher, *The Lights of Liberalism: University Liberals and the Challenge of Democracy, 1860–86* (London: Allen Lane, 1976).

Haslam, Jonathan, *No Virtue Like Necessity: Realist Thought in International Relations Since Machiavelli* (New Haven: Yale University Press, 2002).

Headrick, Daniel, *The Tools of Empire: Technology and European Imperialism in the Nineteenth Century* (New York: Oxford University Press, 1981).

——, *The Tentacles of Progress: Technology Transfer in the Age of Imperialism, 1850–1940* (Oxford: Oxford University Press, 1988).

——, *The Invisible Weapon: Telecommunications and International Politics, 1851–1945* (Oxford: Oxford University Press, 1991).

Held, David, *Global Covenant: The Social Democratic Alternative to the Washington Consensus* (Cambridge: Polity Press, 2004).

Hilton, Boyd, *The Age of Atonement: The Influence of Evangelicalism on Social and Economic Thought, 1795–1865* (Oxford: Clarendon, 1988).

——, *A Mad, Bad, and Dangerous People? England, 1783–1846* (Oxford: Oxford University Press, 2006).

Hingley, Richard, *Roman Officers and English Gentlemen: The Imperial Origins of Roman Archaeology* (London: Routledge, 2000).

Hont, Istvan, *Jealousy of Trade: International Competition and the Nation-State in Historical Perspective* (Cambridge, Mass.: Harvard University Press, 2005).

Hopkins, A. G. (ed.), *Globalization in World History* (London: Pimlico, 2002).

Hörnqvist, Mikael, *Machiavelli and Empire* (Cambridge: Cambridge University Press, 2004).

Howe, Anthony, *Free Trade and Liberal England, 1846–1946* (Oxford: Clarendon, 1997).

Hyam, Ronald, *Britain's Imperial Century: A Study of Empire and Expansion*, 2nd ed. (London: Macmillan, 1992).

Jenkyns, Richard, *The Victorians and Ancient Greece* (Oxford: Blackwell, 1980).

Jones, H. S., *Victorian Political Thought* (Basingstoke: Macmillan, 2000).

Jones, Todd E., *The Broad Church: A Biography of a Movement* (Lanham, Md.: Lexington Books, 2003).

Kelly, George Armstrong, *The Humane Comedy: Constant, Tocqueville, and French Liberalism* (Cambridge: Cambridge University Press, 1992).

Kendle, J. E., *The Colonial and Imperial Conferences, 1887–1911: A Study in Imperial Organization* (London: Longman's, 1967).

——, *The Round Table Movement and Imperial Union* (Toronto: University of Toronto Press, 1975).

————, *Ireland and the Federal Solution: The Debate Over the United Kingdom Constitution, 1870–1921* (Kingston, Ontario: McGill–Queen's University Press, 1989).

————, *Federal Britain: A History* (London: Routledge, 1997).

Kennedy, Paul, *The Rise of Anglo-German Antagonism, 1860–1914* (London: Allen and Unwin, 1982).

Kern, Stephen, *The Culture of Time and Space, 1880–1914* (Cambridge, Mass.: Harvard University Press, 1983).

Kim, Stephen, *John Tyndall's Transcendental Materialism and the Conflict Between Religion and Science in Victorian England* (Lewiston. N.Y.: Mellen Press, 1991).

King, Preston, *Federalism and Federation* (London: Croom Helm, 1982).

Knights, Ben, *The Idea of the Clerisy in the Nineteenth Century* (Cambridge: Cambridge University Press, 1978).

Knorr, Klaus, *British Colonial Theories, 1570–1850* (London: Frank Cass, 1963).

Koebner, Richard, *Empire* (Cambridge: Cambridge University Press, 1961).

Koebner, Richard, and Schmidt, Helmut Dan, *Imperialism: The Story and Significance of a Political Word, 1840–1960* (Cambridge: Cambridge University Press, 1964).

Koot, Gerard M., *English Historical Economics, 1870–1926: The Rise of Economic History and Neomercantalism* (Cambridge: Cambridge University Press, 1987).

Koselleck, Reinhart, *Futures Past: On the Semantics of Historical Time*, trans. Keith Tribe (Cambridge, Mass.: MIT Press, 1988).

Koskenniemi, Martti, *The Gentle Civiliser of Nations: The Rise and Fall of International Law, 1870–1960* (Cambridge: Cambridge University Press, 2001).

Kostal, Rande, *A Jurisprudence of Power: Victorian Empire and the Rule of Law* (Oxford: Oxford University Press, 2005).

Kumar, Krishan, *The Making of English National Identity* (Cambridge: Cambridge University Press, 2003).

Kupperman, Karen Ordahl (ed.), *America in European Consciousness, 1493–1750* (Chapel Hill: University of North Carolina Press, 1995).

Laborde, Cécile, *Pluralist Thought and the State in Britain and France, 1900–1925* (Basingstoke: Macmillan, 2000).

Laborde, Cécile and John Maynor (eds.), *Republicanism and Political Theory* (Oxford: Blackwell, 2007).

Langford, Paul, *Englishness Identified: Manners and Character, 1650–1850* (Oxford: Oxford University Press, 2000).

Lavin, Deborah, *From Empire to International Commonwealth: A Biography of Lionel Curtis* (Oxford: Oxford University Press, 1995).

Lester, Alan, *Imperial Networks: Creating Identities in Nineteenth-Century South Africa and Britain* (London: Routledge, 2001).

Leventhal, Fred M., and Quinault, Roland (eds.), *Anglo-American Attitudes: From Revolution to Partnership* (Aldershot: Ashgate, 2000).

Lillibridge, George, *Beacon of Freedom: The Impact of American Democracy Upon Great Britain, 1830–1870* (Philadelphia: University of Pennsylvania Press, 1955).

Linklater, Andrew, *The Transformation of Political Community: Ethical Foundations of the Post-Westphalian Era* (Cambridge: Polity, 1998).

Livingstone, David N., *The Geographical Tradition: Episodes in the History of a Contested Enterprise* (Oxford: Blackwell, 1992).

Louis, Wm. Roger (ed.), *Oxford History of the British Empire*, 5 vols. (Oxford: Oxford University Press, 1998–99).

Lowe, John, *The Great Powers, Imperialism, and the German Problem, 1865–1925* (London: Routledge, 1994).

Mackenzie, John, *Orientalism: History, Theory, and the Arts* (Manchester: Manchester University Press, 1995).

Mahajan, Sneh, *British Foreign Policy 1874–1914: The Role of India* (London: Routledge, 2001).

Malchow, Howard L., *Population Pressures: Emigration and Government in Late Nineteenth-Century Britain* (Palo Alto: Society for the Promotion of Science and Scholarship, 1979).

Mandler, Peter, *The English National Character: The History of an Idea from Burke to Blair* (London: Yale University Press, 2006).

Marriott, John, *The Other Empire: Metropolis, India and Progress in the Colonial Imagination* (Manchester: Manchester University Press, 2003).

Marsh, Peter, *Joseph Chamberlain: Entrepreneur in Politics* (London: Yale University Press, 1994).

Martin, Ged, *The Durham Report and Colonial Policy: A Critical Essay* (Cambridge: Cambridge University Press, 1972).

Matthew, H.C.G., *The Liberal Imperialists: The Ideas and Politics of a Post-Gladstonian Élite* (Oxford: Oxford University Press, 1973).

———, *Gladstone, 1809–1898* (Oxford: Oxford University Press, 1997).

McKendrick, Neil (ed.), *Historical Perspectives: Studies in English Thought and Society in Honour of J. H. Plumb* (London: Europa, 1974).

Meadowcroft, James, *Conceptualizing the State: Innovation and Dispute in British Political Thought 1880–1914* (Oxford: Clarendon, 1995).

Mehta, Uday Singh, *Liberalism and Empire: A Study in Nineteenth-Century British Liberal Thought* (Chicago: University of Chicago Press, 1999).

Metcalf, Thomas, *An Imperial Vision: Indian Architecture and Britain's Raj* (Berkeley: University of California Press, 1989).

———, *Ideologies of the Raj* (Cambridge: Cambridge University Press, 1994).

Miller, Peter N., *Defining the Common Good: Empire, Religion, and Philosophy in Eighteenth-Century Britain* (Cambridge: Cambridge University Press, 1994).

Millman, Richard, *British Foreign Policy and the Coming of the Franco-Prussian War* (Oxford: Clarendon, 1965).

Mogi, Sobei, *The Problem of Federalism: A Study in the History of Political Theory*, 2 vols. (London: Allen and Unwin, 1931).

Morefield, Jeanne, *Covenants Without Swords: Idealist Liberalism and the Spirit of Empire* (Princeton: Princeton University Press, 2005).

———, "'An Education to Greece': The Round Table, Imperial Theory, and the Uses of History," *HPT* (2007).

Morrell, W. P., *British Colonial Policy in the Age of Peel and Russell* (Oxford: Clarendon Press, 1930).

Morris, Jan, *Pax Britannica: The Climax of an Empire* (London: Faber, 1968).

Morris, Jeremy, *F. D. Maurice and the Crisis of Christian Authority* (Oxford: Oxford University Press, 2005).

Moses, A. Dirk (ed.), *Genocide and Settler Society: Frontier Violence and Stolen Indigenous Children in Australian History* (Oxford: Berghahn Books, 2004).

Mulvey, Christopher, *Transatlantic Manners: Social Patterns in Nineteenth-Century Anglo-American Travel Literature* (Cambridge: Cambridge University Press, 1990).

Nabulsi, Karma, *Traditions of War: Occupation, Resistance, and the Law* (Oxford: Oxford University Press, 1999).

Navari, Cornelia (ed.), *British Politics and the Spirit of the Age: Political Concepts in Action* (Keele: Keele University Press, 1996).

Nelson, Eric, *The Greek Tradition in Republican Thought* (Cambridge, 2004).

Nicholls, David, *The Lost Prime Minister: A Life of Sir Charles Dilke* (London: Hamledon, 1995).

Nimocks, Walter, *Milner's Young Men: The "Kindergarten" in Edwardian Imperial Affairs* (London: Hodder and Stoughton, 1970).

Pagden, Anthony, *Lords of All the World: Ideologies of Empire in Spain, Britain and France c.1500–c.1800* (New Haven: Yale University Press, 1995).

———, *Spanish Imperialism and the Political Imagination* (New Haven: Yale University Press, 1990).

———, *Peoples and Empires* (London: Weidenfeld and Nicholson, 2001).

Parker, W. H., *Mackinder: Geography as an Aid to Statecraft* (Oxford: Clarendon, 1982).

Parry, J. P., *The Politics of Patriotism: English Liberalism, National Identity, and Europe, 1830–1886* (Cambridge: Cambridge University Press, 2006).

———, *Democracy and Religion: Gladstone and the Liberal Party, 1867–1875* (Cambridge: Cambridge University Press, 1986).

Pettit, Phillip, *Republicanism: A Theory of Freedom and Government* (Oxford: Oxford University Press, 1997).

Phillips, Paul, *The Controversialist: An Intellectual Life of Goldwin Smith* (Westport: Praeger, 2002).

Pick, Daniel, *Faces of Degeneration: A European Disorder, c.1848–c.1918* (Cambridge: Cambridge University Press, 1992).

Pitts, Jennifer, *A Turn to Empire: The Rise of Imperial Liberalism in Britain and France* (Princeton: Princeton University Press, 2005).

Pocock, J.G.A., *The Machiavellian Moment: Florentine Political Thought and the Atlantic Republican Tradition* (Princeton: Princeton University Press, 1975).

———, Gordon J. Schochet and Lois G. Schwoerer (eds.), *The Varieties of British Political Thought, 1500–1800* (Cambridge: Cambridge University Press, 1993).

———, *Barbarism and Religion, Vol. 3: The First Decline and Fall* (Cambridge: Cambridge University Press, 2003).

———, *The Discovery of Islands: Essays in British History* (Cambridge: Cambridge University Press, 2005).

Pooley, Colin G., and Turnbull, Jean, *Migration and Mobility in Britain since the Eighteenth Century* (London: UCL Press, 1998).

Porter, Andrew, *Religion Versus Empire?: British Protestant Missionaries and Overseas Expansion* (Manchester: Manchester University Press, 2004).

Porter, Bernard, *Critics of Empire: British Radical Attitudes to Colonialism in Africa, 1895–1914* (London: Macmillan, 1968).

——, *The Absent-Minded Imperialists: Empire, Society, and Culture in Britain* (Oxford: Oxford University Press, 2004).

Potter, Simon, *News and the British World* (Oxford: Oxford University Press, 2003).

Reardon, Bernard, *From Coleridge to Gore: A Century of Religious Thought in Britain* (London: Longman, 1971).

Reese, Trevor, *The History of the Royal Commonwealth Society, 1868–1968* (Oxford: Oxford University Press, 1968).

Reynolds, Matthew, *The Realms of Verse, 1830–1870: English Poetry in a Time of Nation-Building* (Oxford: Oxford University Press, 2001).

Rich, Paul, *Race and Empire in British Politics* (Cambridge: Cambridge University Press, 1986).

Richard, Carl J., *The Founders and the Classics: Greece, Rome, and the American Enlightenment* (Cambridge, Mass.: Harvard University Press, 1994).

Roberts, Andrew, *A History of the English-Speaking Peoples Since 1900* (London: Weidenfeld and Nicholson, 2006).

Rodgers, Daniel, *Atlantic Crossings: Social Politics in a Progressive Age* (Cambridge, Mass.: Harvard University Press, 1998).

Rose, Jonathan, *The Intellectual Life of the English Working Class* (London: Yale University Press, 2001).

Rosen, Fred, *Bentham, Byron, and Greece: Constitutionalism, Nationalism, and Early Liberal Political Thought* (Oxford: Clarendon, 1992).

Runciman, David, *Pluralism and the Personality of the State* (Cambridge: Cambridge University Press, 1997).

Runciman, David, and Magnus Ryan (eds.), *Maitland: State, Trust, and Corporation* (Cambridge: Cambridge University Press, 2003).

Said, Edward, *Orientalism* (London: Routledge, 1978).

——, *Culture and Imperialism* (London: Chatto and Windus, 1993).

Schivelbusch, W., *The Railway Journey: The Industrialization and Perception of Time and Space* (Oxford: Oxford University Press, 1986).

Schofield, Philip, *Utility and Democracy: The Political Thought of Jeremy Bentham* (Oxford: Oxford University Press, 2006).

Schultz, Bart, *Henry Sidgwick, Eye of the Universe: An Intellectual Biography* (Cambridge: Cambridge University Press, 2004).

Searle, G. R., *A New England? Peace and War, 1886–1918* (Oxford: Oxford University Press, 2004).

Sellers, M.N.S., *American Republicanism: Roman Ideology in the United States Constitution* (Basingstoke: Macmillan, 1994).

Semmel, Bernard, *Imperialism and Social Reform: English Social-Imperial Thought, 1895–1914* (London: George Allen and Unwin, 1960).

——, *The Governor Eyre Controversy* (London: MacGibbon and Kee, 1962).

——, *The Rise of Free Trade Imperialism: Classical Political Economy, the Em-*

pire of Free Trade and Imperialism, 1750–1850 (Cambridge: Cambridge University Press, 1970).

———, *Liberalism and Naval Strategy* (London: Allen and Unwin, 1986).

———, *The Liberal Ideal and the Demons of Empire: Theories of Imperialism from Adam Smith to Lenin* (Baltimore: Johns Hopkins University Press, 1993).

Shannon, Richard T., *Gladstone and the Bulgarian Agitation, 1876* (London: Thomas Nelson, 1963).

Simhony, Avital, and D. Weinstein (eds.), *The New Liberalism: Reconciling Liberty and Community* (Cambridge: Cambridge University Press, 2001).

Sinclair, Keith, *Imperial Federation: A Study of New Zealand Policy and Opinion, 1880–1914* (London: Athlone Press, 1955).

Skinner, Quentin, *Liberty Before Liberalism* (Cambridge: Cambridge University Press, 1998).

———, *Visions of Politics*, 3 vols. (Cambridge: Cambridge University Press, 2002).

Soffer, Reba N., *Discipline and Power: The University, History, and the Making of an English Elite, 1870–1930* (Stanford: Stanford University Press, 1994).

Stapleton, Julia, *Political Intellectuals and Public Identities in Britain since 1850* (Manchester: Manchester University Press, 2001).

Stears, Marc, *Progressives, Pluralists, and the Problems of the State: Ideologies of Reform in the United States and Britain, 1909–1926* (Oxford: Oxford University Press, 2002).

Stedman Jones, Gareth, *Outcast London: A Study in the Relationship Between Classes in Victorian Society* (Oxford: Clarendon, 1971).

Steele, David, *Lord Salisbury: A Political Biography* (London: UCL Press, 1999).

Strausz-Hupe, Robert, *Geopolitics: The Struggle for Space and Power* (New York: G. P. Putnam's Sons, 1942).

Suganami, Hidemi, *The Domestic Analogy and World Order Proposals* (Cambridge: Cambridge University Press, 1989).

Thompson, Andrew, *Imperial Britain: The Empire in British Politics, 1880–1932* (Harlow: Longman, 2000).

Thompson, Thomas W., *James Anthony Froude on Nation and Empire: A Study in Victorian Racialism* (London: Garland, 1987).

Thornton, A. P., *Doctrines of Imperialism* (London: J. Wiley and Sons, 1965).

———, *The Imperial Idea and its Enemies: A Study in British Power* (London: Macmillan, 1966 [1959]).

Todorov, Tzetvan, *The Conquest of America: The Question of the Other*, trans. Richard Howard (New York: Harper and Row, 1984).

Turner, Frank M., *Between Science and Religion: The Reaction to Scientific Naturalism in Late Victorian England* (New Haven: Yale University Press, 1974).

———, *The Greek Heritage in Victorian Britain* (New Haven: Yale University Press, 1981).

———, *Contesting Cultural Authority: Essays in Victorian Intellectual Life* (Cambridge: Cambridge University Press, 1993).

Turner, John (ed.), *The Larger Idea: Lord Lothian and the Problem of National Sovereignty* (London: The Historians" Press, 1988).

Tyler, J. E., *The Struggle for Imperial Unity, 1868–1895* (London: Longman's, 1938).

Vance, Norman, *The Victorians and Ancient Rome* (Oxford: Blackwells, 1997).

Varouxakis, Georgios, *Mill on Nationality* (London: Routledge, 2002).

———, *Victorian Political Theory on France and the French* (London: Macmillan, 2002).

Wallace, Elisabeth, *Goldwin Smith: Victorian Liberal* (Toronto: University of Toronto Press, 1957).

Ward, John, *Colonial Self-Government: The British Experience, 1759–1856* (London: Macmillan, 1976).

Weinstock, Daniel, and Christian Nadeau (eds.), *Republicanism: History, Theory and Practice* (London: Frank Cass, 2004).

Wilson, Kathleen (ed.), *A New Imperial History: Culture, Identity, and Modernity in Britain and the Empire, 1660–1840* (Cambridge: Cambridge University Press, 2004).

Winch, Donald, *Classical Political Economy and Colonies* (London: G. Bell and Sons, 1965).

Winner, Langdon, *Autonomous Technology: Technics-Out-of-Control as a Theme in Political Thought* (Cambridge, Mass.: MIT Press, 1977).

Wolffe, John, *God and Greater Britain: Religion and National Life in Britain and Ireland, 1843–1945* (London: Routledge, 1994).

Wood, John Cunningham, *British Economists and the Empire* (London: Croom Helm, 1983).

Worden, Blair, *Roundhead Reputations: The English Civil Wars and the Passions of Posterity* (London: Allen Lane, 2001).

Wormell, Deborah, *Sir John Seeley and the Uses of History* (Cambridge: Cambridge University Press, 1980).

3. Articles and Chapters

Alessio, Dominic David, "Domesticating 'The Heart of the Wild': Female Personifications of the Colonies, 1886–1940," *Women's History Review*, 6 (1997), 239–69.

Armitage, David, "Empire and Liberty: A Republican Dilemma" in Martin van Gelderen and Quentin Skinner (eds.), *Republicanism: A Shared European Heritage, Vol. 2, The Values of Republicanism in Early Modern Europe* (Cambridge: Cambridge University Press, 2003), 29–47.

Ashcraft, Richard, "Liberal Political Theory and Working-Class Radicalism in Nineteenth-Century England," *PT*, 21 (1993), 249–72.

Bayly, C. A., "The First Age of Global Imperialism, c.1760–1830," *JICH*, 27 (1998), 28–48.

Bell, Duncan, "Language, Legitimacy, and the Project of Critique," *Alternatives: Global, Local, Political*, 27 (2002), 327–50.

———, "Globalisation and History: Reflections on Temporality," *International Affairs*, 79 (2003), 801–15.

———, "Unity and Difference: J. R. Seeley and the Political Theology of International Relations," *Review of International Studies*, 31 (2005), 559–79.

———, "Dissolving Distance: Empire, Space, and Technology in British Political Thought, 1770–1900," *JMH*, 77 (2005), 523–63.

———, "The Idea of a Patriot Queen? The Monarchy, the Constitution, and the

Iconographic Order of Greater Britain, 1860–1900," *JICH*, 34 (2006), 1–19.
——, "From Ancient to Modern in Victorian Imperial Thought," *HJ*, 49 (2006), 1–25.
——, "Empire and International Relations in Victorian Political Thought," *HJ*, 49 (2006), 281–98.
——, "Empire and Imperialism" in Claeys and Stedman Jones (eds.), *The Cambridge History of Nineteenth Century Political Thought*, forthcoming.
——, "Virtue and Empire: On Liberal and Republican Imperialisms" in Bell and Quentin Skinner (eds.), *Republicanism and Global Politics* (forthcoming).
Bell, Duncan, and Casper Sylvest, "International Society in Victorian Political Thought: T. H. Green, Herbert Spencer, and Henry Sidgwick," *MIH*, 3 (2006), 1–32.
Bernstein, George L., "Sir Henry Campbell-Bannerman and the Liberal Imperialists," *JBS*, 23 (1983), 105–24.
Betts, Raymond, "The Allusion to Rome in British Imperialist Thought of the Late Nineteenth and Early Twentieth Centuries," *VS*, 15 (1971), 149–59.
——, "Immense Dimensions: The Impact of the American West on Late Nineteenth-Century European Thought about Expansion," *Western Historical Quarterly*, 10 (1979), 149–66.
Biagini, Eugenio, "Neo-Roman Liberalism: 'Republican' Values and British Liberalism, ca.1860–1875," *History of European Ideas*, 29 (2003), 55–72.
Bosco, Andrea, "Lothian, Curtis, Kimber and the Federal Union Movement (1938–40)," *Journal of Contemporary History*, 23 (1988), 465–502.
——, "National Sovereignty and Peace: Lord Lothians's Federalist Thought" in Turner (ed.), *The Larger Idea*, 108–23.
Bowen, H. V., "British Conceptions of Global Empire, 1756–83," *JICH*, 26 (1998), 1–27.
Boyce, George, "Federalism and the Irish Question" in Bosco (ed.), *The Federal Idea*, I, 119–39.
Bremner, G. Alex, "'Some Imperial Institute': Architecture, Symbolism, and the Ideal of Empire in Late-Victorian Britain," *Journal of the Society of Architectural Historians*, 62 (2003), 50–73.
——, "Nation and Empire in the Government Architecture of Mid-Victorian London: The Foreign and India Office Reconsidered," *HJ*, 48 (2005), 703–42.
Bridge, Carl, and Fedorwich, Kent, "Mapping the British World," *JICH*, 31 (2003), 1–15.
Buckner, Phillip, "Whatever Happened to the British Empire?" *Journal of the Canadian Historical Association*, 3 (1993), 3–32.
Bull, Hedley, "What Is the Commonwealth," *World Politics*, 11 (1959), 577–87.
Burgess, Michael, "Imperial Federation: Edward Freeman and the Intellectual Debate on the Consolidation of the British Empire in the Nineteenth-Century," *Trivium*, 13 (1978), 77–95.
——, "The Federal Plan of the Imperial Federation League, 1892: Milestone or Tombstone?" in Bosco (ed.), *The Federal Idea*, I, 139–53.
——, "Federalism and Federation: A Reappraisal" in Burgess and Alain-G Gagnon (eds.), *Comparative Federalism and Federation: Competing Traditions and Future Directions* (London: Harvester Wheatsheaf, 1993), 3–14.

Burroughs, Peter, "John Robert Seeley and British Imperial History," *JICH*, 1 (1973), 191–213.

Burrow, John, "The Village Community and the Uses of History" in Mckendrick (ed.), *Historical Perspectives*, 255–85.

———, "Some British Views of the United States Constitution" in R. C. Simmons (ed.), *The United States Constitution: The First 200 Years: Papers Delivered at a Bicentennial Colloquium at the University of Birmingham* (Manchester: Manchester University Press, 1989), 116–38.

———, "Images of Time: From Carlylean Vulcanism to Sedimentary Gradualism" in Collini, Whatmore, and Young (eds.), *History, Religion, and Culture*, 198–224.

———, "The Age of Reform" in David Reynolds (ed.), *Christ's: A Cambridge College Over Five Centuries* (London: Palgrave, 2004), 111–43.

Cain, Peter, "Capitalism, War, and Internationalism in the Thought of Richard Cobden," *British Journal of International Studies*, 5 (1979), 229–45.

———, "The Economic Philosophy of Constructive Imperialism" in Navari (ed.), *British Politics and the Spirit of the Age*, 41–65.

———, "Character and Imperialism: The British Financial Administration of Egypt, 1878–1914," *JICH*, 34 (2006), 177–200.

———, "Radicalism, Gladstone, and the Liberal Critique of Disraelian Imperialism" in Bell (ed.), *Victorian Visions of Global Order*.

———, "Empire and the Languages of Character and Virtue in Later Victorian and Edwardian Britain," *MIH*, 4 (2007), 1–25.

Ceadel, Martin, "Pacifism and *Pacificism*" in Terence Ball and Richard Bellamy (eds.), *The Cambridge History of Twentieth Century Political Thought* (Cambridge: Cambridge University Press, 2003), 473–93.

Claeys, Gregory, "The 'Left' and the Critique of Empire, c.1865–1900" in Bell (ed.), *Victorian Visions of Global Order*.

Cole, Douglas, "The Problem of 'Nationalism' and 'Imperialism' in British Settlement Colonies," *JBS*, 10 (1971), 160–82.

Colley, Linda, "Britishness and Otherness: An Argument," *JBS*, 31 (1992), 309–29.

———, "What Is Imperial History Today?" in David Cannadine (ed.), *What Is History Today?* (Basingstoke: Palgrave, 2002), 132–47.

Constantine, Stephen, "Empire Migration and Social Reform 1880–1950" in Colin Pooley and Ian Whyte (eds.), *Migrants, Emigrants and Immigrants: A Social History of Migration* (London: Routledge, 1991), 62–86.

Cook, T., "George R. Parkin and the Concept of Britannic Idealism," *Journal of Canadian Studies*, 10 (1975), 15–31.

Darwin, John, "The Fear of Falling: British Political and Imperial Decline since 1900," *Transactions of the Royal Historical Society*, 5th series, 36 (1986), 27–45.

———, "Imperialism and the Victorians: The Dynamics of Territorial Expansion," *EHR*, 112 (1997), 614–42.

Demetriou, K., "In Defence of the British Constitution: Theoretical Implications of the Debate over Athenian Democracy in Britain, 1770–1850," *HPT*, 17 (1996), 280–97.

Dickinson, H. T., "Britain's Imperial Sovereignty: The Ideological Case Against the American Colonists" in Dickinson (ed.), *Britain and the American Revolution*, 64–97.

Durrans, Peter J., "The House of Commons and the British Empire, 1868–1880," *Canadian Journal of History*, 9 (1974), 19–45.

Edwards, Catherine, "Translating Empire: Macaulay's Rome" in Edwards (ed.), *Roman Presences*, 70–88.

Ellis, Heather, "Proconsuls, Guardians, and Great Men: The Indian Civil Service and an Education in Empire," unpublished paper, University of Oxford, 2003.

Epstein, James, "'America' in the Victorian Cultural Imagination" in Leventhal and Quinault (eds.), *Anglo-American Attitudes*, 107–24.

Erickson, Charlotte, "The Encouragement of Emigration by British Trade Unions, 1850–1900," *Population Studies*, 3 (1949), 248–73.

Feldman, David, "Migration" in Martin Daunton (ed.), *The Cambridge Urban History of Britain* (Cambridge: Cambridge University Press, 2000), III, 185–207.

Finley, Moses, "Colonies—An Attempt at a Typology," *TRHS*, 5th series, 6 (1976), 167–88.

Floud, Roderick, "Britain, 1860–1914: A Survey" in Floud and McCloskey (eds.), *The Economic History of Britain Since 1700*, 1–29.

Freeden, Michael, "Ideology, Political Theory and Political Philosophy" in Gerald Gaus and Chandran Kukathas (eds.), *Handbook of Political Theory* (London: Sage, 2004).

——, "What Should the "Political" in Political Theory Explore?" *Journal of Political Philosophy*, 13 (2005), 113–34.

Geuss, Raymond, "Liberalism and Its Discontents," *PT*, 30 (2002), 320–39.

Geyer, Michael, and Bright, Charles, "World History in a Global Age," *AHR*, 100 (1995), 1034–60.

Gildea, Robert, "1848 in European Collective Memory" in Evans and Pogge von Strandmann (eds.), *The Revolutions in Europe*, 207–37.

Gorman, Daniel, "Lionel Curtis, Imperial Citizenship, and the Quest for Unity," *The Historian*, 66 (2004), 67–96.

Gould, Eliga, "A Virtual Nation? Greater Britain and the Imperial Legacy of the American Revolution," *AHR*, 104 (1999), 476–89.

——, "The American Revolution in Britain's Imperial Identity" in Leventhal and Quinault (eds.), *Anglo-American Attitudes*, 23–38.

Green, E.H.H., "The Political Economy of Empire, 1880–1914," *OHBE*, III, 346–71.

Greenlee, J. G., "A 'Succession of Seeleys': The 'Old School' Re-examined," *JICH*, 4 (1976), 266–83.

Gross, John, "Editor's Introduction" to Seeley, *The Expansion of England*, ed. Gross, xi–xxvi.

Guttridge, G. H., "Thomas Pownall's *The Administration of the Colonies*: The Six Editions," *The William and Mary Quarterly*, 26 (1969), 31–46.

Harling, Philip, "Equipoise Regained? Recent Trends in British Political History, 1780–1867," *JMH*, 75 (2003), 890–918.

Harper, Marjory, "British Migration and the Peopling of the Empire," *OHBE*, III, 75–88.

Harris, Jose, "Political Theory and the State" in S.J.D. Green and R. C. Whiting (eds.), *The Boundaries of the State in Modern Britain* (Cambridge, 1996), 15–29.

Harrison, Ross, "Utilitarians and Idealists" in Tom Baldwin (ed.), *The Cambridge History of Philosophy, 1870–1945* (Cambridge, 2003), 255–66.

Harvie, Christopher, "Ideology and Home Rule: James Bryce, A. V. Dicey, and Ireland, 1880–1887," *EHR*, 91 (1976), 298–314.

Herkless, J. L., "Introduction" to Rein, *Sir John Robert Seeley*, i–xxix.

Hickford, M., " 'Decidedly the Most Interesting Savages on the Globe': An Approach to the History of Maori Property Rights, 1837–1853," *HPT*, 46 (2006), 122–67.

Hont, Istvan, "Commerce and Luxury" in Mark Goldie and Robert Wokler (eds.), *The Cambridge History of Eighteenth-Century Political Thought* (Cambridge: Cambridge University Press, 2006), 379–419.

Hopkins, A. G., "Back to the Future: From National History to Imperial Past," *P&P*, 164 (1999), 198–244.

Horn, Pamela, "Agricultural Trade Unionism and Emigration, 1872–1881," *HJ*, 15 (1972), 87–102.

Hörnqvist Mikael, "The Two Myths of Civic Humanism" in James Hankins (ed.), *Renaissance Civic Humanism: Reappraisals and Reflections* (Cambridge: Cambridge University Press, 2000), 105–43.

Howe, Anthony, "Free Trade and Global Order: The Rise and Fall of a Victorian Vision" in Bell (ed.), *Victorian Visions of Global Order*.

Jones, H. S., "The Idea of the Nation in Victorian Political Thought," *EJPT*, 5 (2006), 12–21.

Kearns, Gerry, "*Fin de Siècle* Geopolitics: Mackinder, Hobson and Theories of Global Closure" in Peter Taylor (ed.), *Political Geography of the Twentieth Century: A Global Analysis* (London: Belhaven Press, 1993), 9–25.

Kendle, J. E., "The Round Table Movement and 'Home Rule All Round,'" *HJ*, 11 (1968), 332–53.

Kennedy, Paul, "The Theory and Practice of Imperialism," *HJ*, 20 (1977), 761–69.

Kidd, Colin, "Damnable Deficient," *London Review of Books*, 27 (2005), 30.

Kramer, Paul, "Empires, Exceptions, and Anglo-Saxons: Race and Rule between the British and United States Empires, 1880–1910," *Journal of American History*, 88 (2002), 1315–53.

Laborde, Cécile, "The Concept of the State in British and French Political Thought," *Political Studies*, 48 (2000), 540–57.

Langford, Paul, "Property and 'Virtual Representation' in Eighteenth-Century England," *HJ*, 31 (1988), 83–115.

———, "Manners and Character in Anglo-American Perceptions, 1750–1850" in Leventhal and Quinault (eds.), *Anglo-American Attitudes*, 76–90.

Lester, Alan, "British Settler Discourse and the Circuits of Empire," *History Workshop Journal*, 54 (2002), 25–48.

Levy, Jacob, "Beyond Publius: Montesquieu, Liberal Republicanism and the Small-Republic Thesis," *HPT*, 27 (2006), 50–90.

Majeed, Javeed, "Comparativism and References to Rome in British Imperial Attitudes to India" in Edwards (ed.), *Roman Presences*, 88–110.

Malchow, Howard L, "Trade Unions and Emigration in Late Victorian England: A National Lobby for State Aid," *JBS*, 15 (1976), 92–116.

Mandler, Peter, "Against "Englishness": English Culture and the Limits of Rural Nostalgia, 1850–1940," *Transactions of the Royal Historical Society*, 6th series, 7 (1997), 155–76.

——, "'Race' and 'Nation' in Mid-Victorian Thought" in Collini et al., *History, Religion, and Culture*, 224–45.

——, "The Consciousness of Modernity? Liberalism and the English National Character, 1870–1940" in Daunton and Rieger (eds.), *Meanings of Modernity*, 119–44.

——, "The Problem with Cultural History," *Cultural and Social History*, 1 (2004), 94–118.

——, "What Is 'National Identity'? Definitions and Applications in Modern British Historiography," *MIH*, 3 (2006), 271–97.

Marshall, Peter, "Imperial Britain," *JICH*, 23 (1995), 379–95.

Martin, Ged, "Empire Federalism and Imperial Parliamentary Union, 1820–1870," *HJ*, 16 (1973), 65–92.

——, "The Idea of 'Imperial Federation'" in Ronald Hyam and Ged Martin (eds.), *Reappraisals in British Imperial History* (London: Macmillan, 1975), 121–39.

Mehrota, S. R., "Imperial Federation and India, 1868–1917," *Journal of Commonwealth Political Studies*, 1 (1961), 29–40.

Miller, J.D.B, "The Utopia of Imperial Federation," *Political Studies*, 4 (1956), 195–7.

Mitchell, Leslie, "Britain's Reaction to the Revolutions" in Evans and Pogge von Strandmann (eds.), *The Revolutions in Europe*, 83–99.

Momigliano, Arnaldo, "Time in Ancient Historiography" in *Essays in Ancient and Modern Historiography* (Oxford: Blackwell, 1977), 179–205.

Morefield, Jeanne, "'An Education to Greece': The Round Table, Imperial Theory, and the Uses of History," *HPT* (2007).

Morris, R. J., "Urbanization" in Morris and Richard Rodger (eds.), *The Victorian City* (London: Longman's, 1993), 43–73.

Murray, Oswyn, "Ancient History, 1872–1914" in Brock and Curthoys (eds.), *The History of the University of Oxford*, VII, 333–60.

O'Brien, Karen, "Poetry Against Empire: Milton to Shelley," *Proceedings of the British Academy*, 117 (2002), 269–96.

O'Brien, Patrick K., "Historiographical Traditions and Modern Imperatives for the Restoration of Global History," *Journal of Global History*, 1 (2006), 3–39.

O'Gráda, Cormac, "British Agriculture, 1860–1914" in Floud and McCloskey (eds.), *The Economic History of Britain Since 1700*, 145–72.

Olssen, Erik, "Mr Wakefield and New Zealand as an Experiment in Post-Enlightenment Experimental Practice," *New Zealand Journal of History*, 31 (1997), 197–218.

Otis, Laura, "The Metaphoric Circuit: Organic and Technological Communication in the Nineteenth-Century," *JHI*, 63 (2002), 105–29.

Owen, Nicholas, "Critics of Empire," *OHBE*, IV, 188–212.

Palonen, Kari, "Political Theorizing as a Dimension of Political Life," *EJPT*, 4 (2005), 351–66.

Parekh, Bikhu, "Decolonizing Liberalism" in Aleksandras Shtromas (ed.), *The End of "Isms"? Reflections on the Fate of Ideological Politics After Communism's Collapse* (Oxford: Blackwell, 1994), 85–103.

Parry, J. P., "The Impact of Napoleon III on British Politics, 1851–1880," *Transactions of the Royal Historical Society*, 6th series, 11 (2001), 147–75.

Pinder, John, "Prophet not Without Honour: Lothian and the Federal Idea" in Turner (ed.), *The Larger Idea*, 137–53.

——, "The Federal Idea and the British Liberal Tradition" in Bosco (ed.), *The Federal Idea*, I, 99–118.

Pocock, J.G.A., "British History: A Plea for a New Subject," *JMH*, 47 (1975), 601–21.

——, "Between Gog and Magog: The Republican Thesis and the *Ideologia Americana*," *JHI*, 48 (1987), 325–46.

——, "States, Republics, and Empires: The American Founding in Early Modern Perspective" in Terence Ball and Pocock (eds.), *Conceptual Change and the Constitution* (Lawrence, Kans.: University Press of Kansas, 1988), 55–78.

——, "Political Theory in the English-Speaking Atlantic, 1760–1790: (1) The Imperial Crisis" in Pocock, Schochet and Schwoerer (eds.), *The Varieties of British Political Thought, 1500–1800*, 246–82.

——, "Political Theory in the English-Speaking Atlantic, 1760–1790: (2) Empire, Revolution, and the End of Early Modernity" in Pocock, Schochet and Schwoerer (eds.), *The Varieties of British Political Thought, 1500–1800*, 283–321.

——, "The New British History in Antipodean Perspective: A Commentary," *AHR*, 104 (1999), 490–500.

Pombeni, Paolo, "Starting in Reason, Ending in Passion: Bryce, Lowell, Ostrogorski and the Problem of Democracy," *HJ*, 37 (1994), 319–41.

Pyenson, Lewis, "Science and Imperialism" in R. C. Olby et al. (eds.), *Companion to the History of Modern Science* (London: Routledge, 1996), 920–34.

Richards, Eric, "How Did Poor People Emigrate from the British Isles to Australia in the Nineteenth Century?" *JBS*, 32 (1993), 250–79.

Robinson, Ronald, "Imperial Problems in British Politics, 1880–1895" in Benians, Butler, and Carrington (eds.), *The Cambridge History of the British Empire*, III, 127–79.

Rothschild, Emma, "Political Economy" in Claeys and Stedman Jones (eds.), *The Cambridge History of Nineteenth Century Political Thought*, forthcoming.

——, "Global Commerce and the Question of Sovereignty in the Eighteenth-Century Provinces," *MIH*, 1 (2004), 3–25.

Ryan, Alan, "The Critique of Individualism" in Brian Barry, Archie Brown, and Jack Hayward (eds.), *The British Study of Politics in the Twentieth Century* (Oxford: Oxford University Press, 2003), 89–117.

Shannon, Richard, "John Robert Seeley and the Idea of a National Church: A Study in Churchmanship, Historiography, and Politics" in Robert Robson (ed.), *Ideas and Institutions of Victorian Britain: Essays in Honour of George Kitson Clark* (London: Bell, 1967), 236–67.

Shaw, A.G.L., "British Attitudes to the Colonies, ca. 1820–1850," *JBS*, 9 (1969), 71–95.

Soffer, Reba, "History and Religion: J. R. Seeley and the Burden of the Past" in

R. W. Davis and R. J. Helmstadter (eds.), *Religion and Irreligion in Victorian Society: Essays in Honor of R. K. Webb* (London: Routledge, 1992), 133–51.

Stapleton, Julia, "Citizenship Versus Patriotism in Twentieth-Century England," *HJ*, 48 (2005), 151–78.

Stedman Jones, Gareth, "Introduction" to Karl Marx and Friedrich Engels, *The Communist Manifesto*, 3–190.

Taylor, Miles, "Imperium et Libertas?" Rethinking the Radical Critique of Imperialism During the Nineteenth Century," *JICH*, 19 (1991), 1–23.

———, "The 1848 Revolutions and the British Empire," *P&P*, 166 (2000), 146–80.

———, "Republics Versus Empires: Charles Dilke's Republicanism Reconsidered" in David Nash and Anthony Taylor (eds.), *Republicanism in Victorian Society* (Stroud: Sutton Publishing, 2003), 25–34.

Thompson, Andrew S., "The Language of Imperialism and the Meanings of Empire: Imperial Discourse in British Politics, 1895–1914," *JBS*, 26 (1997), 147–77.

Trentman, Frank, "The Strange Death of Free Trade: The Erosion of the 'Liberal Consensus' in Great Britain, c.1903–1932" in Biagini (ed.), *Citizenship and Community*, 219–51.

Tuck, Richard, "The Making and Unmaking of Boundaries from the Natural Law Perspective" in Allen Buchanan and Margaret Moore (eds.), *States, Nations, and Borders: The Ethics of Making Boundaries* (Cambridge: Cambridge University Press, 2003), 143–71.

Tulloch, Hugh, "Changing British Attitudes Towards the United States in the 1880's," *HJ*, 20 (1977), 825–40.

Tully, James, "The Kantian Idea of Europe: Critical and Cosmopolitan Perspectives" in Anthony Pagden (ed.), *The Idea of Europe: From Antiquity to the European Union* (Cambridge: Cambridge University Press, 2002), 331–58.

Tunstall, W.C.B., "Imperial Defence, 1870–1897" in Benians, Butler, and Carrington (eds.), *The Cambridge History of the British Empire*, III, 230–53.

Turner, Frank, "British Politics and the Demise of the Roman Republic, 1700–1939," *HJ* 29 (1986), 577–99.

Turner, John, and Michael Dockrill, "Philip Kerr at 10 Downing Street, 1916–1921" in Turner (ed.), *The Larger Idea*, 42–52.

Turner, Michael J., "Radical Agitation and the Canada Question in British Politics, 1837–41," *Historical Research*, 79 (2006), 90–114.

Varouxakis, Giorgios, "'Patriotism,' 'Cosmopolitanism' and 'Humanity' in Victorian Political Thought,"*EJPT*, 5 (2006), 100–18.

Vasunia, Phiroze, "Greater Britain and Greater Rome" in Barbara Goff (ed.), *Classics and Colonialism* (London: Duckworth, 2005), 34–68.

———, "Greek, Latin, and the Indian Civil Service," *Proceedings of the Cambridge Philological Society*, 51 (2005), 35–69.

Vernon, James, "Notes Towards an Introduction" in Vernon (ed.), *Re-Reading the Constitution: New Narratives in the Political History of England's Long Nineteenth Century* (Cambridge: Cambridge University Press, 1996), 1–22.

Walsh, W. H., "The Zenith of Greats" in Brock and Curthoys (eds.), *The History of the University of Oxford*, VII, 311–26.

Weber, Max, "Politics as a Vocation" [1918/19], in Weber, *Political Writings*, ed. Peter Lassman, trans. Ronald Speirs (Cambridge: Cambridge University Press, 1994), 309–10.

White, Donald, "Changing Views of the *Adventus Saxonum* in Nineteenth- and Twentieth-Century English Scholarship," *JHI*, 32 (1971), 585–94.

Winterer, Caroline, "From Royal to Republican: The Classical Image in Early America," *Journal of American History*, 91 (2005), 1264–90.

York, Neil, "Federalism and the Failure of Imperial Reform, 1774–1775," *History*, 86 (2001), 155–79.

Index

Lightning Source UK Ltd.
Milton Keynes UK
UKHW011016110322
399878UK00004BA/297